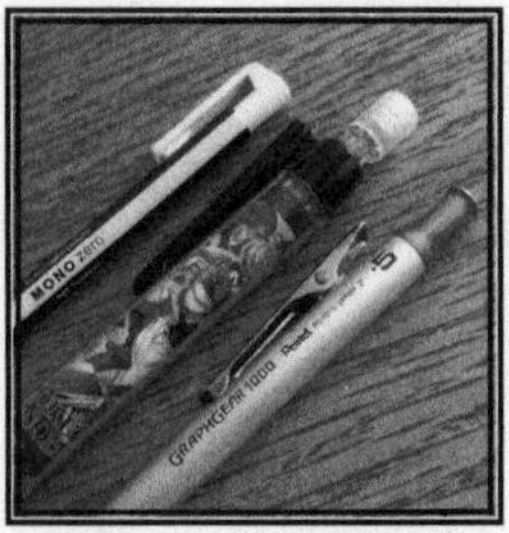
MONO zero
GRAPHGEAR 1000

Yuto Tsukuda

My goal for the latter half of this year: fixing my night owl tendencies and getting my sleep patterns back on track!

Shun Saeki

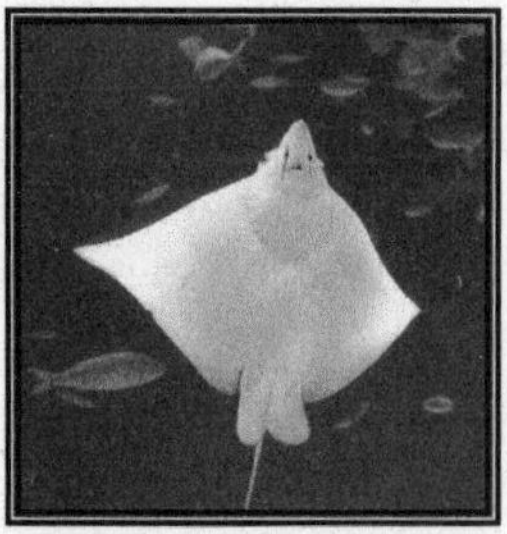

I really love visiting zoos, but aquariums are right up there too. It's my personal dream to someday build my own animal kingdom (i.e., have various kinds of pets), but once that's done, I want to create an aquatic empire (i.e., have an aquarium) too. Then I can live my life surrounded by living creatures of all kinds.

About the authors

Yuto Tsukuda won the 34th Jump Juniketsu Newcomers' Manga Award for his one-shot story *Kiba ni Naru*. He made his *Weekly Shonen Jump* debut in 2010 with the series *Shonen Shikku*. His follow-up series, *Food Wars!: Shokugeki no Soma*, is his first English-language release.

Shun Saeki made his *Jump NEXT!* debut in 2011 with the one-shot story *Kimi to Watashi no Renai Soudan. Food Wars!: Shokugeki no Soma* is his first *Shonen Jump* series.

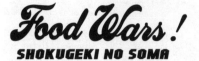

Food Wars!
SHOKUGEKI NO SOMA

Volume 25
Shonen Jump Advanced Manga Edition
Story by Yuto Tsukuda, Art by Shun Saeki
Contributor Yuki Morisaki

Translation: Adrienne Beck
Touch-Up Art & Lettering: James Gaubatz, Mara Coman
Design: Alice Lewis
Editor: Jennifer LeBlanc

Printed in the U.S.A.

Published by VIZ Media, LLC
P.O. Box 77010
San Francisco, CA 94107

10 9 8 7 6 5 4 3 2 1
First printing, August 2018

ratings.viz.com RATED T+ OLDER TEEN

PARENTAL ADVISORY
FOOD WARS! is rated T+ for Older Teen and is recommended for ages 16 and up. This volume contains sexual situations/humor.

VIZ MEDIA
viz.com

SHONEN JUMP ADVANCED
shonenjump.com

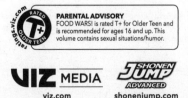

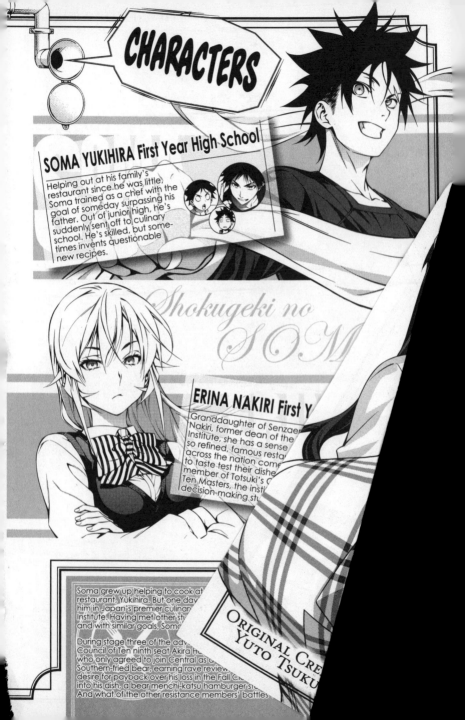

CHARACTERS

SOMA YUKIHIRA First Year High School

Helping out at his family's restaurant since he was little, Soma trained as a chef with the goal of someday surpassing his father. Out of junior high, he's suddenly sent off to culinary school. He's skilled, but sometimes invents questionable new recipes.

Shokugeki no SOM

ERINA NAKIRI First Y

Granddaughter of Senzaer Nakiri, former dean of the Institute, she has a sense so refined, famous resta across the nation come to taste test their dishe member of Totsuki's Ten Masters, the insti decision-making st

Soma grew up helping to cook at restaurant, Yukihira. But one day him in Japan's premier culinary Institute. Having met other st and with similar goals, Som

During stage three of the adv Council of Ten ninth seat Akira Hu who only agreed to join Central as c Southern-fried bear, earning rave review desire for payback over his loss in the Fall Cl into his dish, a bear menchi-katsu hamburger st And what of the other resistance members' battles

ORIGINAL CRE
YUTO TSUKU

THE LIFE OF A REJECT

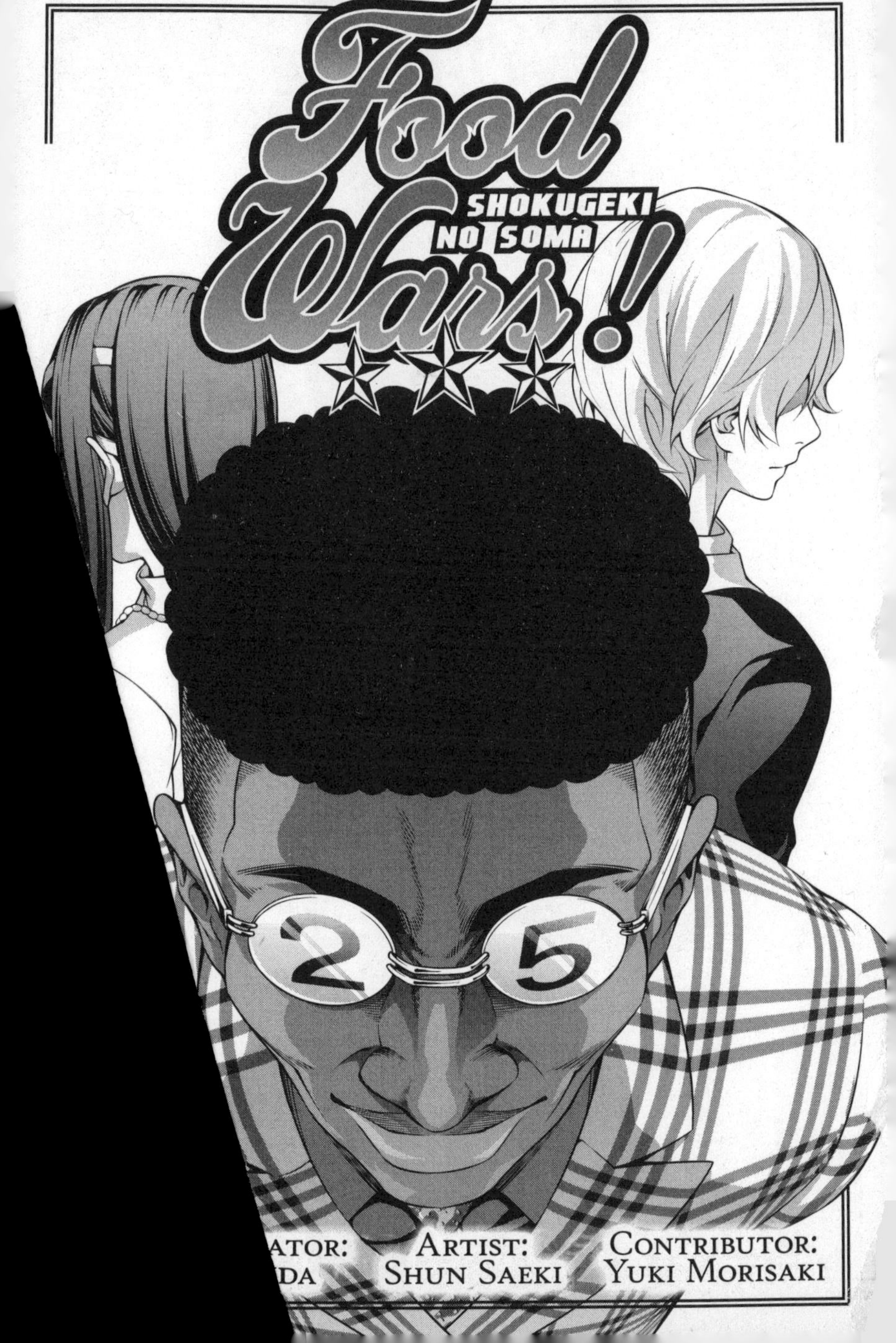
Food Wars!
SHOKUGEKI NO SOMA
25
ATOR:
DA
ARTIST:
SHUN SAEKI
CONTRIBUTOR:
YUKI MORISAKI

Shokugeki no SOMA

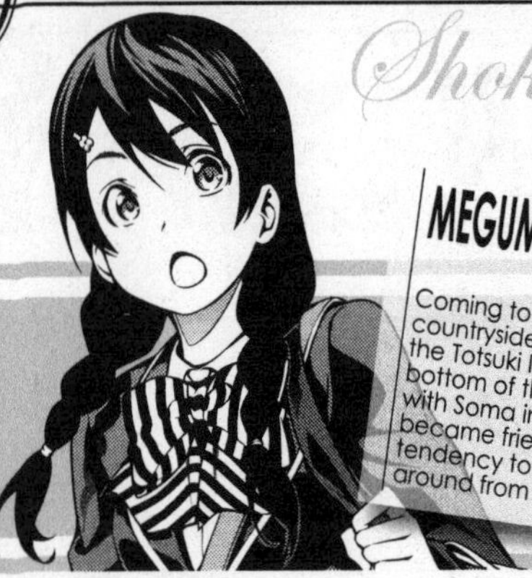

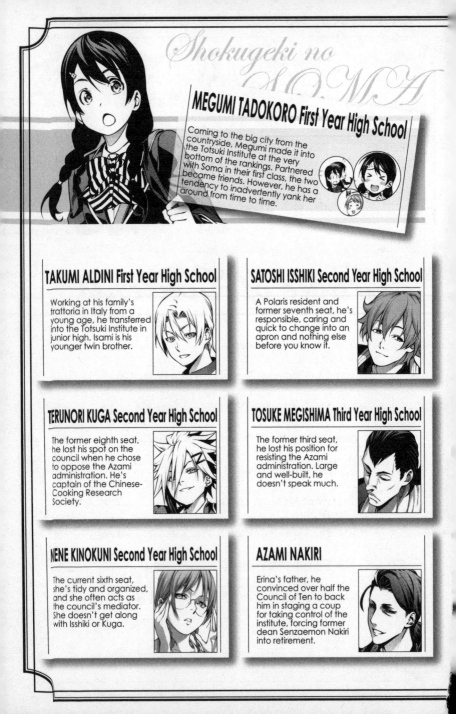

MEGUMI TADOKORO First Year High School

Coming to the big city from the countryside, Megumi made it into the Totsuki Institute at the very bottom of the rankings. Partnered with Soma in their first class, the two became friends. However, he has a tendency to inadvertently yank her around from time to time.

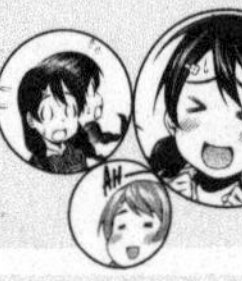

TAKUMI ALDINI First Year High School

Working at his family's trattoria in Italy from a young age, he transferred into the Totsuki Institute in junior high. Isami is his younger twin brother.

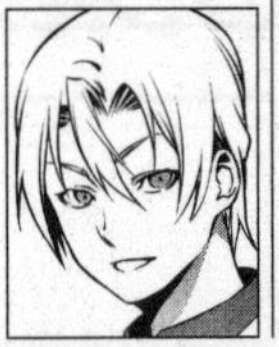

SATOSHI ISSHIKI Second Year High School

A Polaris resident and former seventh seat, he's responsible, caring and quick to change into an apron and nothing else before you know it.

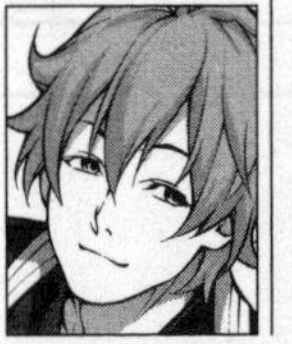

TERUNORI KUGA Second Year High School

The former eighth seat, he lost his spot on the council when he chose to oppose the Azami administration. He's captain of the Chinese-Cooking Research Society.

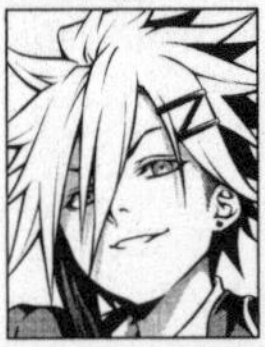

TOSUKE MEGISHIMA Third Year High School

The former third seat, he lost his position for resisting the Azami administration. Large and well-built, he doesn't speak much.

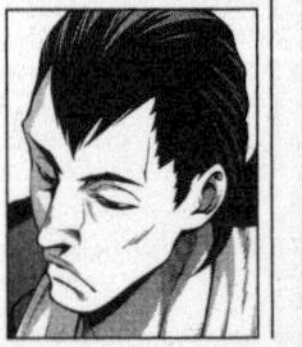

NENE KINOKUNI Second Year High School

The current sixth seat, she's tidy and organized, and she often acts as the council's mediator. She doesn't get along with Isshiki or Kuga.

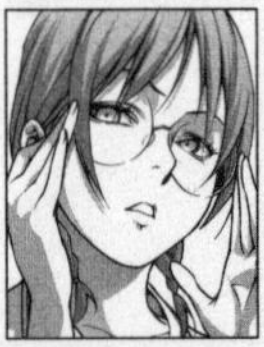

AZAMI NAKIRI

Erina's father, he convinced over half the Council of Ten to back him in staging a coup for taking control of the institute, forcing former dean Senzaemon Nakiri into retirement.

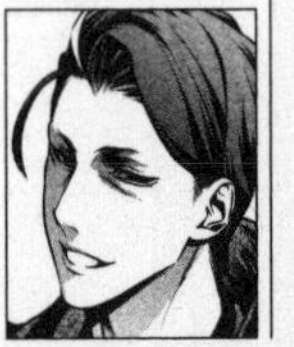

Food Wars!
SHOKUGEKI NO SOMA

25

Table of Contents

#209 THE LIFE OF A REJECT

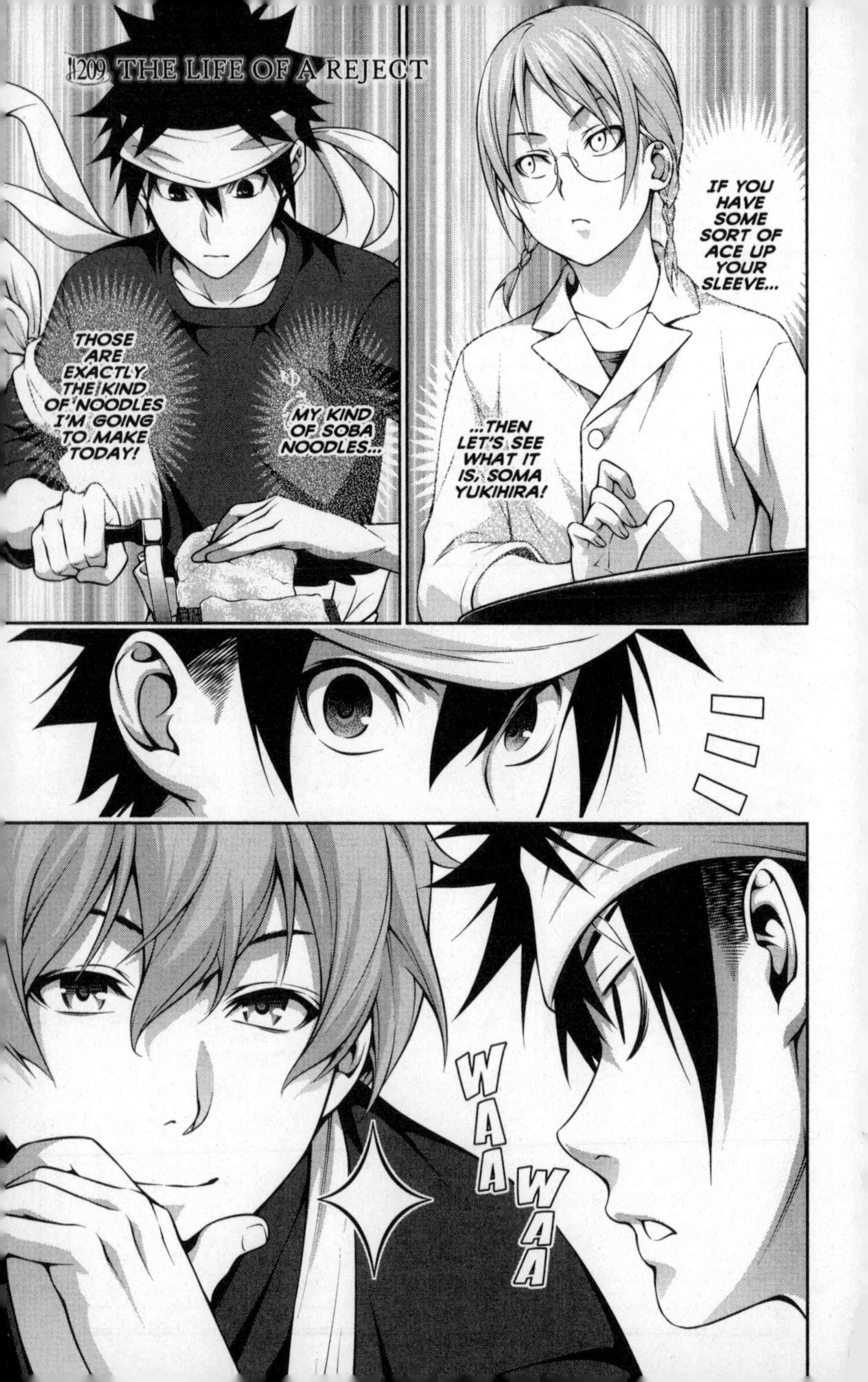

IF YOU HAVE SOME SORT OF ACE UP YOUR SLEEVE...
...THEN LET'S SEE WHAT IT IS, SOMA YUKIHIRA!
MY KIND OF SOBA NOODLES...
THOSE ARE EXACTLY THE KIND OF NOODLES I'M GOING TO MAKE TODAY!
WAA
WAA

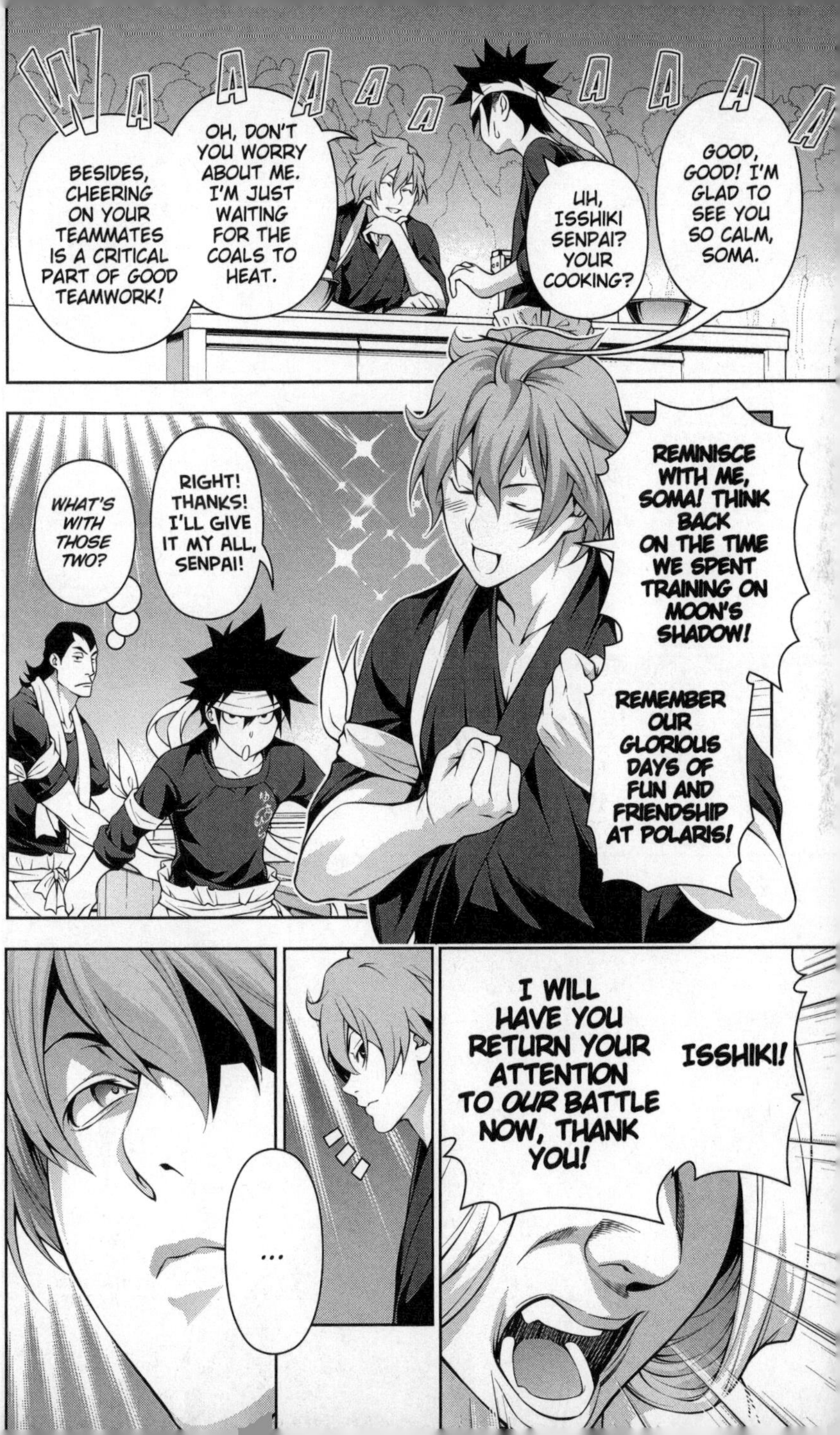
WAAAAAAAAA
GOOD, GOOD! I'M GLAD TO SEE YOU SO CALM, SOMA.
UH, ISSHIKI SENPAI? YOUR COOKING?
OH, DON'T YOU WORRY ABOUT ME. I'M JUST WAITING FOR THE COALS TO HEAT.
BESIDES, CHEERING ON YOUR TEAMMATES IS A CRITICAL PART OF GOOD TEAMWORK!
REMINISCE WITH ME, SOMA! THINK BACK ON THE TIME WE SPENT TRAINING ON MOON'S SHADOW!
REMEMBER OUR GLORIOUS DAYS OF FUN AND FRIENDSHIP AT POLARIS!
RIGHT! THANKS! I'LL GIVE IT MY ALL, SENPAI!
WHAT'S WITH THOSE TWO?
ISSHIKI!
I WILL HAVE YOU RETURN YOUR ATTENTION TO *OUR* BATTLE NOW, THANK YOU!
...
...

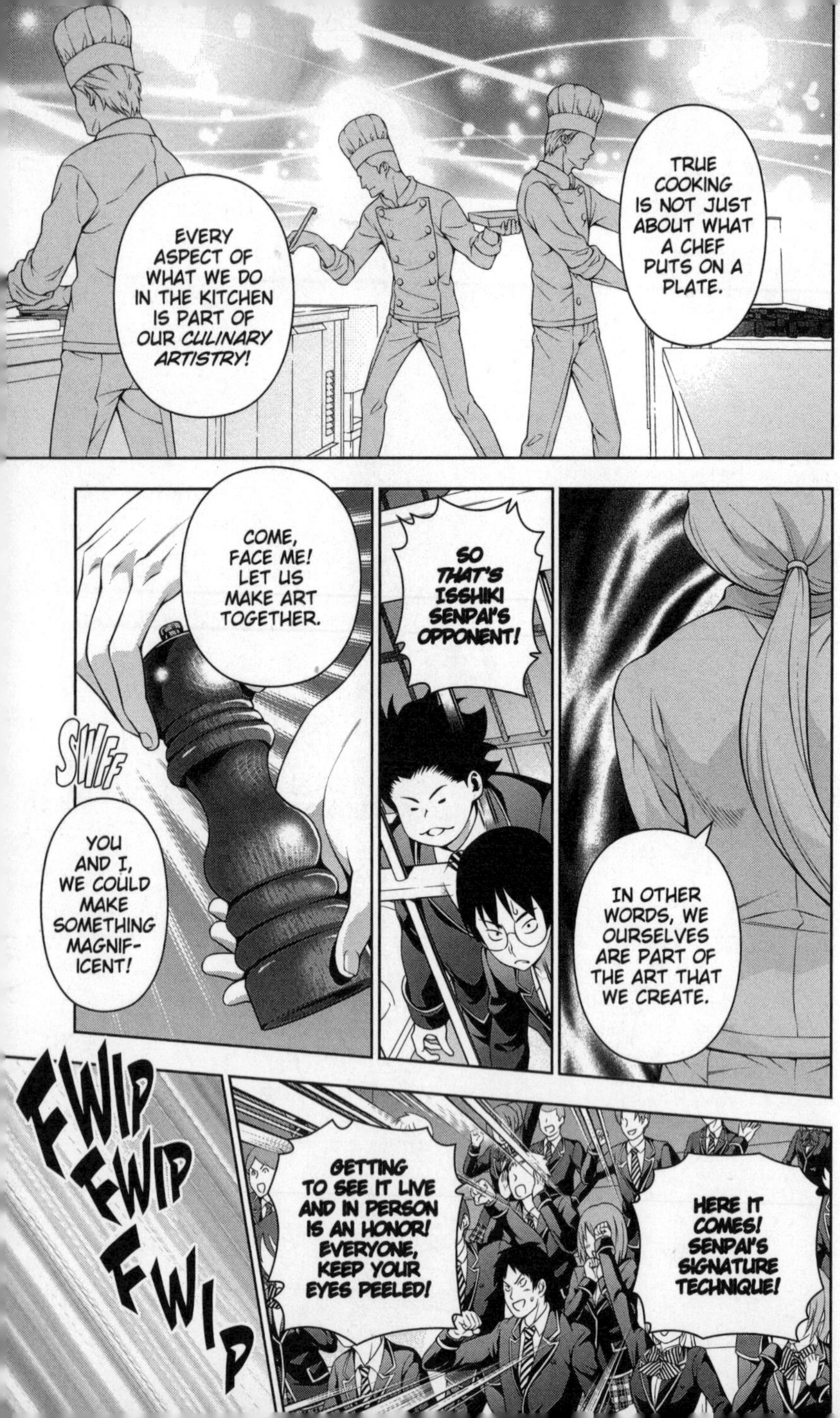
TRUE COOKING IS NOT JUST ABOUT WHAT A CHEF PUTS ON A PLATE.
EVERY ASPECT OF WHAT WE DO IN THE KITCHEN IS PART OF OUR *CULINARY ARTISTRY!*
IN OTHER WORDS, WE OURSELVES ARE PART OF THE ART THAT WE CREATE.
SO *THAT'S* ISSHIKI SENPAI'S OPPONENT!
COME, FACE ME! LET US MAKE ART TOGETHER.
SWFF
YOU AND I, WE COULD MAKE SOMETHING MAGNIF-ICENT!
HERE IT COMES! SENPAI'S SIGNATURE TECHNIQUE!
GETTING TO SEE IT LIVE AND IN PERSON IS AN HONOR! EVERYONE, KEEP YOUR EYES PEELED!
FWIP FWIP FWIP FWIP

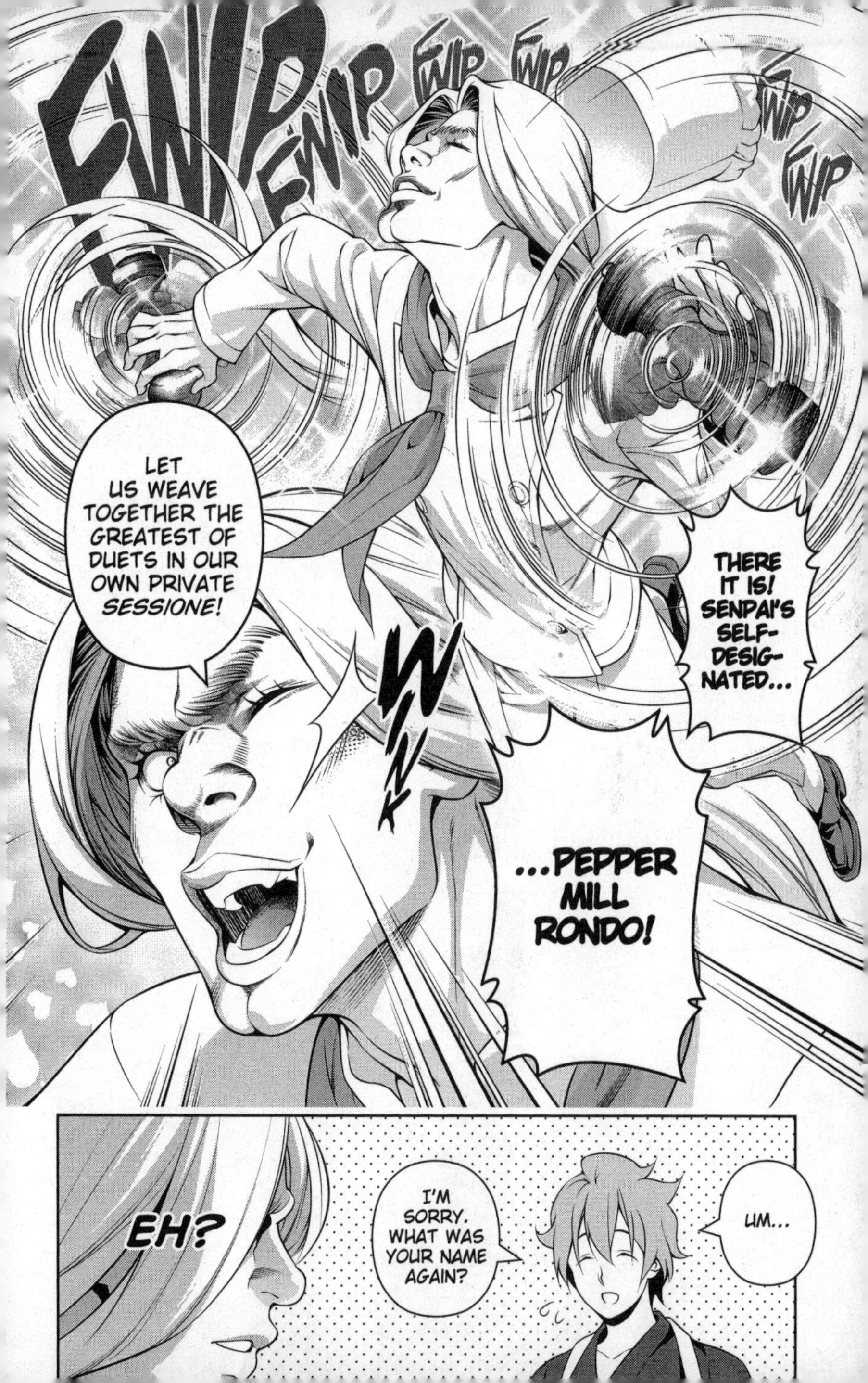
FWIP FWIP FWIP FWIP FWIP FWIP FWIP
LET US WEAVE TOGETHER THE GREATEST OF DUETS IN OUR OWN PRIVATE *SESSIONE*!
WINK
THERE IT IS! SENPAI'S SELF-DESIGNATED...
...PEPPER MILL RONDO!
UM...
I'M SORRY. WHAT WAS YOUR NAME AGAIN?
EH?

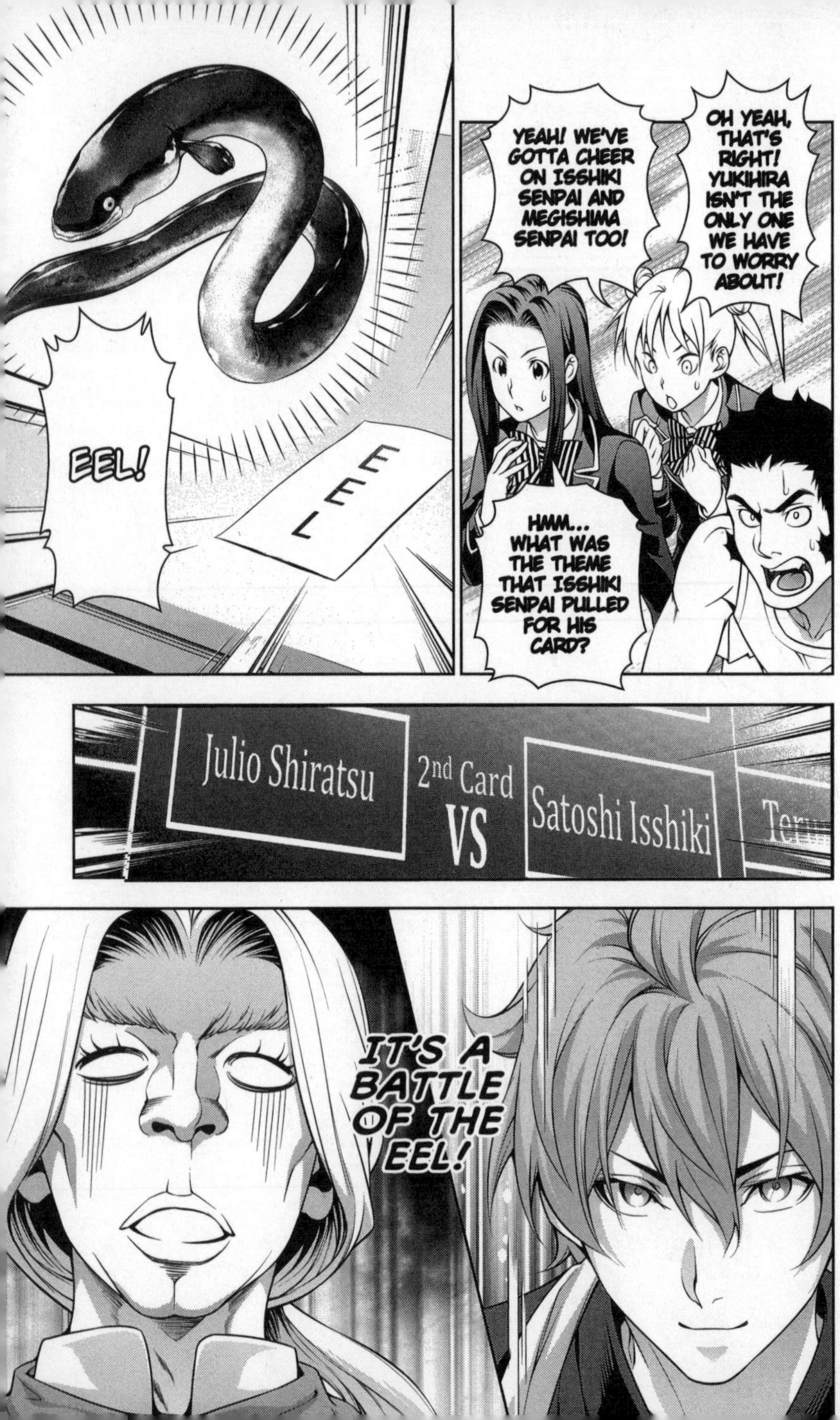
OH YEAH, THAT'S RIGHT! YUKIHIRA ISN'T THE ONLY ONE WE HAVE TO WORRY ABOUT!
YEAH! WE'VE GOTTA CHEER ON ISSHIKI SENPAI AND MEGISHIMA SENPAI TOO!
HMM... WHAT WAS THE THEME THAT ISSHIKI SENPAI PULLED FOR HIS CARD?
EEL!
EEL
Julio Shiratsu
2nd Card
VS
Satoshi Isshiki
IT'S A BATTLE OF THE EEL!

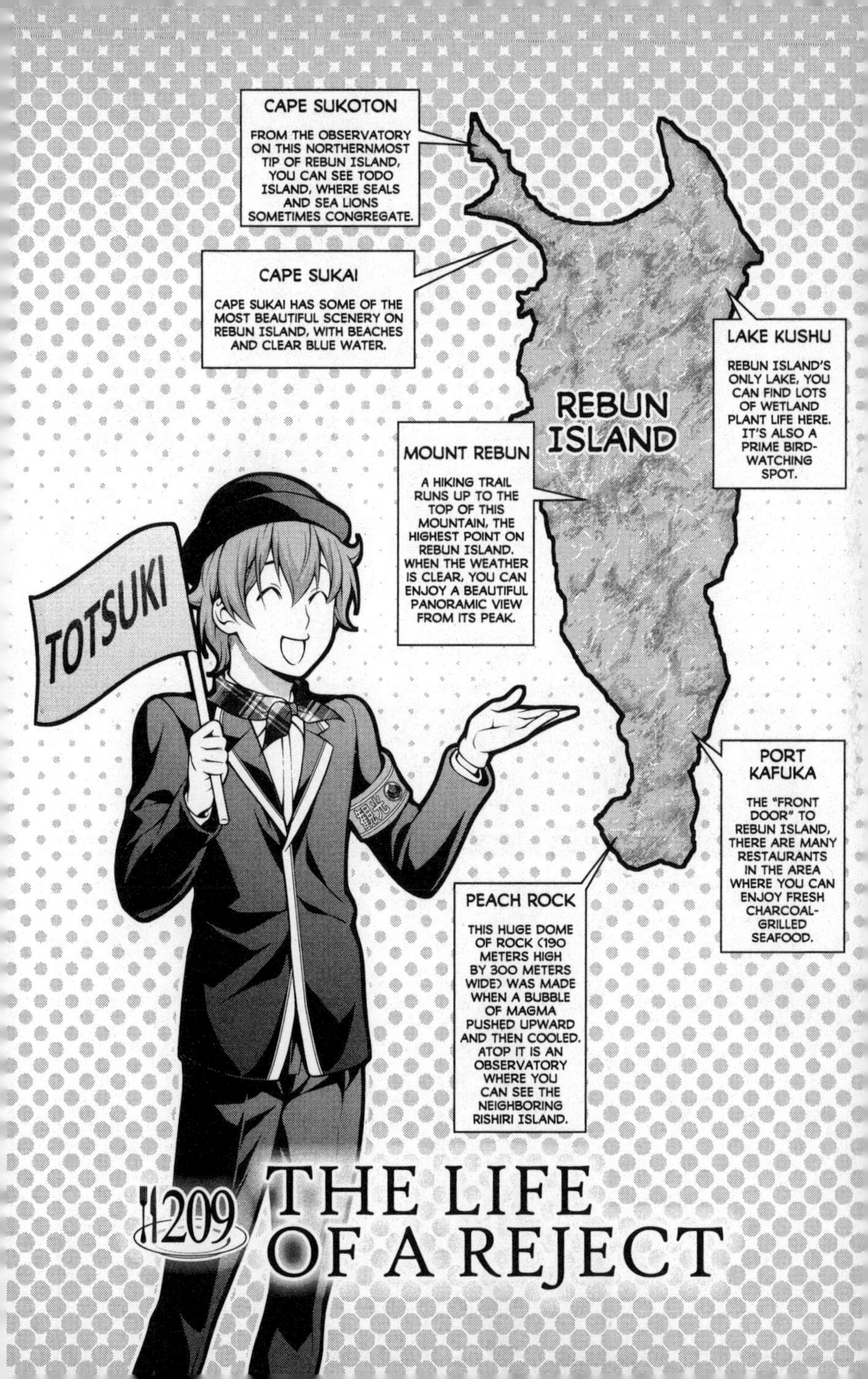
CAPE SUKOTON
FROM THE OBSERVATORY ON THIS NORTHERNMOST TIP OF REBUN ISLAND, YOU CAN SEE TODO ISLAND, WHERE SEALS AND SEA LIONS SOMETIMES CONGREGATE.
CAPE SUKAI
CAPE SUKAI HAS SOME OF THE MOST BEAUTIFUL SCENERY ON REBUN ISLAND, WITH BEACHES AND CLEAR BLUE WATER.
LAKE KUSHU
REBUN ISLAND'S ONLY LAKE, YOU CAN FIND LOTS OF WETLAND PLANT LIFE HERE. IT'S ALSO A PRIME BIRD-WATCHING SPOT.
REBUN ISLAND
MOUNT REBUN
A HIKING TRAIL RUNS UP TO THE TOP OF THIS MOUNTAIN, THE HIGHEST POINT ON REBUN ISLAND. WHEN THE WEATHER IS CLEAR, YOU CAN ENJOY A BEAUTIFUL PANORAMIC VIEW FROM ITS PEAK.
TOTSUKI
PORT KAFUKA
THE "FRONT DOOR" TO REBUN ISLAND, THERE ARE MANY RESTAURANTS IN THE AREA WHERE YOU CAN ENJOY FRESH CHARCOAL-GRILLED SEAFOOD.
PEACH ROCK
THIS HUGE DOME OF ROCK (190 METERS HIGH BY 300 METERS WIDE) WAS MADE WHEN A BUBBLE OF MAGMA PUSHED UPWARD AND THEN COOLED. ATOP IT IS AN OBSERVATORY WHERE YOU CAN SEE THE NEIGHBORING RISHIRI ISLAND.
209 THE LIFE OF A REJECT

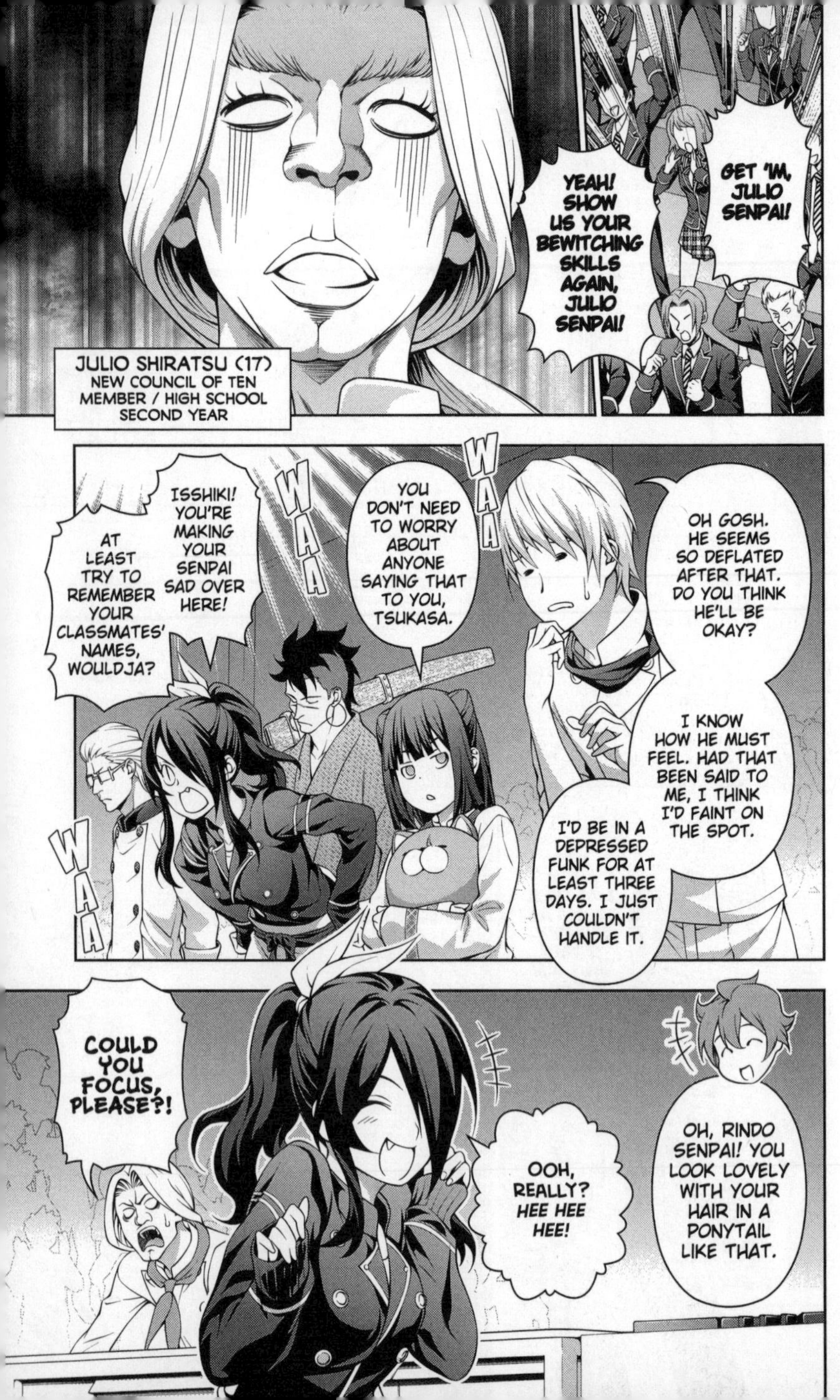
GET 'IM, JULIO SENPAI!
YEAH! SHOW US YOUR BEWITCHING SKILLS AGAIN, JULIO SENPAI!
JULIO SHIRATSU (17) NEW COUNCIL OF TEN MEMBER / HIGH SCHOOL SECOND YEAR
OH GOSH. HE SEEMS SO DEFLATED AFTER THAT. DO YOU THINK HE'LL BE OKAY?
I KNOW HOW HE MUST FEEL. HAD THAT BEEN SAID TO ME, I THINK I'D FAINT ON THE SPOT.
I'D BE IN A DEPRESSED FUNK FOR AT LEAST THREE DAYS. I JUST COULDN'T HANDLE IT.
WAA
YOU DON'T NEED TO WORRY ABOUT ANYONE SAYING THAT TO YOU, TSUKASA.
WAA
ISSHIKI! YOU'RE MAKING YOUR SENPAI SAD OVER HERE!
AT LEAST TRY TO REMEMBER YOUR CLASSMATES' NAMES, WOULDJA?
WAA
OH, RINDO SENPAI! YOU LOOK LOVELY WITH YOUR HAIR IN A PONYTAIL LIKE THAT.
OOH, REALLY? HEE HEE HEE!
COULD YOU FOCUS, PLEASE?!

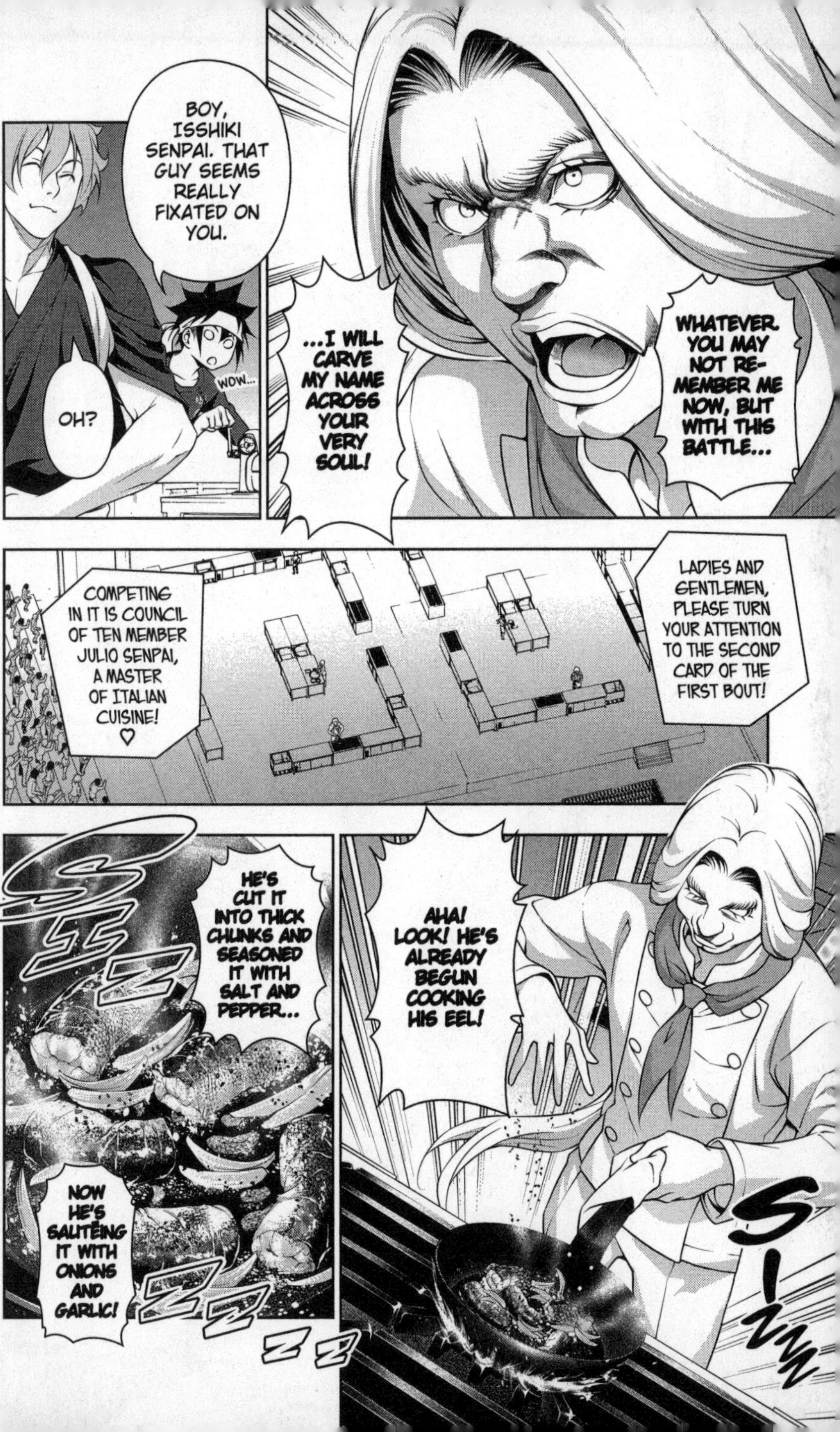

WHATEVER. YOU MAY NOT REMEMBER ME NOW, BUT WITH THIS BATTLE...
...I WILL CARVE MY NAME ACROSS YOUR VERY SOUL!
BOY, ISSHIKI SENPAI. THAT GUY SEEMS REALLY FIXATED ON YOU.
WOW...
OH?
LADIES AND GENTLEMEN, PLEASE TURN YOUR ATTENTION TO THE SECOND CARD OF THE FIRST BOUT!
COMPETING IN IT IS COUNCIL OF TEN MEMBER JULIO SENPAI, A MASTER OF ITALIAN CUISINE! ♡
AHA! LOOK! HE'S ALREADY BEGUN COOKING HIS EEL!
SIZZZ
HE'S CUT IT INTO THICK CHUNKS AND SEASONED IT WITH SALT AND PEPPER...
SIZZ
NOW HE'S SAUTÉING IT WITH ONIONS AND GARLIC!
ZZZZZ

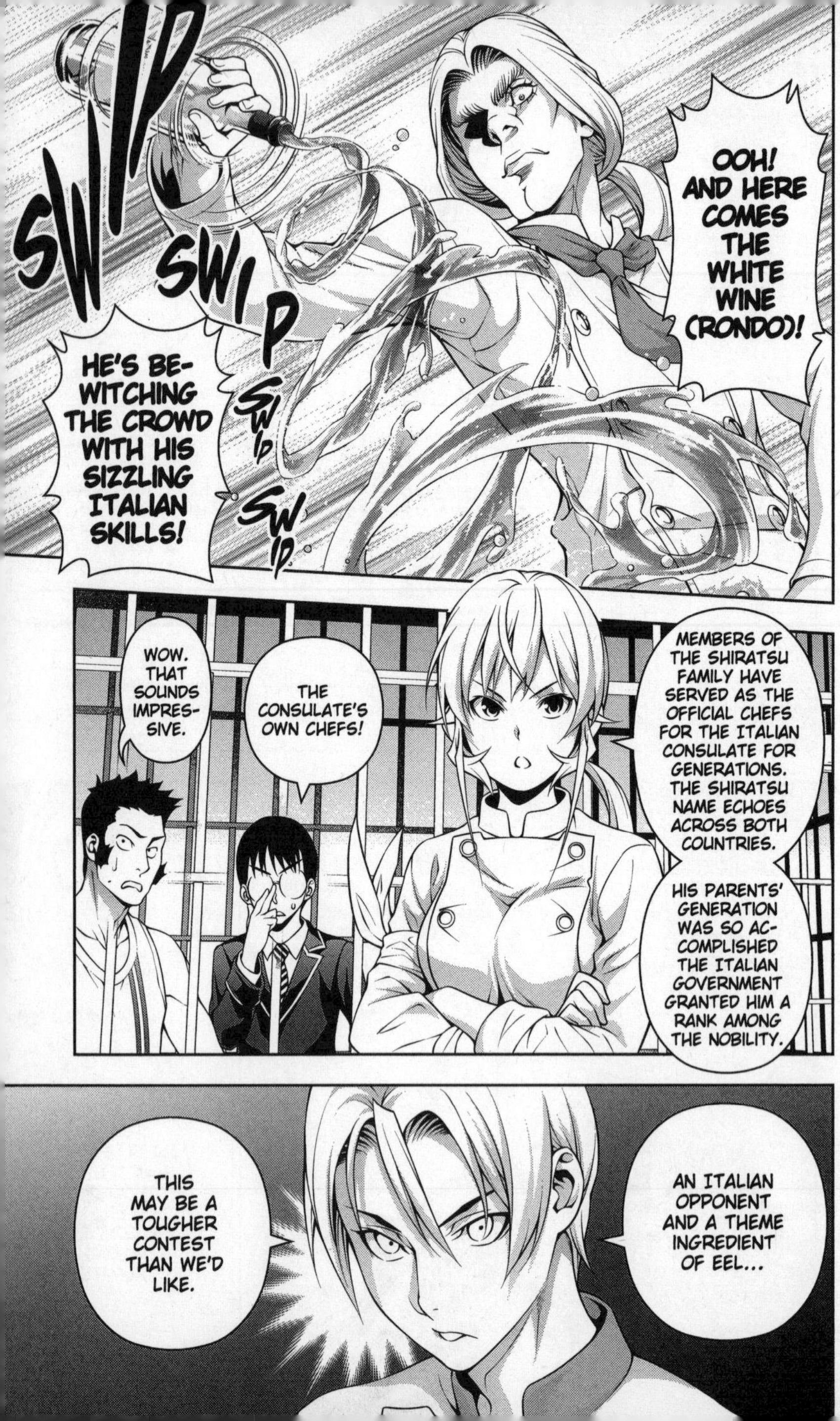
OOH! AND HERE COMES THE WHITE WINE (RONDO)!
SWIP
SWIP
HE'S BE-WITCHING THE CROWD WITH HIS SIZZLING ITALIAN SKILLS!
SWIP
SWIP
MEMBERS OF THE SHIRATSU FAMILY HAVE SERVED AS THE OFFICIAL CHEFS FOR THE ITALIAN CONSULATE FOR GENERATIONS. THE SHIRATSU NAME ECHOES ACROSS BOTH COUNTRIES.
HIS PARENTS' GENERATION WAS SO AC-COMPLISHED THE ITALIAN GOVERNMENT GRANTED HIM A RANK AMONG THE NOBILITY.
THE CONSULATE'S OWN CHEFS!
WOW. THAT SOUNDS IMPRES-SIVE.
AN ITALIAN OPPONENT AND A THEME INGREDIENT OF EEL...
THIS MAY BE A TOUGHER CONTEST THAN WE'D LIKE.

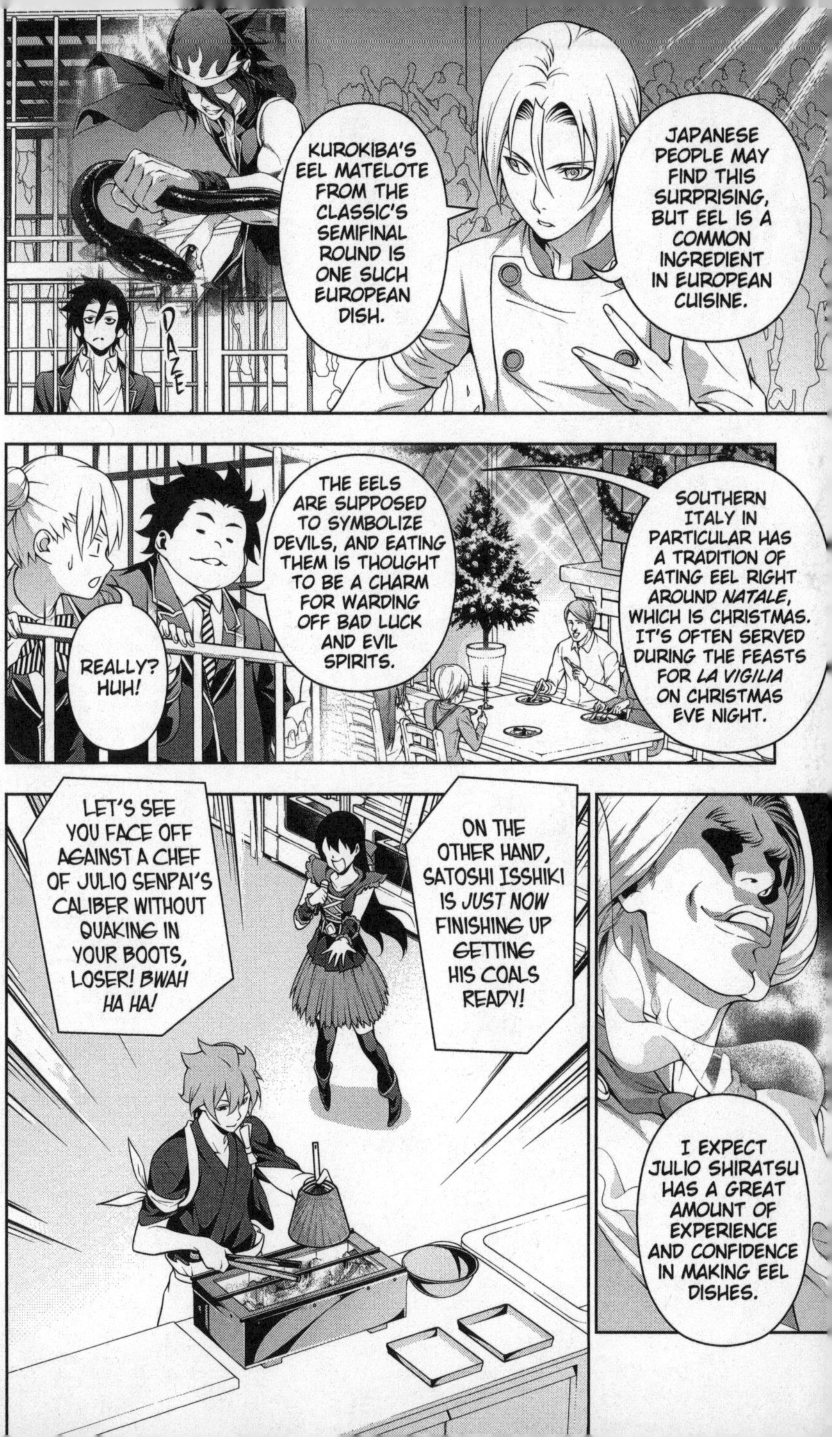
JAPANESE PEOPLE MAY FIND THIS SURPRISING, BUT EEL IS A COMMON INGREDIENT IN EUROPEAN CUISINE.
KUROKIBA'S EEL MATELOTE FROM THE CLASSIC'S SEMIFINAL ROUND IS ONE SUCH EUROPEAN DISH.
DAZE
SOUTHERN ITALY IN PARTICULAR HAS A TRADITION OF EATING EEL RIGHT AROUND *NATALE*, WHICH IS CHRISTMAS. IT'S OFTEN SERVED DURING THE FEASTS FOR *LA VIGILIA* ON CHRISTMAS EVE NIGHT.
THE EELS ARE SUPPOSED TO SYMBOLIZE DEVILS, AND EATING THEM IS THOUGHT TO BE A CHARM FOR WARDING OFF BAD LUCK AND EVIL SPIRITS.
REALLY? HUH!
I EXPECT JULIO SHIRATSU HAS A GREAT AMOUNT OF EXPERIENCE AND CONFIDENCE IN MAKING EEL DISHES.
ON THE OTHER HAND, SATOSHI ISSHIKI IS *JUST NOW* FINISHING UP GETTING HIS COALS READY!
LET'S SEE YOU FACE OFF AGAINST A CHEF OF JULIO SENPAI'S CALIBER WITHOUT QUAKING IN YOUR BOOTS, LOSER! *BWAH HA HA!*

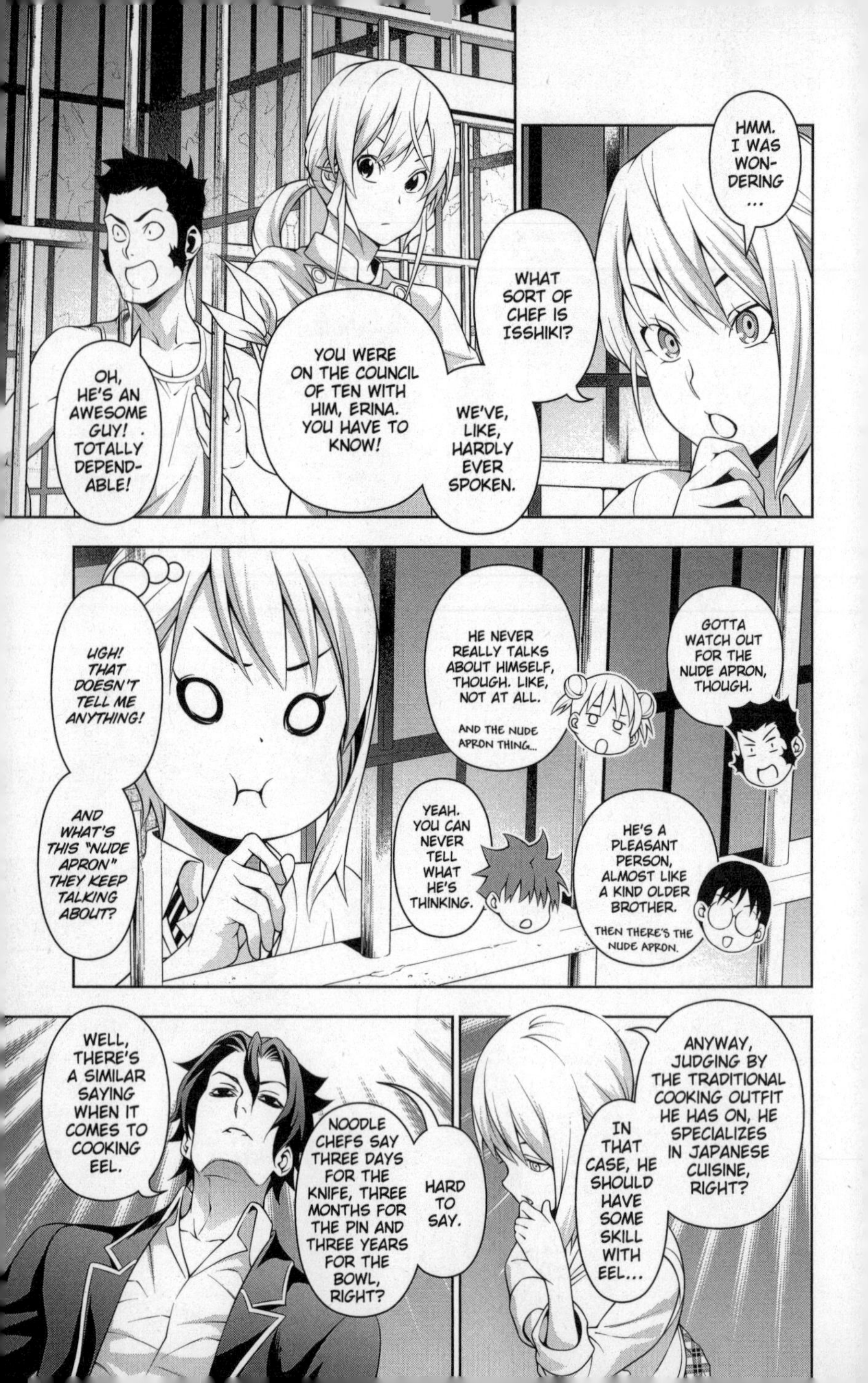
HMM. I WAS WON-DERING ...
WHAT SORT OF CHEF IS ISSHIKI?
YOU WERE ON THE COUNCIL OF TEN WITH HIM, ERINA. YOU HAVE TO KNOW!
WE'VE, LIKE, HARDLY EVER SPOKEN.
OH, HE'S AN AWESOME GUY! TOTALLY DEPEND-ABLE!
GOTTA WATCH OUT FOR THE NUDE APRON, THOUGH.
HE NEVER REALLY TALKS ABOUT HIMSELF, THOUGH. LIKE, NOT AT ALL.
AND THE NUDE APRON THING...
HE'S A PLEASANT PERSON, ALMOST LIKE A KIND OLDER BROTHER.
THEN THERE'S THE NUDE APRON.
YEAH. YOU CAN NEVER TELL WHAT HE'S THINKING.
UGH! THAT DOESN'T TELL ME ANYTHING!
AND WHAT'S THIS "NUDE APRON" THEY KEEP TALKING ABOUT?
ANYWAY, JUDGING BY THE TRADITIONAL COOKING OUTFIT HE HAS ON, HE SPECIALIZES IN JAPANESE CUISINE, RIGHT?
IN THAT CASE, HE SHOULD HAVE SOME SKILL WITH EEL...
HARD TO SAY.
NOODLE CHEFS SAY THREE DAYS FOR THE KNIFE, THREE MONTHS FOR THE PIN AND THREE YEARS FOR THE BOWL, RIGHT?
WELL, THERE'S A SIMILAR SAYING WHEN IT COMES TO COOKING EEL.

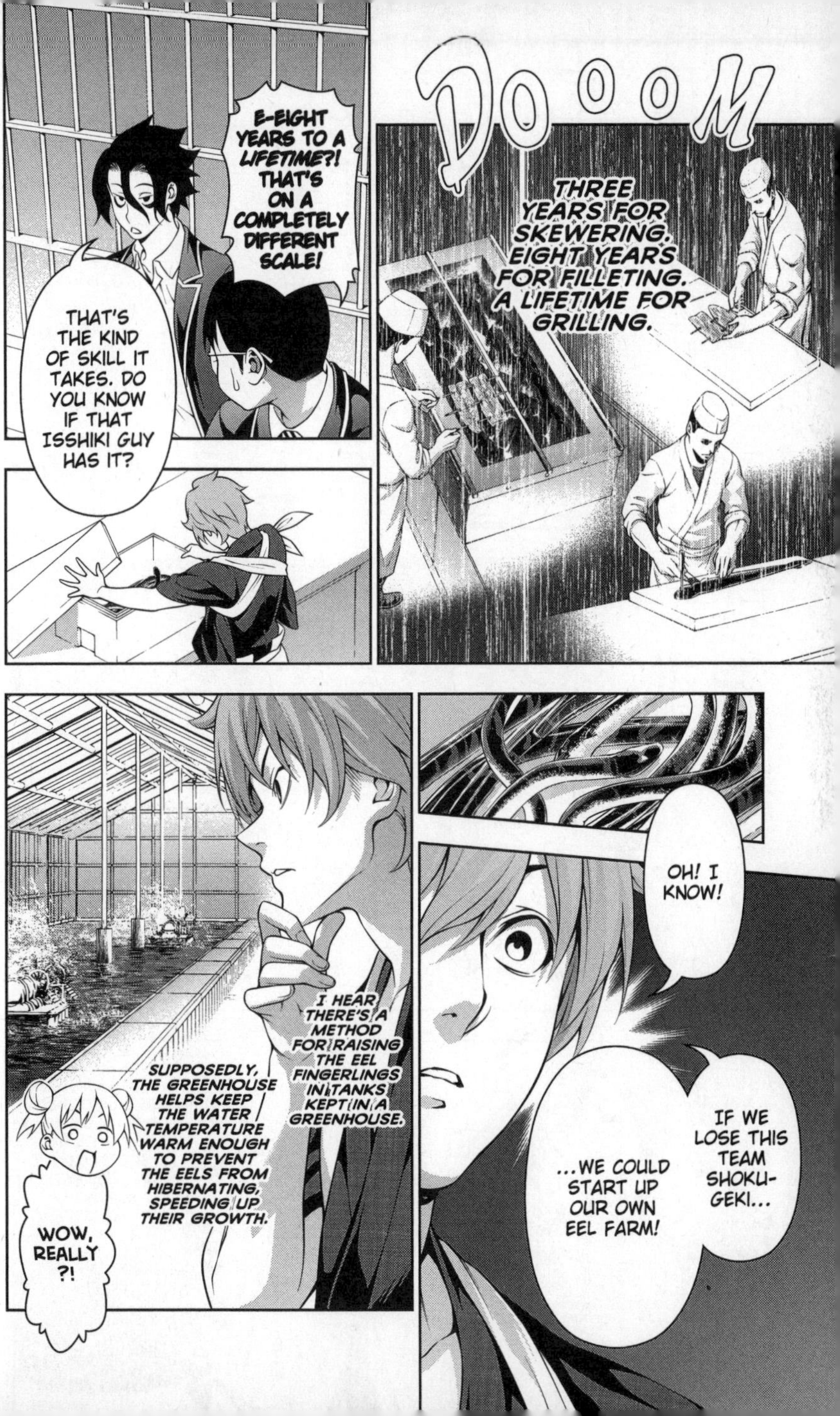
DOOOOM
THREE YEARS FOR SKEWERING. EIGHT YEARS FOR FILLETING. A LIFETIME FOR GRILLING.
E-EIGHT YEARS TO A LIFETIME?! THAT'S ON A COMPLETELY DIFFERENT SCALE!
THAT'S THE KIND OF SKILL IT TAKES. DO YOU KNOW IF THAT ISSHIKI GUY HAS IT?
OH! I KNOW!
IF WE LOSE THIS TEAM SHOKU-GEKI...
...WE COULD START UP OUR OWN EEL FARM!
I HEAR THERE'S A METHOD FOR RAISING THE EEL FINGERLINGS IN TANKS KEPT IN A GREENHOUSE.
SUPPOSEDLY, THE GREENHOUSE HELPS KEEP THE WATER TEMPERATURE WARM ENOUGH TO PREVENT THE EELS FROM HIBERNATING, SPEEDING UP THEIR GROWTH.
WOW, REALLY ?!

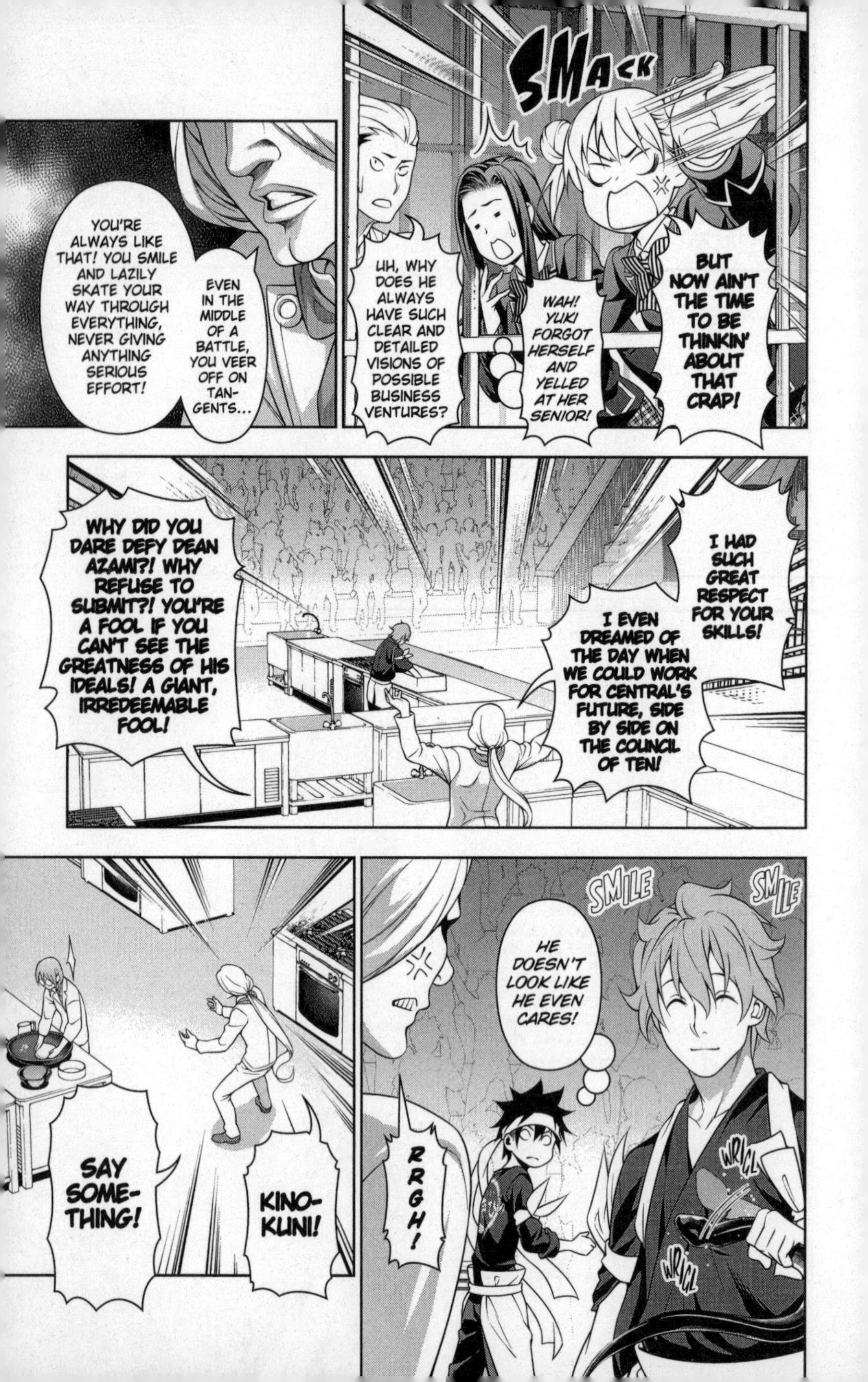
SMACK
BUT NOW AIN'T THE TIME TO BE THINKIN' ABOUT THAT CRAP!
WAH! YUKI FORGOT HERSELF AND YELLED AT HER SENIOR!
UH, WHY DOES HE ALWAYS HAVE SUCH CLEAR AND DETAILED VISIONS OF POSSIBLE BUSINESS VENTURES?
EVEN IN THE MIDDLE OF A BATTLE, YOU VEER OFF ON TAN-GENTS...
YOU'RE ALWAYS LIKE THAT! YOU SMILE AND LAZILY SKATE YOUR WAY THROUGH EVERYTHING, NEVER GIVING ANYTHING SERIOUS EFFORT!
I HAD SUCH GREAT RESPECT FOR YOUR SKILLS!
I EVEN DREAMED OF THE DAY WHEN WE COULD WORK FOR CENTRAL'S FUTURE, SIDE BY SIDE ON THE COUNCIL OF TEN!
WHY DID YOU DARE DEFY DEAN AZAMI?! WHY REFUSE TO SUBMIT?! YOU'RE A FOOL IF YOU CAN'T SEE THE GREATNESS OF HIS IDEALS! A GIANT, IRREDEEMABLE FOOL!
SMILE
SMILE
HE DOESN'T LOOK LIKE HE EVEN CARES!
RRGH!
WRIGL
WRIGL
KINO-KUNI!
SAY SOME-THING!

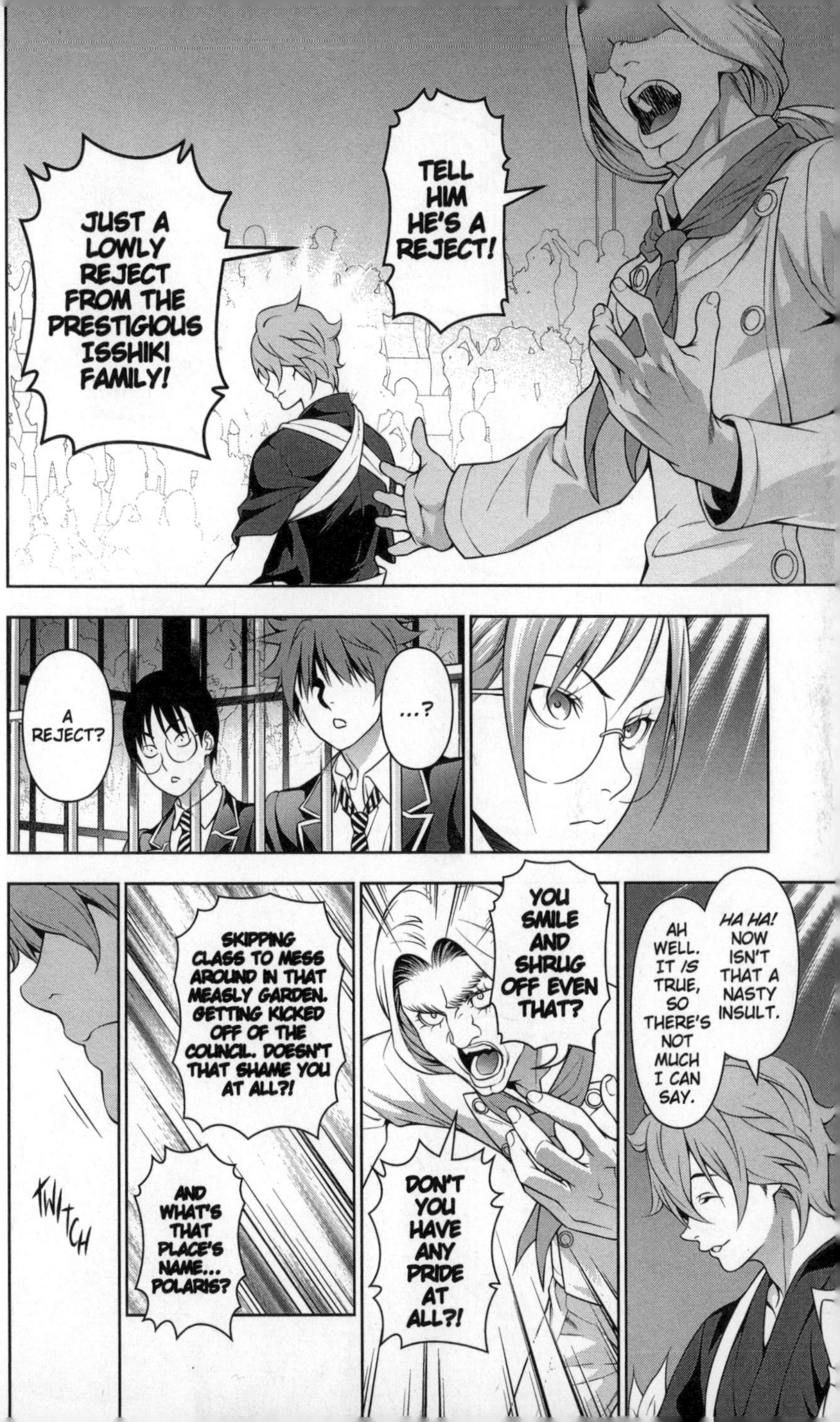
TELL HIM HE'S A REJECT!
JUST A LOWLY REJECT FROM THE PRESTIGIOUS ISSHIKI FAMILY!
...?
A REJECT?
HA HA! NOW ISN'T THAT A NASTY INSULT.
AH WELL. IT *IS* TRUE, SO THERE'S NOT MUCH I CAN SAY.
YOU SMILE AND SHRUG OFF EVEN THAT?
DON'T YOU HAVE ANY PRIDE AT ALL?!
SKIPPING CLASS TO MESS AROUND IN THAT MEASLY GARDEN. GETTING KICKED OFF OF THE COUNCIL. DOESN'T THAT SHAME YOU AT ALL?!
AND WHAT'S THAT PLACE'S NAME... POLARIS?
TWITCH

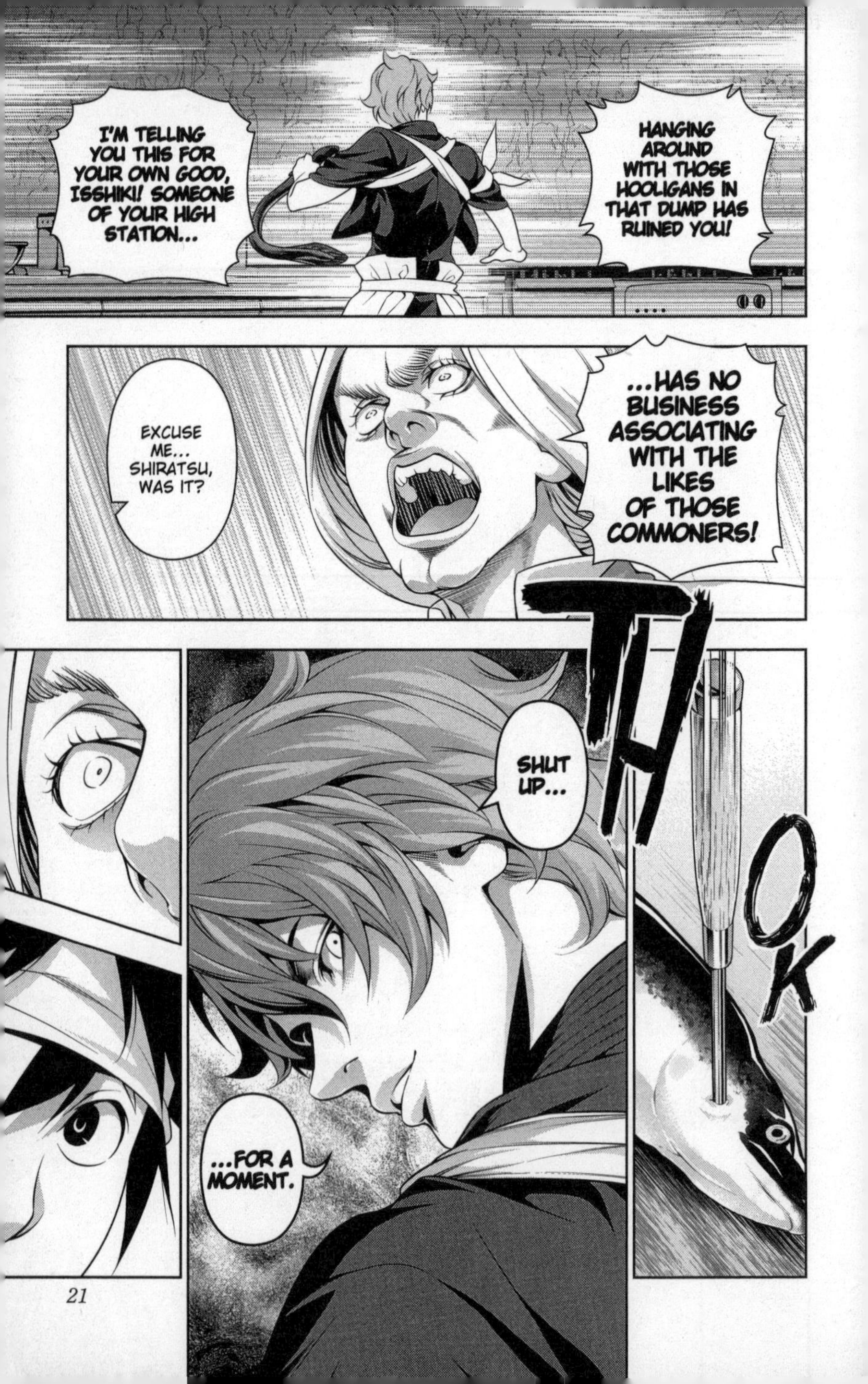
HANGING AROUND WITH THOSE HOOLIGANS IN THAT DUMP HAS RUINED YOU!
I'M TELLING YOU THIS FOR YOUR OWN GOOD, ISSHIKI! SOMEONE OF YOUR HIGH STATION...
...HAS NO BUSINESS ASSOCIATING WITH THE LIKES OF THOSE COMMONERS!
EXCUSE ME... SHIRATSU, WAS IT?
THOK
SHUT UP...
...FOR A MOMENT.

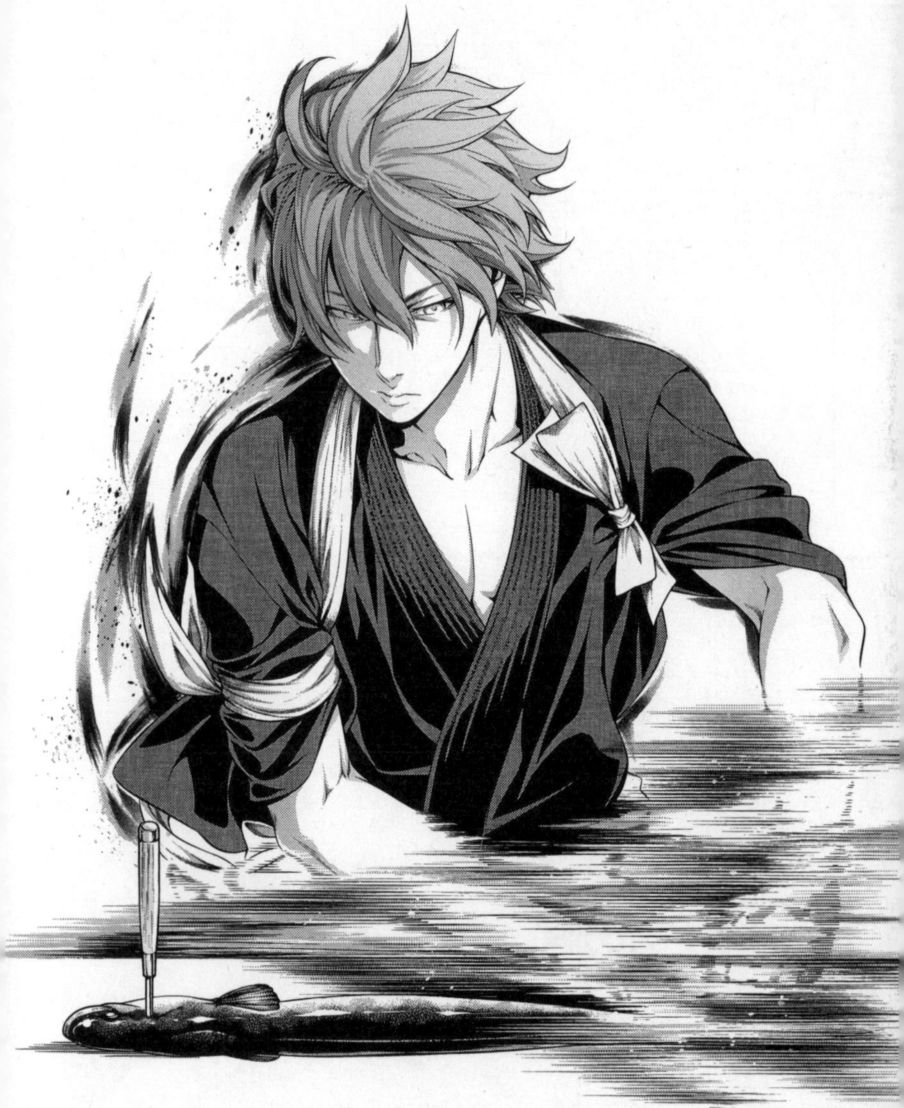

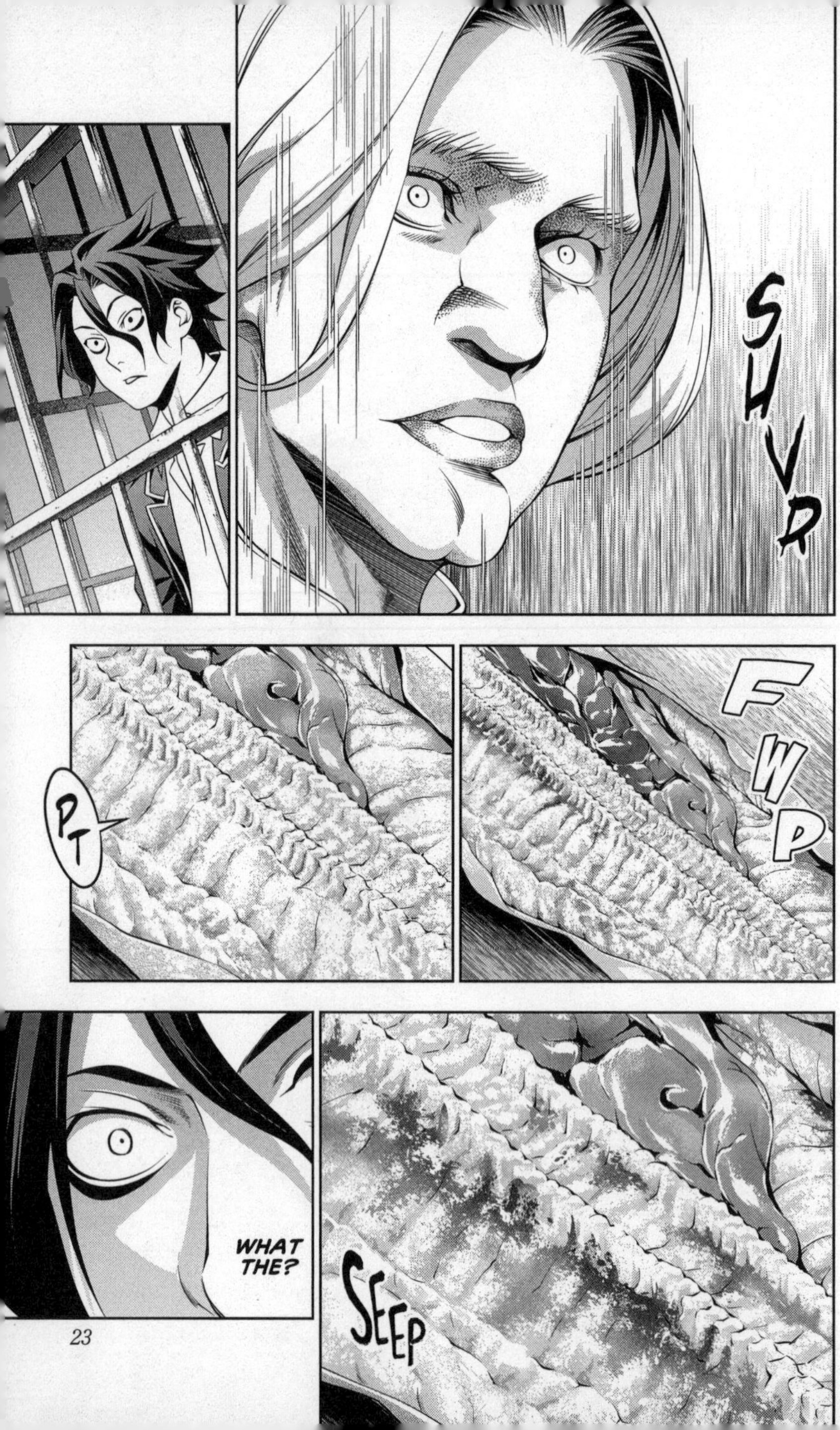
SHVR
FWP
PT
SEEP
WHAT THE?

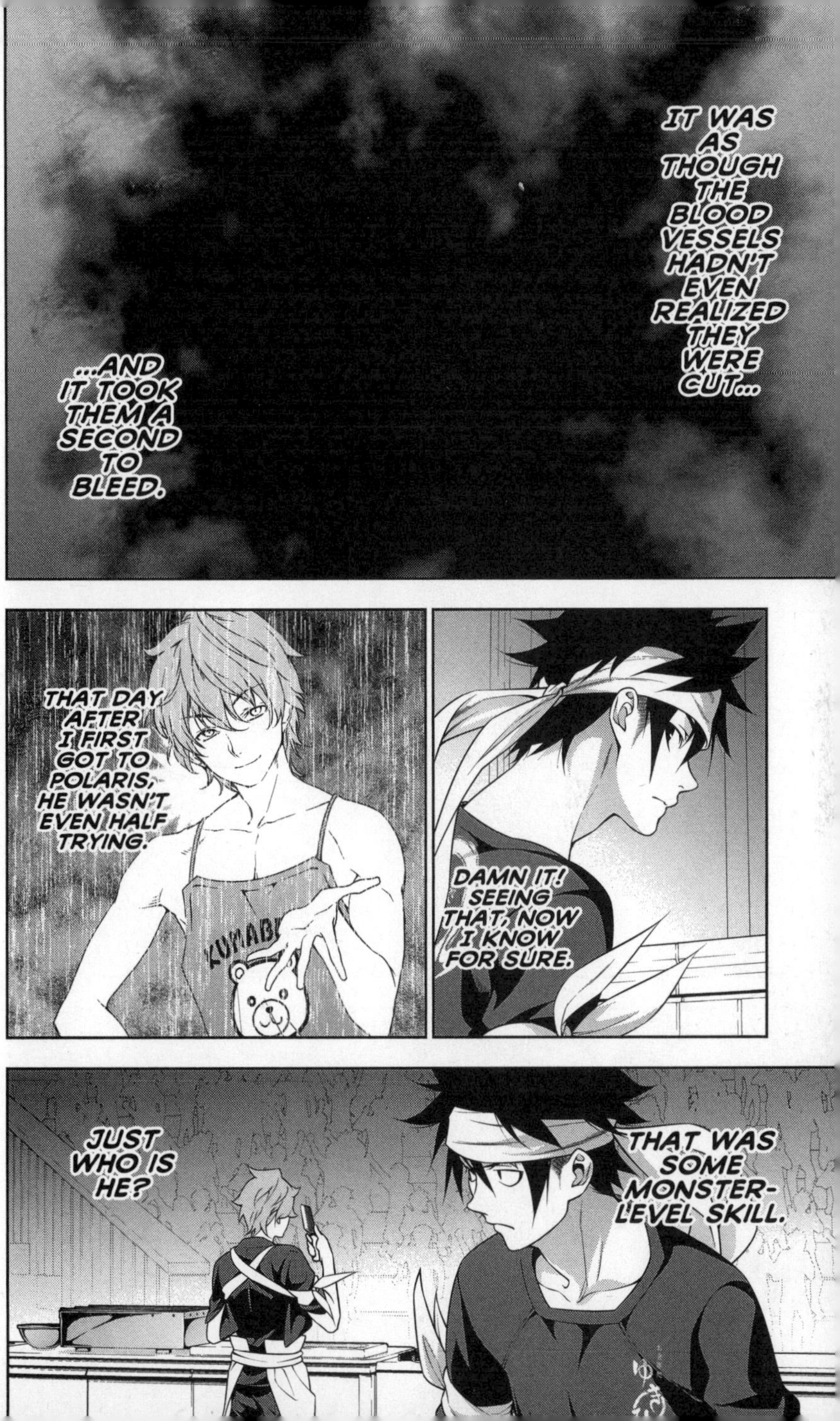
IT WAS AS THOUGH THE BLOOD VESSELS HADN'T EVEN REALIZED THEY WERE CUT...
...AND IT TOOK THEM A SECOND TO BLEED.
DAMN IT! SEEING THAT, NOW I KNOW FOR SURE.
THAT DAY AFTER I FIRST GOT TO POLARIS, HE WASN'T EVEN HALF TRYING.
THAT WAS SOME MONSTER-LEVEL SKILL.
JUST WHO IS HE?

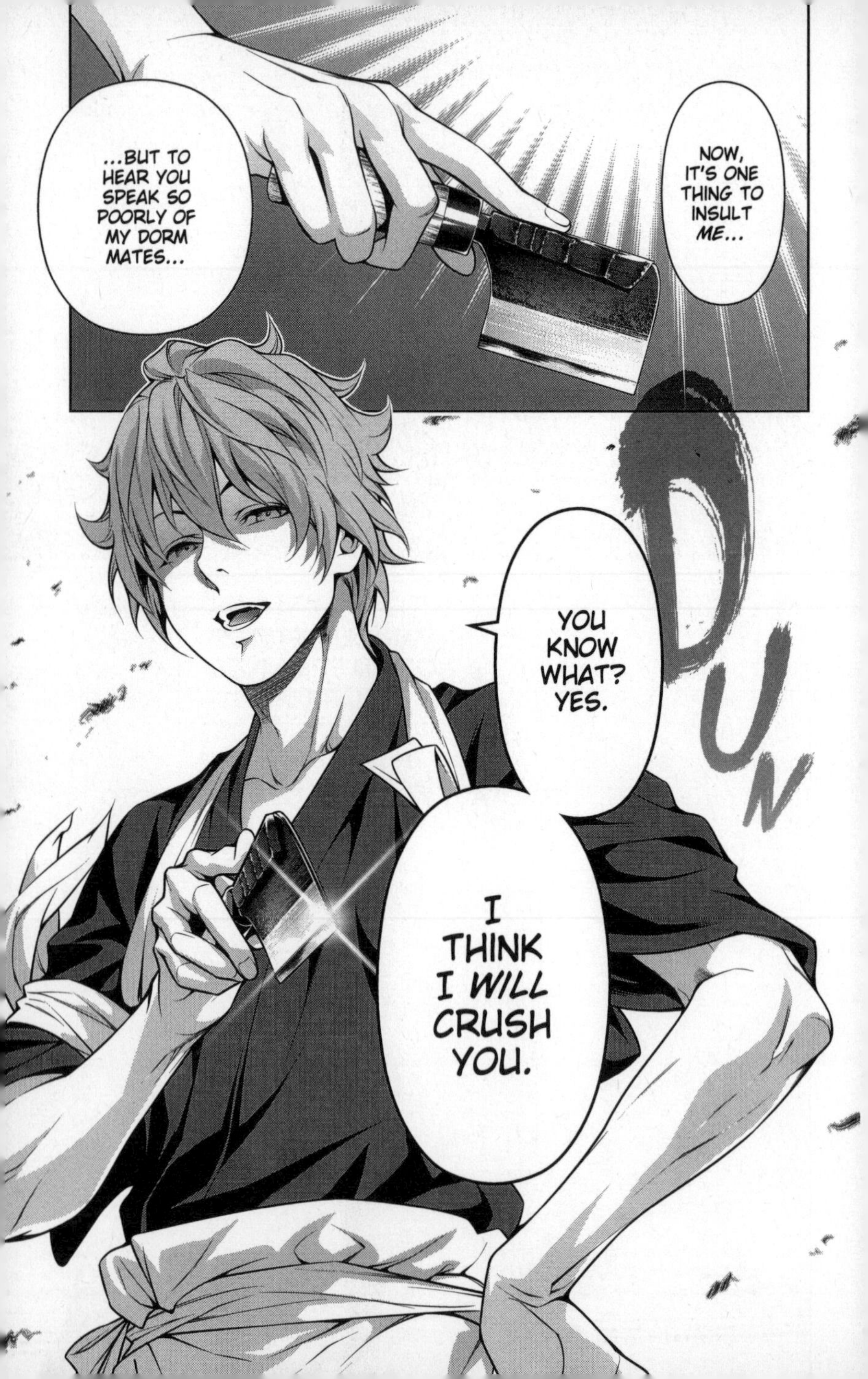
NOW, IT'S ONE THING TO INSULT *ME*...
...BUT TO HEAR YOU SPEAK SO POORLY OF MY DORM MATES...
DUN
YOU KNOW WHAT? YES.
I THINK I *WILL* CRUSH YOU.

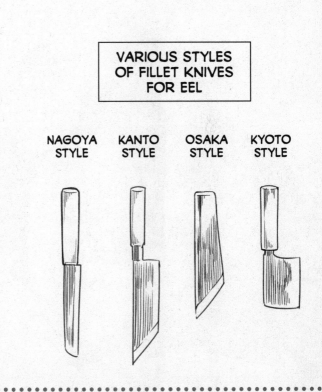

VARIOUS STYLES
OF FILLET KNIVES
FOR EEL

NAGOYA
STYLE

KANTO
STYLE

OSAKA
STYLE

KYOTO
STYLE

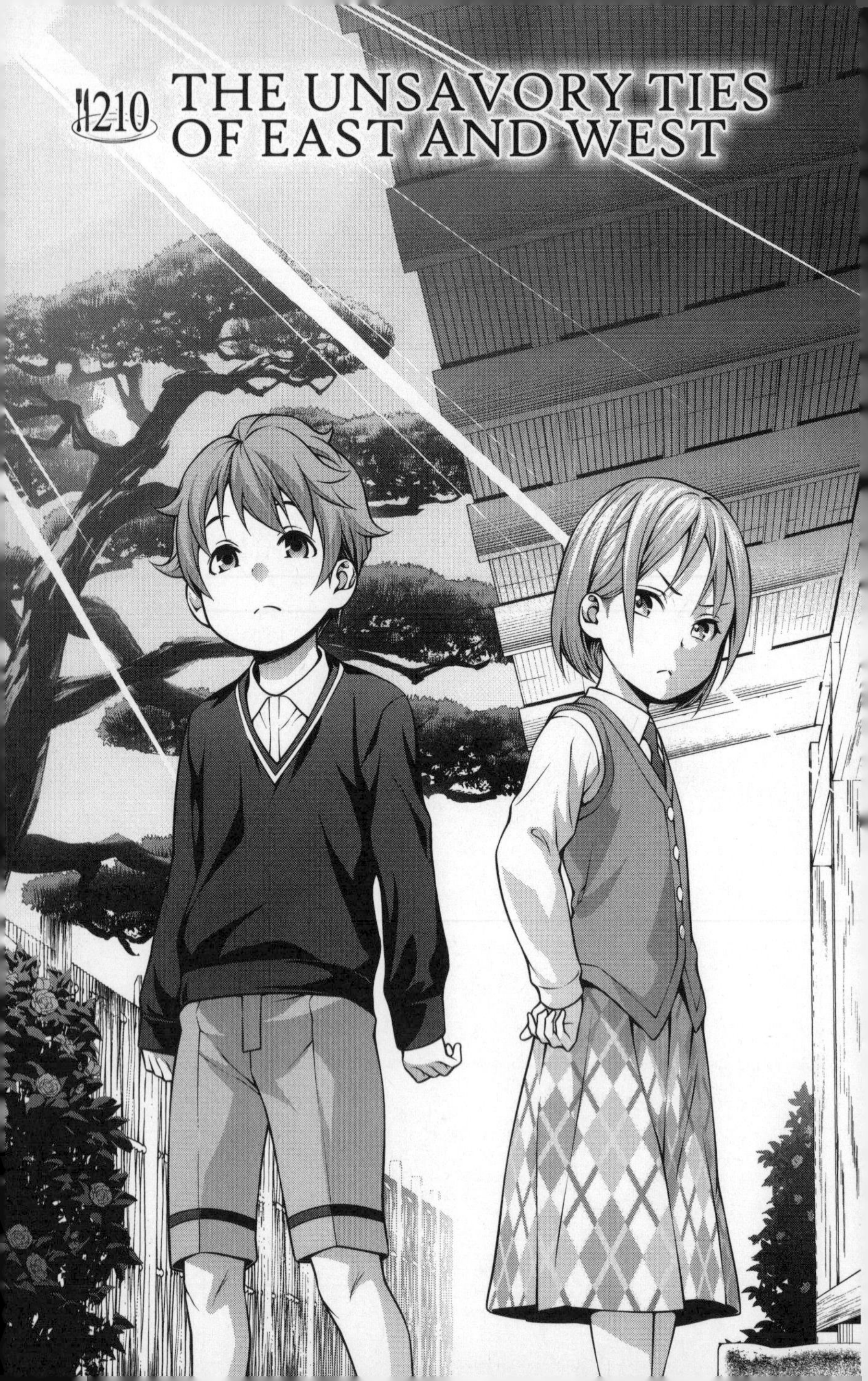
210
THE UNSAVORY TIES
OF EAST AND WEST

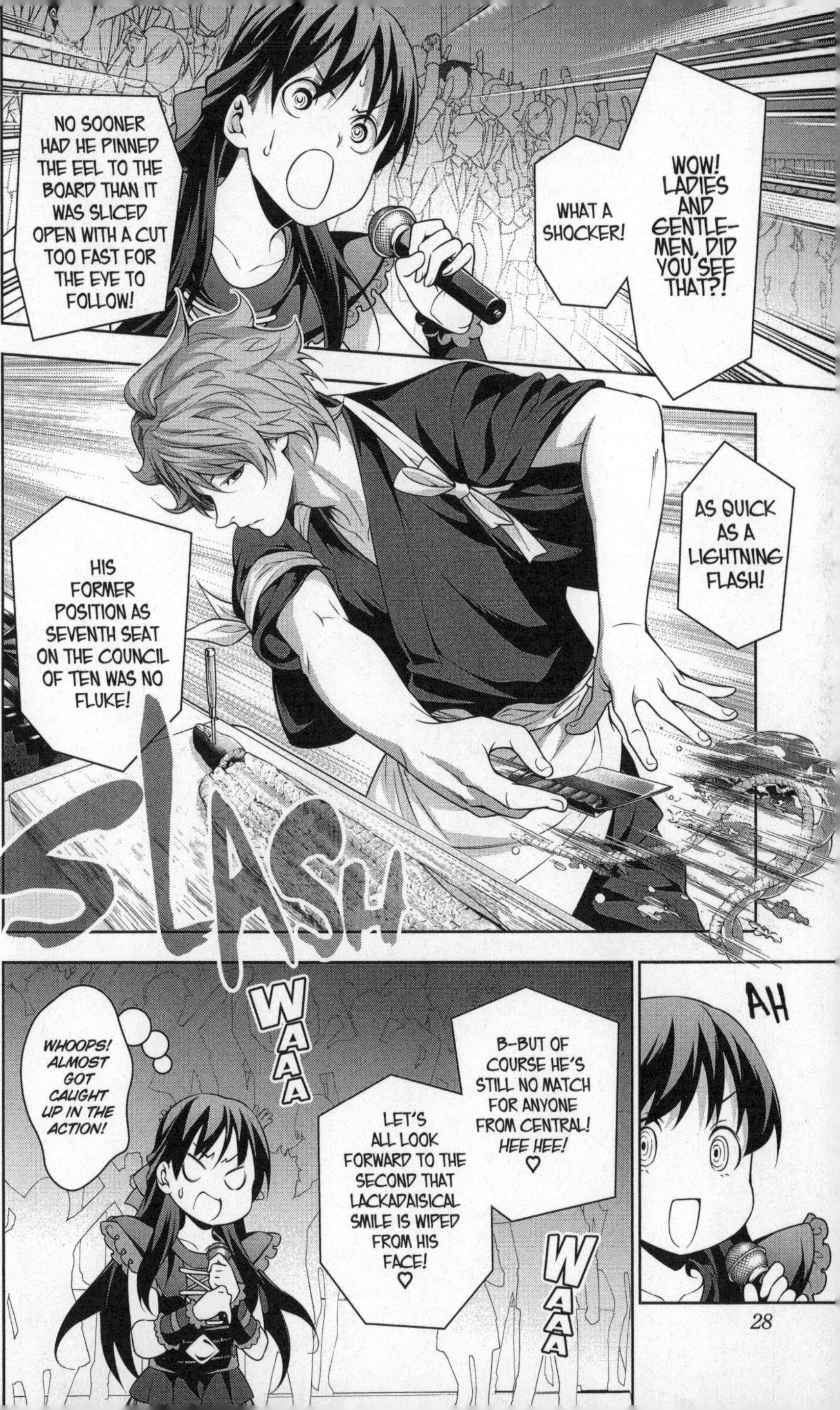
WOW! LADIES AND GENTLEMEN, DID YOU SEE THAT?!
WHAT A SHOCKER!
NO SOONER HAD HE PINNED THE EEL TO THE BOARD THAN IT WAS SLICED OPEN WITH A CUT TOO FAST FOR THE EYE TO FOLLOW!
AS QUICK AS A LIGHTNING FLASH!
HIS FORMER POSITION AS SEVENTH SEAT ON THE COUNCIL OF TEN WAS NO FLUKE!
SLASH
AH
B-BUT OF COURSE HE'S STILL NO MATCH FOR ANYONE FROM CENTRAL! HEE HEE! ♡
LET'S ALL LOOK FORWARD TO THE SECOND THAT LACKADAISICAL SMILE IS WIPED FROM HIS FACE! ♡
WAAA
WAAA
WHOOPS! ALMOST GOT CAUGHT UP IN THE ACTION!

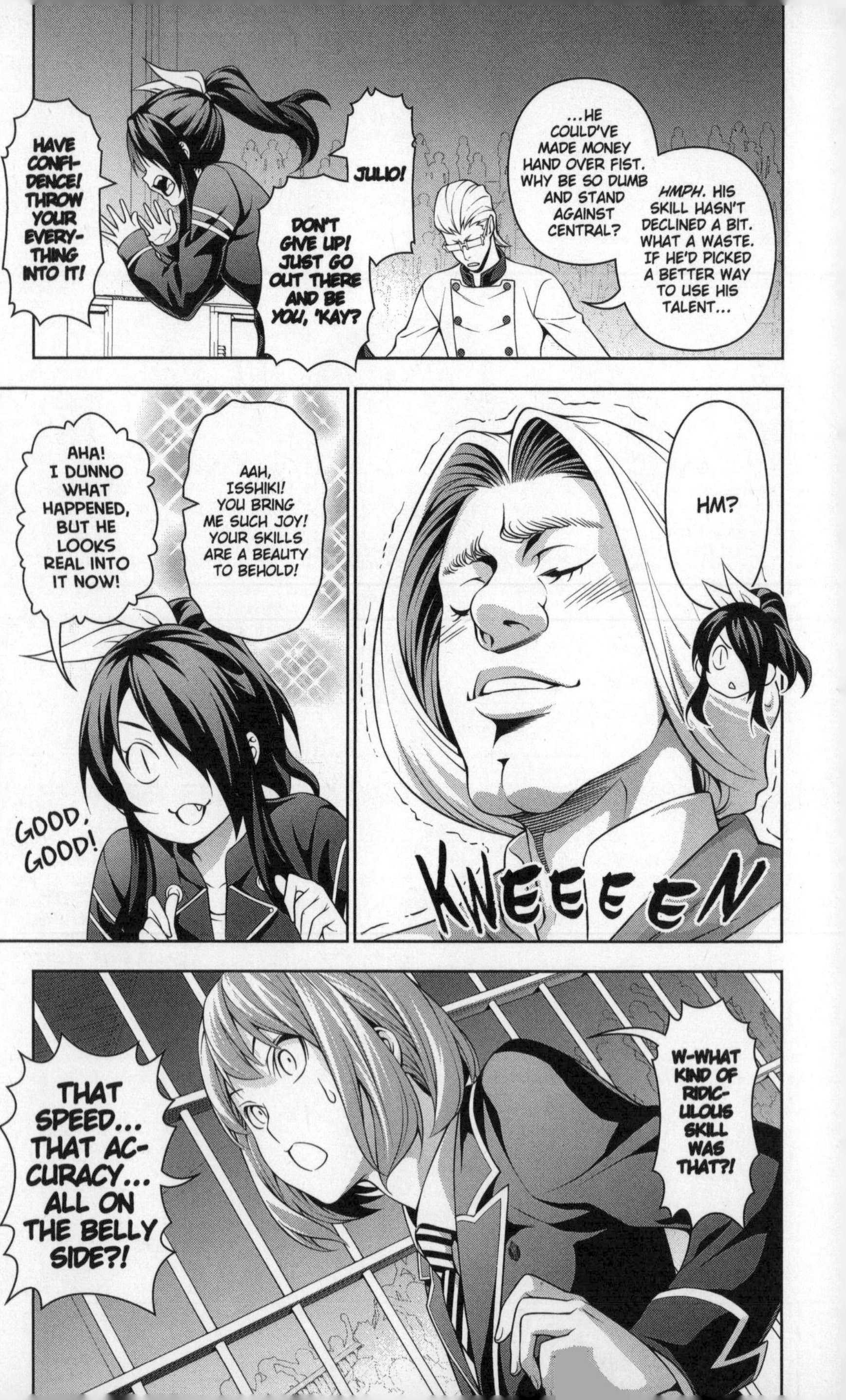
HMPH. HIS SKILL HASN'T DECLINED A BIT. WHAT A WASTE. IF HE'D PICKED A BETTER WAY TO USE HIS TALENT...
...HE COULD'VE MADE MONEY HAND OVER FIST. WHY BE SO DUMB AND STAND AGAINST CENTRAL?
JULIO!
DON'T GIVE UP! JUST GO OUT THERE AND BE YOU, 'KAY?
HAVE CONFIDENCE! THROW YOUR EVERYTHING INTO IT!
HM?
KWEEEEEN
AAH, ISSHIKI! YOU BRING ME SUCH JOY! YOUR SKILLS ARE A BEAUTY TO BEHOLD!
AHA! I DUNNO WHAT HAPPENED, BUT HE LOOKS REAL INTO IT NOW!
GOOD, GOOD!
W-WHAT KIND OF RIDICULOUS SKILL WAS THAT?!
THAT SPEED... THAT ACCURACY... ALL ON THE BELLY SIDE?!

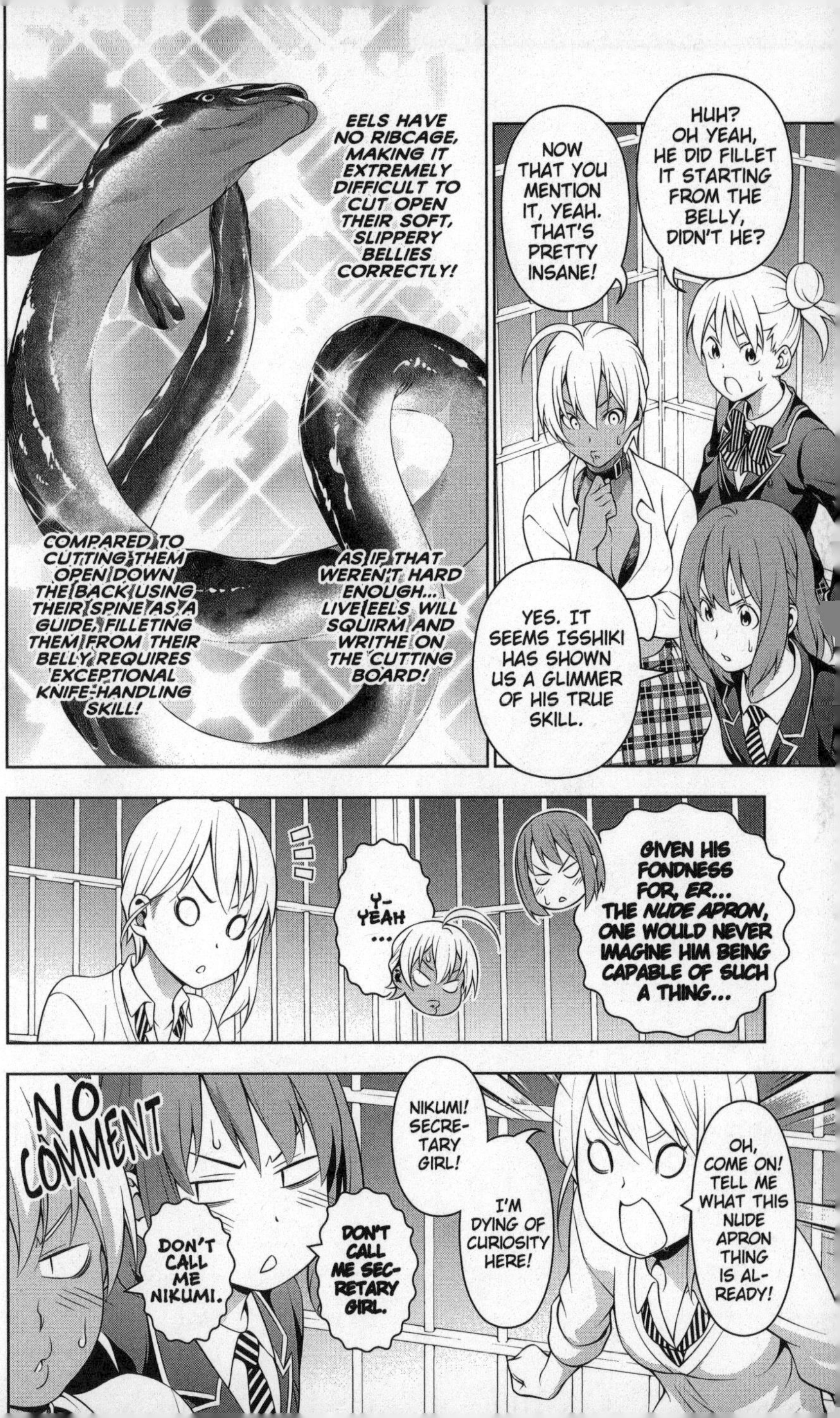
HUH? OH YEAH, HE DID FILLET IT STARTING FROM THE BELLY, DIDN'T HE?
NOW THAT YOU MENTION IT, YEAH. THAT'S PRETTY INSANE!
YES. IT SEEMS ISSHIKI HAS SHOWN US A GLIMMER OF HIS TRUE SKILL.
EELS HAVE NO RIBCAGE, MAKING IT EXTREMELY DIFFICULT TO CUT OPEN THEIR SOFT, SLIPPERY BELLIES CORRECTLY!
AS IF THAT WEREN'T HARD ENOUGH... LIVE EELS WILL SQUIRM AND WRITHE ON THE CUTTING BOARD!
COMPARED TO CUTTING THEM OPEN DOWN THE BACK USING THEIR SPINE AS A GUIDE, FILLETING THEM FROM THEIR BELLY REQUIRES EXCEPTIONAL KNIFE-HANDLING SKILL!
GIVEN HIS FONDNESS FOR, ER... THE NUDE APRON, ONE WOULD NEVER IMAGINE HIM BEING CAPABLE OF SUCH A THING...
Y-YEAH...
OH, COME ON! TELL ME WHAT THIS NUDE APRON THING IS ALREADY!
NIKUMI! SECRETARY GIRL!
I'M DYING OF CURIOSITY HERE!
DON'T CALL ME SECRETARY GIRL.
DON'T CALL ME NIKUMI.
NO COMMENT

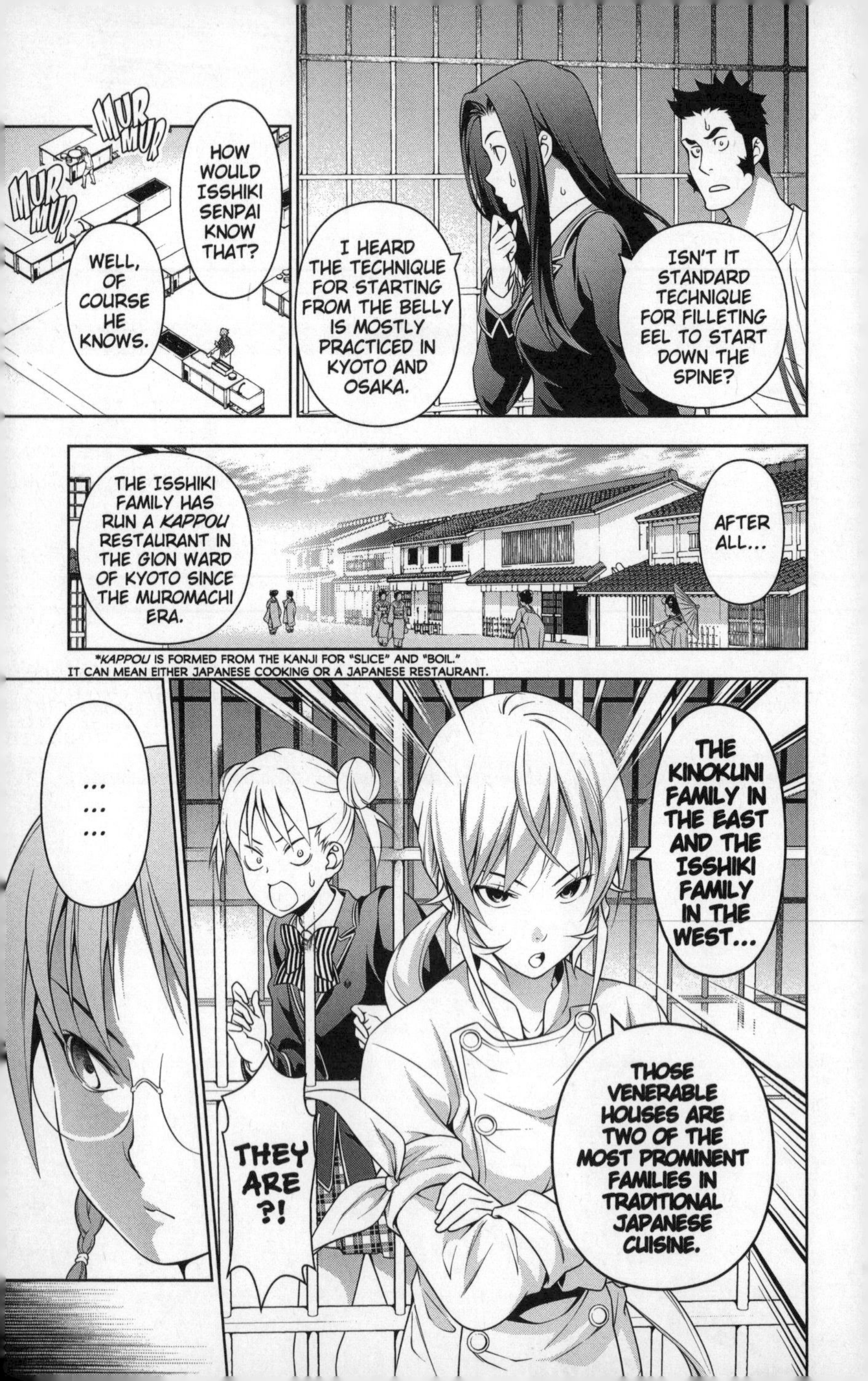
ISN'T IT STANDARD TECHNIQUE FOR FILLETING EEL TO START DOWN THE SPINE?
I HEARD THE TECHNIQUE FOR STARTING FROM THE BELLY IS MOSTLY PRACTICED IN KYOTO AND OSAKA.
HOW WOULD ISSHIKI SENPAI KNOW THAT?
MUR MUR
MUR MUR
WELL, OF COURSE HE KNOWS.
AFTER ALL...
THE ISSHIKI FAMILY HAS RUN A *KAPPOU* RESTAURANT IN THE GION WARD OF KYOTO SINCE THE MUROMACHI ERA.
THE KINOKUNI FAMILY IN THE EAST AND THE ISSHIKI FAMILY IN THE WEST...
THOSE VENERABLE HOUSES ARE TWO OF THE MOST PROMINENT FAMILIES IN TRADITIONAL JAPANESE CUISINE.
THEY ARE ?!
... ...

**KAPPOU* IS FORMED FROM THE KANJI FOR "SLICE" AND "BOIL." IT CAN MEAN EITHER JAPANESE COOKING OR A JAPANESE RESTAURANT.

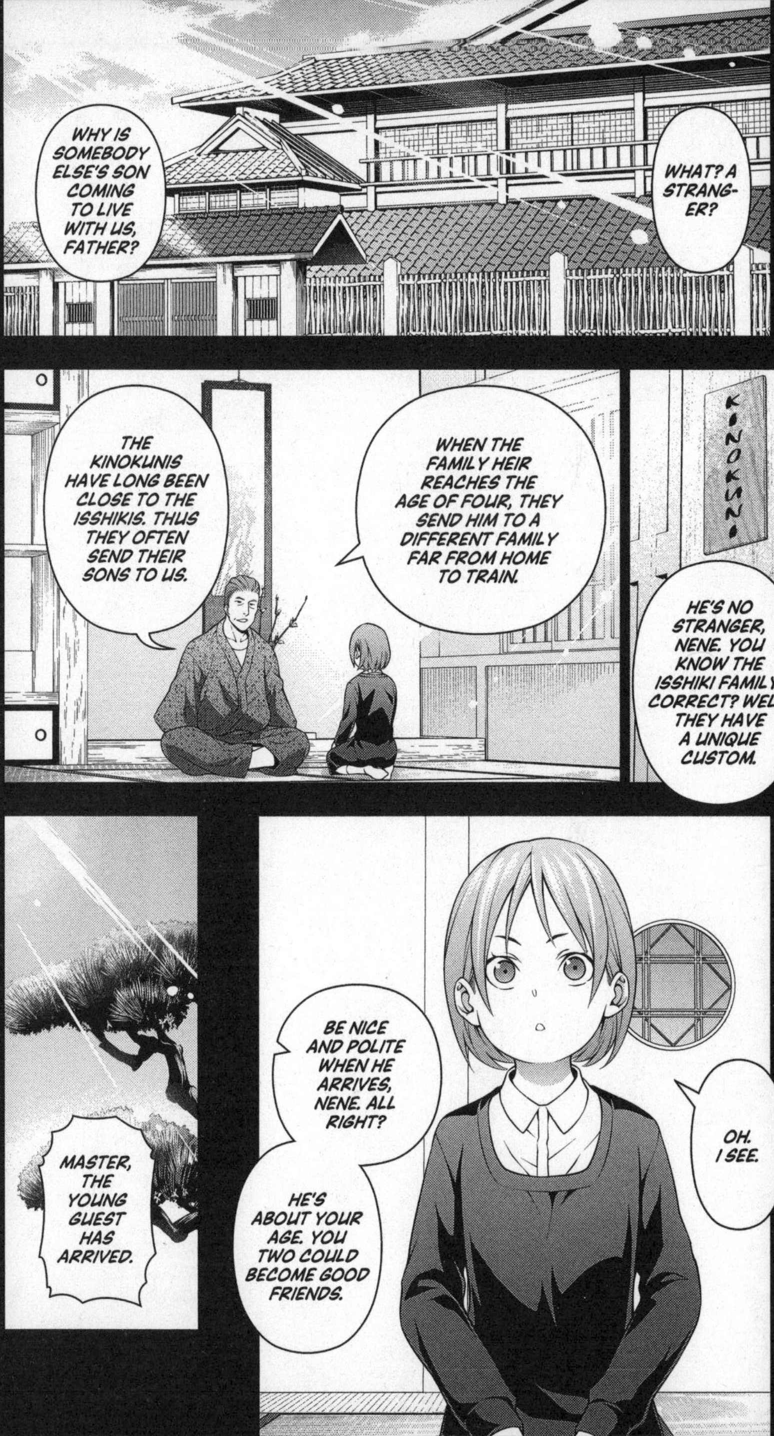
WHAT? A STRANGER?
WHY IS SOMEBODY ELSE'S SON COMING TO LIVE WITH US, FATHER?
KINOKUNI
HE'S NO STRANGER, NENE. YOU KNOW THE ISSHIKI FAMILY, CORRECT? WELL, THEY HAVE A UNIQUE CUSTOM.
WHEN THE FAMILY HEIR REACHES THE AGE OF FOUR, THEY SEND HIM TO A DIFFERENT FAMILY FAR FROM HOME TO TRAIN.
THE KINOKUNIS HAVE LONG BEEN CLOSE TO THE ISSHIKIS. THUS THEY OFTEN SEND THEIR SONS TO US.
OH. I SEE.
BE NICE AND POLITE WHEN HE ARRIVES, NENE. ALL RIGHT?
HE'S ABOUT YOUR AGE. YOU TWO COULD BECOME GOOD FRIENDS.
MASTER, THE YOUNG GUEST HAS ARRIVED.

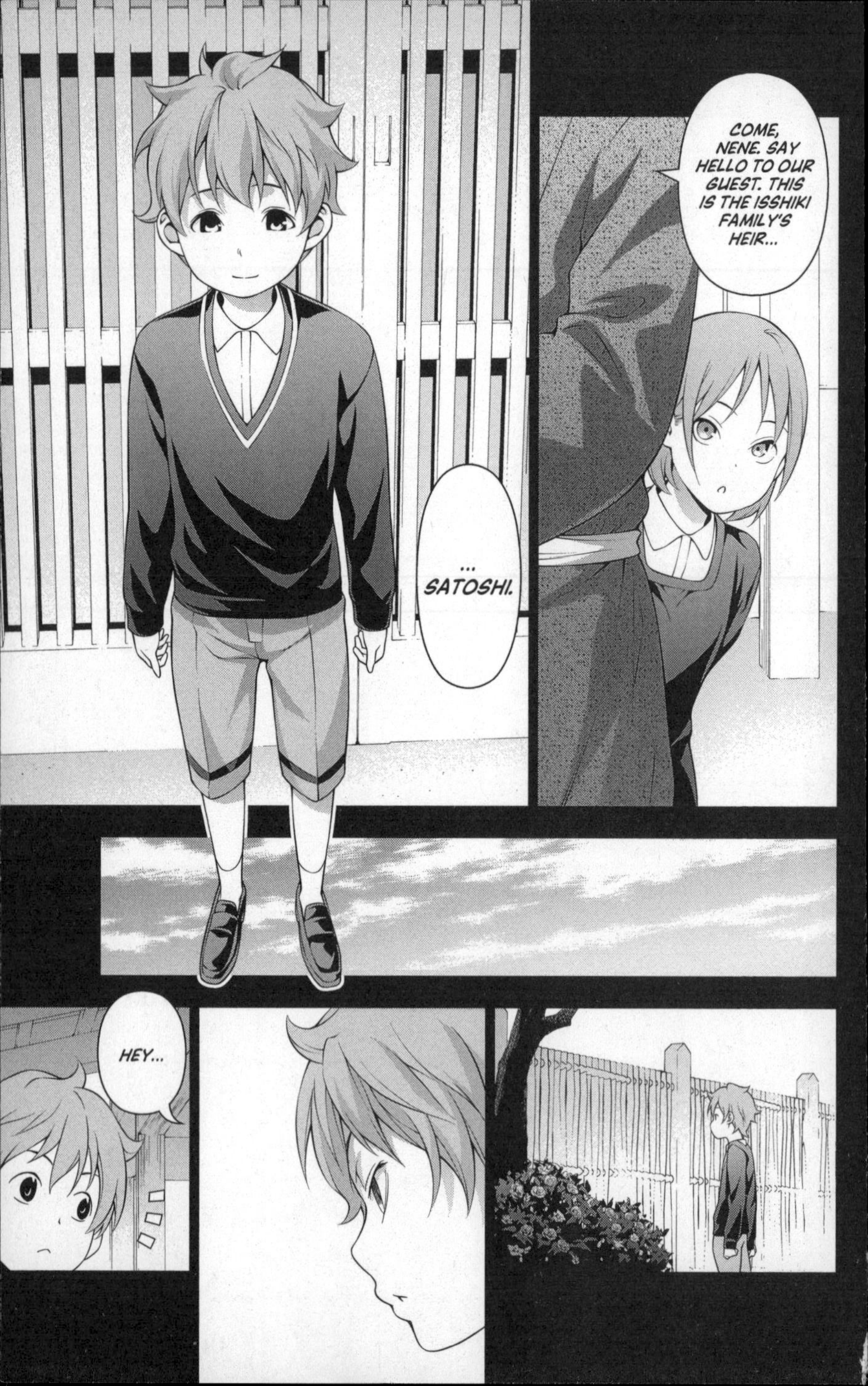
COME, NENE. SAY HELLO TO OUR GUEST. THIS IS THE ISSHIKI FAMILY'S HEIR...
... SATOSHI.
HEY...

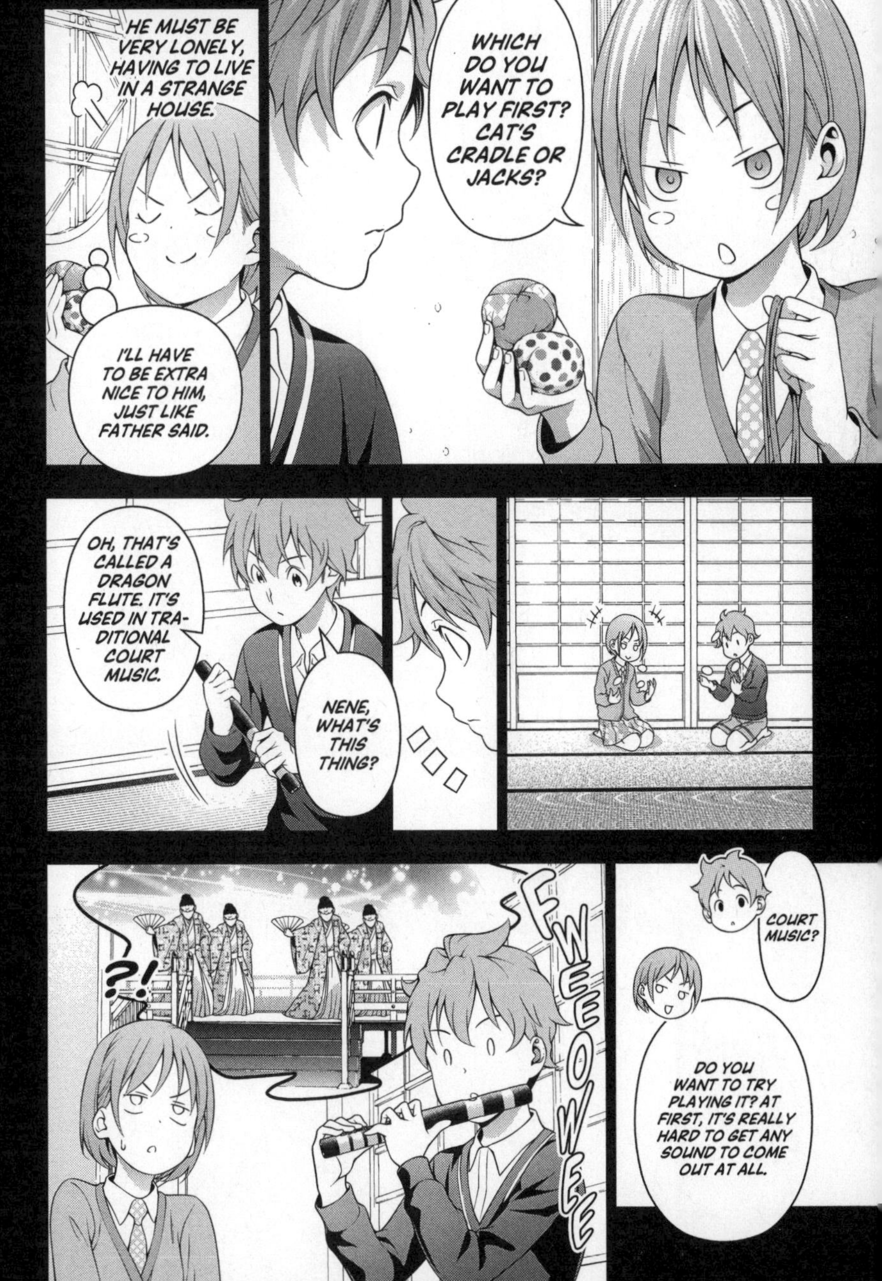
WHICH DO YOU WANT TO PLAY FIRST? CAT'S CRADLE OR JACKS?
HE MUST BE VERY LONELY, HAVING TO LIVE IN A STRANGE HOUSE.
I'LL HAVE TO BE EXTRA NICE TO HIM, JUST LIKE FATHER SAID.
NENE, WHAT'S THIS THING?
OH, THAT'S CALLED A DRAGON FLUTE. IT'S USED IN TRA-DITIONAL COURT MUSIC.
COURT MUSIC?
DO YOU WANT TO TRY PLAYING IT? AT FIRST, IT'S REALLY HARD TO GET ANY SOUND TO COME OUT AT ALL.
FWEEOWEE
?!

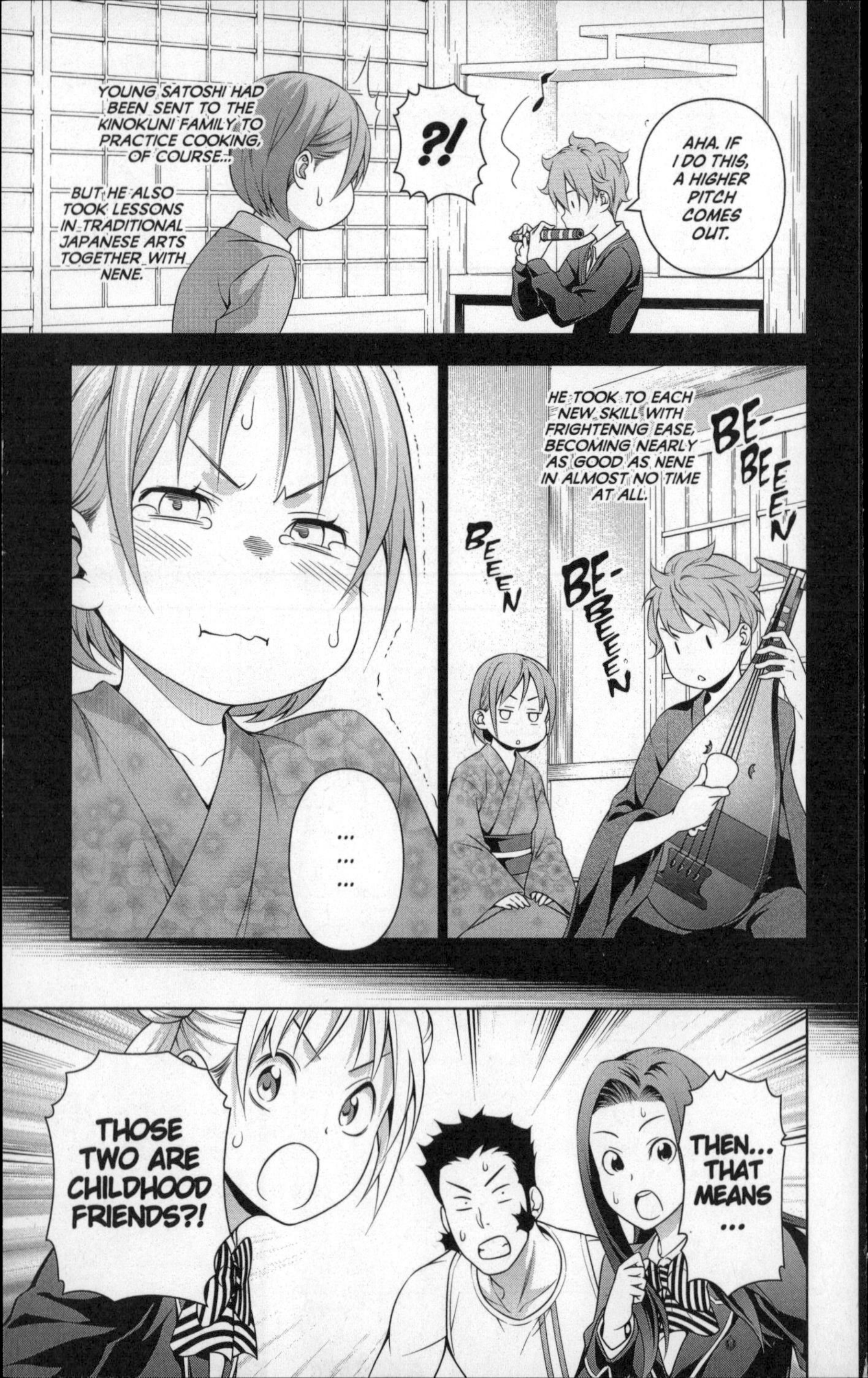
AHA. IF I DO THIS, A HIGHER PITCH COMES OUT.
?!
YOUNG SATOSHI HAD BEEN SENT TO THE KINOKUNI FAMILY TO PRACTICE COOKING, OF COURSE...
BUT HE ALSO TOOK LESSONS IN TRADITIONAL JAPANESE ARTS TOGETHER WITH NENE.
HE TOOK TO EACH NEW SKILL WITH FRIGHTENING EASE, BECOMING NEARLY AS GOOD AS NENE IN ALMOST NO TIME AT ALL.
BE-BEEEN
BE-BEEEEN
BEEEN
...
...
...
THEN... THAT MEANS ...
THOSE TWO ARE CHILDHOOD FRIENDS?!

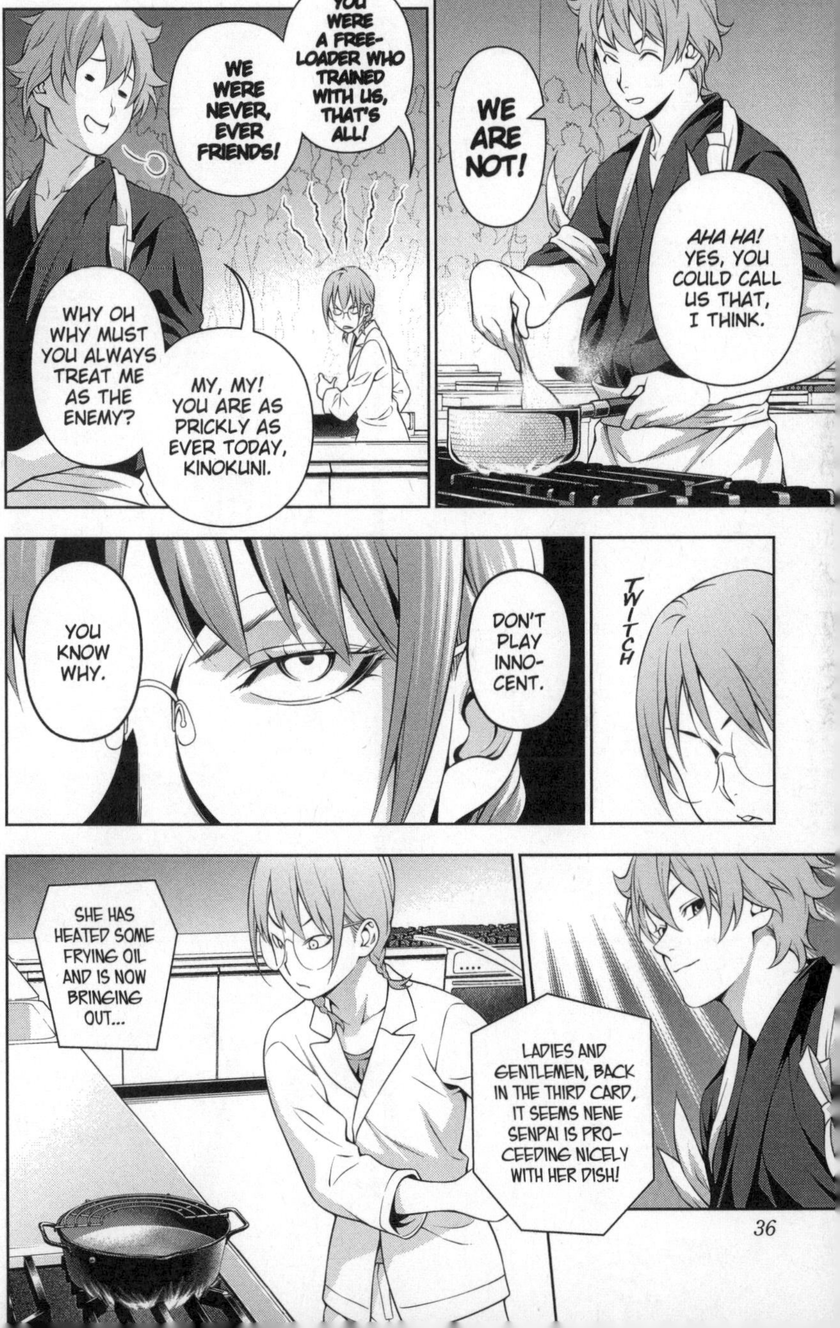
AHA HA! YES, YOU COULD CALL US THAT, I THINK.
WE ARE NOT!
YOU WERE A FREE-LOADER WHO TRAINED WITH US, THAT'S ALL!
WE WERE NEVER, EVER FRIENDS!
MY, MY! YOU ARE AS PRICKLY AS EVER TODAY, KINOKUNI.
WHY OH WHY MUST YOU ALWAYS TREAT ME AS THE ENEMY?
TWITCH
DON'T PLAY INNO-CENT.
YOU KNOW WHY.
LADIES AND GENTLEMEN, BACK IN THE THIRD CARD, IT SEEMS NENE SENPAI IS PRO-CEEDING NICELY WITH HER DISH!
SHE HAS HEATED SOME FRYING OIL AND IS NOW BRINGING OUT...

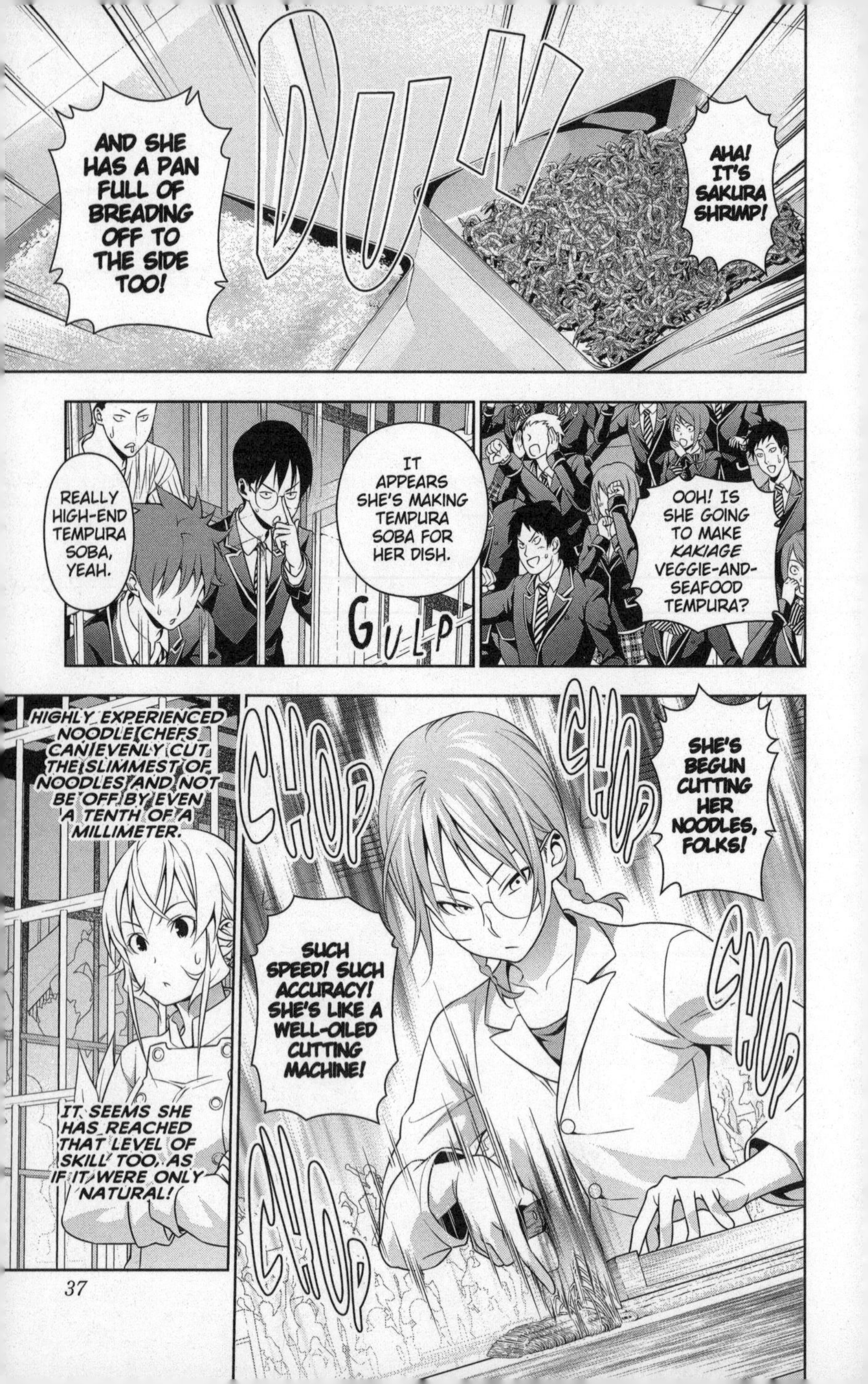
AHA! IT'S SAKURA SHRIMP!
DUN
AND SHE HAS A PAN FULL OF BREADING OFF TO THE SIDE TOO!
OOH! IS SHE GOING TO MAKE *KAKIAGE* VEGGIE-AND-SEAFOOD TEMPURA?
IT APPEARS SHE'S MAKING TEMPURA SOBA FOR HER DISH.
REALLY HIGH-END TEMPURA SOBA, YEAH.
GULP
CHOP
SHE'S BEGUN CUTTING HER NOODLES, FOLKS!
CHOP
CHOP
CHOP
SUCH SPEED! SUCH ACCURACY! SHE'S LIKE A WELL-OILED CUTTING MACHINE!
CHOP
HIGHLY EXPERIENCED NOODLE CHEFS CAN EVENLY CUT THE SLIMMEST OF NOODLES AND NOT BE OFF BY EVEN A TENTH OF A MILLIMETER.
IT SEEMS SHE HAS REACHED THAT LEVEL OF SKILL TOO, AS IF IT WERE ONLY NATURAL!

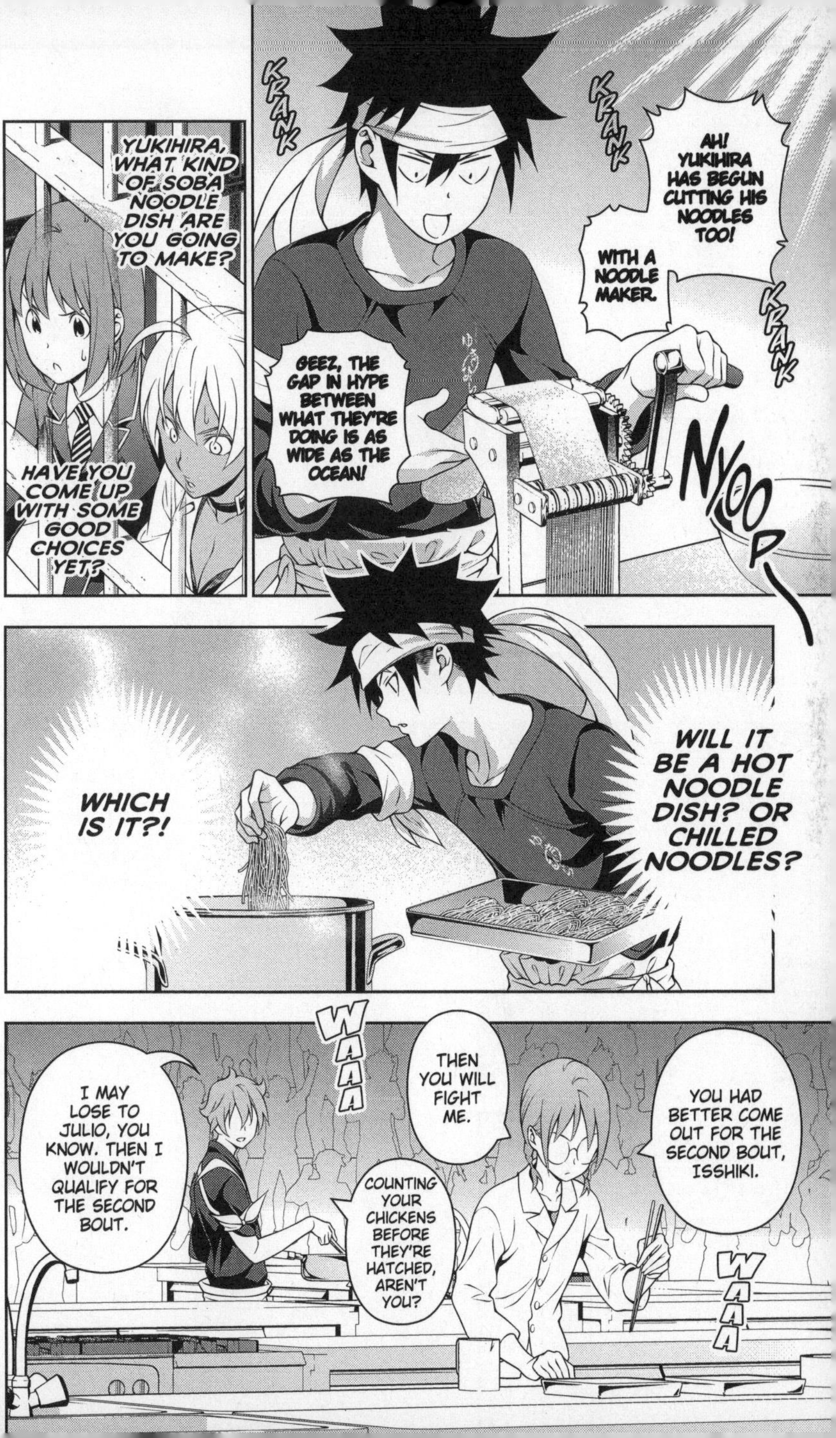
KRAAK
KRAAK
AH! YUKIHIRA HAS BEGUN CUTTING HIS NOODLES TOO!
WITH A NOODLE MAKER.
KRAAK
GEEZ, THE GAP IN HYPE BETWEEN WHAT THEY'RE DOING IS AS WIDE AS THE OCEAN!
NYOOP
YUKIHIRA, WHAT KIND OF SOBA NOODLE DISH ARE YOU GOING TO MAKE?
HAVE YOU COME UP WITH SOME GOOD CHOICES YET?
WILL IT BE A HOT NOODLE DISH? OR CHILLED NOODLES?
WHICH IS IT?!
WAAA
YOU HAD BETTER COME OUT FOR THE SECOND BOUT, ISSHIKI.
THEN YOU WILL FIGHT ME.
WAAA
I MAY LOSE TO JULIO, YOU KNOW. THEN I WOULDN'T QUALIFY FOR THE SECOND BOUT.
COUNTING YOUR CHICKENS BEFORE THEY'RE HATCHED, AREN'T YOU?

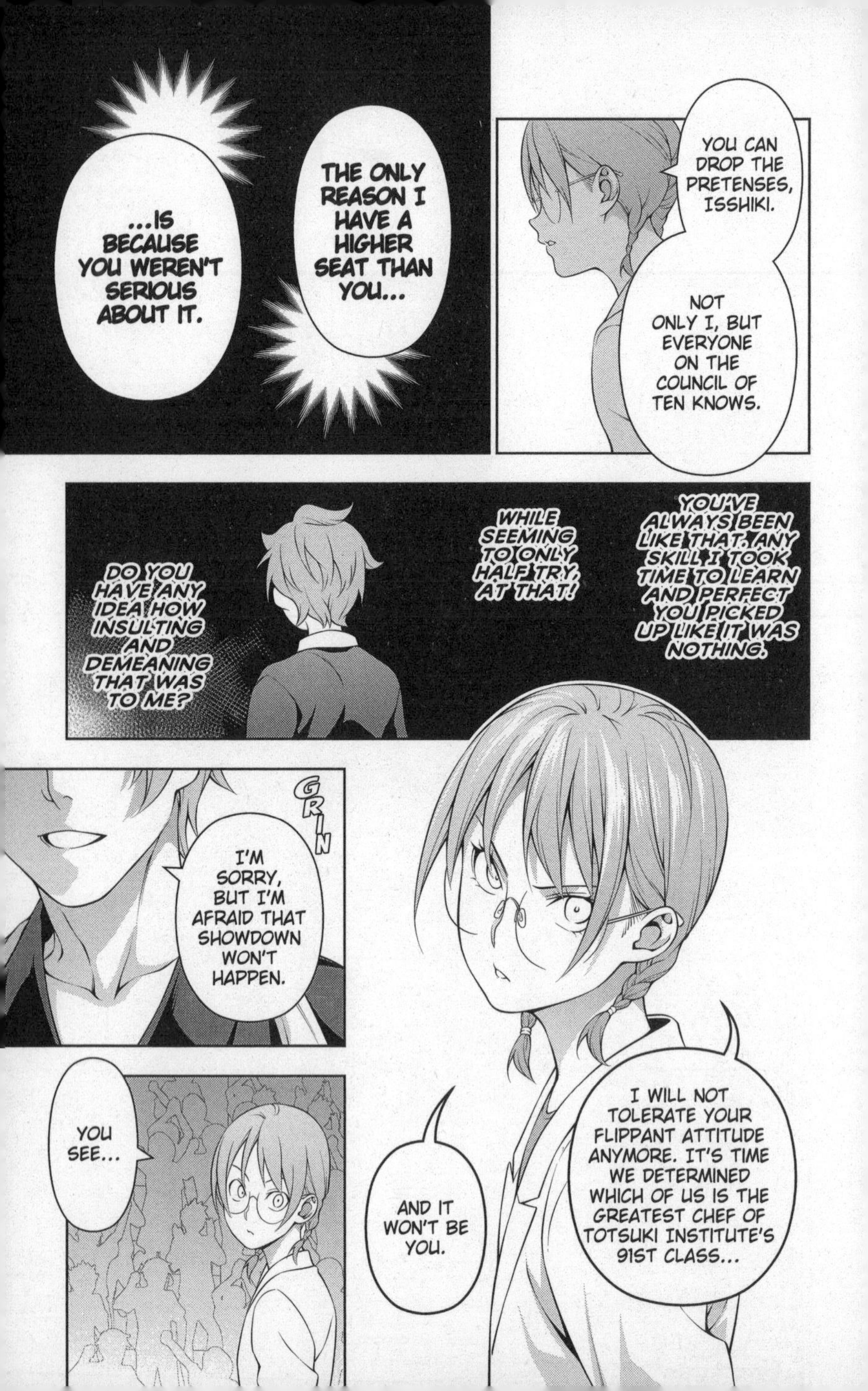
YOU CAN DROP THE PRETENSES, ISSHIKI.
NOT ONLY I, BUT EVERYONE ON THE COUNCIL OF TEN KNOWS.
THE ONLY REASON I HAVE A HIGHER SEAT THAN YOU...
...IS BECAUSE YOU WEREN'T SERIOUS ABOUT IT.
YOU'VE ALWAYS BEEN LIKE THAT. ANY SKILL I TOOK TIME TO LEARN AND PERFECT YOU PICKED UP LIKE IT WAS NOTHING.
WHILE SEEMING TO ONLY HALF TRY, AT THAT!
DO YOU HAVE ANY IDEA HOW INSULTING AND DEMEANING THAT WAS TO ME?
I WILL NOT TOLERATE YOUR FLIPPANT ATTITUDE ANYMORE. IT'S TIME WE DETERMINED WHICH OF US IS THE GREATEST CHEF OF TOTSUKI INSTITUTE'S 91ST CLASS...
AND IT WON'T BE YOU.
GRIN
I'M SORRY, BUT I'M AFRAID THAT SHOWDOWN WON'T HAPPEN.
YOU SEE...

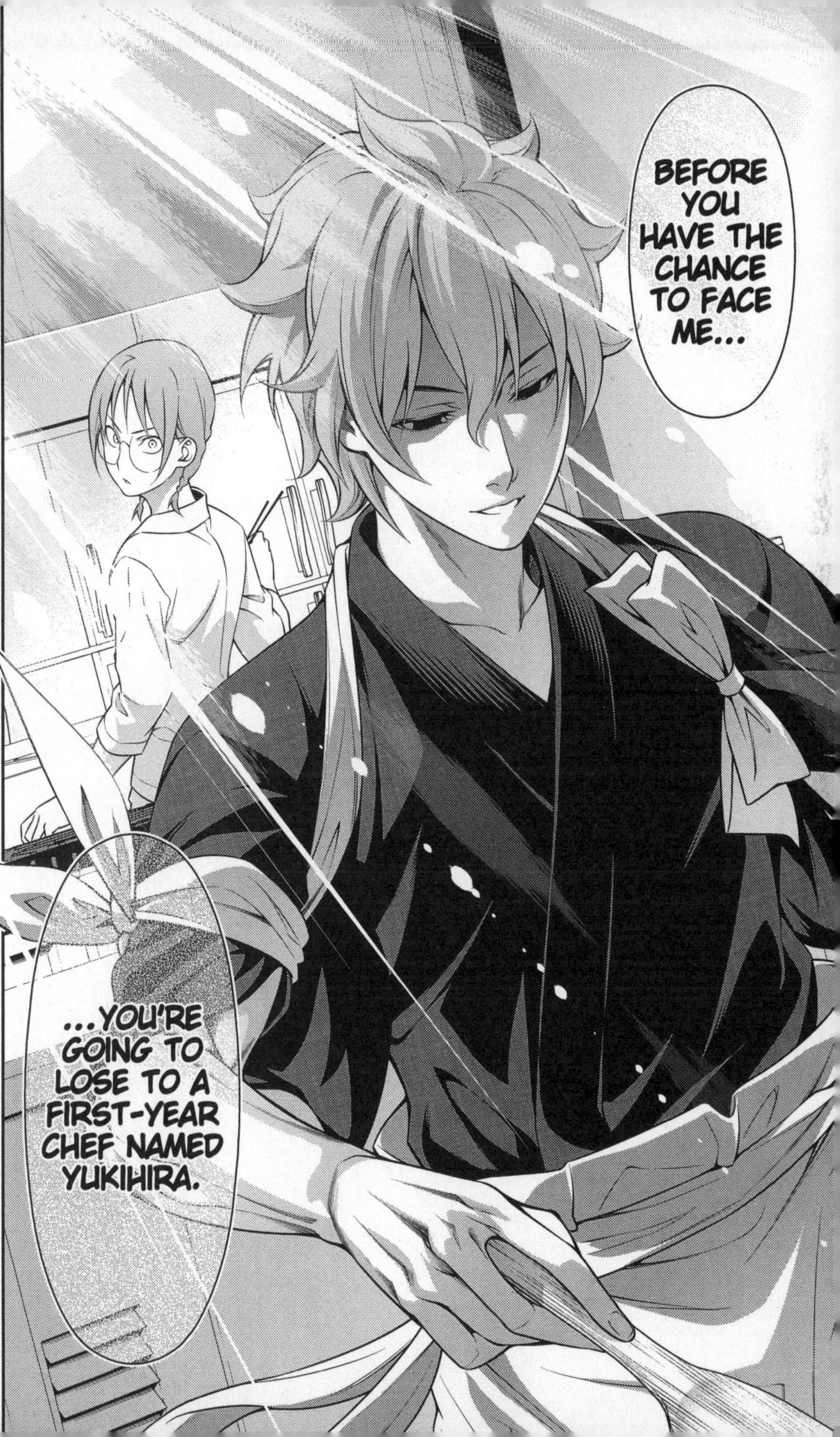
BEFORE YOU HAVE THE CHANCE TO FACE ME...
...YOU'RE GOING TO LOSE TO A FIRST-YEAR CHEF NAMED YUKIHIRA.

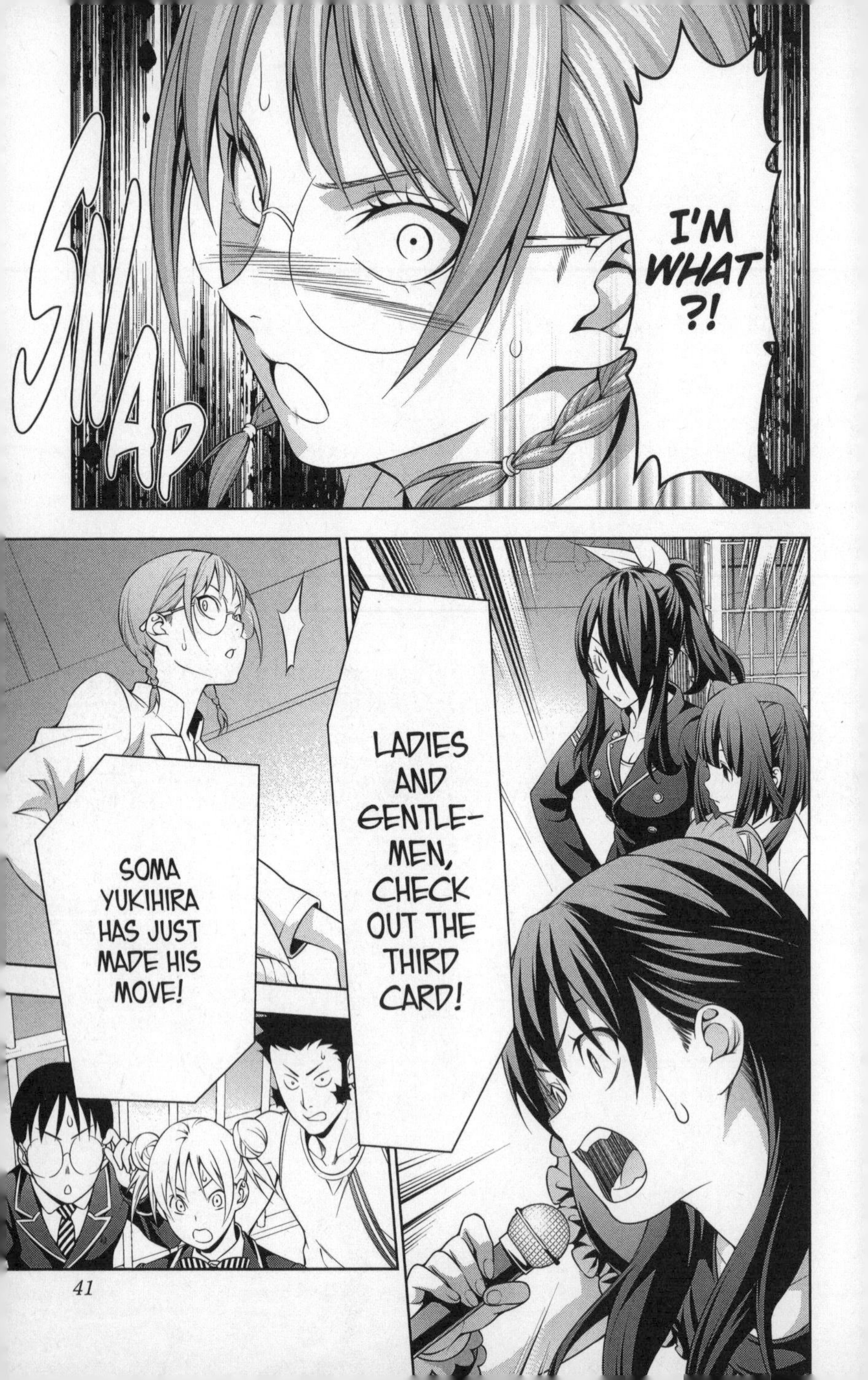
SNAP
I'M WHAT?!
LADIES AND GENTLEMEN, CHECK OUT THE THIRD CARD!
SOMA YUKIHIRA HAS JUST MADE HIS MOVE!

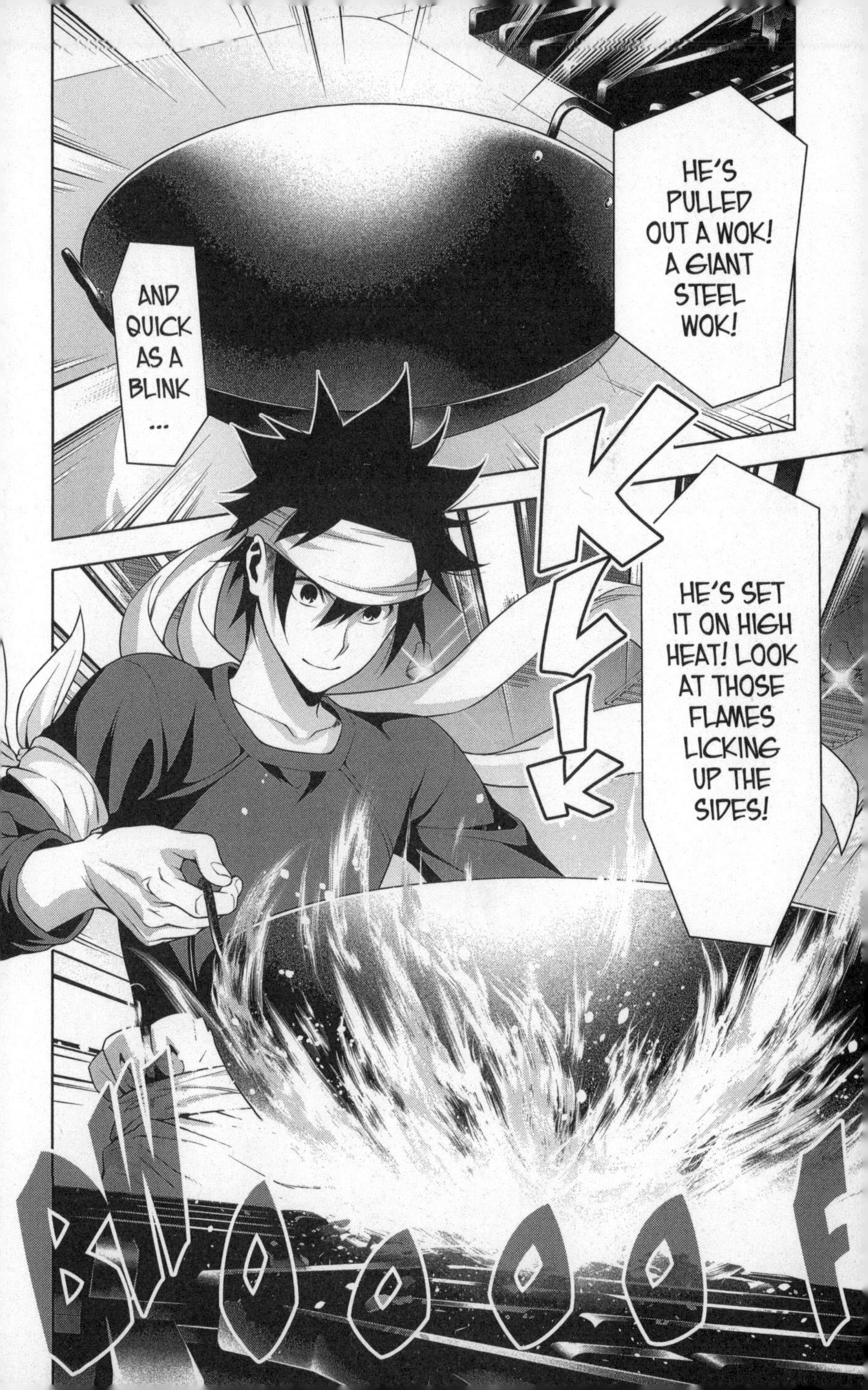
HE'S PULLED OUT A WOK! A GIANT STEEL WOK!
AND QUICK AS A BLINK ...
KLIK
HE'S SET IT ON HIGH HEAT! LOOK AT THOSE FLAMES LICKING UP THE SIDES!
BWOOOF

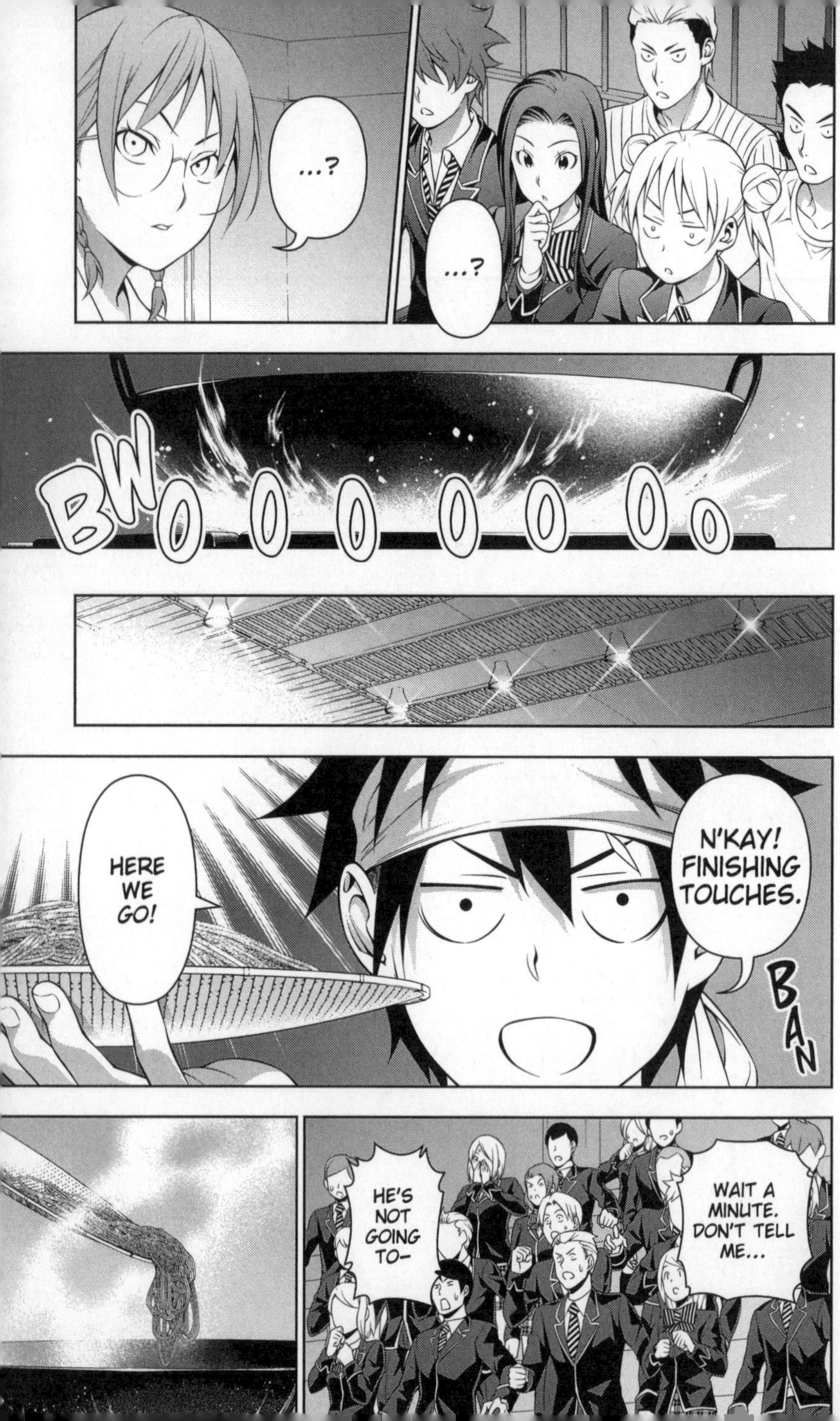
...?
...?
BWOOOOOOO
N'KAY! FINISHING TOUCHES.
BAN
HERE WE GO!
WAIT A MINUTE. DON'T TELL ME...
HE'S NOT GOING TO-

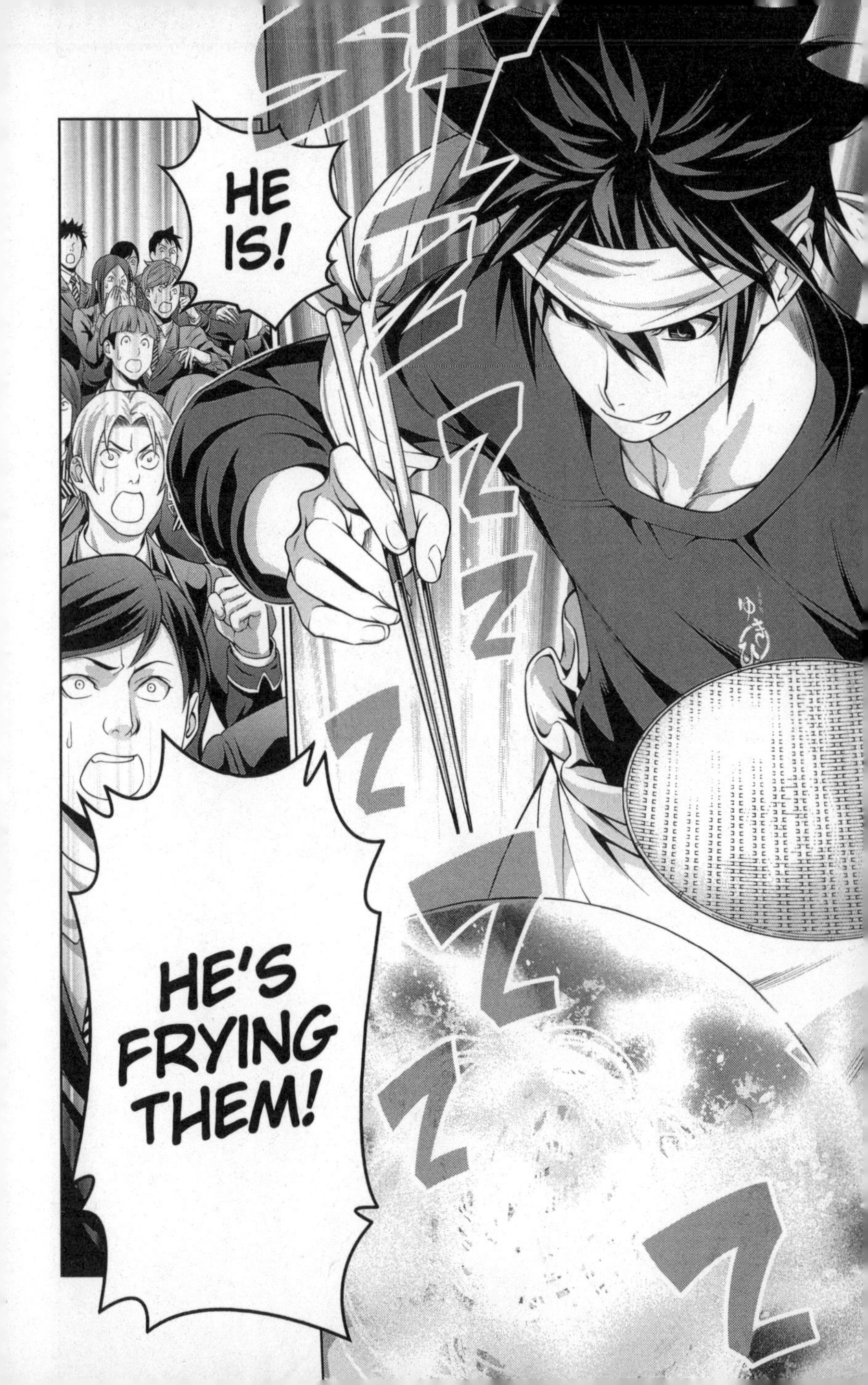
HE IS!
HE'S FRYING THEM!

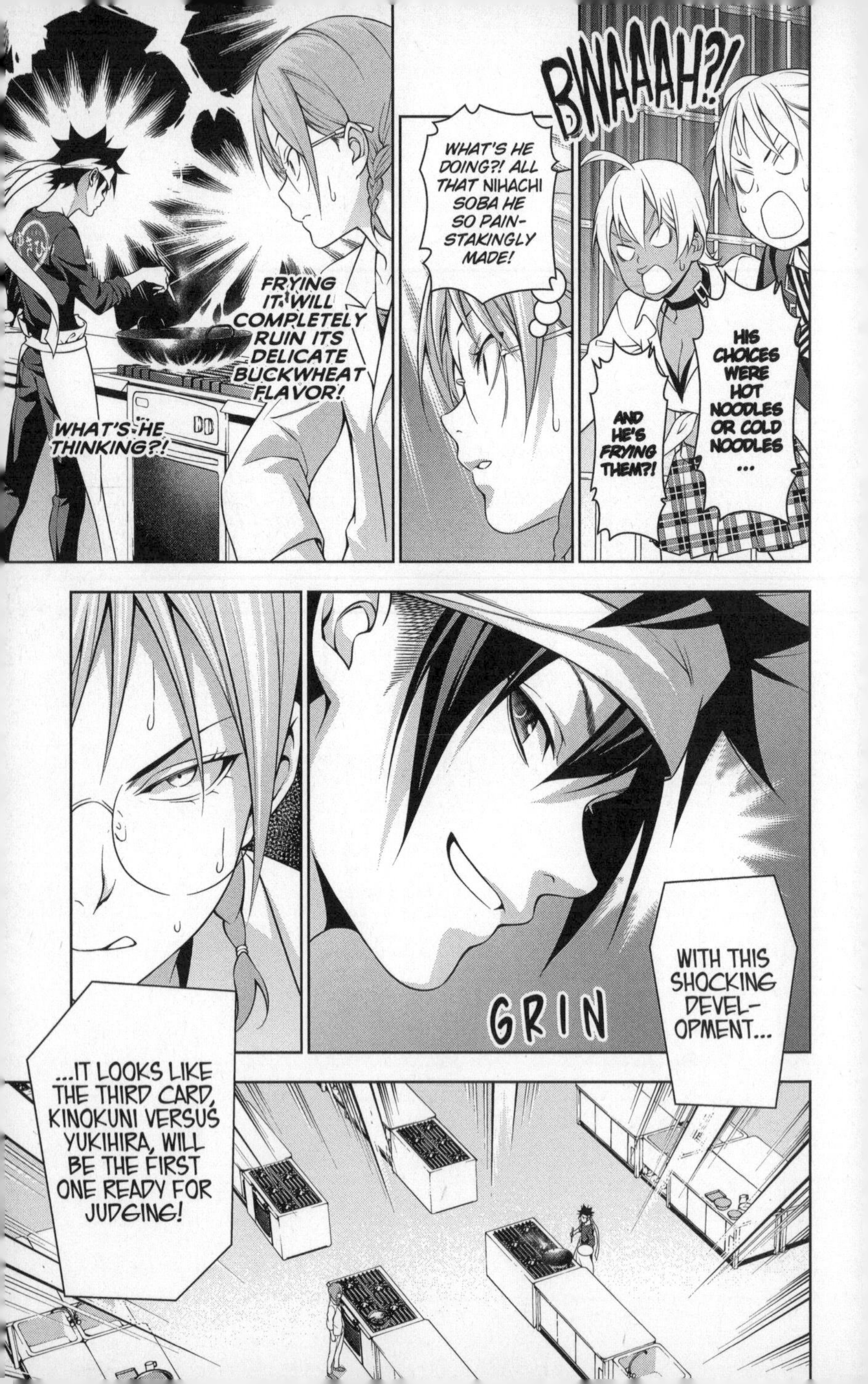
BWAAAH?!
HIS CHOICES WERE HOT NOODLES OR COLD NOODLES...
AND HE'S FRYING THEM?!
WHAT'S HE DOING?! ALL THAT NIHACHI SOBA HE SO PAIN-STAKINGLY MADE!
FRYING IT WILL COMPLETELY RUIN ITS DELICATE BUCKWHEAT FLAVOR!
WHAT'S HE THINKING?!
GRIN
WITH THIS SHOCKING DEVEL-OPMENT...
...IT LOOKS LIKE THE THIRD CARD, KINOKUNI VERSUS YUKIHIRA, WILL BE THE FIRST ONE READY FOR JUDGING!

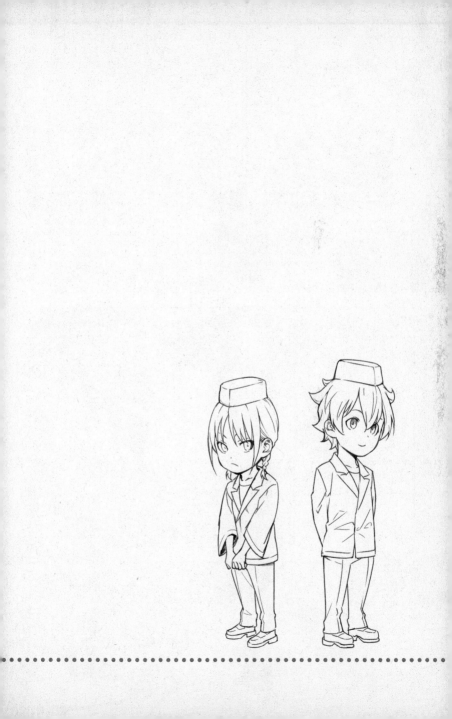

211 ABSOLUTE JUDGES

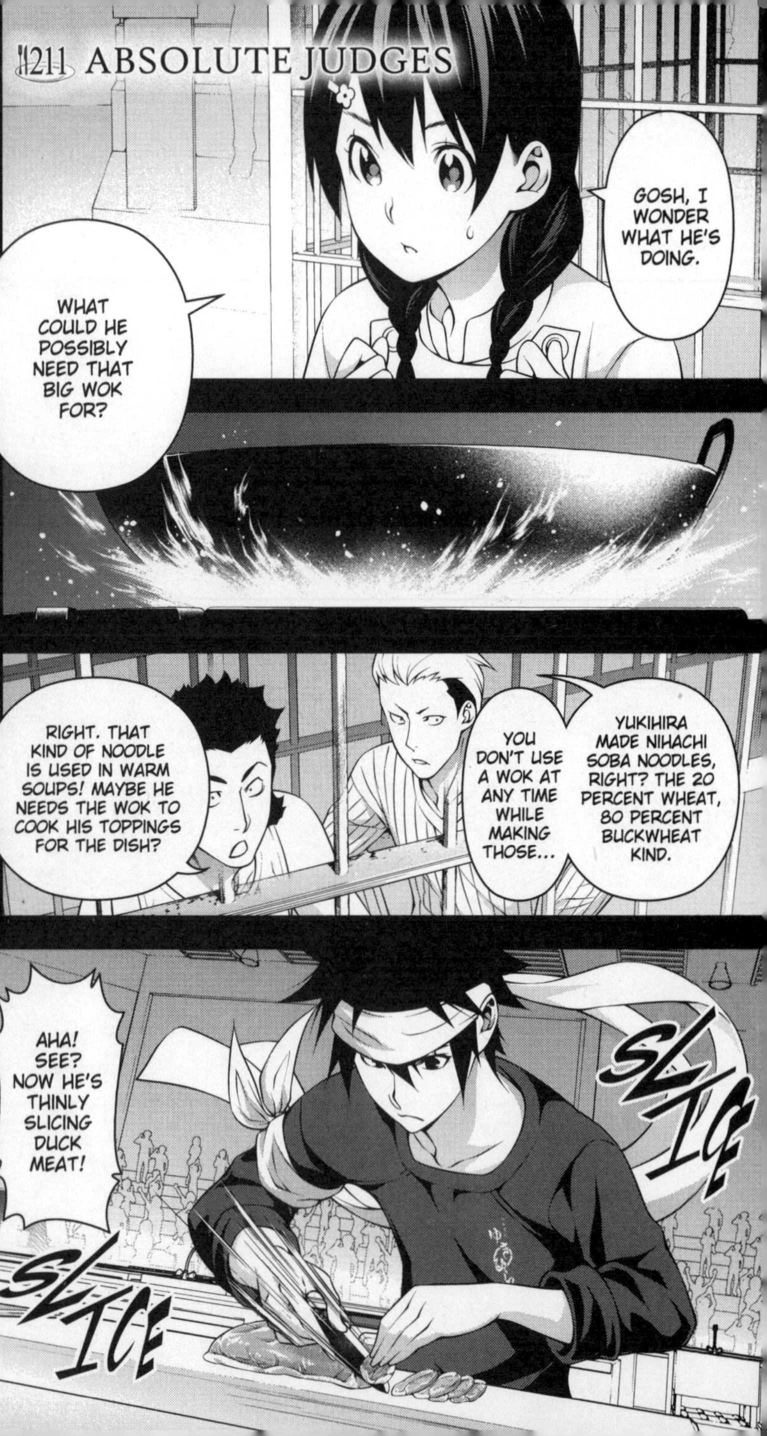
GOSH, I WONDER WHAT HE'S DOING.
WHAT COULD HE POSSIBLY NEED THAT BIG WOK FOR?
YUKIHIRA MADE NIHACHI SOBA NOODLES, RIGHT? THE 20 PERCENT WHEAT, 80 PERCENT BUCKWHEAT KIND.
YOU DON'T USE A WOK AT ANY TIME WHILE MAKING THOSE...
RIGHT. THAT KIND OF NOODLE IS USED IN WARM SOUPS! MAYBE HE NEEDS THE WOK TO COOK HIS TOPPINGS FOR THE DISH?
SLICE
AHA! SEE? NOW HE'S THINLY SLICING DUCK MEAT!
SLICE

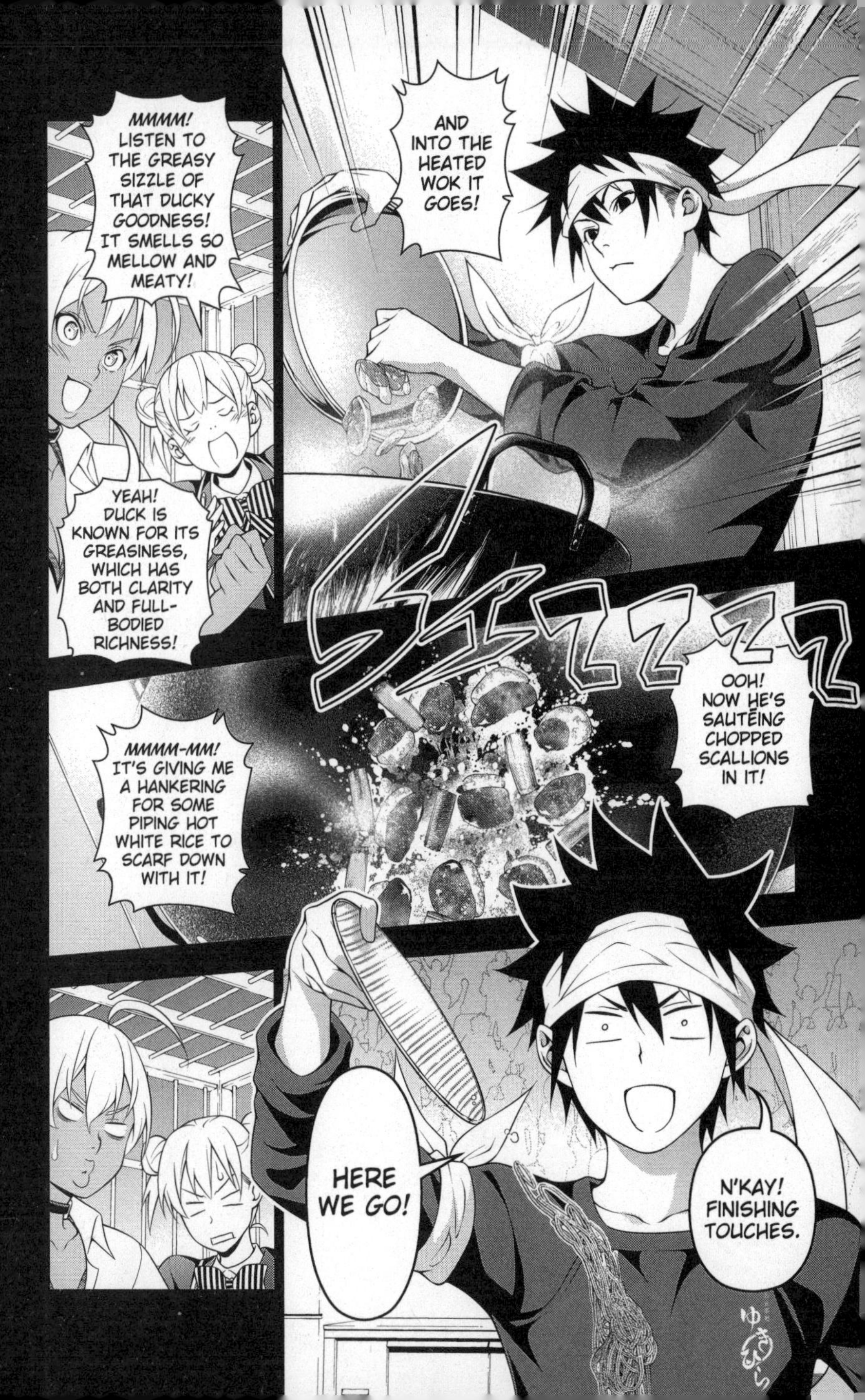

AND INTO THE HEATED WOK IT GOES!
SIZZZZZZ
MMMM! LISTEN TO THE GREASY SIZZLE OF THAT DUCKY GOODNESS! IT SMELLS SO MELLOW AND MEATY!
YEAH! DUCK IS KNOWN FOR ITS GREASINESS, WHICH HAS BOTH CLARITY AND FULL-BODIED RICHNESS!
OOH! NOW HE'S SAUTÉING CHOPPED SCALLIONS IN IT!
MMMM-MM! IT'S GIVING ME A HANKERING FOR SOME PIPING HOT WHITE RICE TO SCARF DOWN WITH IT!
N'KAY! FINISHING TOUCHES.
HERE WE GO!

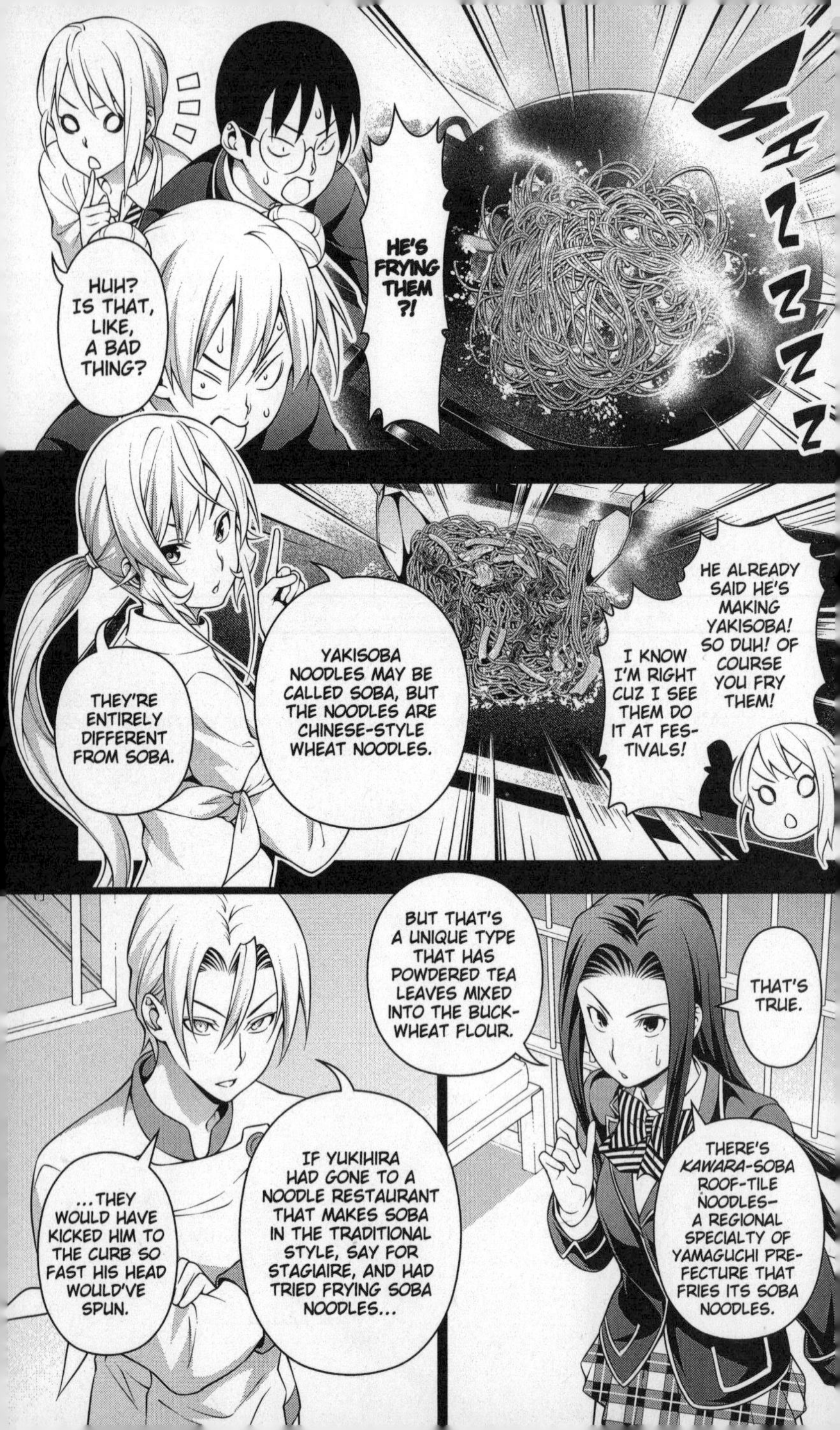
SHZZZZ
HE'S FRYING THEM?!
HUH? IS THAT, LIKE, A BAD THING?
HE ALREADY SAID HE'S MAKING YAKISOBA! SO DUH! OF COURSE YOU FRY THEM!
I KNOW I'M RIGHT CUZ I SEE THEM DO IT AT FES-TIVALS!
YAKISOBA NOODLES MAY BE CALLED SOBA, BUT THE NOODLES ARE CHINESE-STYLE WHEAT NOODLES.
THEY'RE ENTIRELY DIFFERENT FROM SOBA.
THAT'S TRUE.
THERE'S *KAWARA-SOBA* ROOF-TILE NOODLES—A REGIONAL SPECIALTY OF YAMAGUCHI PRE-FECTURE THAT FRIES ITS SOBA NOODLES.
BUT THAT'S A UNIQUE TYPE THAT HAS POWDERED TEA LEAVES MIXED INTO THE BUCK-WHEAT FLOUR.
IF YUKIHIRA HAD GONE TO A NOODLE RESTAURANT THAT MAKES SOBA IN THE TRADITIONAL STYLE, SAY FOR STAGIAIRE, AND HAD TRIED FRYING SOBA NOODLES...
...THEY WOULD HAVE KICKED HIM TO THE CURB SO FAST HIS HEAD WOULD'VE SPUN.

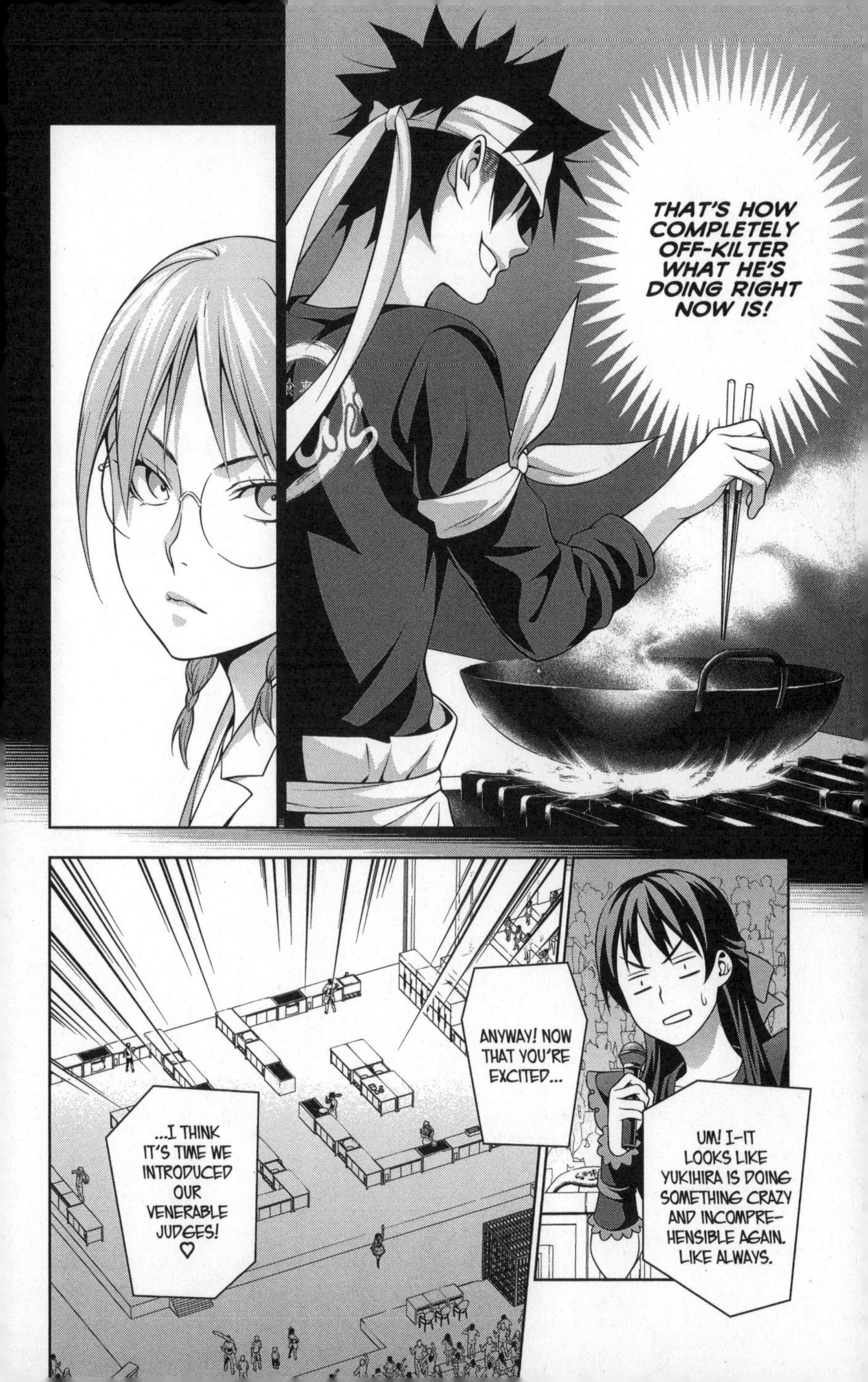
THAT'S HOW COMPLETELY OFF-KILTER WHAT HE'S DOING RIGHT NOW IS!
UM! I-IT LOOKS LIKE YUKIHIRA IS DOING SOMETHING CRAZY AND INCOMPRE-HENSIBLE AGAIN. LIKE ALWAYS.
ANYWAY! NOW THAT YOU'RE EXCITED...
...I THINK IT'S TIME WE INTRODUCED OUR VENERABLE JUDGES! ♡

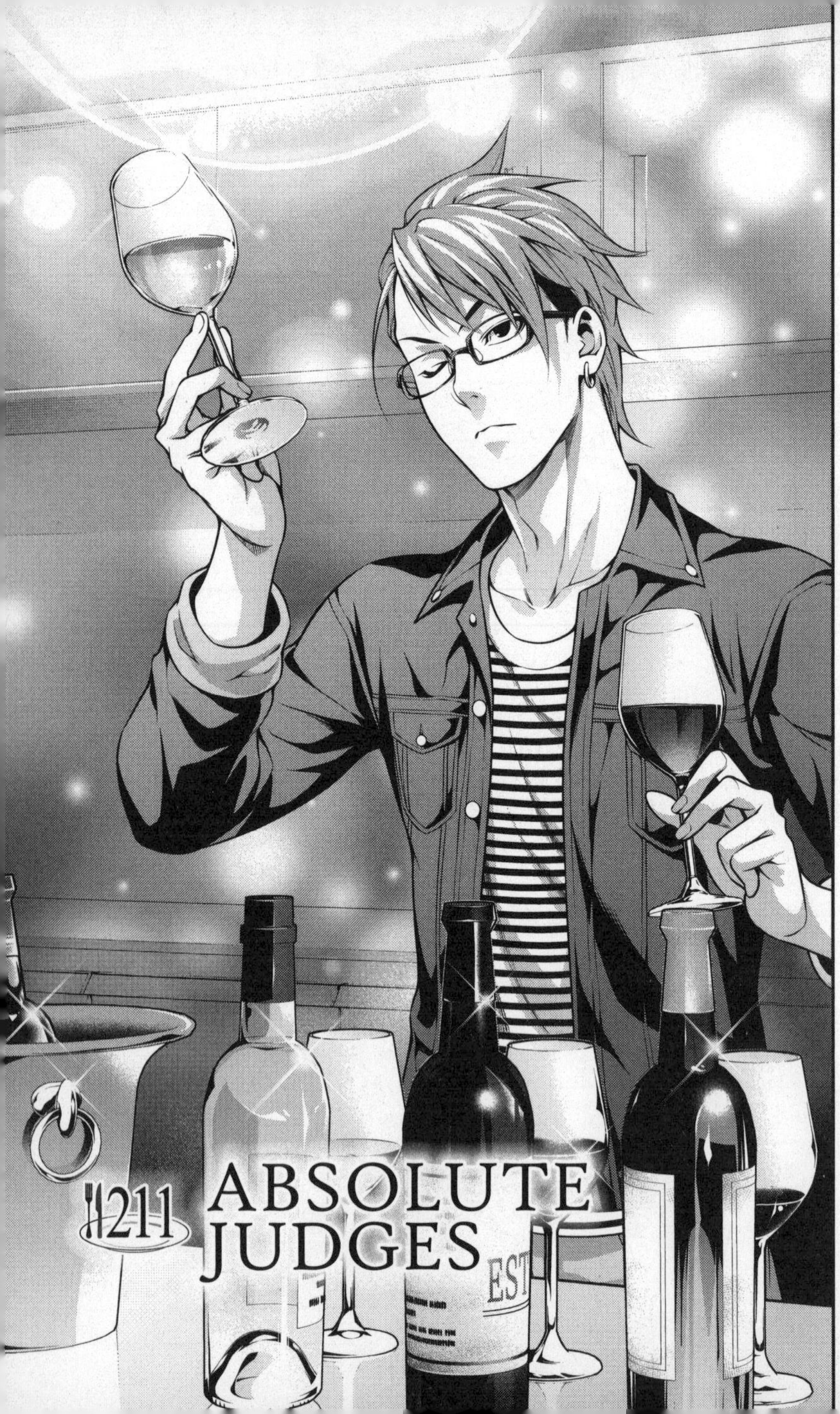
211
ABSOLUTE JUDGES
EST

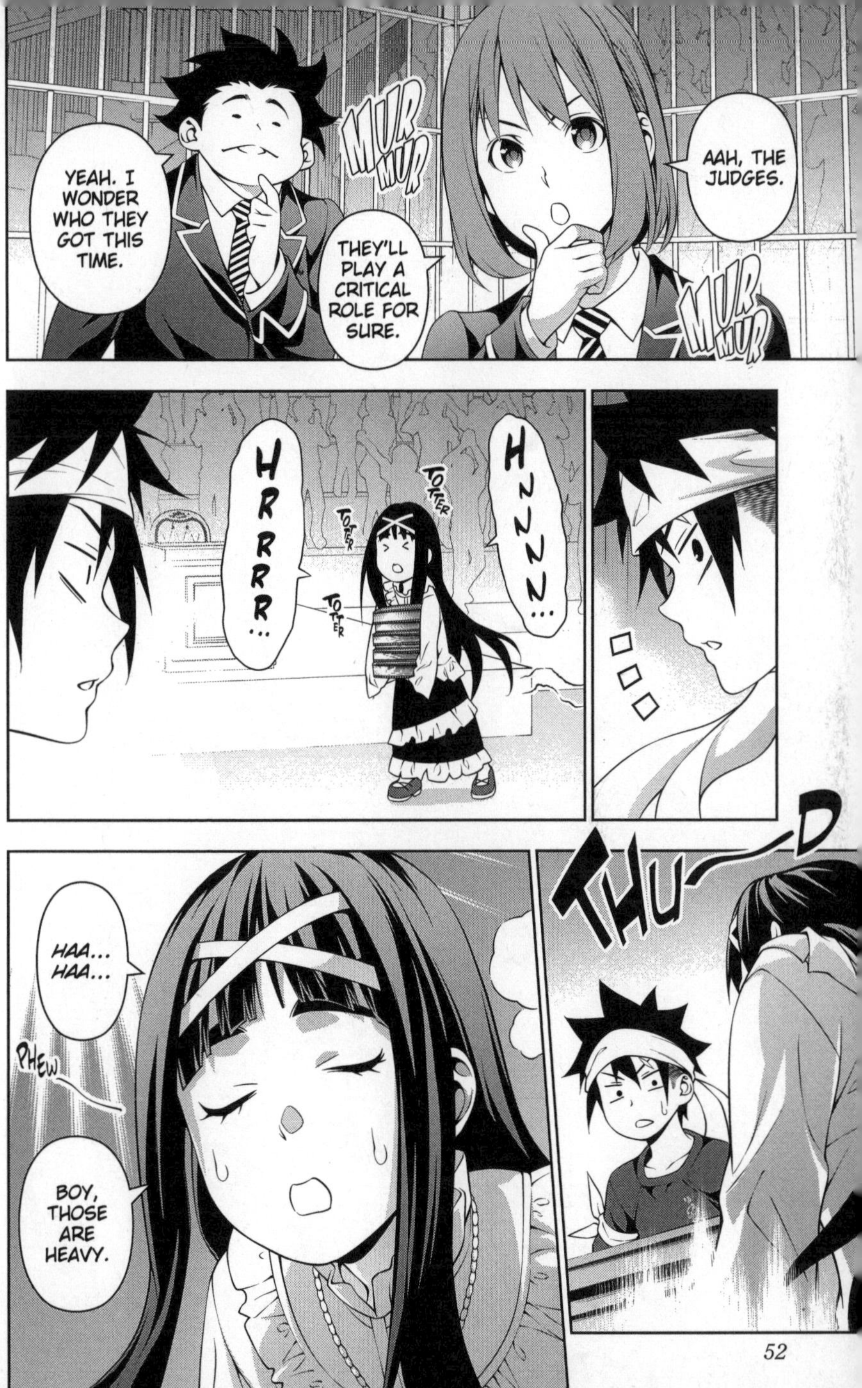
AAH, THE JUDGES.
MUR MUR
THEY'LL PLAY A CRITICAL ROLE FOR SURE.
MUR MUR
YEAH. I WONDER WHO THEY GOT THIS TIME.
HNNNN...
TOTTER
HRRRR...
TOTTER
TOTTER
THU—D
HAA... HAA...
PHEW
BOY, THOSE ARE HEAVY.

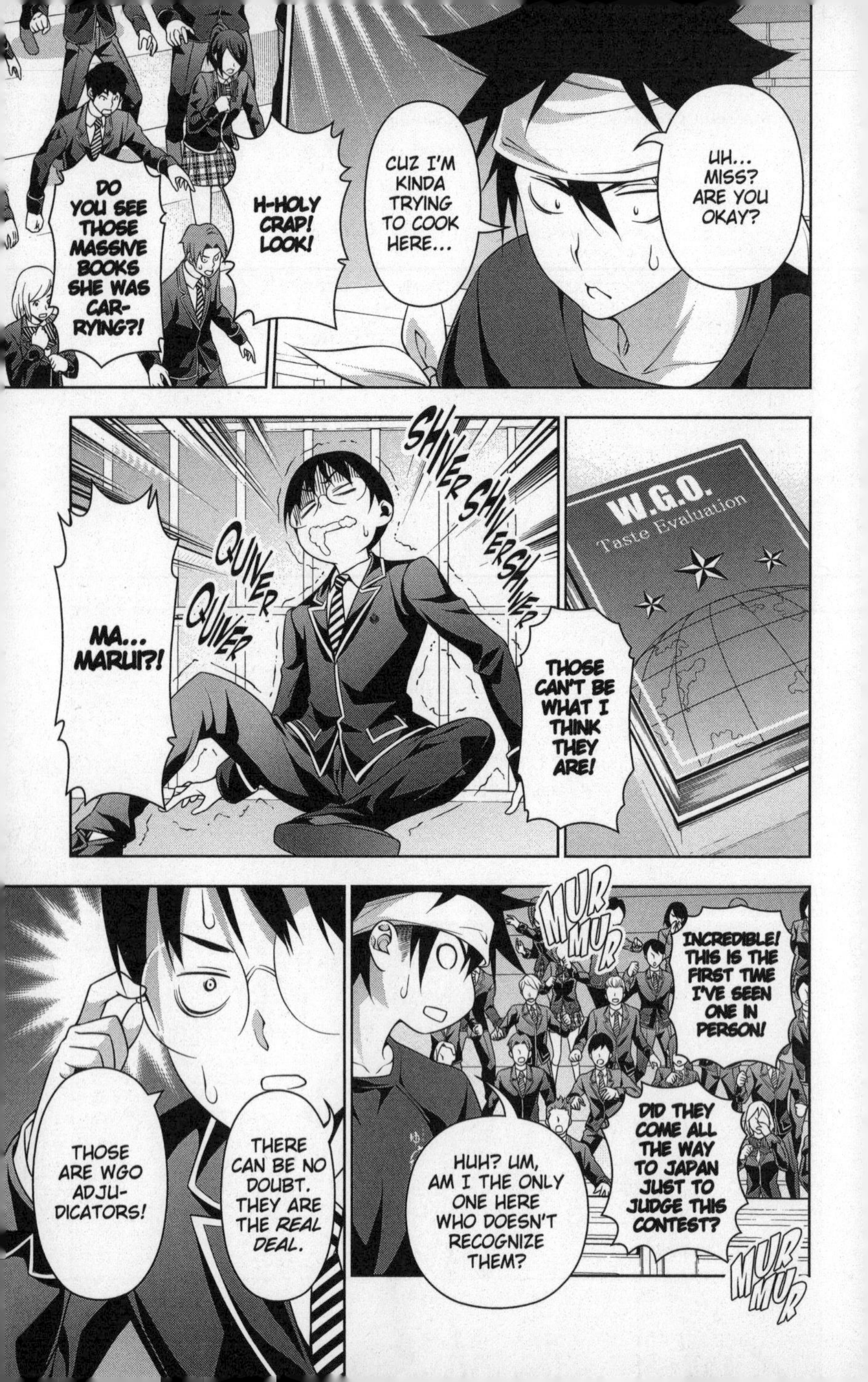

UH... MISS? ARE YOU OKAY?
CUZ I'M KINDA TRYING TO COOK HERE...
H-HOLY CRAP! LOOK!
DO YOU SEE THOSE MASSIVE BOOKS SHE WAS CAR-RYING?!
W.G.O.
Taste Evaluation
THOSE CAN'T BE WHAT I THINK THEY ARE!
SHIVER SHIVER SHIVER SHIVER
QUIVER QUIVER
MA... MARUI?!
MUR MUR
INCREDIBLE! THIS IS THE FIRST TIME I'VE SEEN ONE IN PERSON!
DID THEY COME ALL THE WAY TO JAPAN JUST TO JUDGE THIS CONTEST?
HUH? UM, AM I THE ONLY ONE HERE WHO DOESN'T RECOGNIZE THEM?
MUR MUR
THERE CAN BE NO DOUBT. THEY ARE THE *REAL* DEAL.
THOSE ARE WGO ADJU-DICATORS!

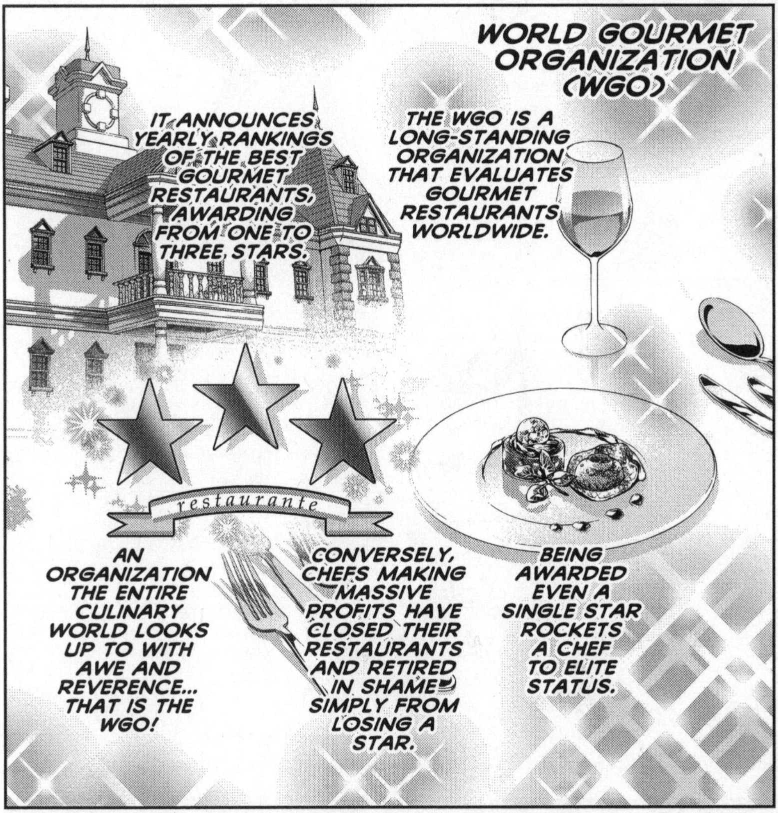
WORLD GOURMET ORGANIZATION (WGO)
THE WGO IS A LONG-STANDING ORGANIZATION THAT EVALUATES GOURMET RESTAURANTS WORLDWIDE.
IT ANNOUNCES YEARLY RANKINGS OF THE BEST GOURMET RESTAURANTS, AWARDING FROM ONE TO THREE STARS.
restaurante
BEING AWARDED EVEN A SINGLE STAR ROCKETS A CHEF TO ELITE STATUS.
CONVERSELY, CHEFS MAKING MASSIVE PROFITS HAVE CLOSED THEIR RESTAURANTS AND RETIRED IN SHAME SIMPLY FROM LOSING A STAR.
AN ORGANIZATION THE ENTIRE CULINARY WORLD LOOKS UP TO WITH AWE AND REVERENCE... THAT IS THE WGO!

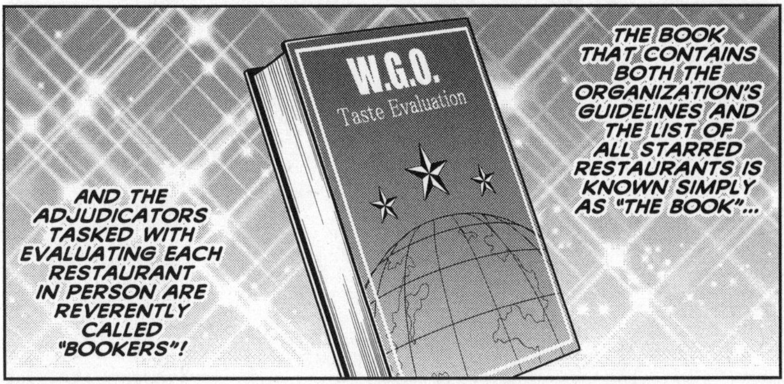
THE BOOK THAT CONTAINS BOTH THE ORGANIZATION'S GUIDELINES AND THE LIST OF ALL STARRED RESTAURANTS IS KNOWN SIMPLY AS "THE BOOK"...
W.G.O.
Taste Evaluation
AND THE ADJUDICATORS TASKED WITH EVALUATING EACH RESTAURANT IN PERSON ARE REVERENTLY CALLED "BOOKERS"!

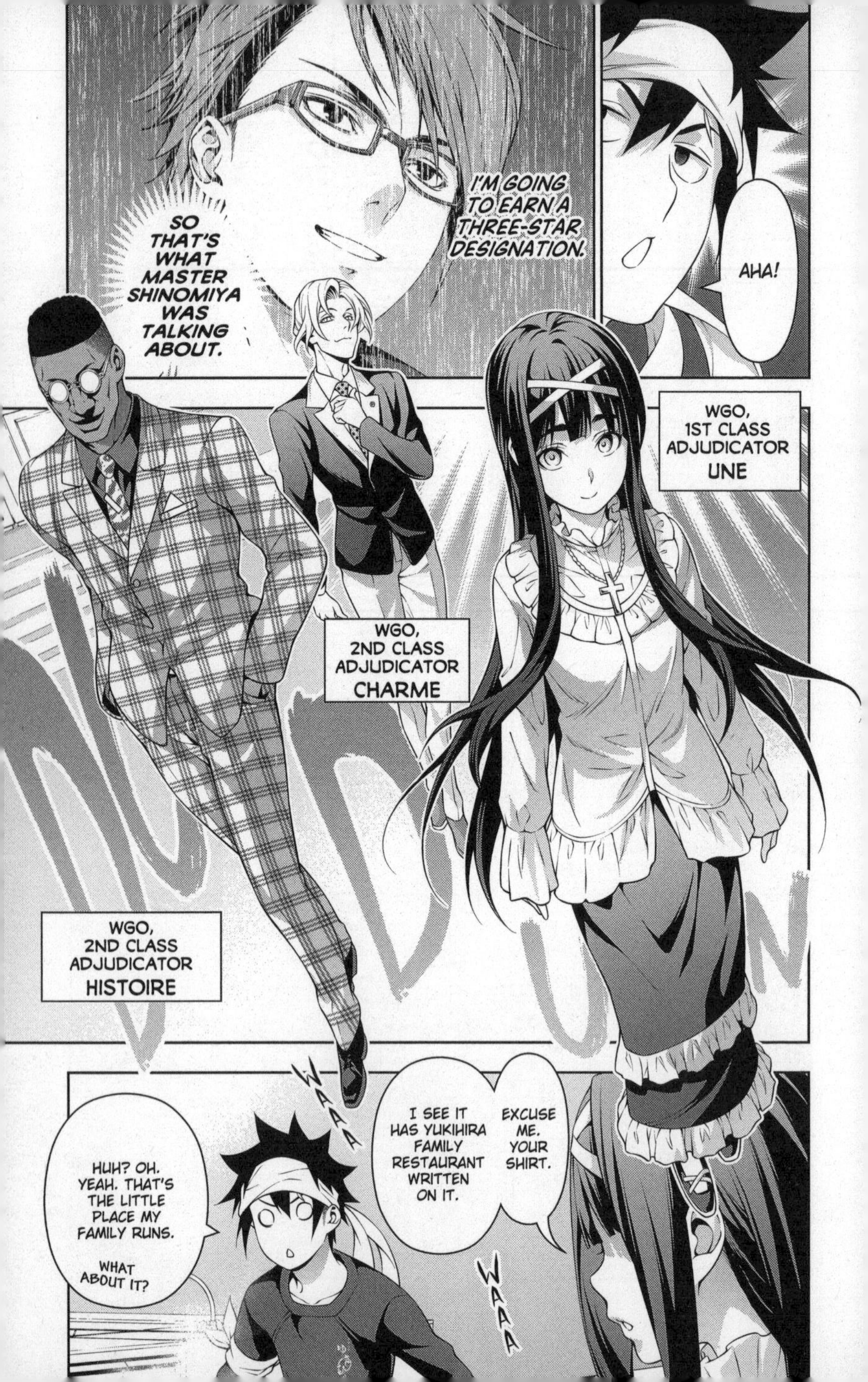
AHA!
I'M GOING TO EARN A THREE-STAR DESIGNATION.
SO THAT'S WHAT MASTER SHINOMIYA WAS TALKING ABOUT.
WGO, 1ST CLASS ADJUDICATOR UNE
WGO, 2ND CLASS ADJUDICATOR CHARME
WGO, 2ND CLASS ADJUDICATOR HISTOIRE
WAAA
EXCUSE ME. YOUR SHIRT.
I SEE IT HAS YUKIHIRA FAMILY RESTAURANT WRITTEN ON IT.
HUH? OH. YEAH. THAT'S THE LITTLE PLACE MY FAMILY RUNS.
WHAT ABOUT IT?
WAAA

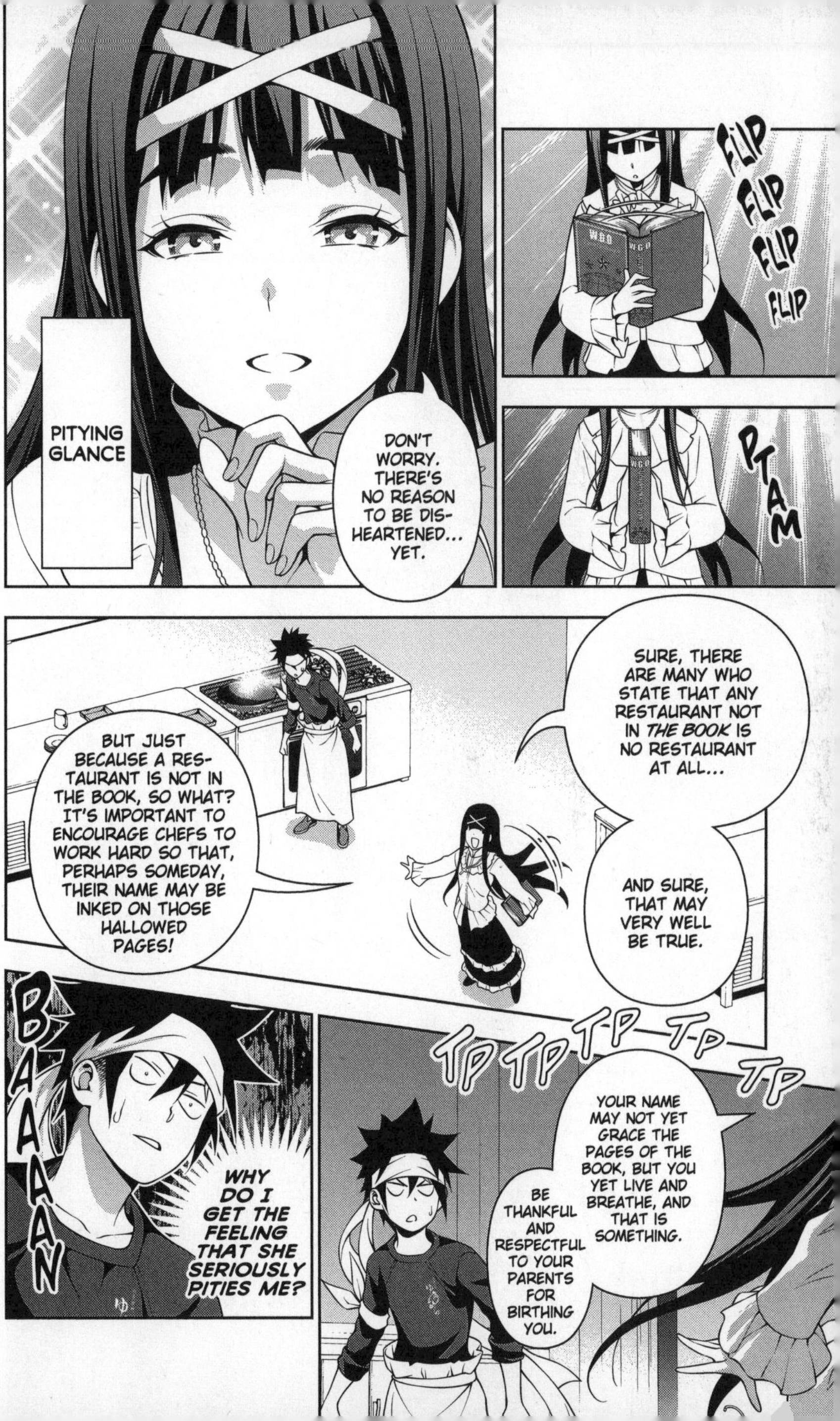
FLIP FLIP FLIP FLIP
PTAM
DON'T WORRY. THERE'S NO REASON TO BE DIS-HEARTENED... YET.
PITYING GLANCE
SURE, THERE ARE MANY WHO STATE THAT ANY RESTAURANT NOT IN *THE BOOK* IS NO RESTAURANT AT ALL...
AND SURE, THAT MAY VERY WELL BE TRUE.
BUT JUST BECAUSE A RES-TAURANT IS NOT IN THE BOOK, SO WHAT? IT'S IMPORTANT TO ENCOURAGE CHEFS TO WORK HARD SO THAT, PERHAPS SOMEDAY, THEIR NAME MAY BE INKED ON THOSE HALLOWED PAGES!
TP TP TP TP TP
YOUR NAME MAY NOT YET GRACE THE PAGES OF THE BOOK, BUT YOU YET LIVE AND BREATHE, AND THAT IS SOMETHING.
BE THANKFUL AND RESPECTFUL TO YOUR PARENTS FOR BIRTHING YOU.
BAAAAAN
WHY DO I GET THE FEELING THAT SHE SERIOUSLY PITIES ME?

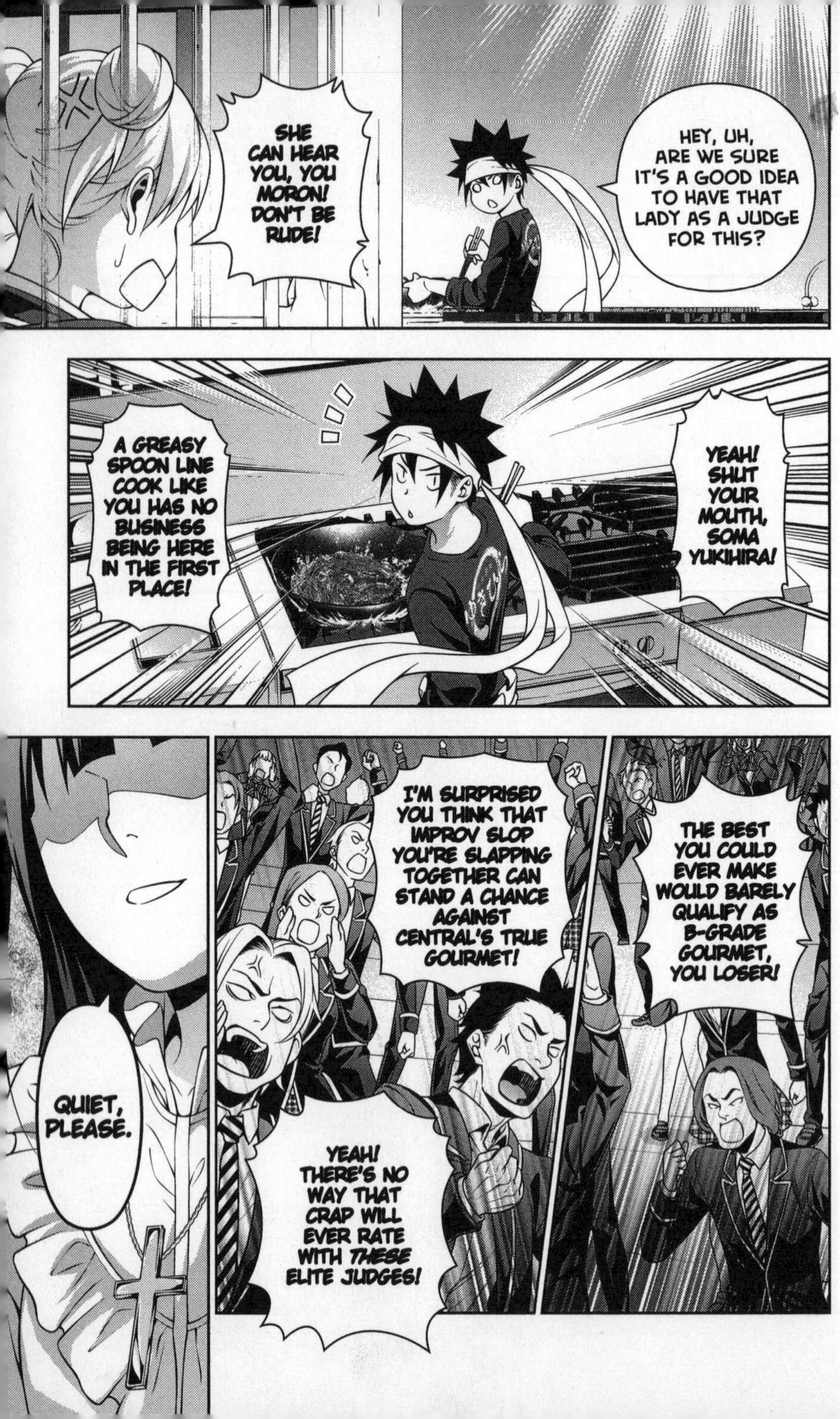
HEY, UH, ARE WE SURE IT'S A GOOD IDEA TO HAVE THAT LADY AS A JUDGE FOR THIS?
SHE CAN HEAR YOU, YOU MORON! DON'T BE RUDE!
YEAH! SHUT YOUR MOUTH, SOMA YUKIHIRA!
A GREASY SPOON LINE COOK LIKE YOU HAS NO BUSINESS BEING HERE IN THE FIRST PLACE!
THE BEST YOU COULD EVER MAKE WOULD BARELY QUALIFY AS B-GRADE GOURMET, YOU LOSER!
I'M SURPRISED YOU THINK THAT IMPROV SLOP YOU'RE SLAPPING TOGETHER CAN STAND A CHANCE AGAINST CENTRAL'S TRUE GOURMET!
YEAH! THERE'S NO WAY THAT CRAP WILL EVER RATE WITH *THESE* ELITE JUDGES!
QUIET, PLEASE.

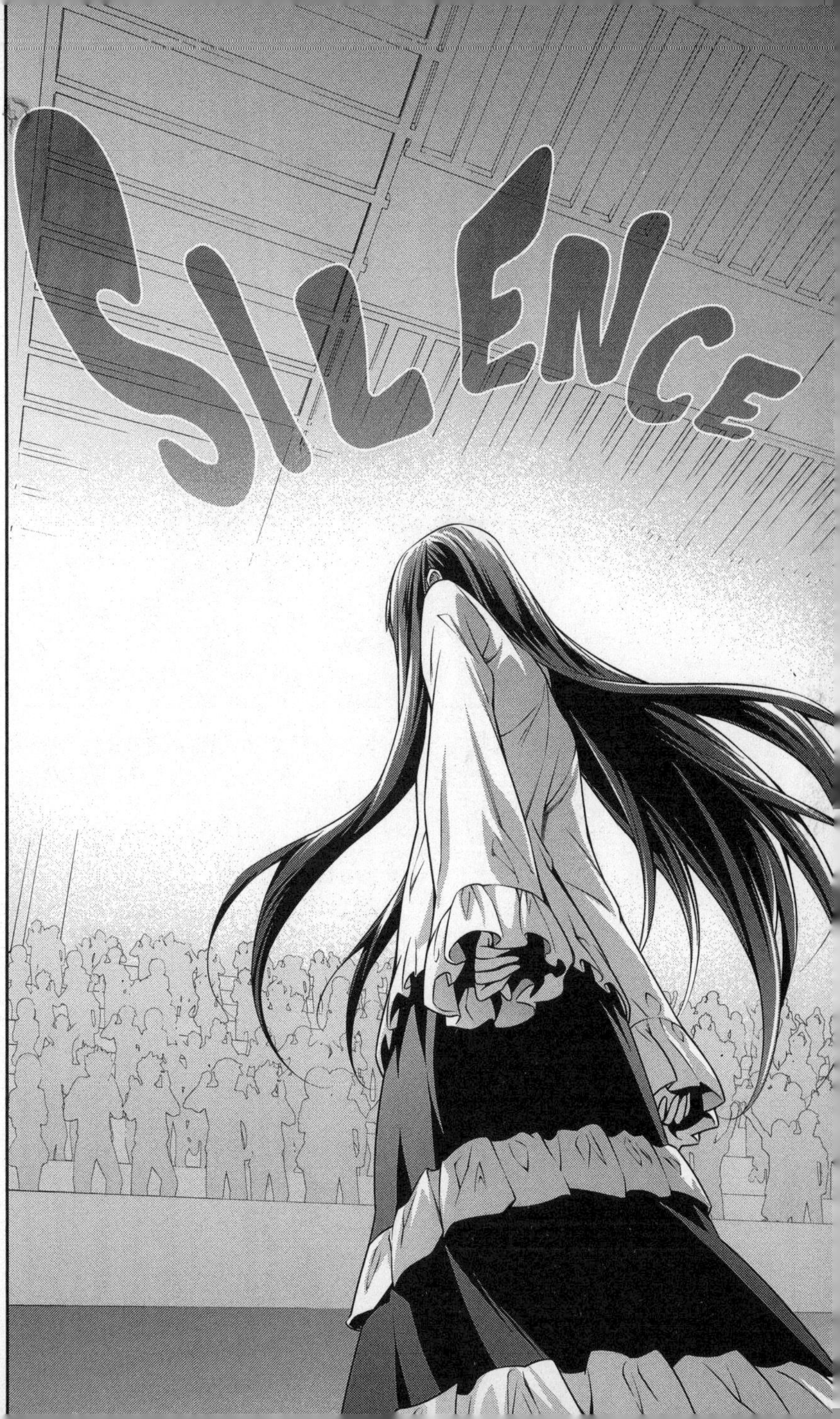
SILENCE

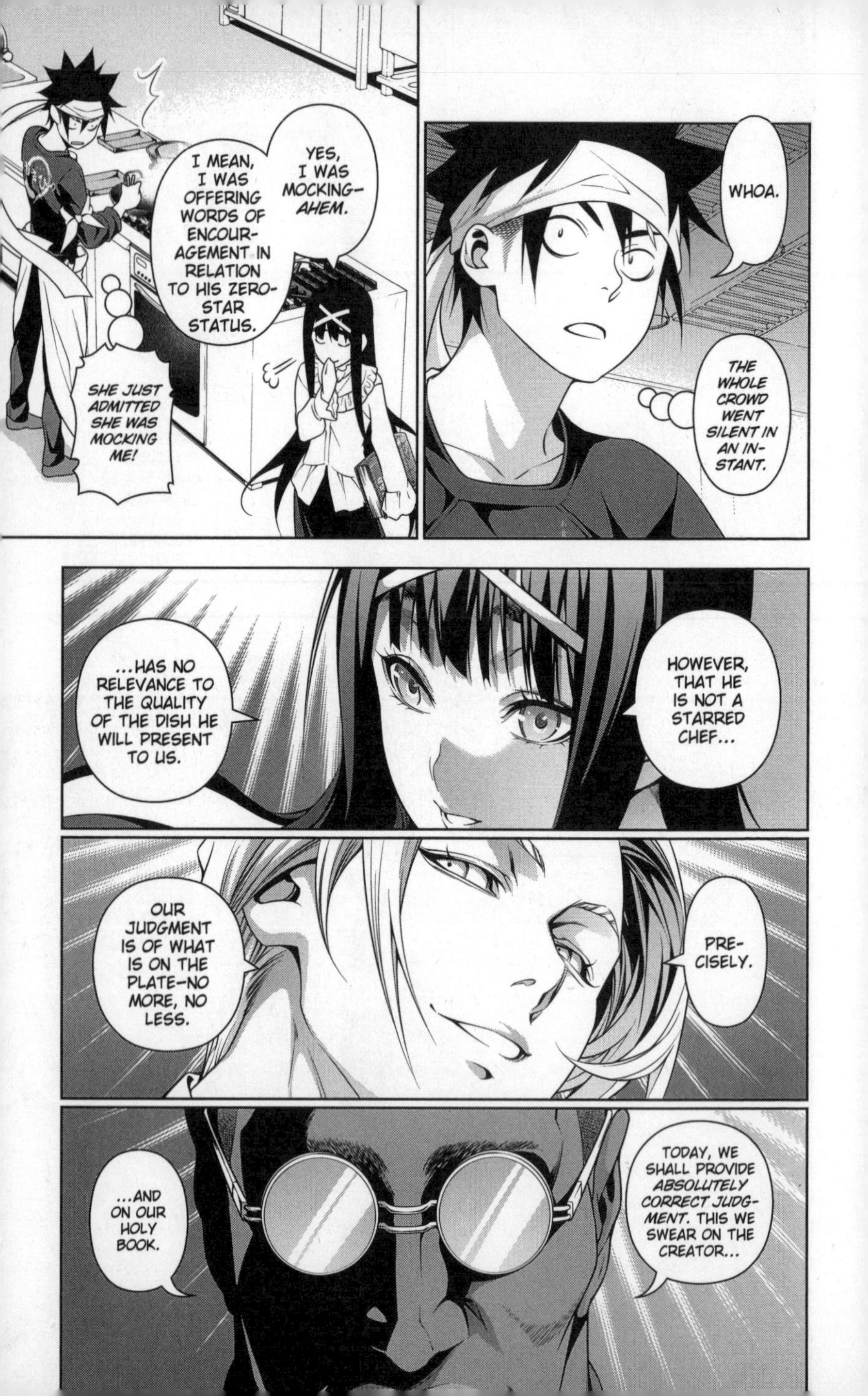
WHOA.
THE WHOLE CROWD WENT SILENT IN AN INSTANT.
YES, I WAS MOCKING—AHEM.
I MEAN, I WAS OFFERING WORDS OF ENCOURAGEMENT IN RELATION TO HIS ZERO-STAR STATUS.
SHE JUST ADMITTED SHE WAS MOCKING ME!
HOWEVER, THAT HE IS NOT A STARRED CHEF...
...HAS NO RELEVANCE TO THE QUALITY OF THE DISH HE WILL PRESENT TO US.
PRECISELY.
OUR JUDGMENT IS OF WHAT IS ON THE PLATE—NO MORE, NO LESS.
TODAY, WE SHALL PROVIDE *ABSOLUTELY CORRECT JUDGMENT*. THIS WE SWEAR ON THE CREATOR...
...AND ON OUR HOLY BOOK.

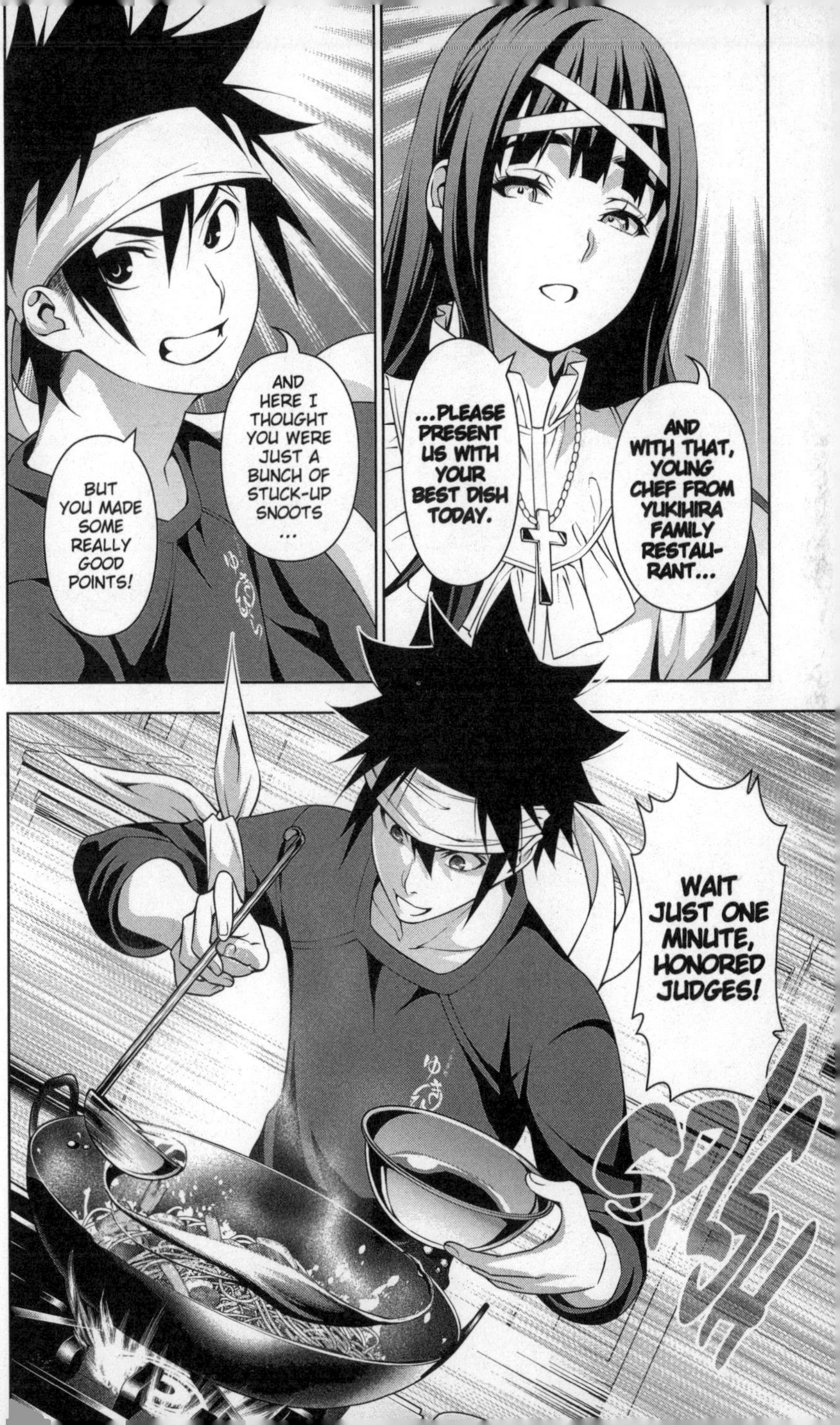
AND WITH THAT, YOUNG CHEF FROM YUKIHIRA FAMILY RESTAU-RANT...
...PLEASE PRESENT US WITH YOUR BEST DISH TODAY.
AND HERE I THOUGHT YOU WERE JUST A BUNCH OF STUCK-UP SNOOTS ...
BUT YOU MADE SOME REALLY GOOD POINTS!
WAIT JUST ONE MINUTE, HONORED JUDGES!

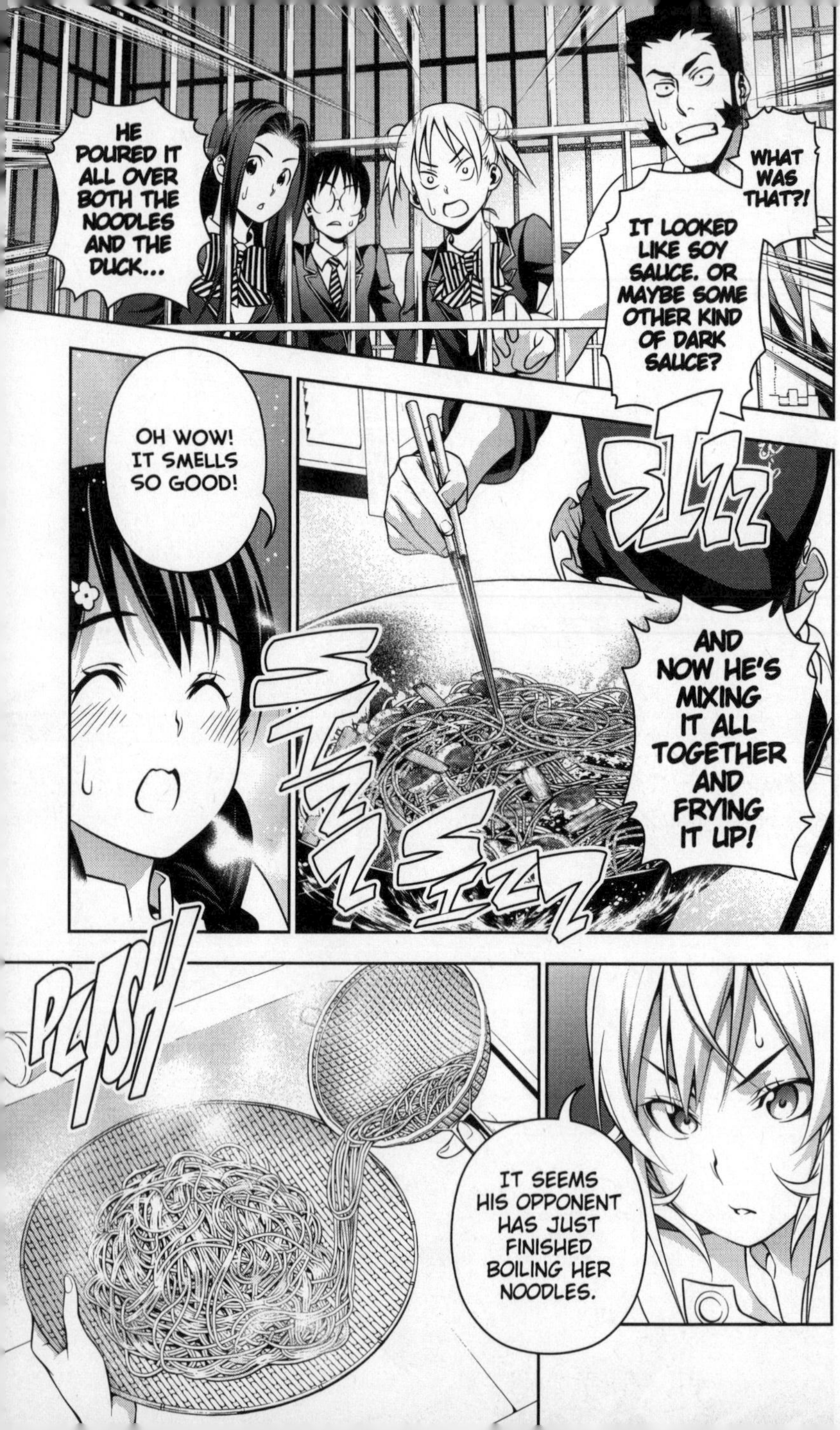
WHAT WAS THAT?!
IT LOOKED LIKE SOY SAUCE. OR MAYBE SOME OTHER KIND OF DARK SAUCE?
HE POURED IT ALL OVER BOTH THE NOODLES AND THE DUCK...
SIZZ
AND NOW HE'S MIXING IT ALL TOGETHER AND FRYING IT UP!
SIZZZ
SIZZZ
OH WOW! IT SMELLS SO GOOD!
IT SEEMS HIS OPPONENT HAS JUST FINISHED BOILING HER NOODLES.
PLISH

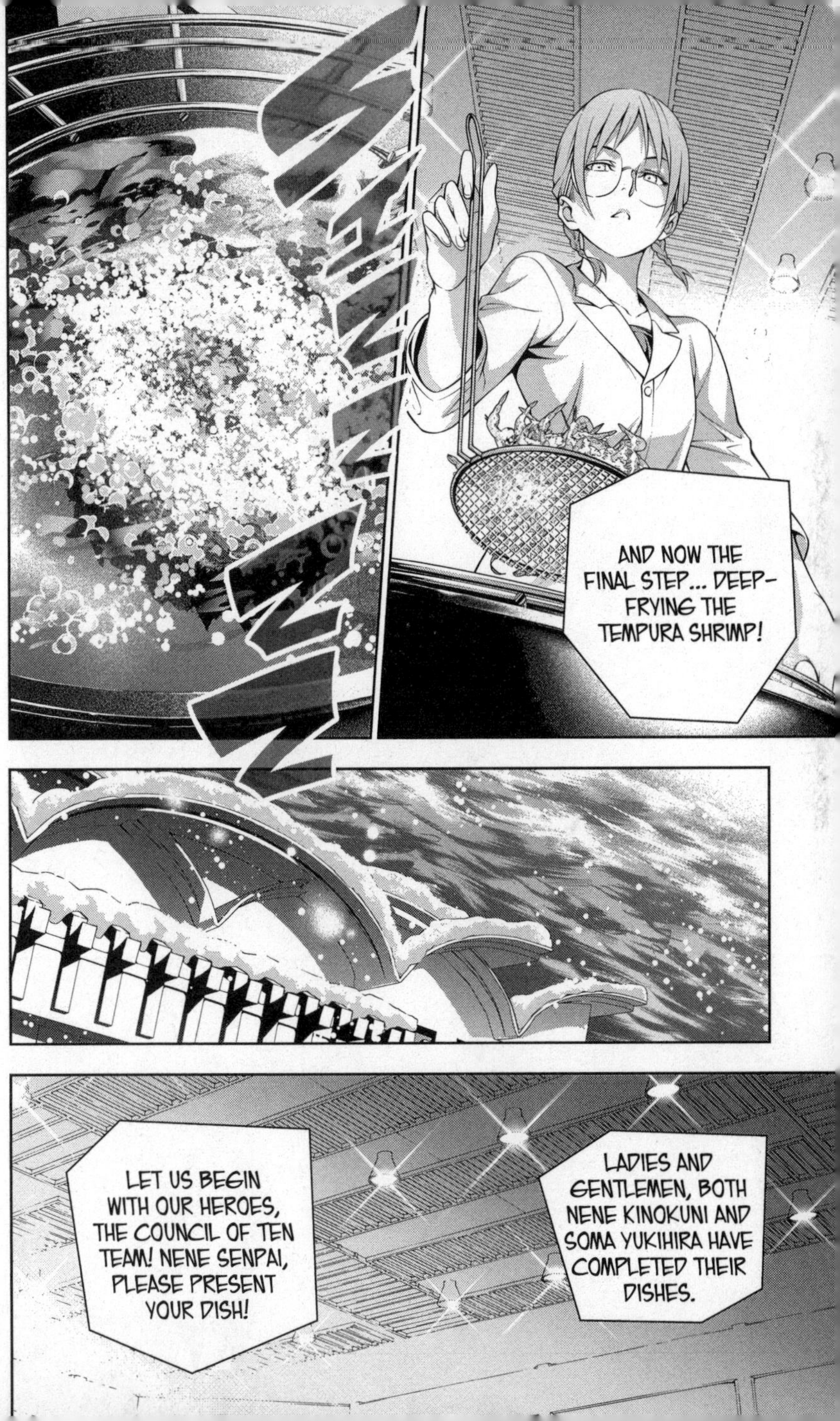
AND NOW THE FINAL STEP... DEEP-FRYING THE TEMPURA SHRIMP!
LADIES AND GENTLEMEN, BOTH NENE KINOKUNI AND SOMA YUKIHIRA HAVE COMPLETED THEIR DISHES.
LET US BEGIN WITH OUR HEROES, THE COUNCIL OF TEN TEAM! NENE SENPAI, PLEASE PRESENT YOUR DISH!

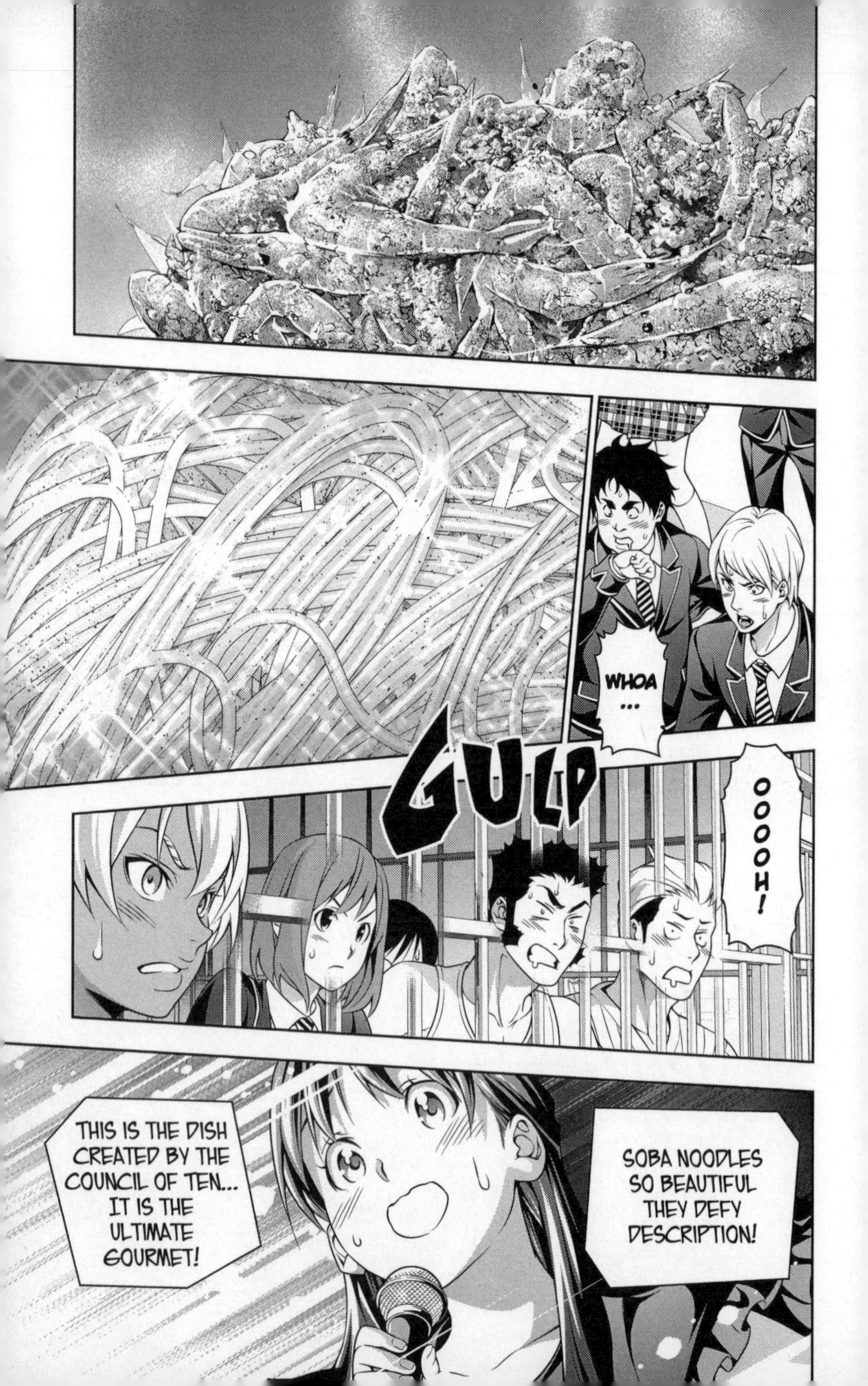
WHOA ...
GULP
OOOOOH!
SOBA NOODLES SO BEAUTIFUL THEY DEFY DESCRIPTION!
THIS IS THE DISH CREATED BY THE COUNCIL OF TEN... IT IS THE ULTIMATE GOURMET!

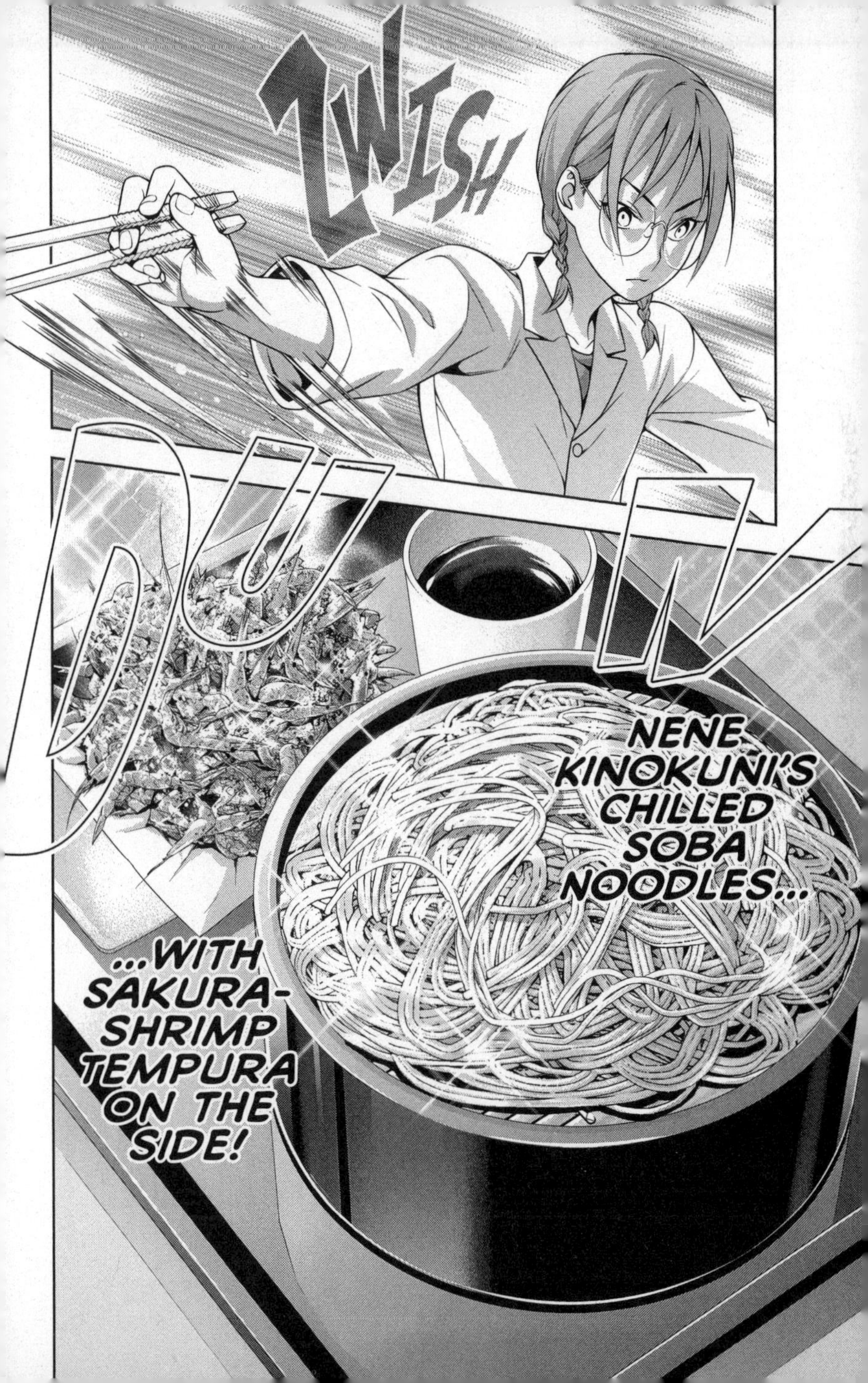
ZWISH
DUN
NENE KINOKUNI'S CHILLED SOBA NOODLES...
...WITH SAKURA-SHRIMP TEMPURA ON THE SIDE!

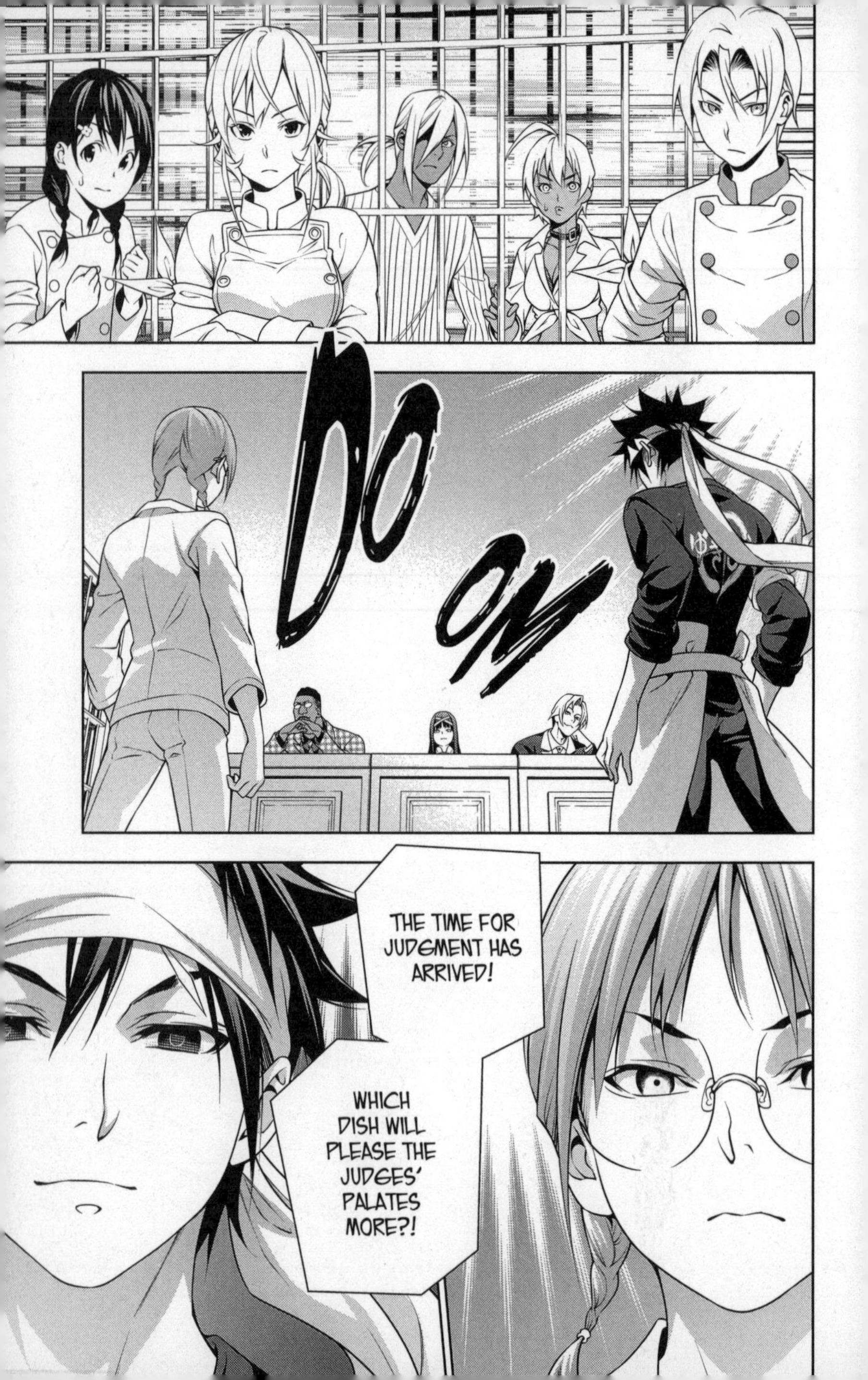
DOOM
THE TIME FOR JUDGMENT HAS ARRIVED!
WHICH DISH WILL PLEASE THE JUDGES' PALATES MORE?!

THE BOOK

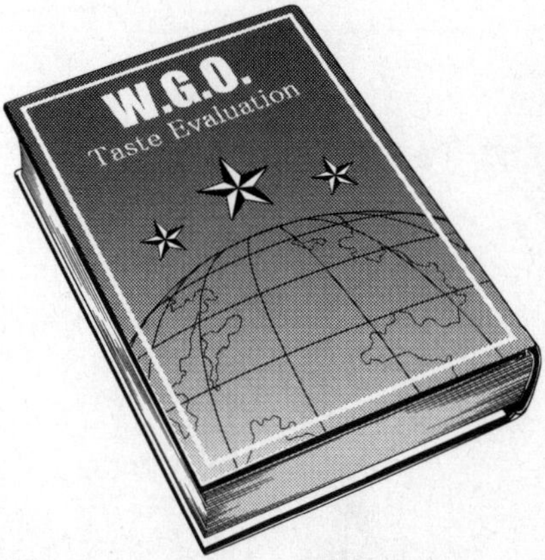
W.G.O.
Taste Evaluation

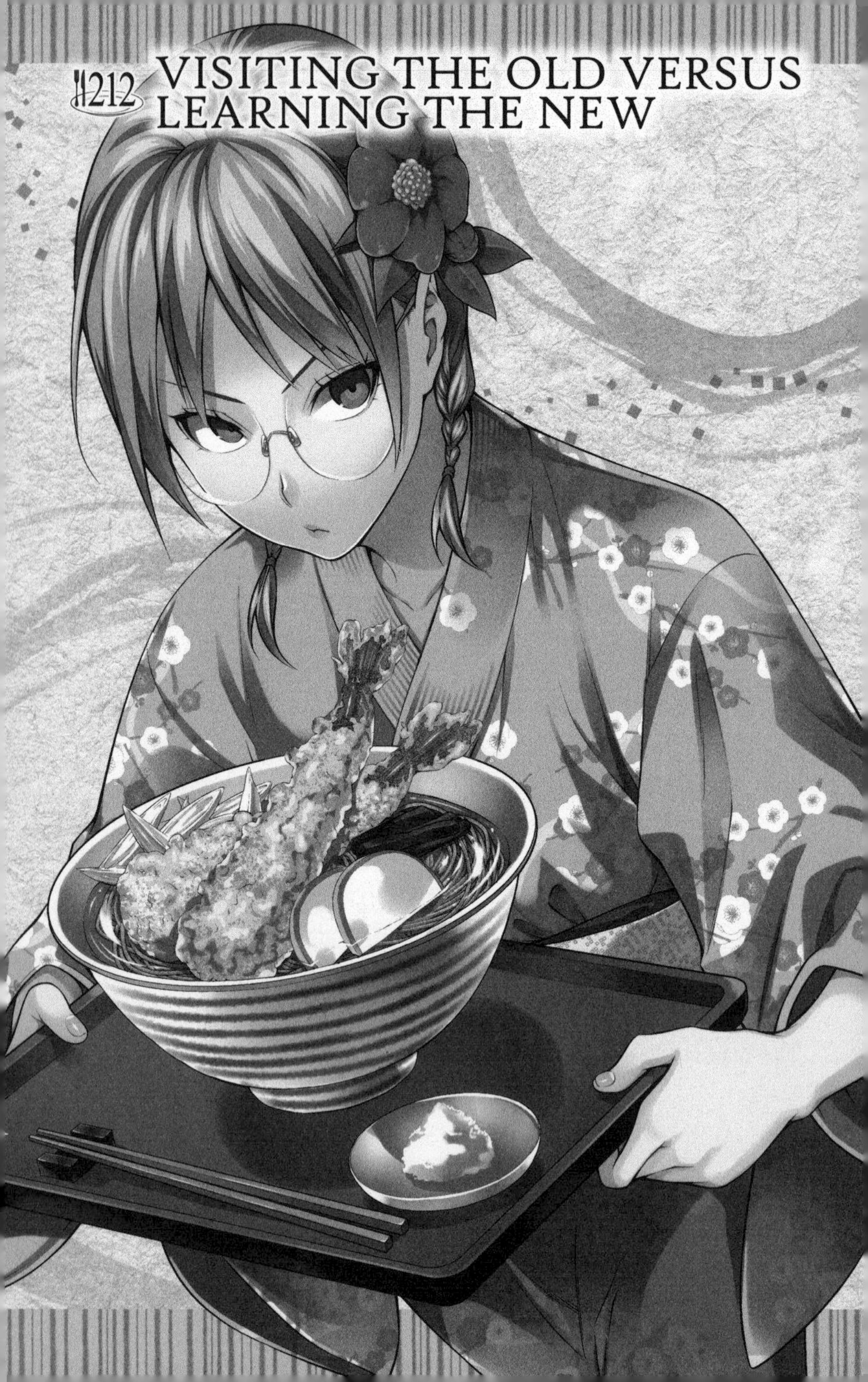

212
VISITING THE OLD VERSUS
LEARNING THE NEW

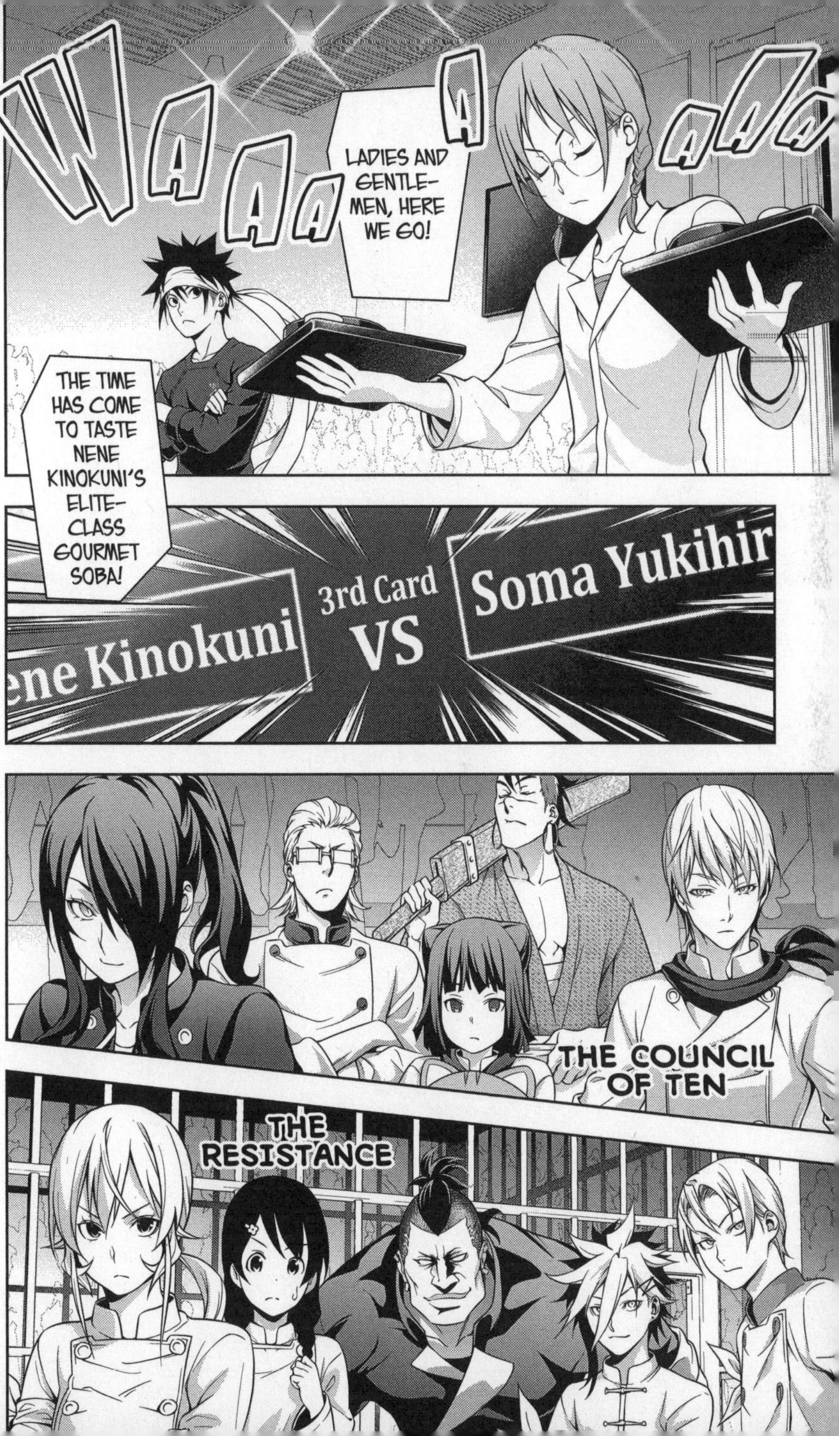
WAAAAAAAAA
LADIES AND GENTLE-MEN, HERE WE GO!
THE TIME HAS COME TO TASTE NENE KINOKUNI'S ELITE-CLASS GOURMET SOBA!
Soma Yukihir
3rd Card
VS
ene Kinokuni
THE COUNCIL OF TEN
THE RESISTANCE

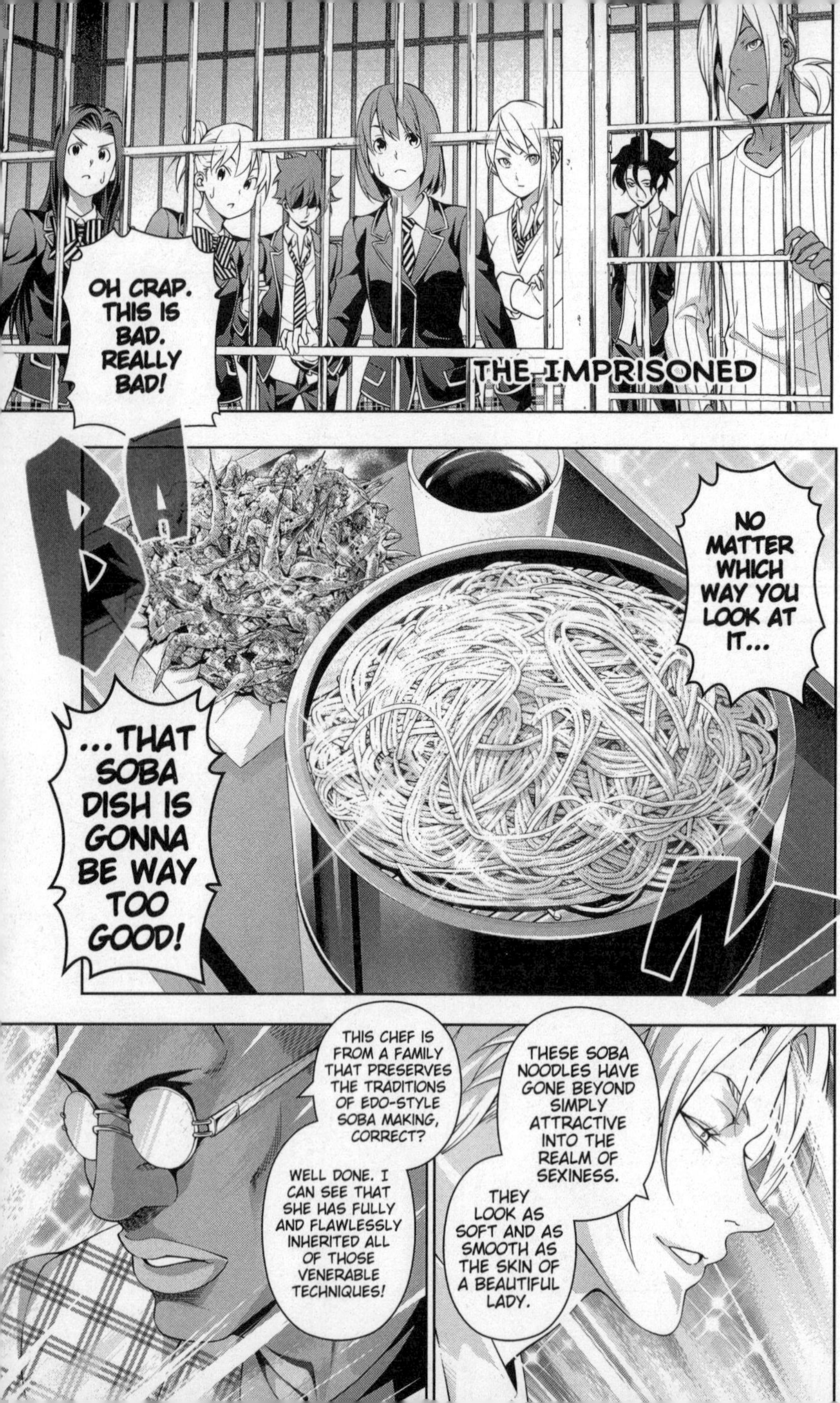
OH CRAP. THIS IS BAD. REALLY BAD!
THE IMPRISONED
NO MATTER WHICH WAY YOU LOOK AT IT...
...THAT SOBA DISH IS GONNA BE WAY TOO GOOD!
THESE SOBA NOODLES HAVE GONE BEYOND SIMPLY ATTRACTIVE INTO THE REALM OF SEXINESS.
THEY LOOK AS SOFT AND AS SMOOTH AS THE SKIN OF A BEAUTIFUL LADY.
THIS CHEF IS FROM A FAMILY THAT PRESERVES THE TRADITIONS OF EDO-STYLE SOBA MAKING, CORRECT?
WELL DONE. I CAN SEE THAT SHE HAS FULLY AND FLAWLESSLY INHERITED ALL OF THOSE VENERABLE TECHNIQUES!

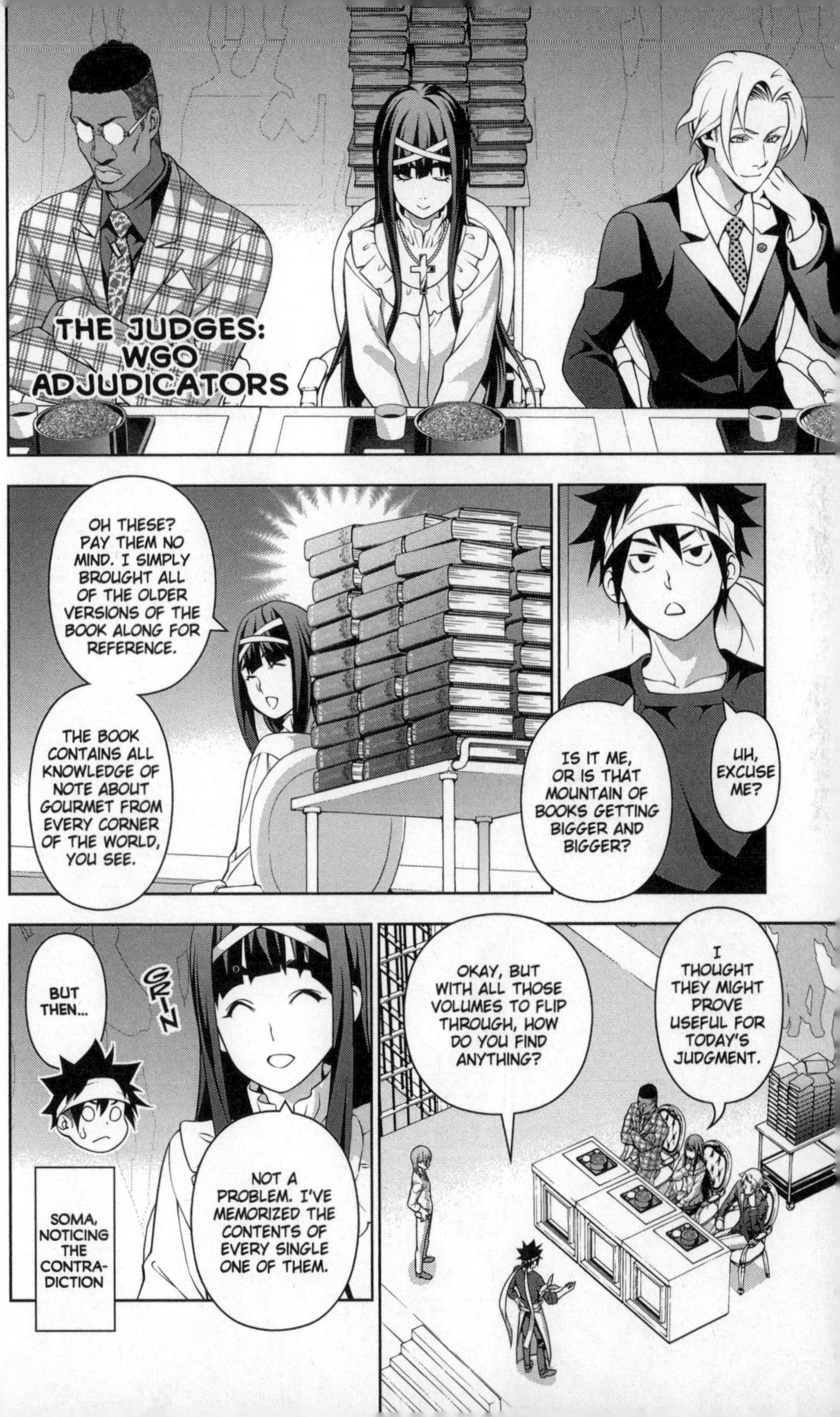
THE JUDGES: WGO ADJUDICATORS
UH, EXCUSE ME?
IS IT ME, OR IS THAT MOUNTAIN OF BOOKS GETTING BIGGER AND BIGGER?
OH THESE? PAY THEM NO MIND. I SIMPLY BROUGHT ALL OF THE OLDER VERSIONS OF THE BOOK ALONG FOR REFERENCE.
THE BOOK CONTAINS ALL KNOWLEDGE OF NOTE ABOUT GOURMET FROM EVERY CORNER OF THE WORLD, YOU SEE.
I THOUGHT THEY MIGHT PROVE USEFUL FOR TODAY'S JUDGMENT.
OKAY, BUT WITH ALL THOSE VOLUMES TO FLIP THROUGH, HOW DO YOU FIND ANYTHING?
GRIN
BUT THEN...
NOT A PROBLEM. I'VE MEMORIZED THE CONTENTS OF EVERY SINGLE ONE OF THEM.
SOMA, NOTICING THE CONTRA-DICTION

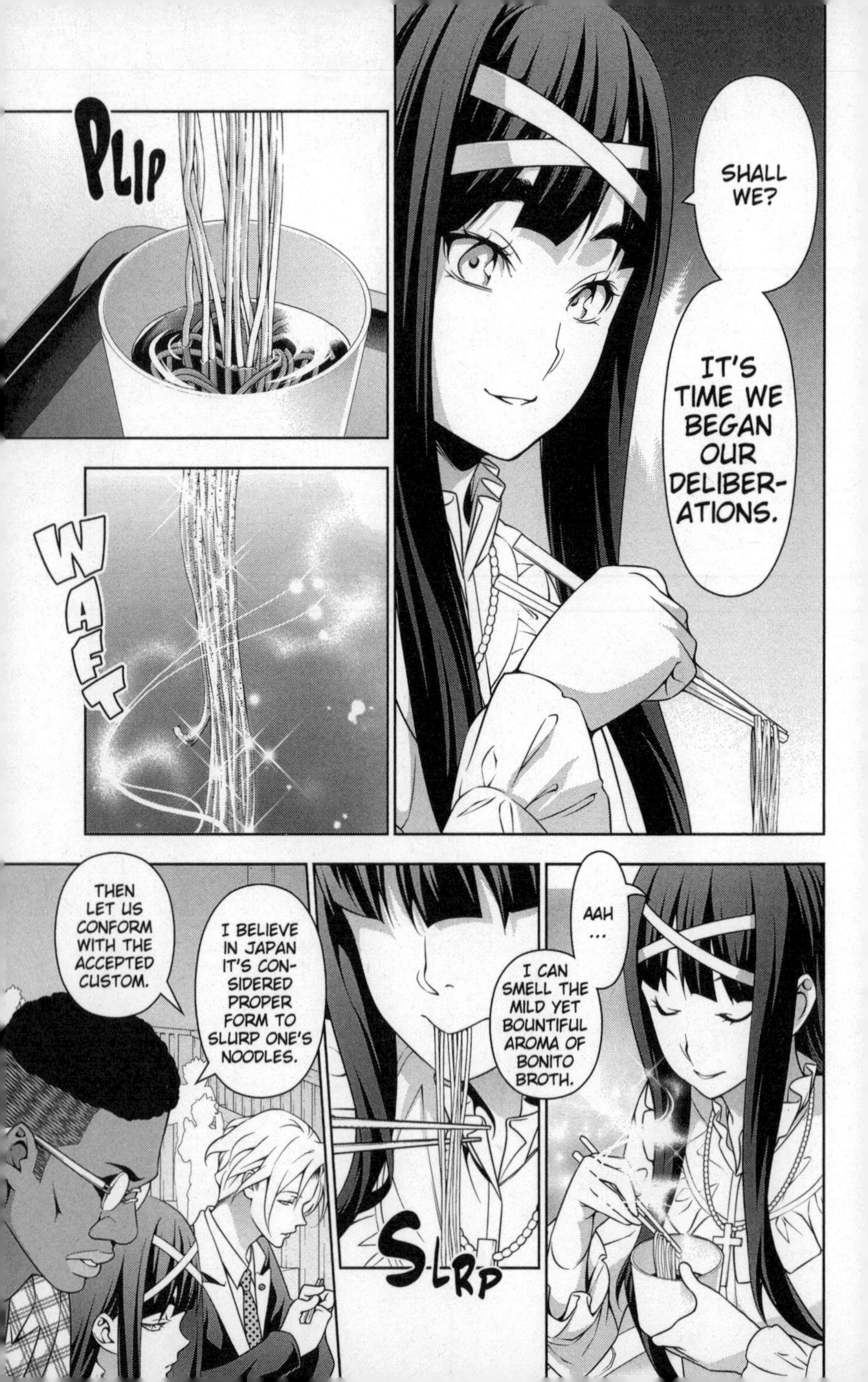
SHALL WE?
IT'S TIME WE BEGAN OUR DELIBER-ATIONS.
PLIP
WAFT
AAH ...
I CAN SMELL THE MILD YET BOUNTIFUL AROMA OF BONITO BROTH.
SLRP
I BELIEVE IN JAPAN IT'S CON-SIDERED PROPER FORM TO SLURP ONE'S NOODLES.
THEN LET US CONFORM WITH THE ACCEPTED CUSTOM.

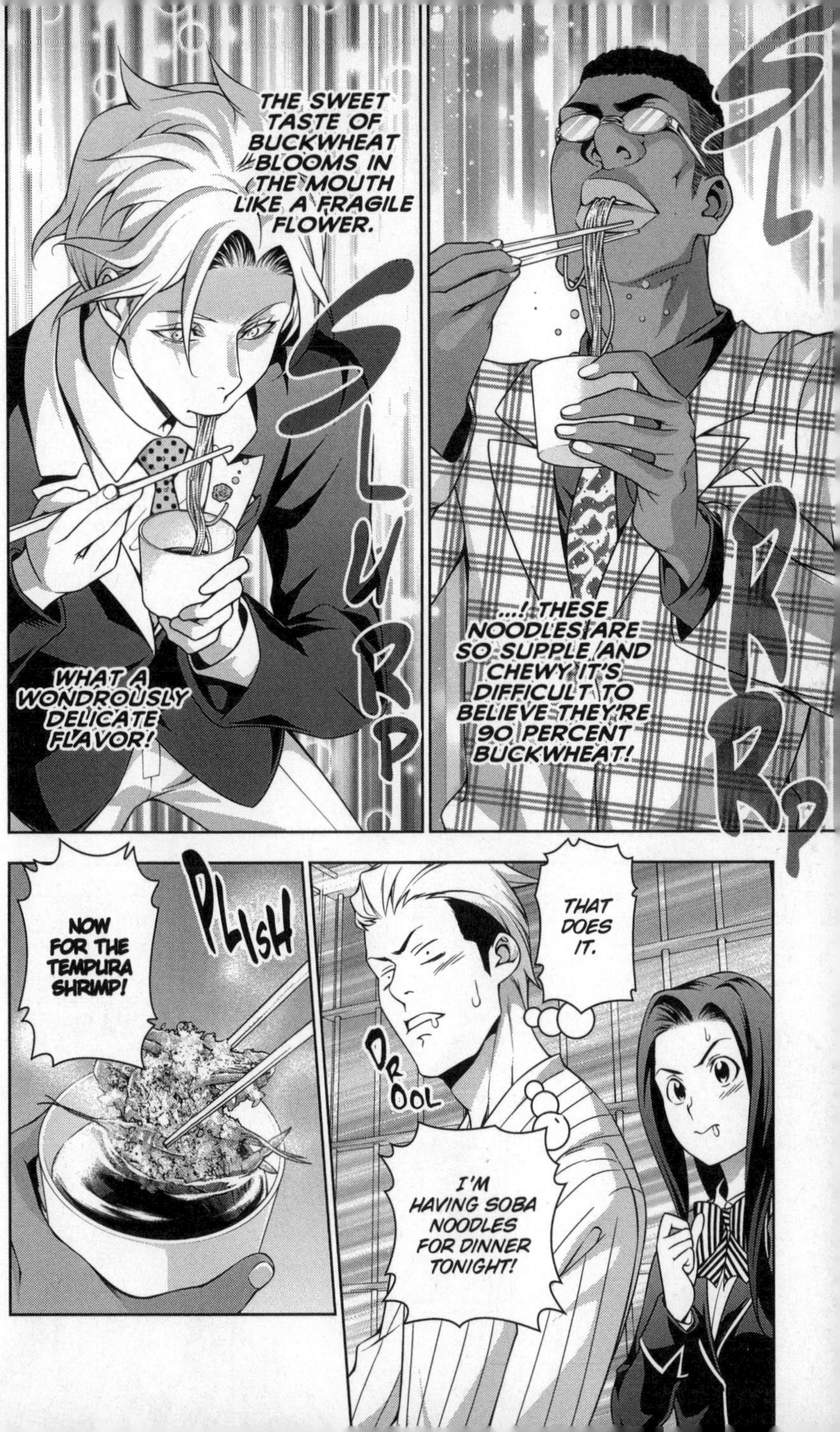
SLURRP
...! THESE NOODLES ARE SO SUPPLE AND CHEWY IT'S DIFFICULT TO BELIEVE THEY'RE 90 PERCENT BUCKWHEAT!
THE SWEET TASTE OF BUCKWHEAT BLOOMS IN THE MOUTH LIKE A FRAGILE FLOWER.
SLURP
WHAT A WONDROUSLY DELICATE FLAVOR!
THAT DOES IT.
I'M HAVING SOBA NOODLES FOR DINNER TONIGHT!
DROOL
PLISH
NOW FOR THE TEMPURA SHRIMP!

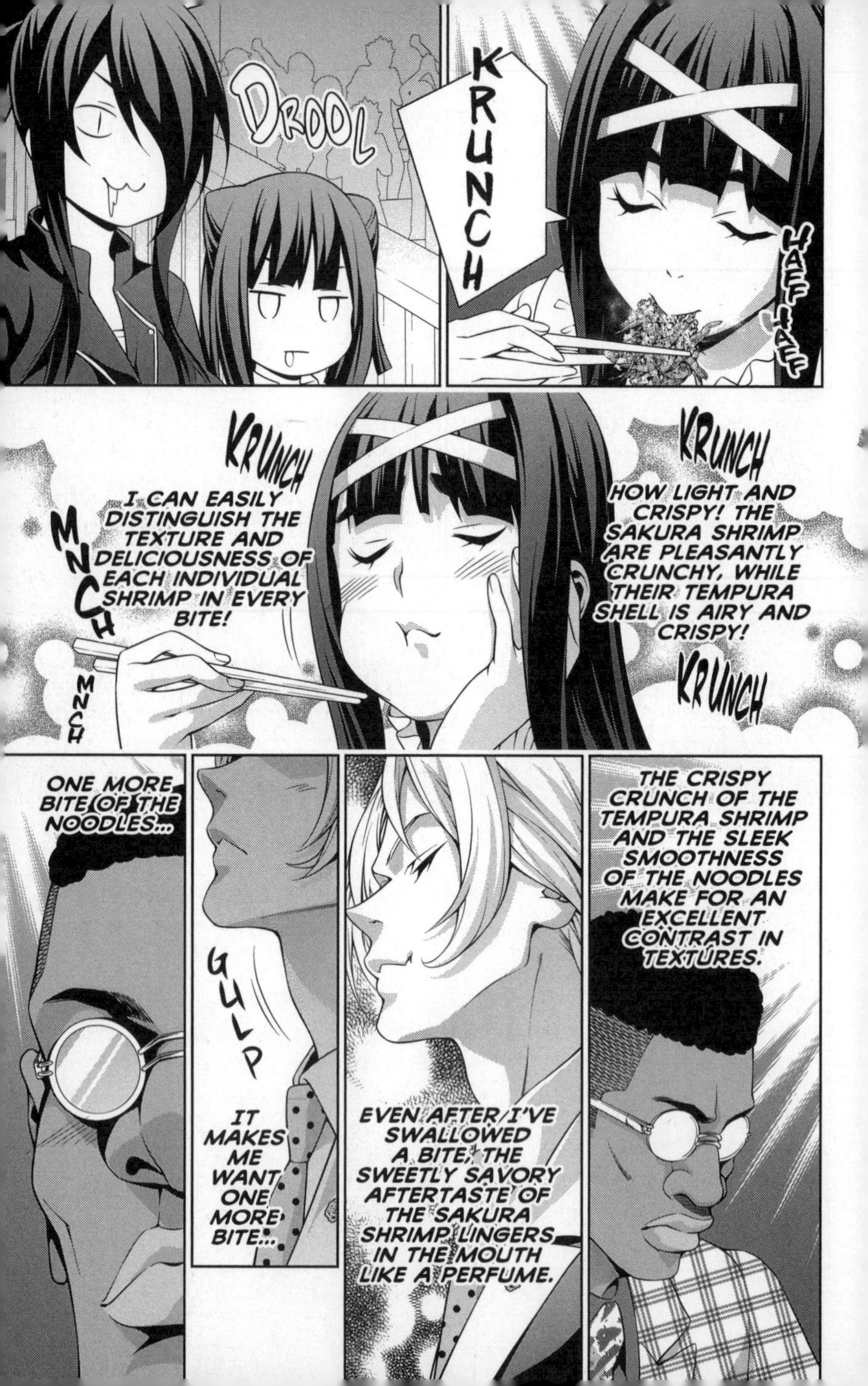
KRUNCH
HAFF HAFF
DROOL
KRUNCH
HOW LIGHT AND CRISPY! THE SAKURA SHRIMP ARE PLEASANTLY CRUNCHY, WHILE THEIR TEMPURA SHELL IS AIRY AND CRISPY!
KRUNCH
KRUNCH
I CAN EASILY DISTINGUISH THE TEXTURE AND DELICIOUSNESS OF EACH INDIVIDUAL SHRIMP IN EVERY BITE!
MNCH
MNCH MNCH
THE CRISPY CRUNCH OF THE TEMPURA SHRIMP AND THE SLEEK SMOOTHNESS OF THE NOODLES MAKE FOR AN EXCELLENT CONTRAST IN TEXTURES.
EVEN AFTER I'VE SWALLOWED A BITE, THE SWEETLY SAVORY AFTERTASTE OF THE SAKURA SHRIMP LINGERS IN THE MOUTH LIKE A PERFUME.
GULP
IT MAKES ME WANT ONE MORE BITE...
ONE MORE BITE OF THE NOODLES...

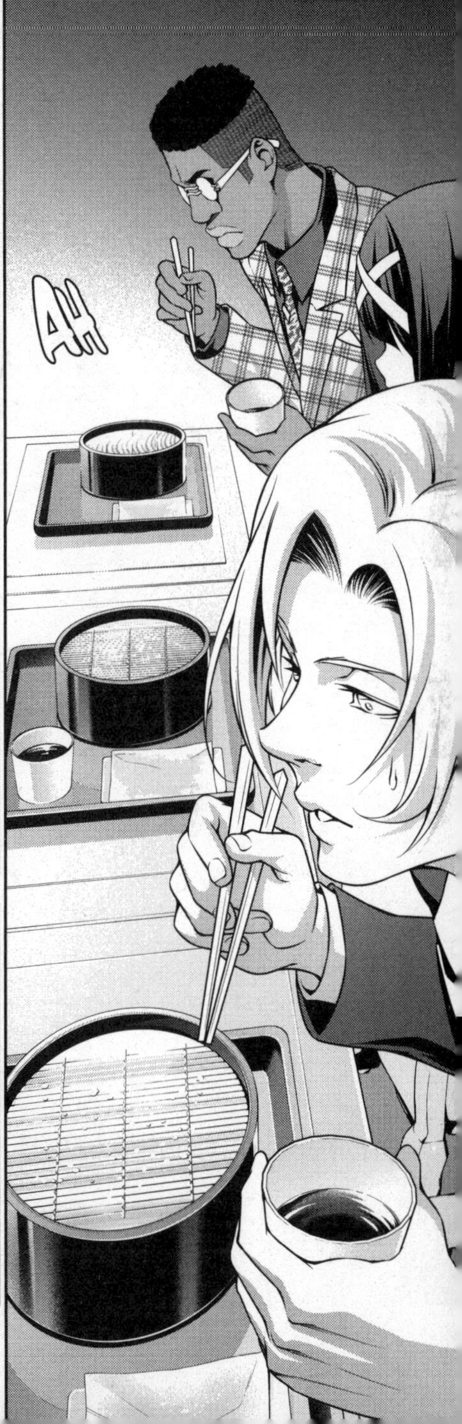
AH

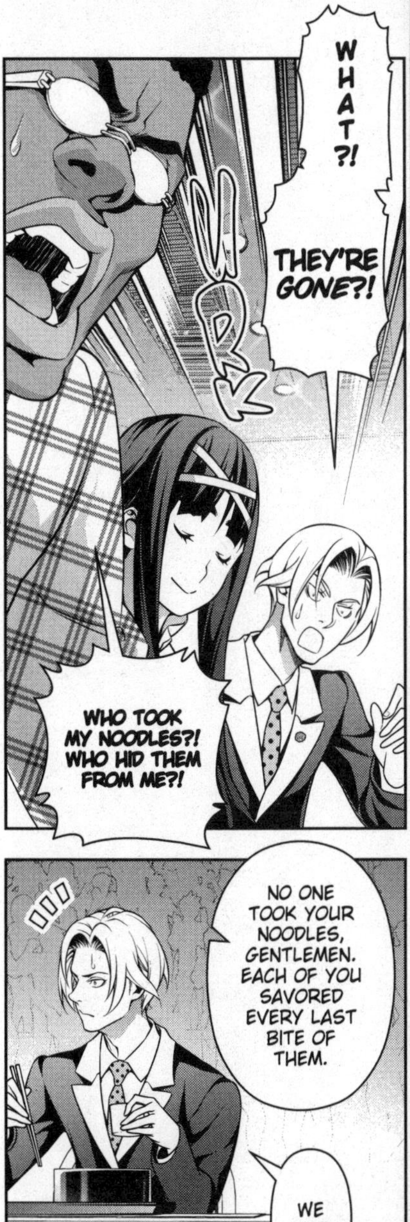
WHAT?!
THEY'RE GONE?!
URRK
WHO TOOK MY NOODLES?! WHO HID THEM FROM ME?!
NO ONE TOOK YOUR NOODLES, GENTLEMEN. EACH OF YOU SAVORED EVERY LAST BITE OF THEM.
WE DID?

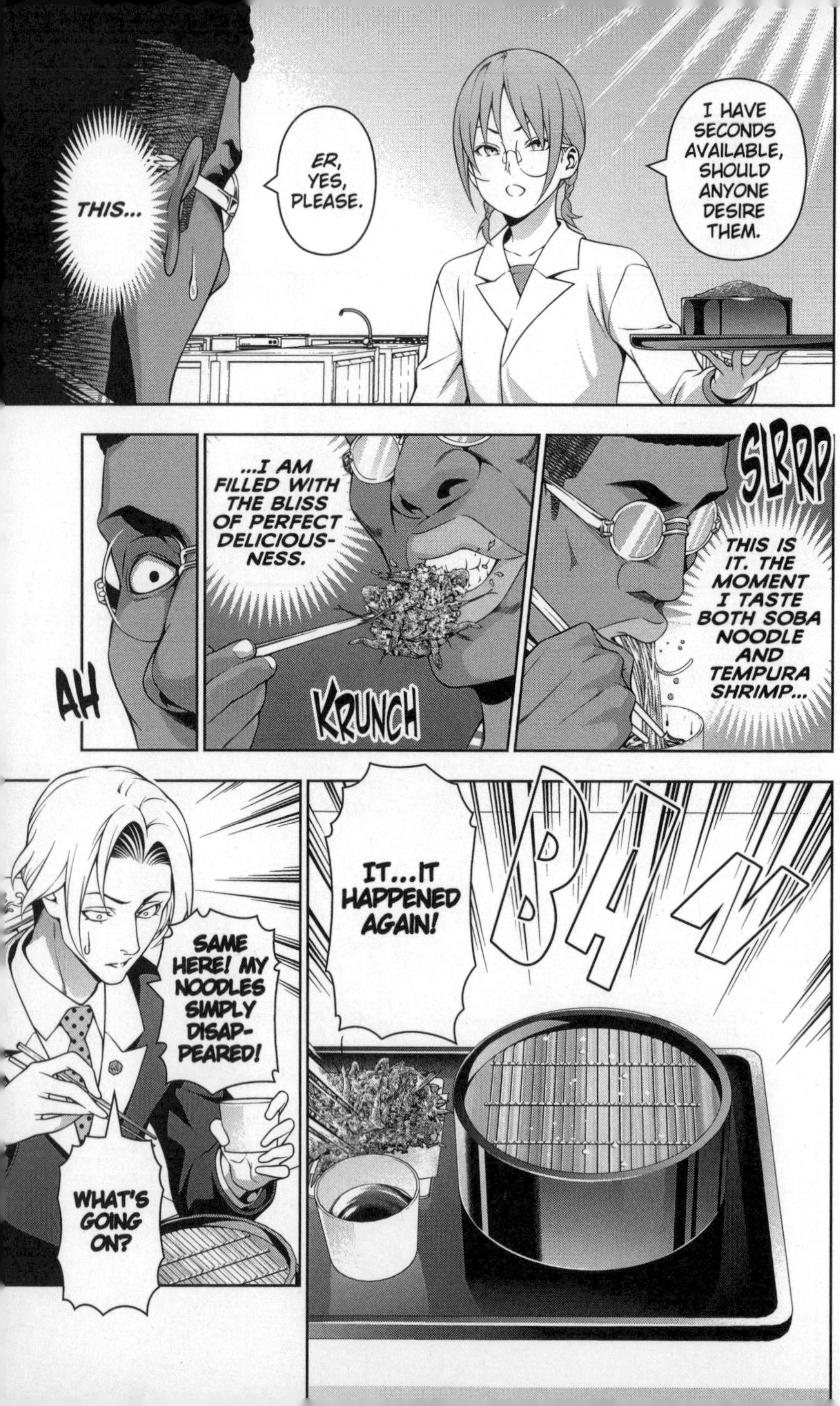
I HAVE SECONDS AVAILABLE, SHOULD ANYONE DESIRE THEM.
ER, YES, PLEASE.
THIS...
SLRRP
THIS IS IT. THE MOMENT I TASTE BOTH SOBA NOODLE AND TEMPURA SHRIMP...
...I AM FILLED WITH THE BLISS OF PERFECT DELICIOUSNESS.
KRUNCH
AH
BAN
IT...IT HAPPENED AGAIN!
SAME HERE! MY NOODLES SIMPLY DISAPPEARED!
WHAT'S GOING ON?

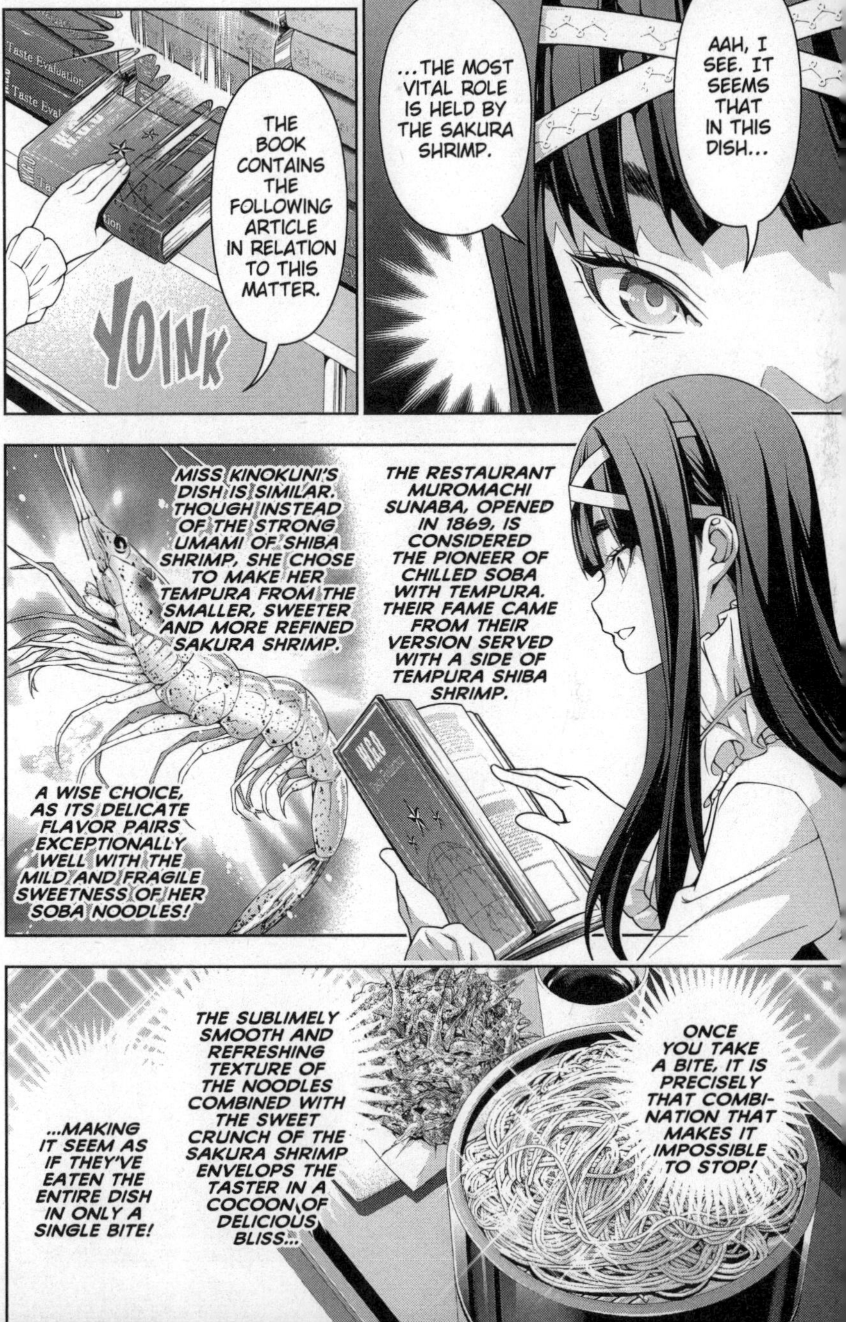
AAH, I SEE. IT SEEMS THAT IN THIS DISH...
...THE MOST VITAL ROLE IS HELD BY THE SAKURA SHRIMP.
THE BOOK CONTAINS THE FOLLOWING ARTICLE IN RELATION TO THIS MATTER.
YOINK
THE RESTAURANT MUROMACHI SUNABA, OPENED IN 1869, IS CONSIDERED THE PIONEER OF CHILLED SOBA WITH TEMPURA. THEIR FAME CAME FROM THEIR VERSION SERVED WITH A SIDE OF TEMPURA SHIBA SHRIMP.
MISS KINOKUNI'S DISH IS SIMILAR. THOUGH INSTEAD OF THE STRONG UMAMI OF SHIBA SHRIMP, SHE CHOSE TO MAKE HER TEMPURA FROM THE SMALLER, SWEETER AND MORE REFINED SAKURA SHRIMP.
A WISE CHOICE, AS ITS DELICATE FLAVOR PAIRS EXCEPTIONALLY WELL WITH THE MILD AND FRAGILE SWEETNESS OF HER SOBA NOODLES!
ONCE YOU TAKE A BITE, IT IS PRECISELY THAT COMBINATION THAT MAKES IT IMPOSSIBLE TO STOP!
THE SUBLIMELY SMOOTH AND REFRESHING TEXTURE OF THE NOODLES COMBINED WITH THE SWEET CRUNCH OF THE SAKURA SHRIMP ENVELOPS THE TASTER IN A COCOON OF DELICIOUS BLISS...
...MAKING IT SEEM AS IF THEY'VE EATEN THE ENTIRE DISH IN ONLY A SINGLE BITE!

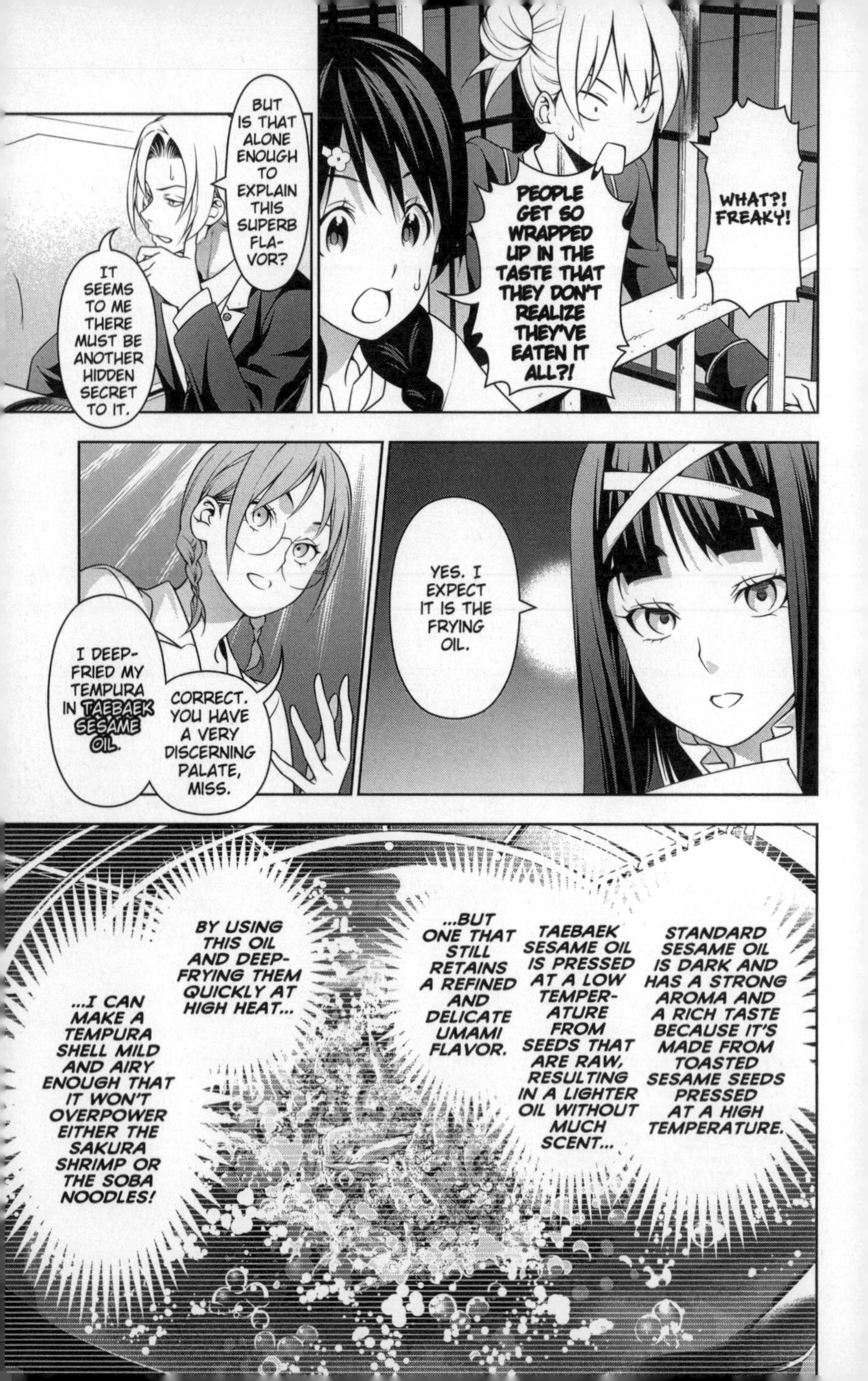
WHAT?! FREAKY!
PEOPLE GET SO WRAPPED UP IN THE TASTE THAT THEY DON'T REALIZE THEY'VE EATEN IT ALL?!
BUT IS THAT ALONE ENOUGH TO EXPLAIN THIS SUPERB FLA-VOR?
IT SEEMS TO ME THERE MUST BE ANOTHER HIDDEN SECRET TO IT.
YES. I EXPECT IT IS THE FRYING OIL.
CORRECT. YOU HAVE A VERY DISCERNING PALATE, MISS.
I DEEP-FRIED MY TEMPURA IN TAEBAEK SESAME OIL.
STANDARD SESAME OIL IS DARK AND HAS A STRONG AROMA AND A RICH TASTE BECAUSE IT'S MADE FROM TOASTED SESAME SEEDS PRESSED AT A HIGH TEMPERATURE.
TAEBAEK SESAME OIL IS PRESSED AT A LOW TEMPER-ATURE FROM SEEDS THAT ARE RAW, RESULTING IN A LIGHTER OIL WITHOUT MUCH SCENT...
...BUT ONE THAT STILL RETAINS A REFINED AND DELICATE UMAMI FLAVOR.
BY USING THIS OIL AND DEEP-FRYING THEM QUICKLY AT HIGH HEAT...
...I CAN MAKE A TEMPURA SHELL MILD AND AIRY ENOUGH THAT IT WON'T OVERPOWER EITHER THE SAKURA SHRIMP OR THE SOBA NOODLES!

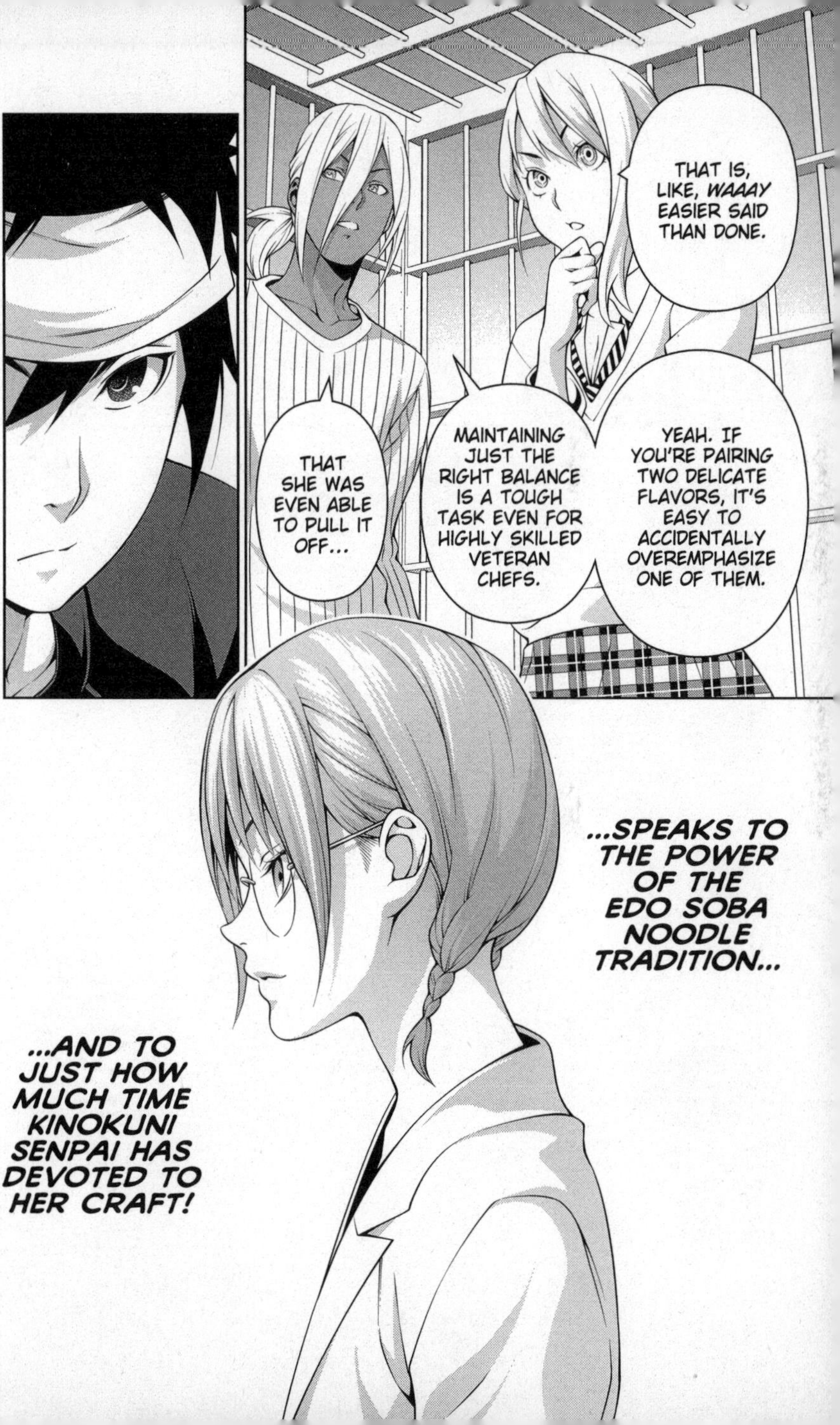
THAT IS, LIKE, *WAAAY* EASIER SAID THAN DONE.
YEAH. IF YOU'RE PAIRING TWO DELICATE FLAVORS, IT'S EASY TO ACCIDENTALLY OVEREMPHASIZE ONE OF THEM.
MAINTAINING JUST THE RIGHT BALANCE IS A TOUGH TASK EVEN FOR HIGHLY SKILLED VETERAN CHEFS.
THAT SHE WAS EVEN ABLE TO PULL IT OFF...
...SPEAKS TO THE POWER OF THE EDO SOBA NOODLE TRADITION...
...AND TO JUST HOW MUCH TIME KINOKUNI SENPAI HAS DEVOTED TO HER CRAFT!

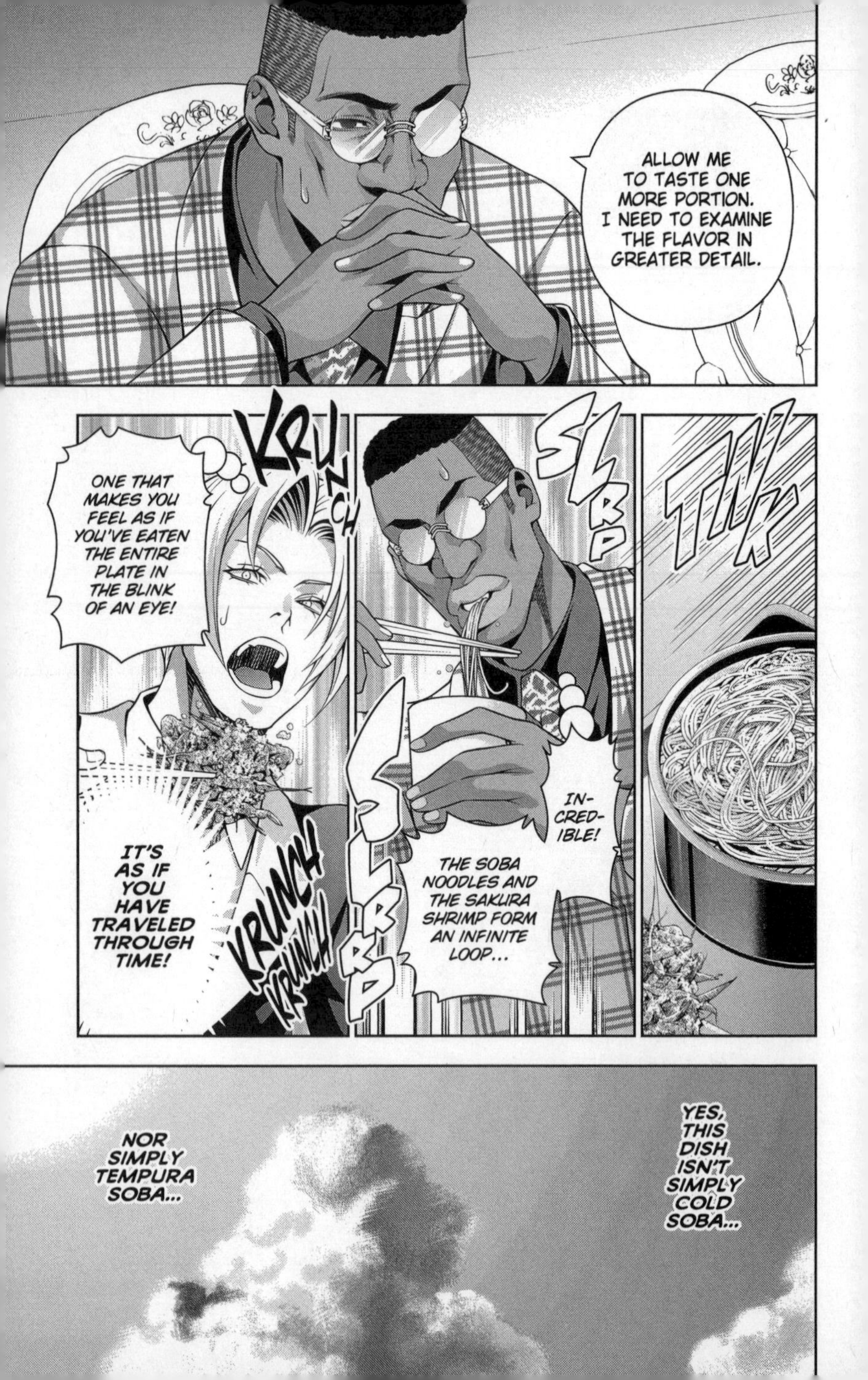
ALLOW ME TO TASTE ONE MORE PORTION. I NEED TO EXAMINE THE FLAVOR IN GREATER DETAIL.
TINK
SLRP
IN-CREDIBLE!
THE SOBA NOODLES AND THE SAKURA SHRIMP FORM AN INFINITE LOOP...
SLRRP
KRUNCH
ONE THAT MAKES YOU FEEL AS IF YOU'VE EATEN THE ENTIRE PLATE IN THE BLINK OF AN EYE!
IT'S AS IF YOU HAVE TRAVELED THROUGH TIME!
KRUNCH KRUNCH
YES, THIS DISH ISN'T SIMPLY COLD SOBA...
NOR SIMPLY TEMPURA SOBA...

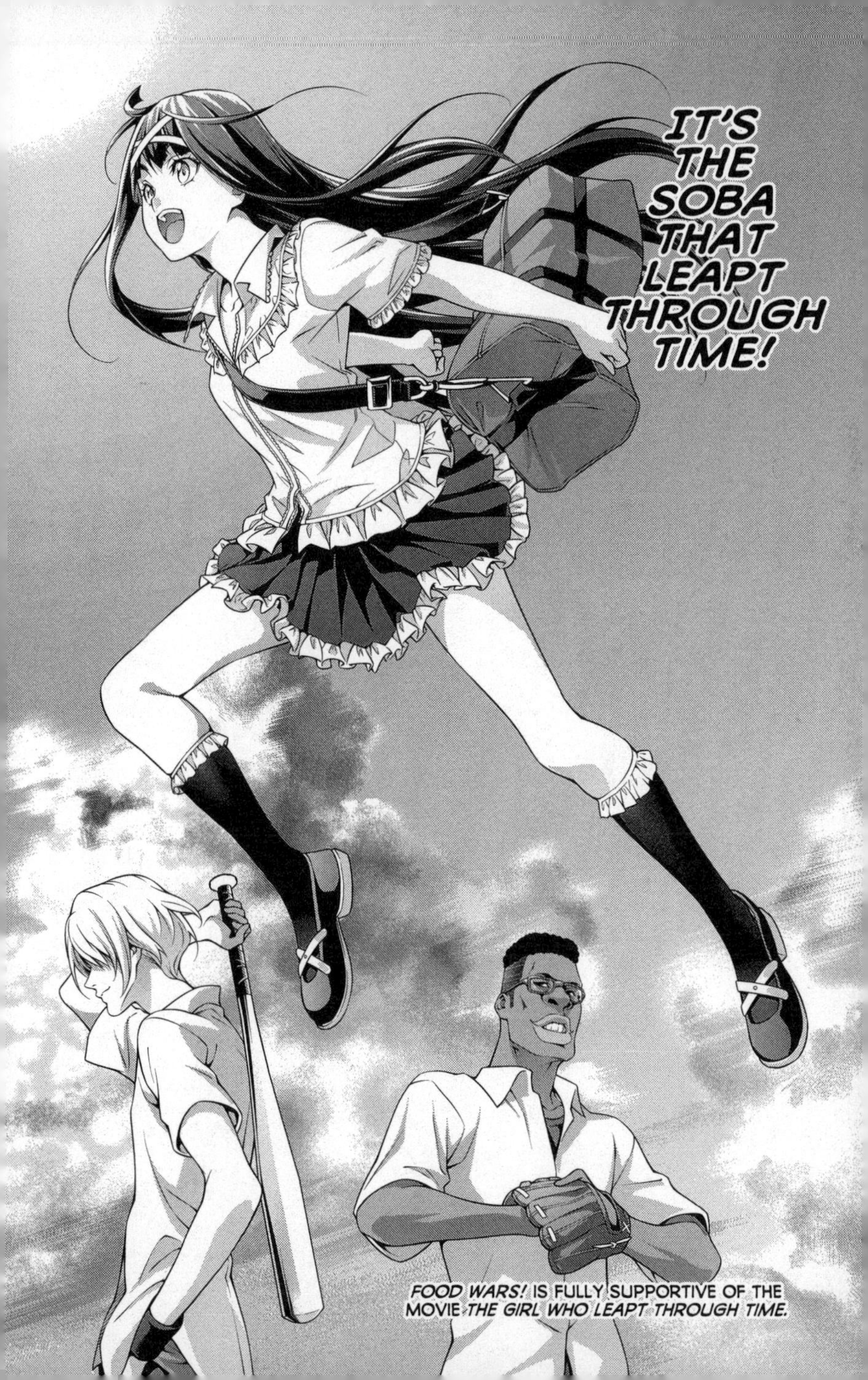
IT'S THE SOBA THAT LEAPT THROUGH TIME!

FOOD WARS! IS FULLY SUPPORTIVE OF THE MOVIE *THE GIRL WHO LEAPT THROUGH TIME.*

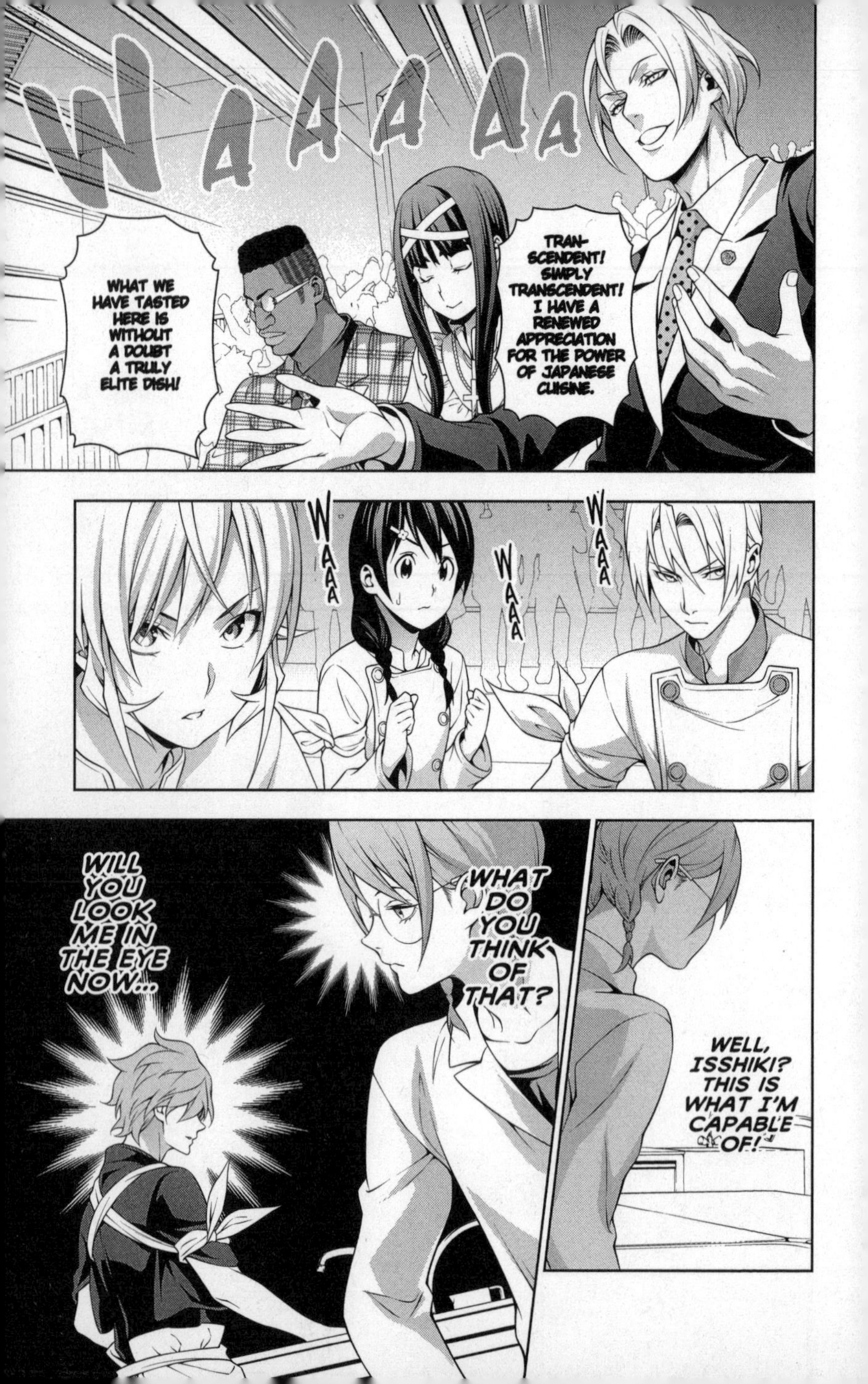
WAAAAAA
TRAN-SCENDENT! SIMPLY TRANSCENDENT! I HAVE A RENEWED APPRECIATION FOR THE POWER OF JAPANESE CUISINE.
WHAT WE HAVE TASTED HERE IS WITHOUT A DOUBT A TRULY ELITE DISH!
WAAA
WAAA
WAAA
WELL, ISSHIKI? THIS IS WHAT I'M CAPABLE OF!
WHAT DO YOU THINK OF THAT?
WILL YOU LOOK ME IN THE EYE NOW...

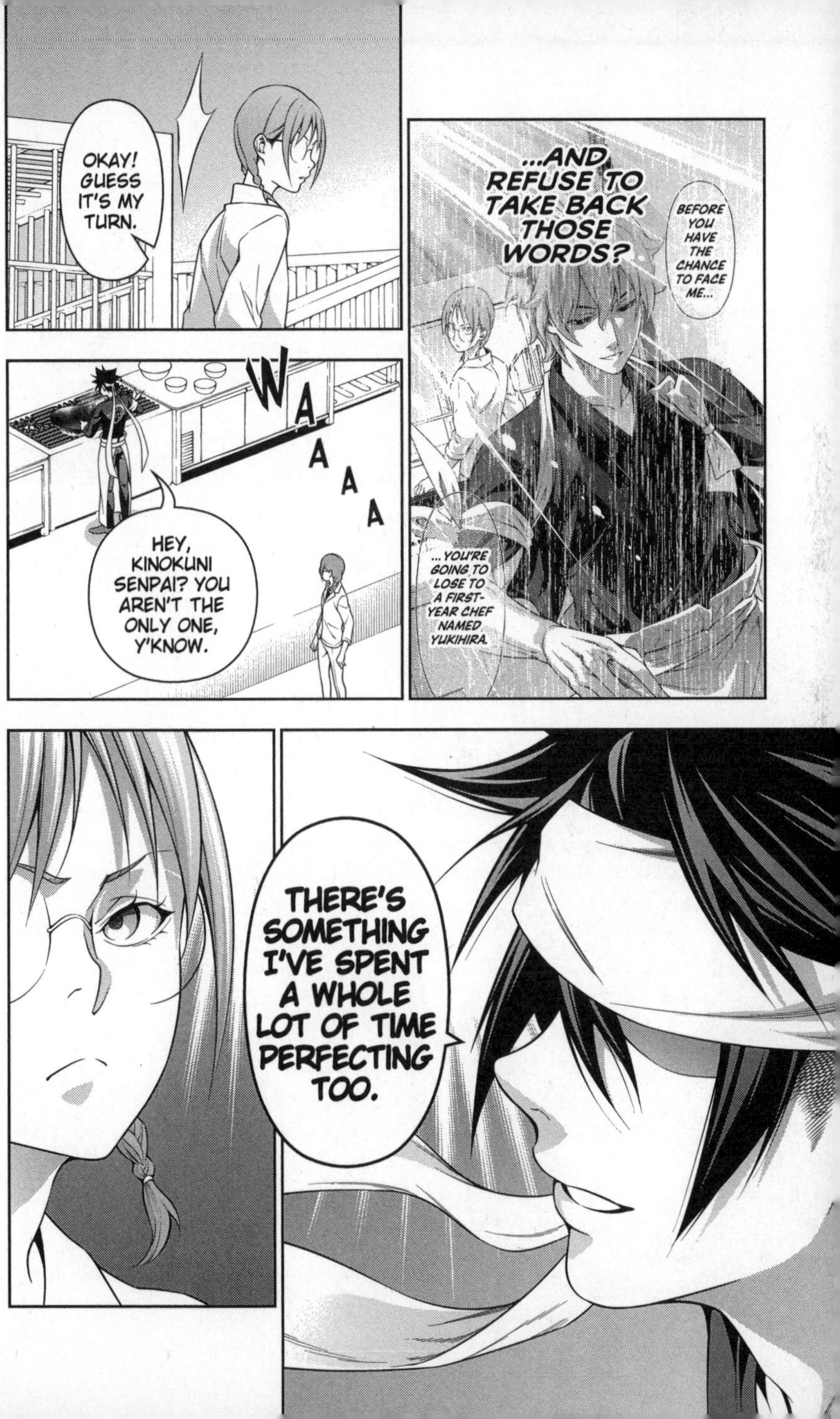
...AND REFUSE TO TAKE BACK THOSE WORDS?
BEFORE YOU HAVE THE CHANCE TO FACE ME...
...YOU'RE GOING TO LOSE TO A FIRST-YEAR CHEF NAMED YUKIHIRA.
OKAY! GUESS IT'S MY TURN.
WAAAAA
HEY, KINOKUNI SENPAI? YOU AREN'T THE ONLY ONE, Y'KNOW.
THERE'S SOMETHING I'VE SPENT A WHOLE LOT OF TIME PERFECTING TOO.

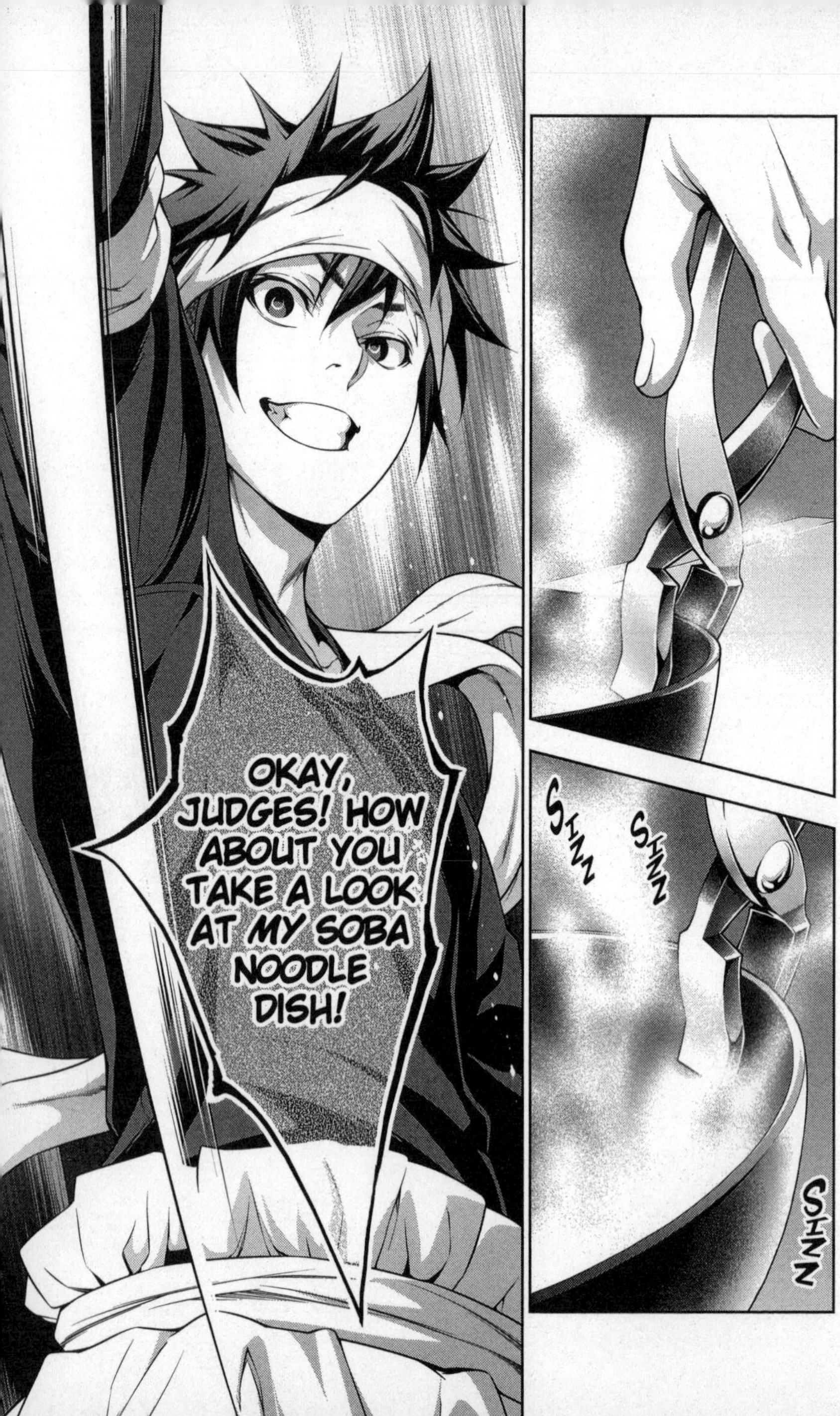
SIZZ
SIZZ
SIZZ
OKAY, JUDGES! HOW ABOUT YOU TAKE A LOOK AT MY SOBA NOODLE DISH!

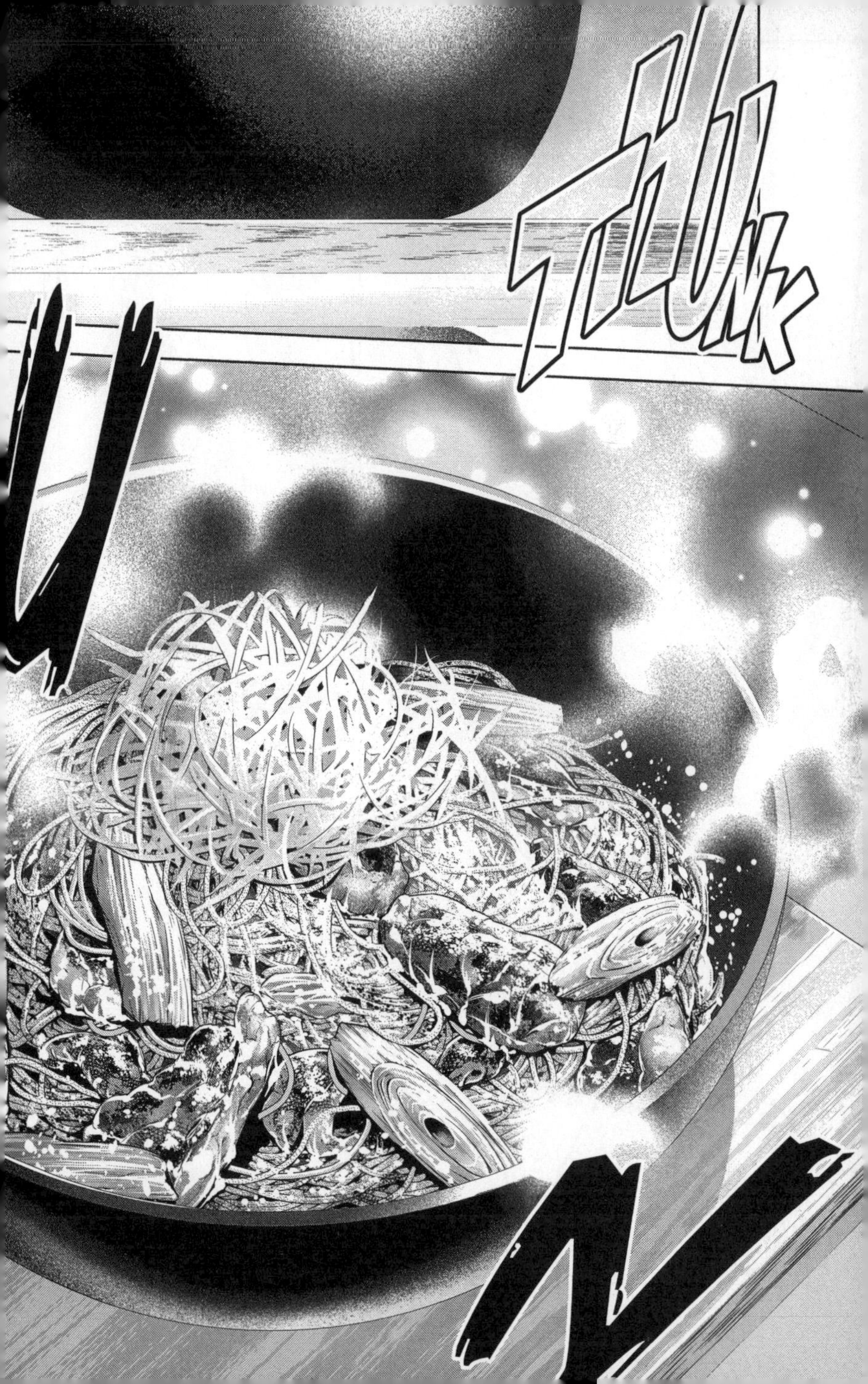
TUNK

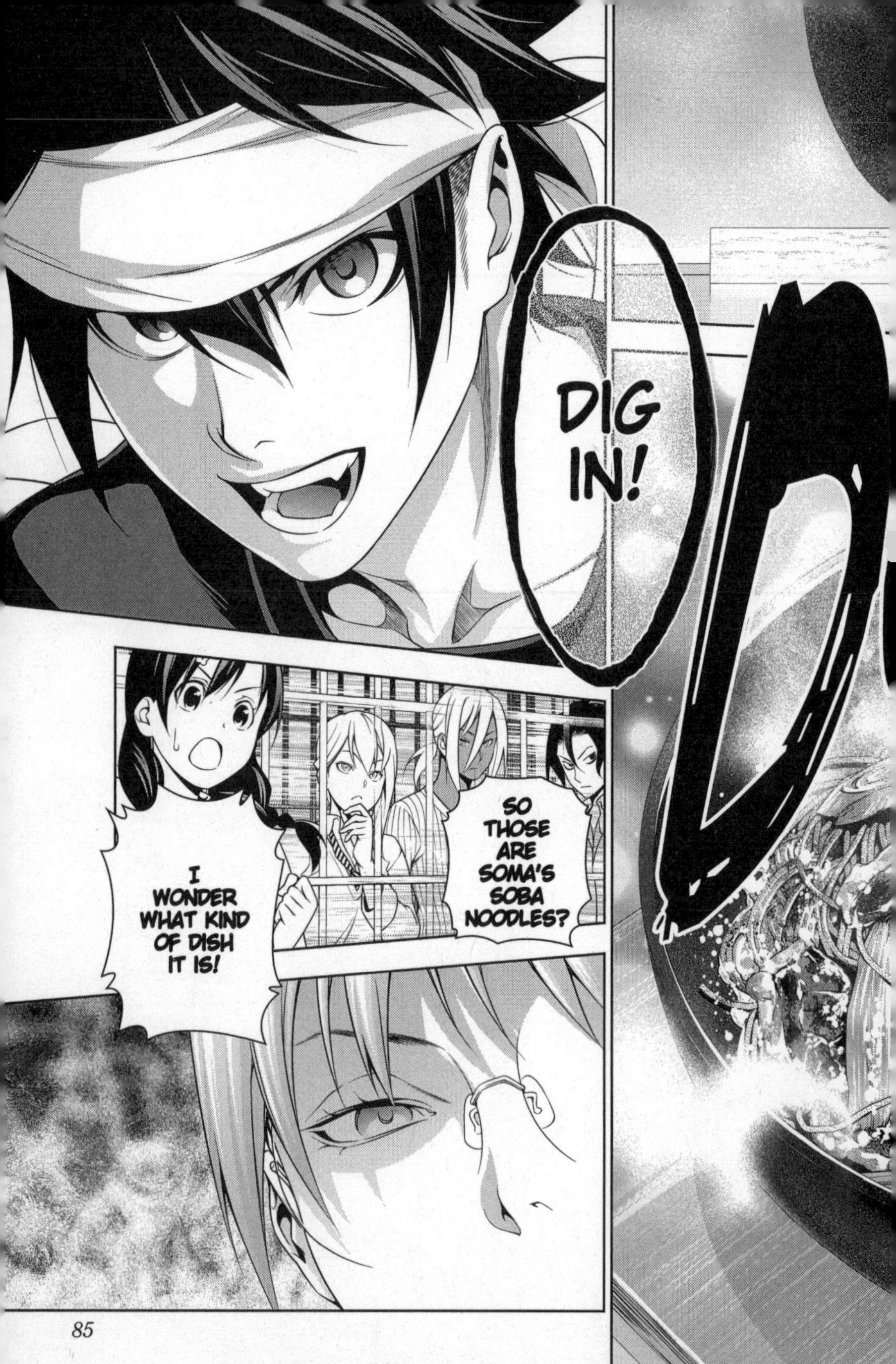
DIG IN!
SO THOSE ARE SOMA'S SOBA NOODLES?
I WONDER WHAT KIND OF DISH IT IS!

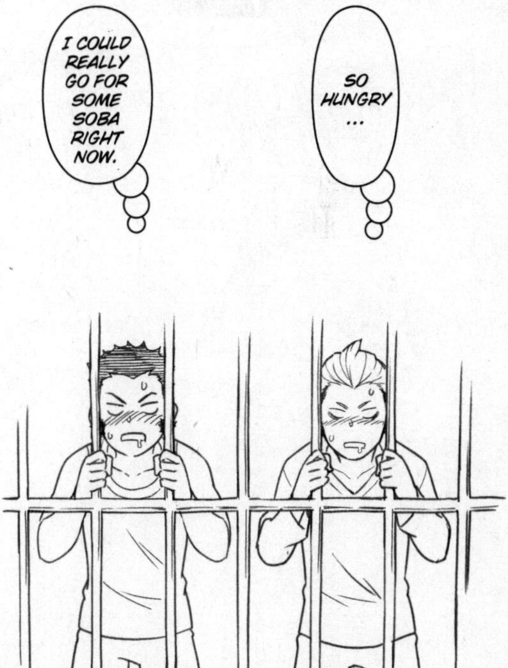
SO HUNGRY...
I COULD REALLY GO FOR SOME SOBA RIGHT NOW.

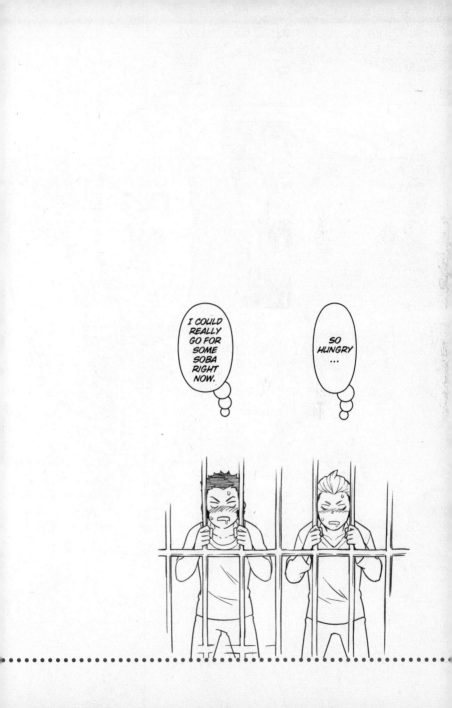

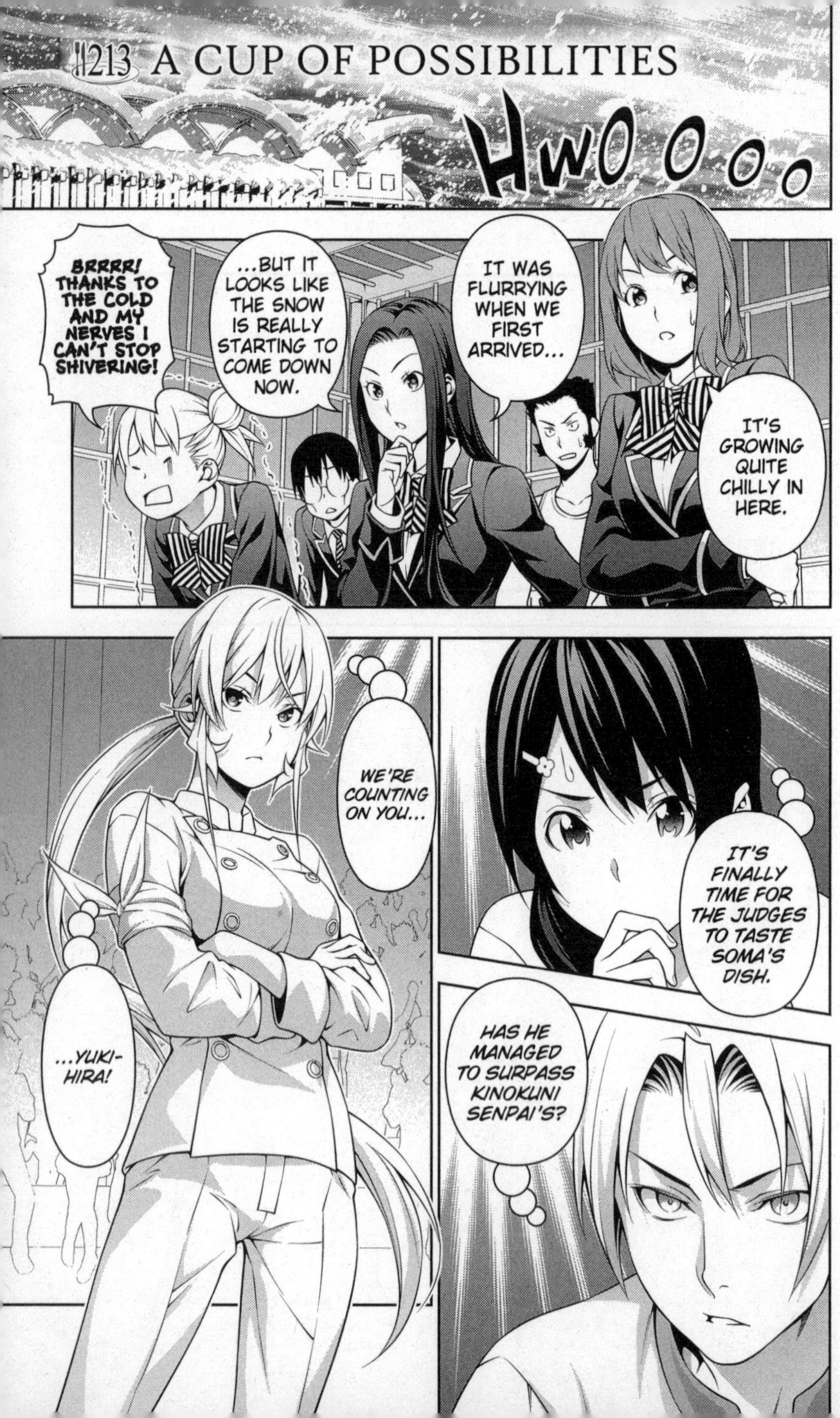

#213 A CUP OF POSSIBILITIES
HWOOOOO
IT'S GROWING QUITE CHILLY IN HERE.
IT WAS FLURRYING WHEN WE FIRST ARRIVED...
...BUT IT LOOKS LIKE THE SNOW IS REALLY STARTING TO COME DOWN NOW.
BRRRR! THANKS TO THE COLD AND MY NERVES I CAN'T STOP SHIVERING!
IT'S FINALLY TIME FOR THE JUDGES TO TASTE SOMA'S DISH.
HAS HE MANAGED TO SURPASS KINOKUNI SENPAI'S?
WE'RE COUNTING ON YOU...
...YUKIHIRA!

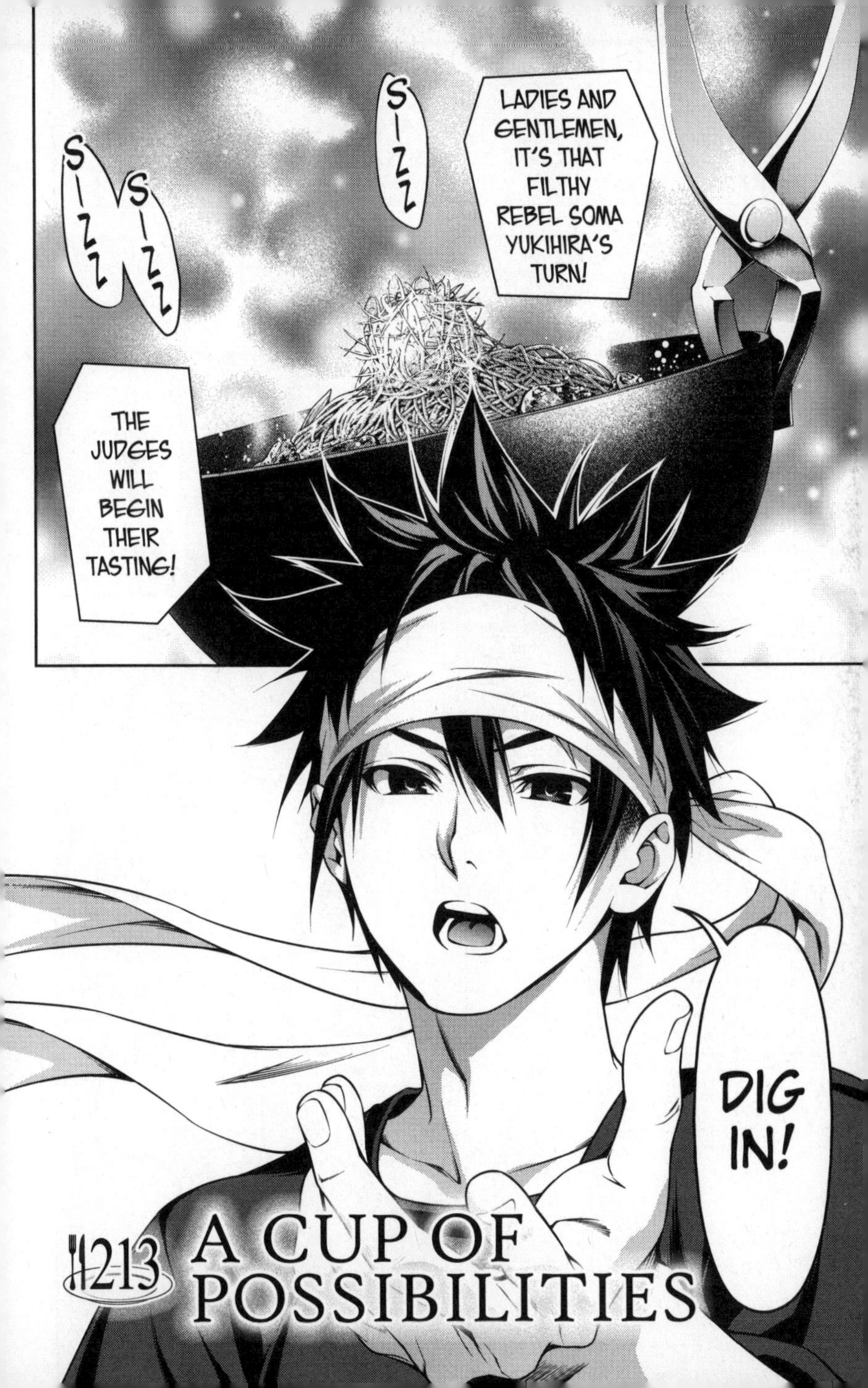
LADIES AND GENTLEMEN, IT'S THAT FILTHY REBEL SOMA YUKIHIRA'S TURN!
SIZZ
SIZZ SIZZ
THE JUDGES WILL BEGIN THEIR TASTING!
DIG IN!

213 A CUP OF POSSIBILITIES

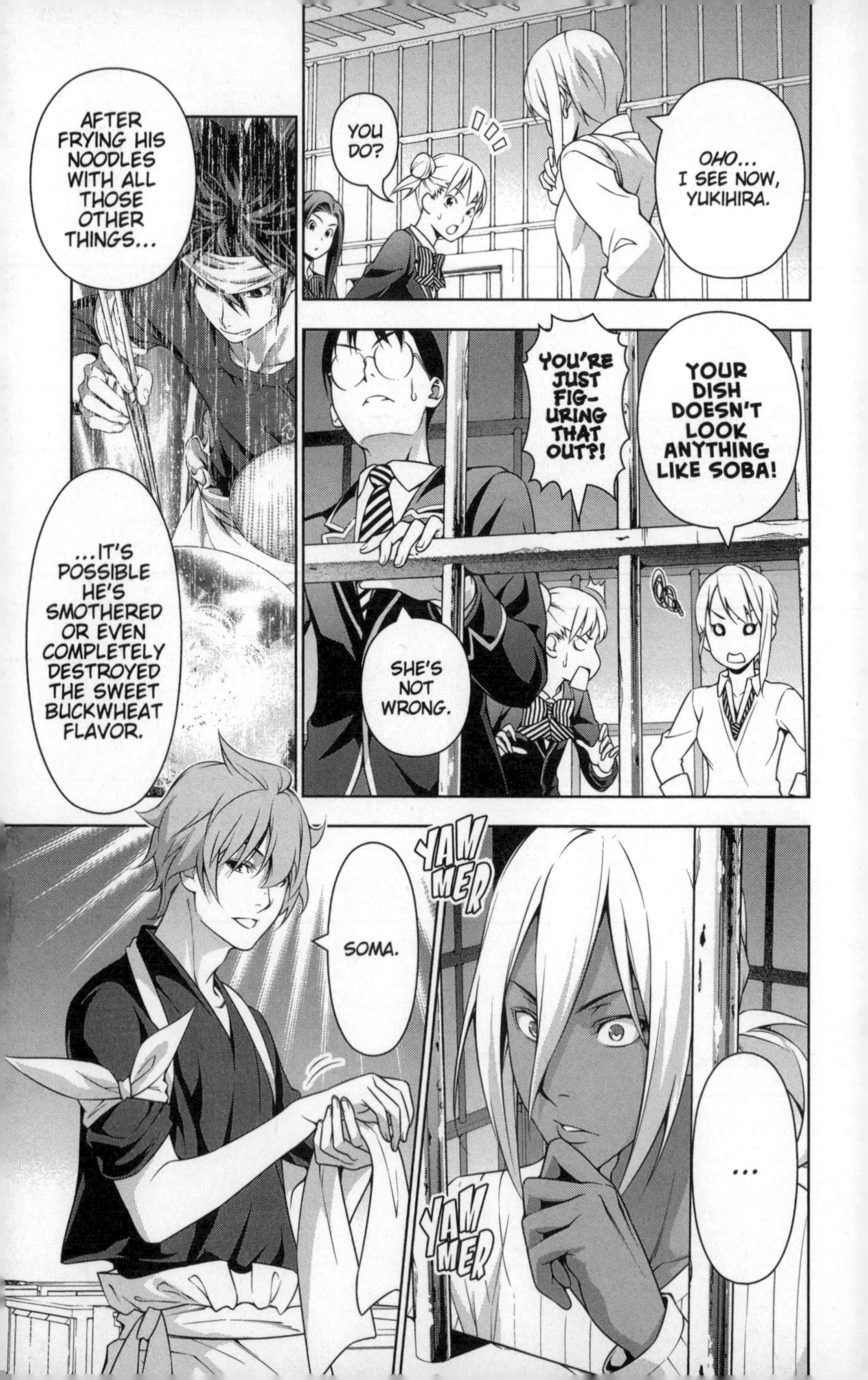

OHO... I SEE NOW, YUKIHIRA.
YOU DO?
YOUR DISH DOESN'T LOOK ANYTHING LIKE SOBA!
YOU'RE JUST FIG-URING THAT OUT?!
SHE'S NOT WRONG.
AFTER FRYING HIS NOODLES WITH ALL THOSE OTHER THINGS...
...IT'S POSSIBLE HE'S SMOTHERED OR EVEN COMPLETELY DESTROYED THE SWEET BUCKWHEAT FLAVOR.
SOMA.
YAMMER
...
YAMMER

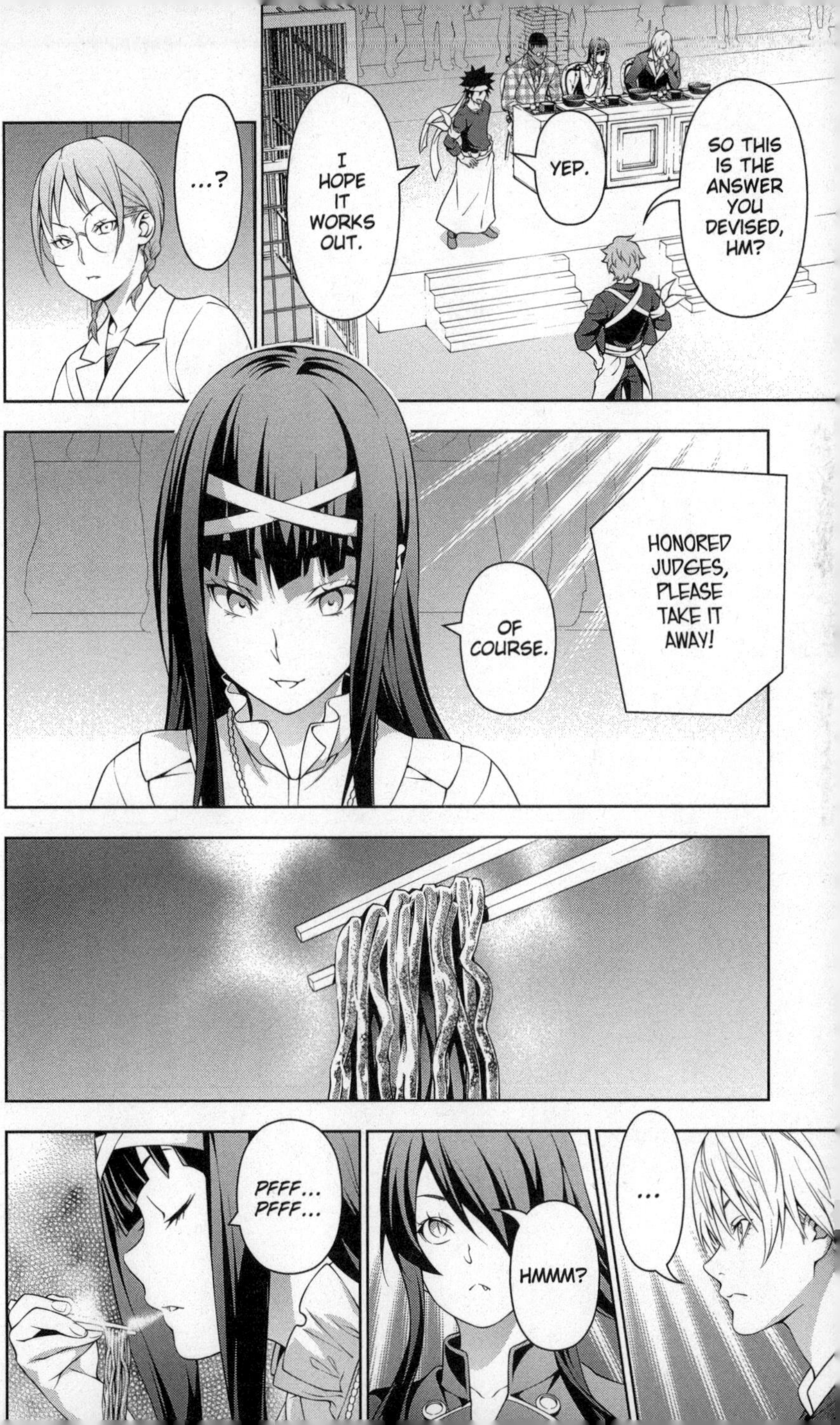
SO THIS IS THE ANSWER YOU DEVISED, HM?
YEP.
I HOPE IT WORKS OUT.
...?
HONORED JUDGES, PLEASE TAKE IT AWAY!
OF COURSE.
...
HMMM?
PFFF... PFFF...

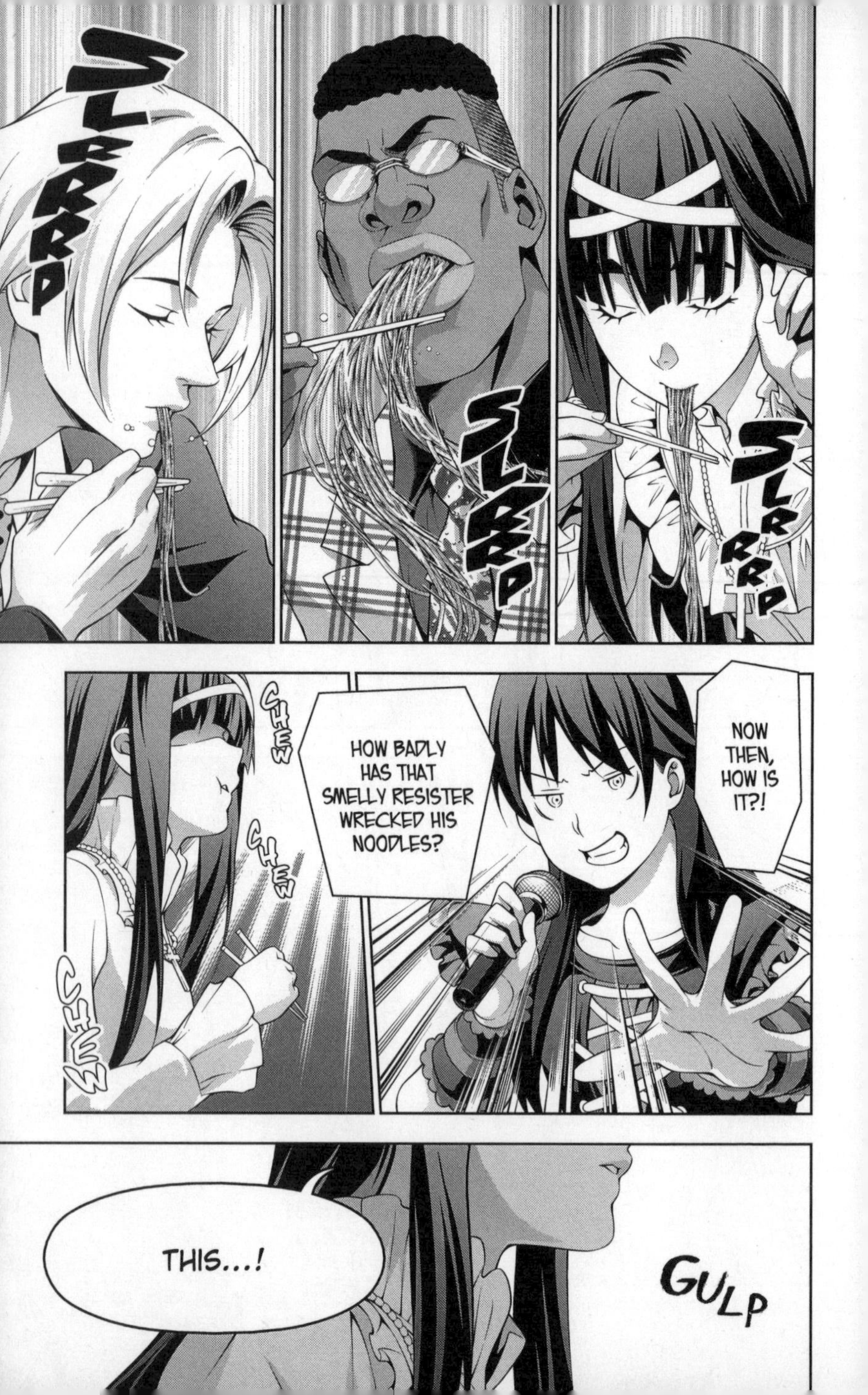
SLRRRP
SLRRP
SLRRRP
NOW THEN, HOW IS IT?!
HOW BADLY HAS THAT SMELLY RESISTER WRECKED HIS NOODLES?
CHEW
CHEW
CHEW
GULP
THIS...!

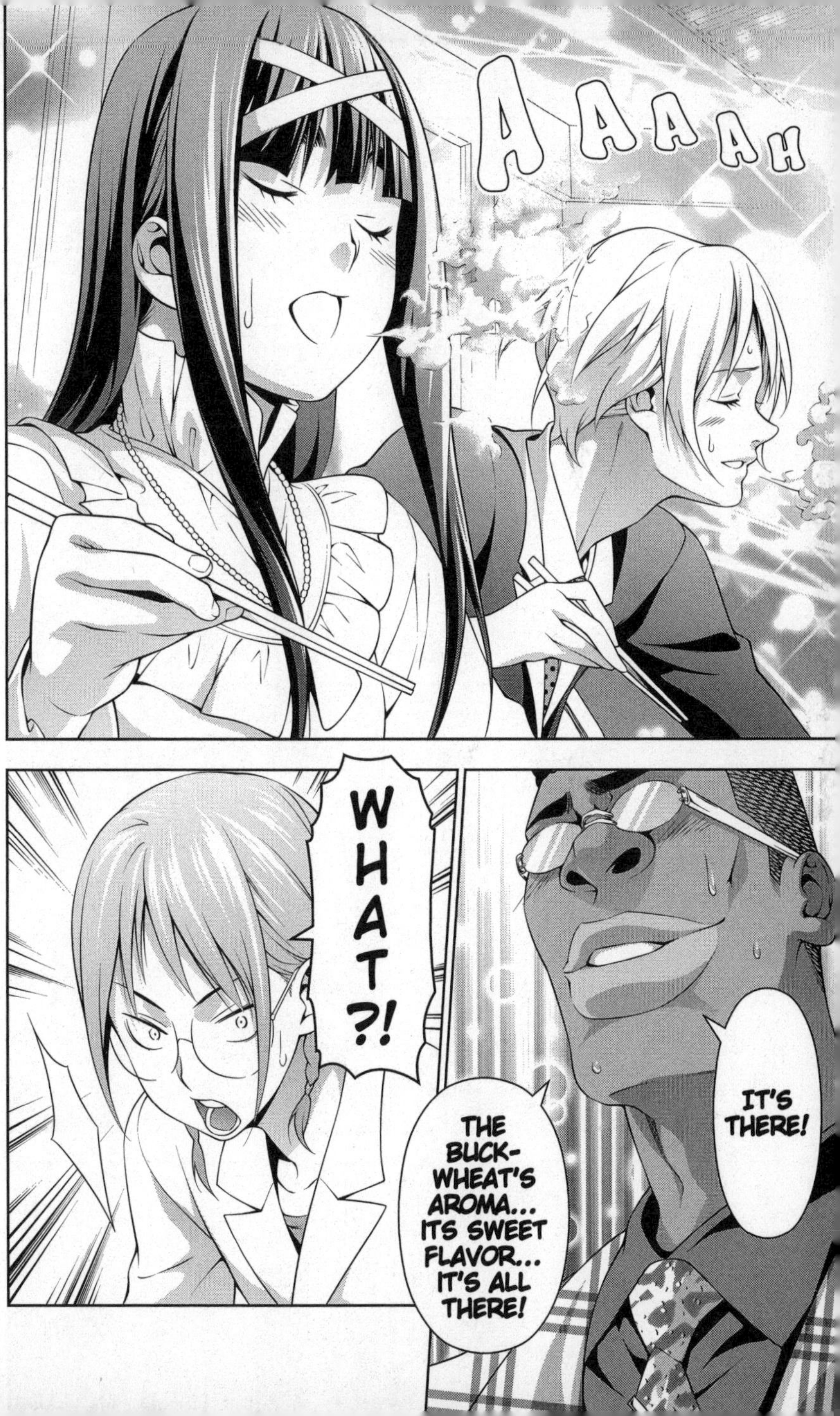
AAAAH
IT'S THERE!
THE BUCK-WHEAT'S AROMA... ITS SWEET FLAVOR... IT'S ALL THERE!
WHAT?!

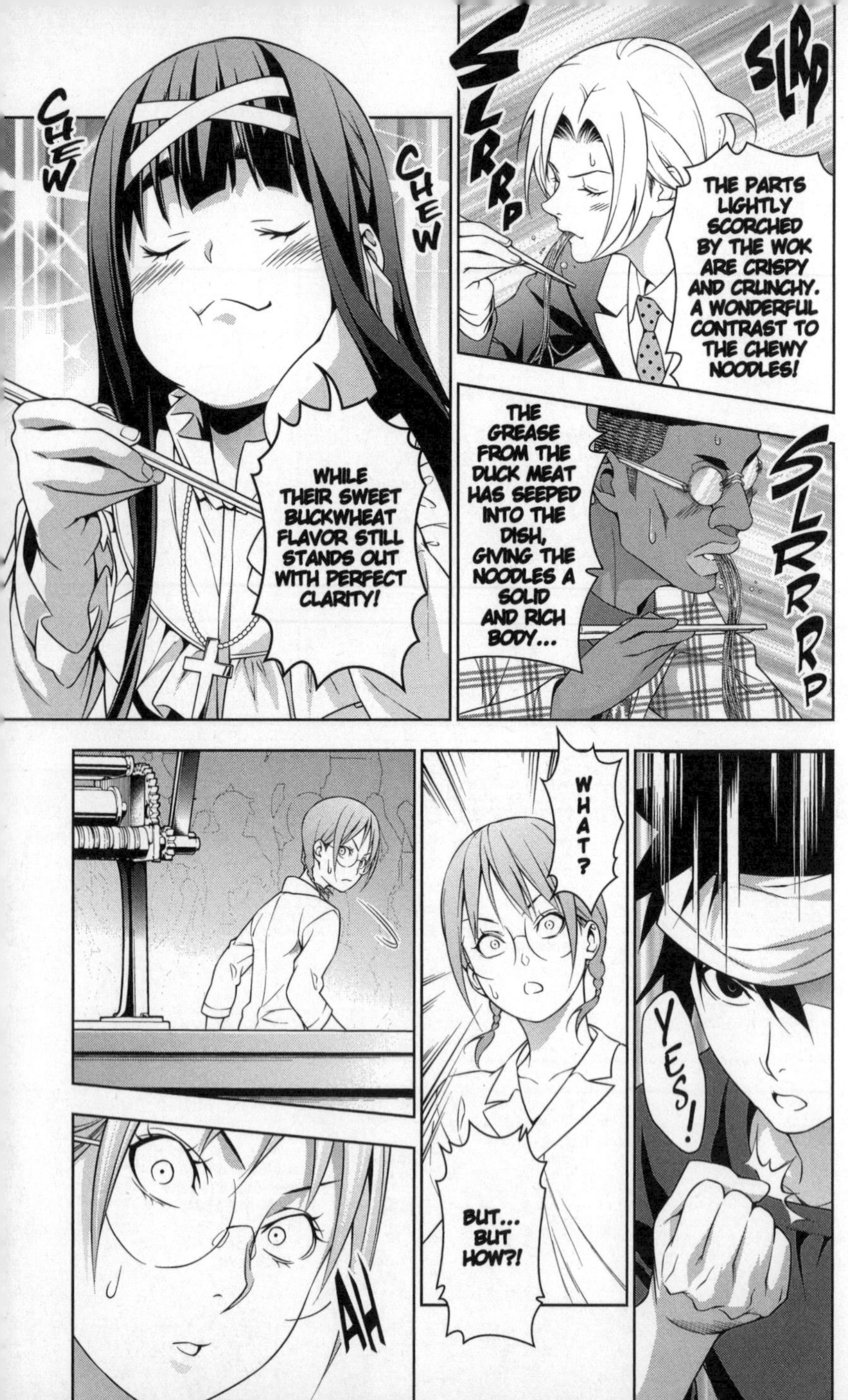
SLRP
THE PARTS LIGHTLY SCORCHED BY THE WOK ARE CRISPY AND CRUNCHY. A WONDERFUL CONTRAST TO THE CHEWY NOODLES!
SLRRP
SLRRRRP
THE GREASE FROM THE DUCK MEAT HAS SEEPED INTO THE DISH, GIVING THE NOODLES A SOLID AND RICH BODY...
CHEW
WHILE THEIR SWEET BUCKWHEAT FLAVOR STILL STANDS OUT WITH PERFECT CLARITY!
CHEW
YES!
WHAT?
BUT... BUT HOW?!
AH

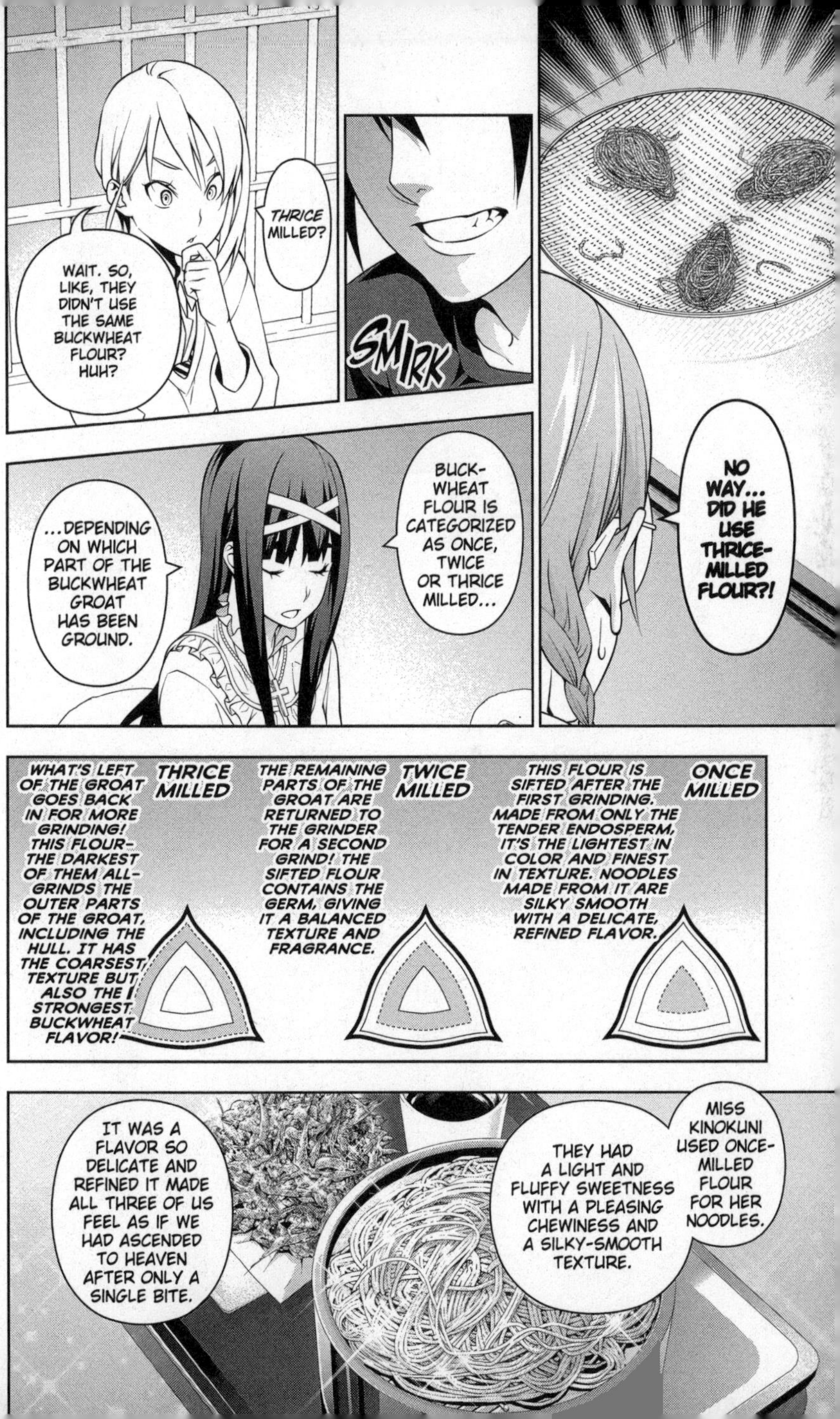
NO WAY... DID HE USE THRICE-MILLED FLOUR?!
THRICE MILLED?
WAIT. SO, LIKE, THEY DIDN'T USE THE SAME BUCKWHEAT FLOUR? HUH?
SMIRK
BUCK-WHEAT FLOUR IS CATEGORIZED AS ONCE, TWICE OR THRICE MILLED...
...DEPENDING ON WHICH PART OF THE BUCKWHEAT GROAT HAS BEEN GROUND.
ONCE MILLED
THIS FLOUR IS SIFTED AFTER THE FIRST GRINDING. MADE FROM ONLY THE TENDER ENDOSPERM, IT'S THE LIGHTEST IN COLOR AND FINEST IN TEXTURE. NOODLES MADE FROM IT ARE SILKY SMOOTH WITH A DELICATE, REFINED FLAVOR.
TWICE MILLED
THE REMAINING PARTS OF THE GROAT ARE RETURNED TO THE GRINDER FOR A SECOND GRIND! THE SIFTED FLOUR CONTAINS THE GERM, GIVING IT A BALANCED TEXTURE AND FRAGRANCE.
THRICE MILLED
WHAT'S LEFT OF THE GROAT GOES BACK IN FOR MORE GRINDING! THIS FLOUR–THE DARKEST OF THEM ALL–GRINDS THE OUTER PARTS OF THE GROAT, INCLUDING THE HULL. IT HAS THE COARSEST TEXTURE BUT ALSO THE STRONGEST BUCKWHEAT FLAVOR!
MISS KINOKUNI USED ONCE-MILLED FLOUR FOR HER NOODLES.
THEY HAD A LIGHT AND FLUFFY SWEETNESS WITH A PLEASING CHEWINESS AND A SILKY-SMOOTH TEXTURE.
IT WAS A FLAVOR SO DELICATE AND REFINED IT MADE ALL THREE OF US FEEL AS IF WE HAD ASCENDED TO HEAVEN AFTER ONLY A SINGLE BITE.

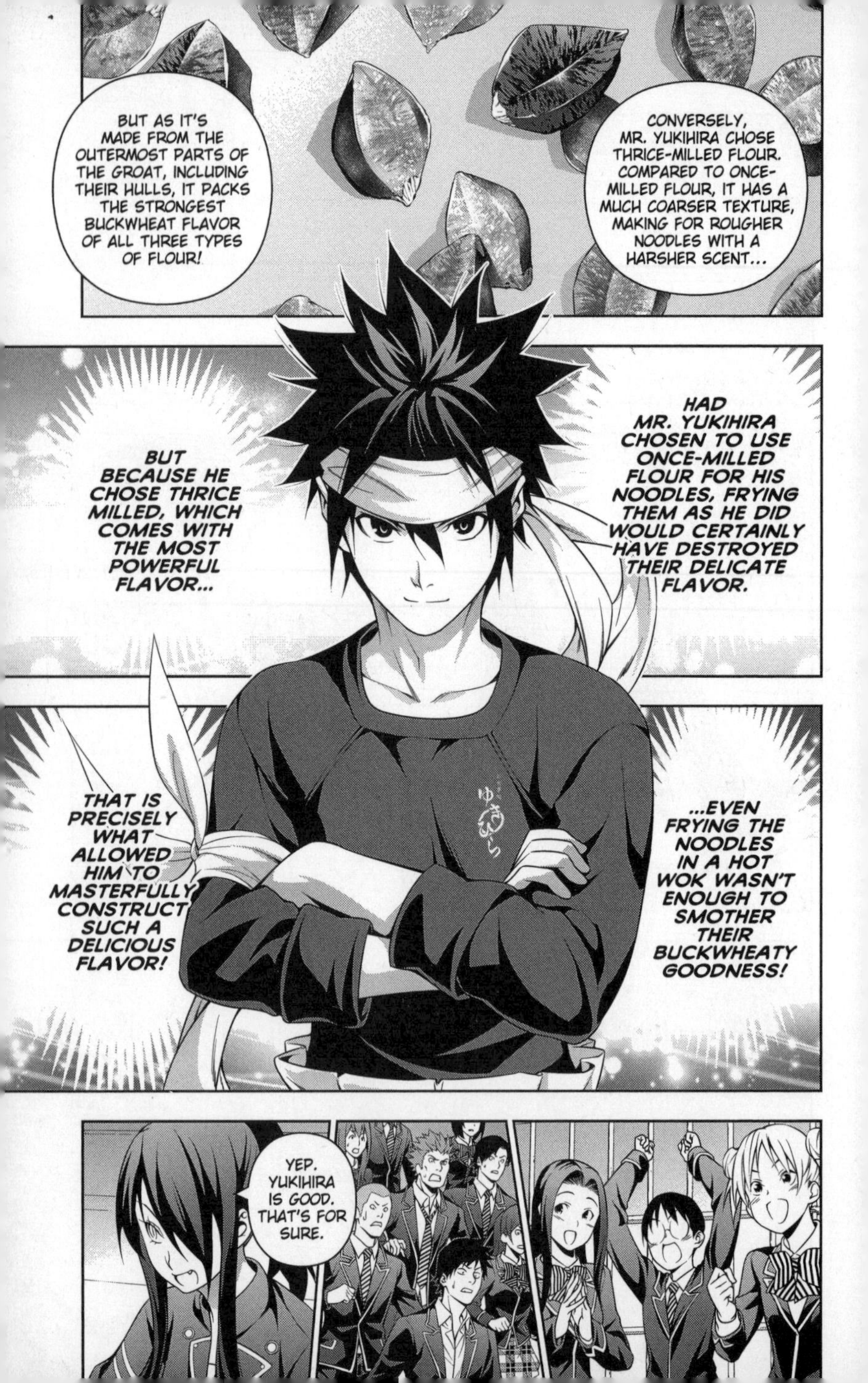
CONVERSELY, MR. YUKIHIRA CHOSE THRICE-MILLED FLOUR. COMPARED TO ONCE-MILLED FLOUR, IT HAS A MUCH COARSER TEXTURE, MAKING FOR ROUGHER NOODLES WITH A HARSHER SCENT...
BUT AS IT'S MADE FROM THE OUTERMOST PARTS OF THE GROAT, INCLUDING THEIR HULLS, IT PACKS THE STRONGEST BUCKWHEAT FLAVOR OF ALL THREE TYPES OF FLOUR!
HAD MR. YUKIHIRA CHOSEN TO USE ONCE-MILLED FLOUR FOR HIS NOODLES, FRYING THEM AS HE DID WOULD CERTAINLY HAVE DESTROYED THEIR DELICATE FLAVOR.
BUT BECAUSE HE CHOSE THRICE MILLED, WHICH COMES WITH THE MOST POWERFUL FLAVOR...
...EVEN FRYING THE NOODLES IN A HOT WOK WASN'T ENOUGH TO SMOTHER THEIR BUCKWHEATY GOODNESS!
THAT IS PRECISELY WHAT ALLOWED HIM TO MASTERFULLY CONSTRUCT SUCH A DELICIOUS FLAVOR!
YEP. YUKIHIRA IS GOOD. THAT'S FOR SURE.

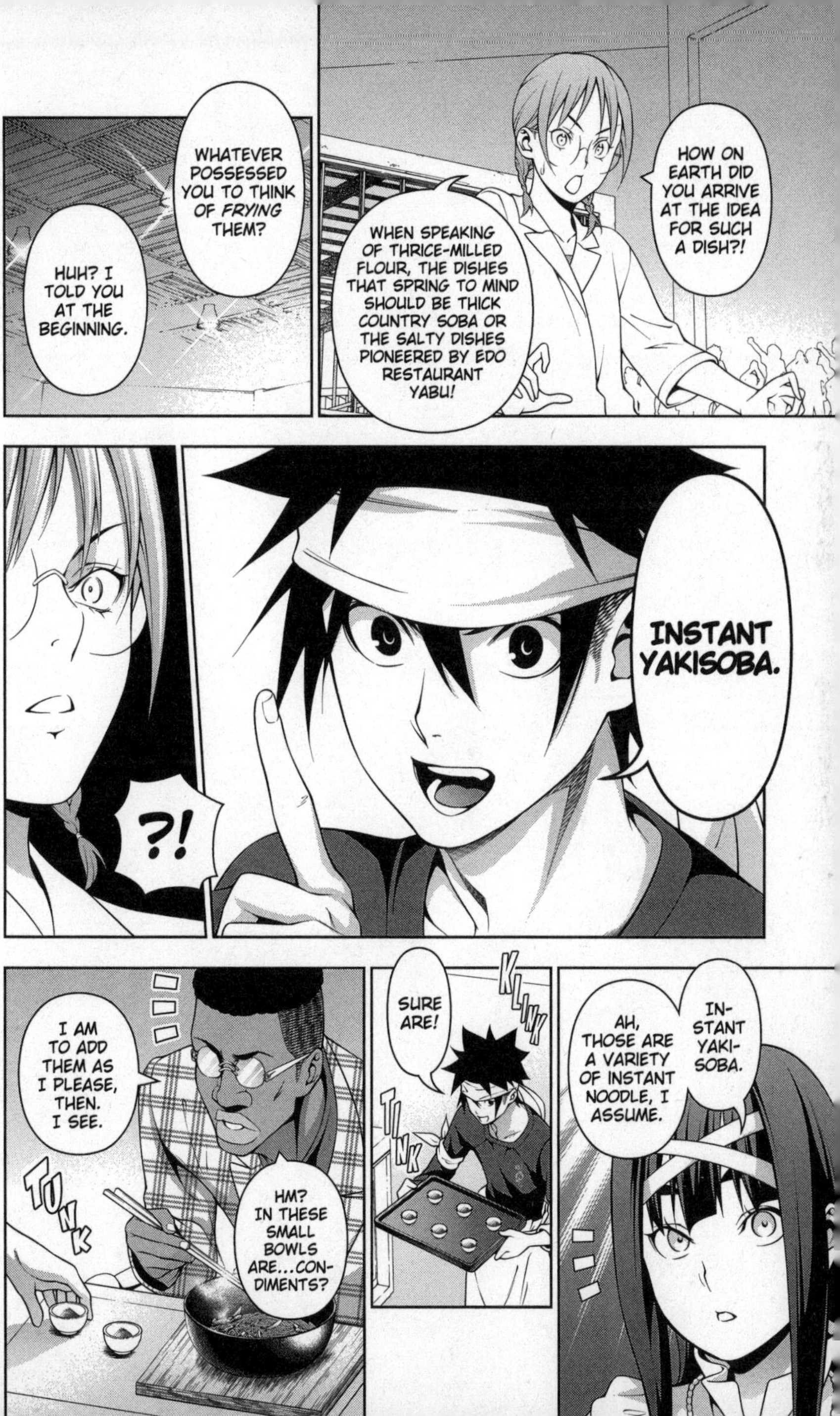

HOW ON EARTH DID YOU ARRIVE AT THE IDEA FOR SUCH A DISH?!
WHEN SPEAKING OF THRICE-MILLED FLOUR, THE DISHES THAT SPRING TO MIND SHOULD BE THICK COUNTRY SOBA OR THE SALTY DISHES PIONEERED BY EDO RESTAURANT YABU!
WHATEVER POSSESSED YOU TO THINK OF *FRYING* THEM?
HUH? I TOLD YOU AT THE BEGINNING.
INSTANT YAKISOBA.
?!
IN-STANT YAKI-SOBA.
AH, THOSE ARE A VARIETY OF INSTANT NOODLE, I ASSUME.
SURE ARE!
KLINK
TINK
I AM TO ADD THEM AS I PLEASE, THEN. I SEE.
HM? IN THESE SMALL BOWLS ARE...CON-DIMENTS?
TONK

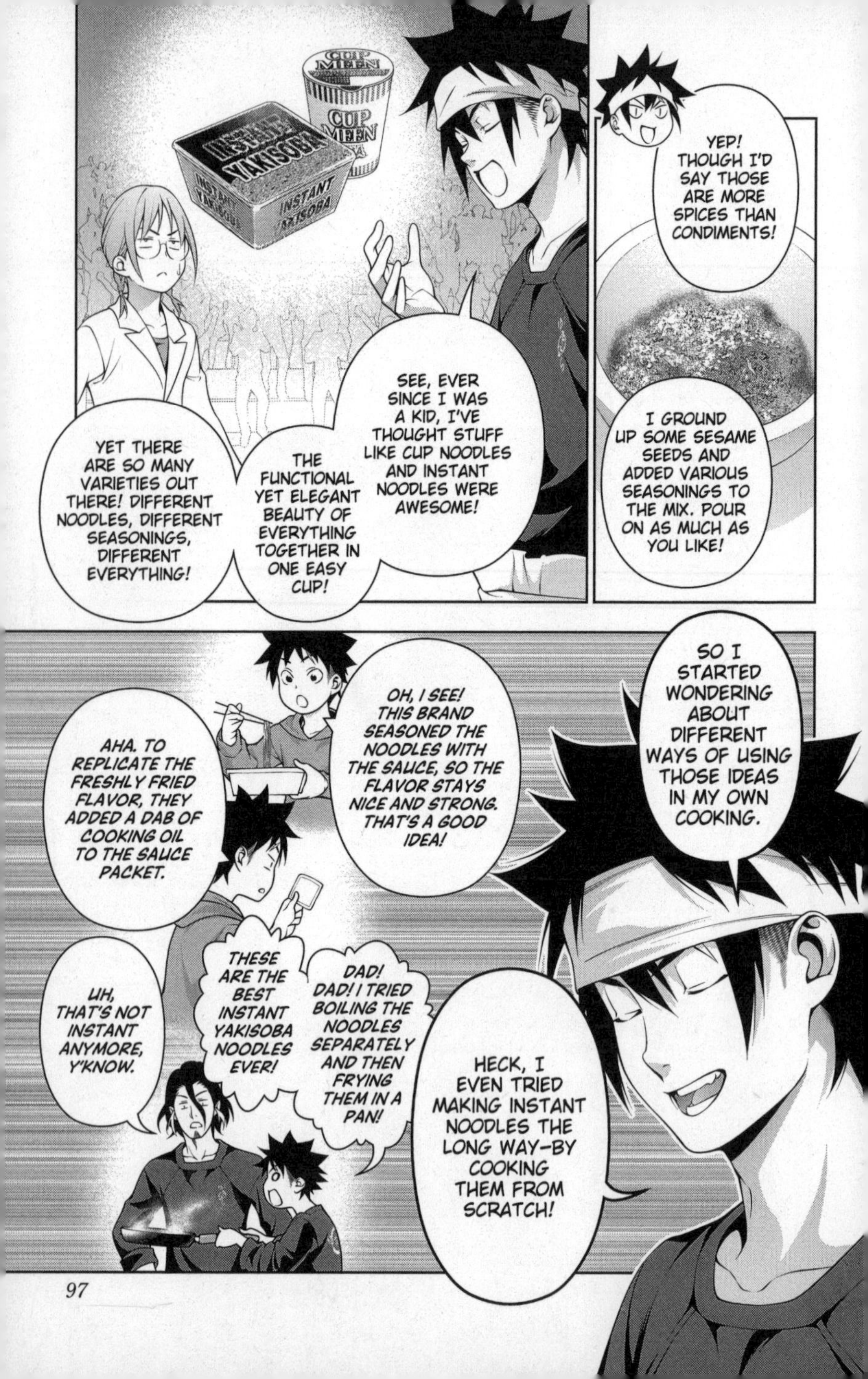
CUP MEEN
CUP MEEN
INSTANT YAKISOBA
INSTANT YAKISOBA
INSTANT YAKISOBA
YEP! THOUGH I'D SAY THOSE ARE MORE SPICES THAN CONDIMENTS!
I GROUND UP SOME SESAME SEEDS AND ADDED VARIOUS SEASONINGS TO THE MIX. POUR ON AS MUCH AS YOU LIKE!
SEE, EVER SINCE I WAS A KID, I'VE THOUGHT STUFF LIKE CUP NOODLES AND INSTANT NOODLES WERE AWESOME!
THE FUNCTIONAL YET ELEGANT BEAUTY OF EVERYTHING TOGETHER IN ONE EASY CUP!
YET THERE ARE SO MANY VARIETIES OUT THERE! DIFFERENT NOODLES, DIFFERENT SEASONINGS, DIFFERENT EVERYTHING!
SO I STARTED WONDERING ABOUT DIFFERENT WAYS OF USING THOSE IDEAS IN MY OWN COOKING.
OH, I SEE! THIS BRAND SEASONED THE NOODLES WITH THE SAUCE, SO THE FLAVOR STAYS NICE AND STRONG. THAT'S A GOOD IDEA!
AHA. TO REPLICATE THE FRESHLY FRIED FLAVOR, THEY ADDED A DAB OF COOKING OIL TO THE SAUCE PACKET.
HECK, I EVEN TRIED MAKING INSTANT NOODLES THE LONG WAY—BY COOKING THEM FROM SCRATCH!
DAD! DAD! I TRIED BOILING THE NOODLES SEPARATELY AND THEN FRYING THEM IN A PAN!
THESE ARE THE BEST INSTANT YAKISOBA NOODLES EVER!
UH, THAT'S NOT INSTANT ANYMORE, Y'KNOW.

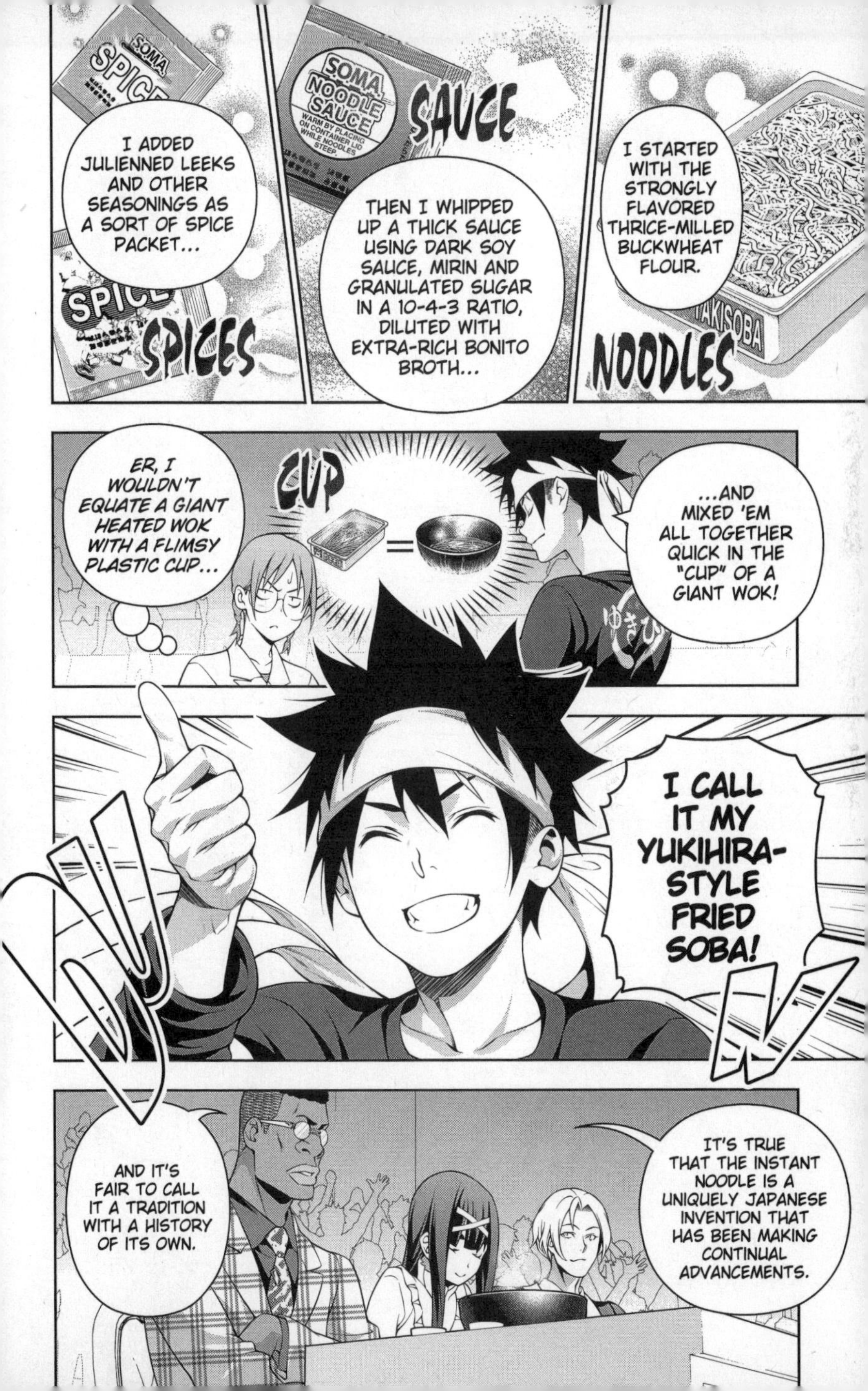
I STARTED WITH THE STRONGLY FLAVORED THRICE-MILLED BUCKWHEAT FLOUR.
NOODLES
YAKISOBA
THEN I WHIPPED UP A THICK SAUCE USING DARK SOY SAUCE, MIRIN AND GRANULATED SUGAR IN A 10-4-3 RATIO, DILUTED WITH EXTRA-RICH BONITO BROTH...
SAUCE
SOMA NOODLE SAUCE
WARM BY PLACING ON CONTAINER LID WHILE NOODLES STEEP.
I ADDED JULIENNED LEEKS AND OTHER SEASONINGS AS A SORT OF SPICE PACKET...
SPICES
SOMA SPICE
SPICE
...AND MIXED 'EM ALL TOGETHER QUICK IN THE "CUP" OF A GIANT WOK!
CUP
ER, I WOULDN'T EQUATE A GIANT HEATED WOK WITH A FLIMSY PLASTIC CUP...
I CALL IT MY YUKIHIRA-STYLE FRIED SOBA!
IT'S TRUE THAT THE INSTANT NOODLE IS A UNIQUELY JAPANESE INVENTION THAT HAS BEEN MAKING CONTINUAL ADVANCEMENTS.
AND IT'S FAIR TO CALL IT A TRADITION WITH A HISTORY OF ITS OWN.

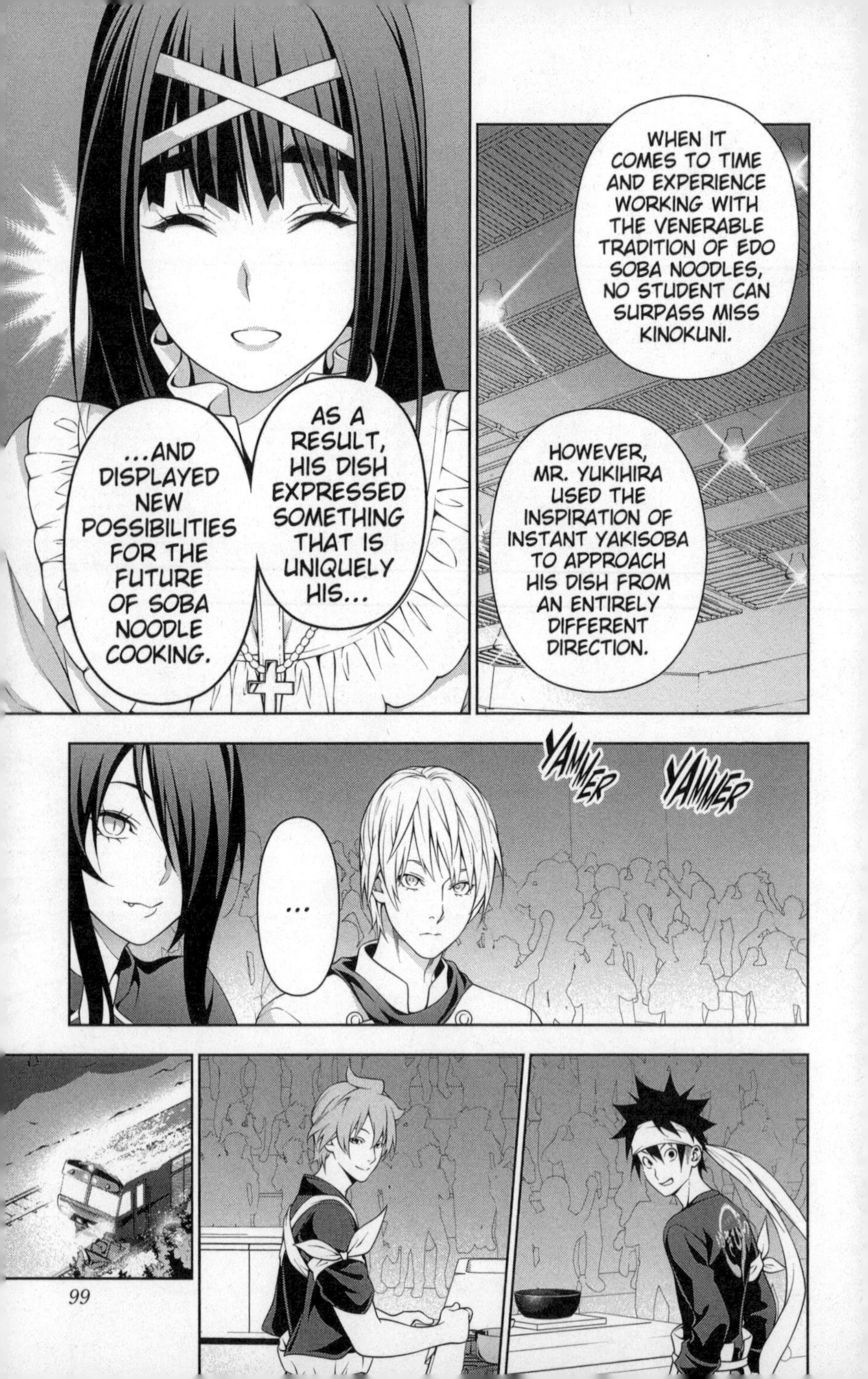
WHEN IT COMES TO TIME AND EXPERIENCE WORKING WITH THE VENERABLE TRADITION OF EDO SOBA NOODLES, NO STUDENT CAN SURPASS MISS KINOKUNI.
HOWEVER, MR. YUKIHIRA USED THE INSPIRATION OF INSTANT YAKISOBA TO APPROACH HIS DISH FROM AN ENTIRELY DIFFERENT DIRECTION.
AS A RESULT, HIS DISH EXPRESSED SOMETHING THAT IS UNIQUELY HIS...
...AND DISPLAYED NEW POSSIBILITIES FOR THE FUTURE OF SOBA NOODLE COOKING.
YAMMER
YAMMER
...

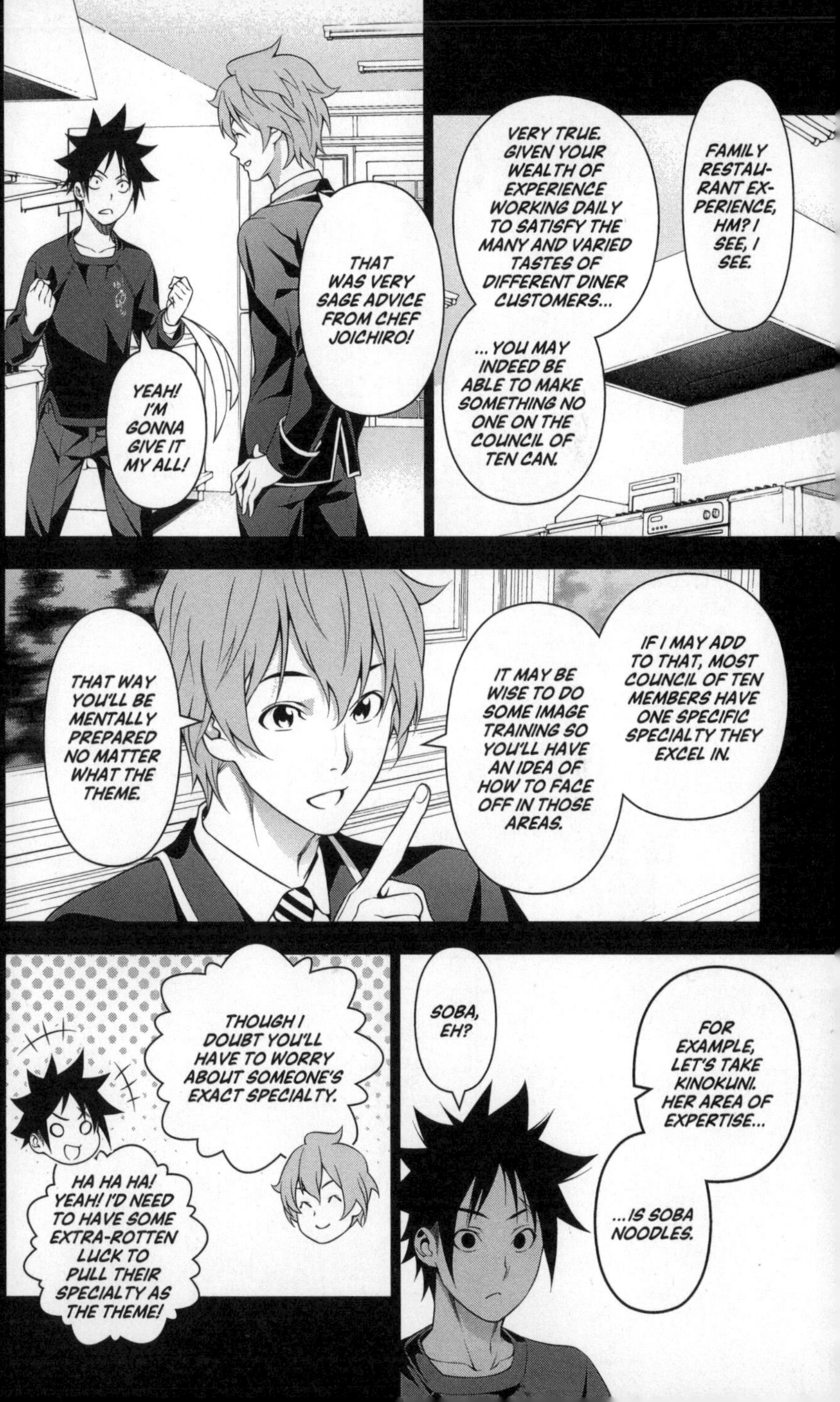
FAMILY RESTAURANT EXPERIENCE, HM? I SEE, I SEE.
VERY TRUE. GIVEN YOUR WEALTH OF EXPERIENCE WORKING DAILY TO SATISFY THE MANY AND VARIED TASTES OF DIFFERENT DINER CUSTOMERS...
...YOU MAY INDEED BE ABLE TO MAKE SOMETHING NO ONE ON THE COUNCIL OF TEN CAN.
THAT WAS VERY SAGE ADVICE FROM CHEF JOICHIRO!
YEAH! I'M GONNA GIVE IT MY ALL!
IF I MAY ADD TO THAT, MOST COUNCIL OF TEN MEMBERS HAVE ONE SPECIFIC SPECIALTY THEY EXCEL IN.
IT MAY BE WISE TO DO SOME IMAGE TRAINING SO YOU'LL HAVE AN IDEA OF HOW TO FACE OFF IN THOSE AREAS.
THAT WAY YOU'LL BE MENTALLY PREPARED NO MATTER WHAT THE THEME.
FOR EXAMPLE, LET'S TAKE KINOKUNI. HER AREA OF EXPERTISE...
...IS SOBA NOODLES.
SOBA, EH?
THOUGH I DOUBT YOU'LL HAVE TO WORRY ABOUT SOMEONE'S EXACT SPECIALTY.
HA HA HA! YEAH! I'D NEED TO HAVE SOME EXTRA-ROTTEN LUCK TO PULL THEIR SPECIALTY AS THE THEME!

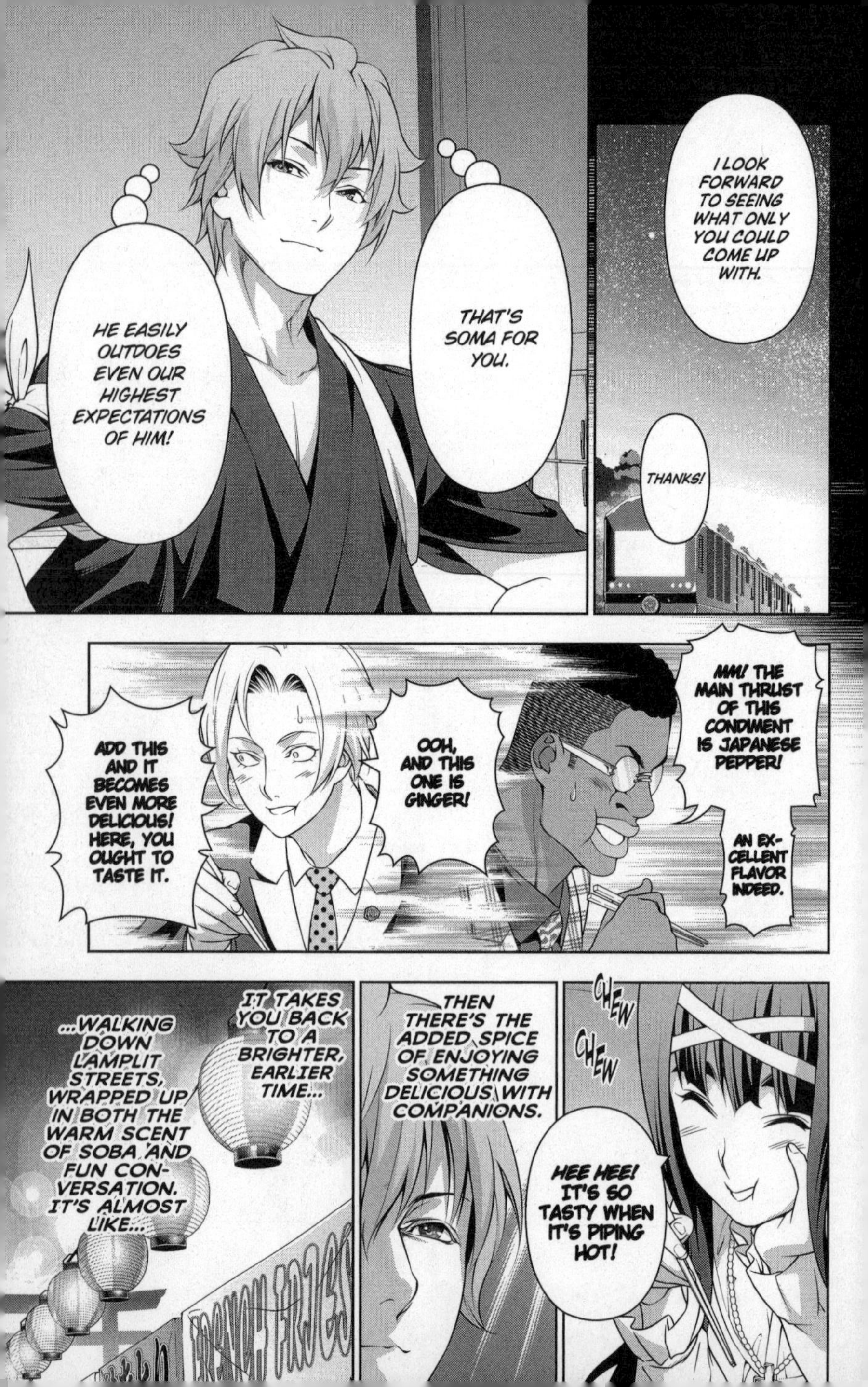
I LOOK FORWARD TO SEEING WHAT ONLY YOU COULD COME UP WITH.
THANKS!
THAT'S SOMA FOR YOU.
HE EASILY OUTDOES EVEN OUR HIGHEST EXPECTATIONS OF HIM!
MM! THE MAIN THRUST OF THIS CONDIMENT IS JAPANESE PEPPER!
AN EXCELLENT FLAVOR INDEED.
OOH, AND THIS ONE IS GINGER!
ADD THIS AND IT BECOMES EVEN MORE DELICIOUS! HERE, YOU OUGHT TO TASTE IT.
CHEW
CHEW
HEE HEE! IT'S SO TASTY WHEN IT'S PIPING HOT!
THEN THERE'S THE ADDED SPICE OF ENJOYING SOMETHING DELICIOUS WITH COMPANIONS.
...WALKING DOWN LAMPLIT STREETS, WRAPPED UP IN BOTH THE WARM SCENT OF SOBA AND FUN CONVERSATION. IT'S ALMOST LIKE...
IT TAKES YOU BACK TO A BRIGHTER, EARLIER TIME...

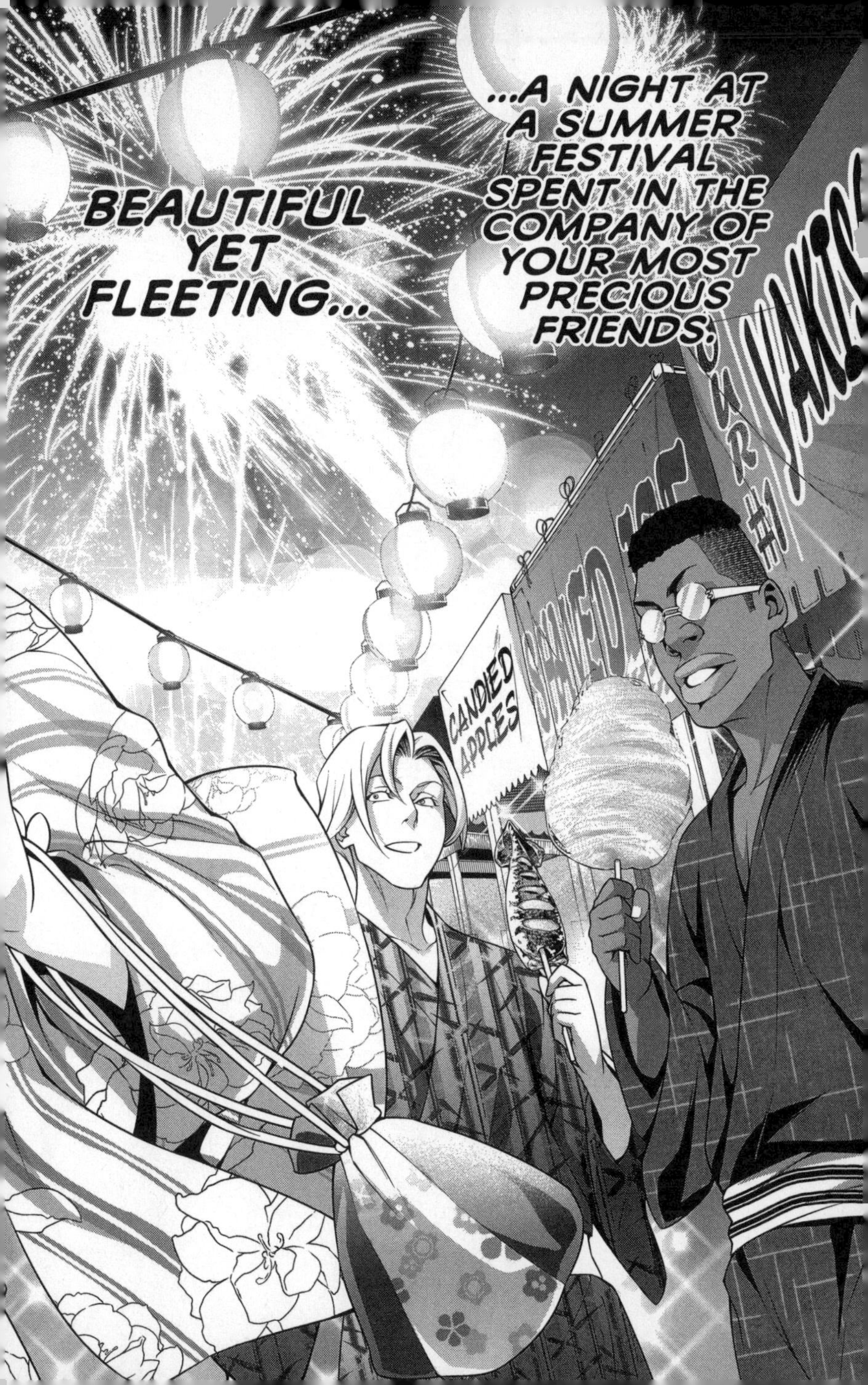
BEAUTIFUL YET FLEETING...
...A NIGHT AT A SUMMER FESTIVAL SPENT IN THE COMPANY OF YOUR MOST PRECIOUS FRIENDS.
CANDIED APPLES

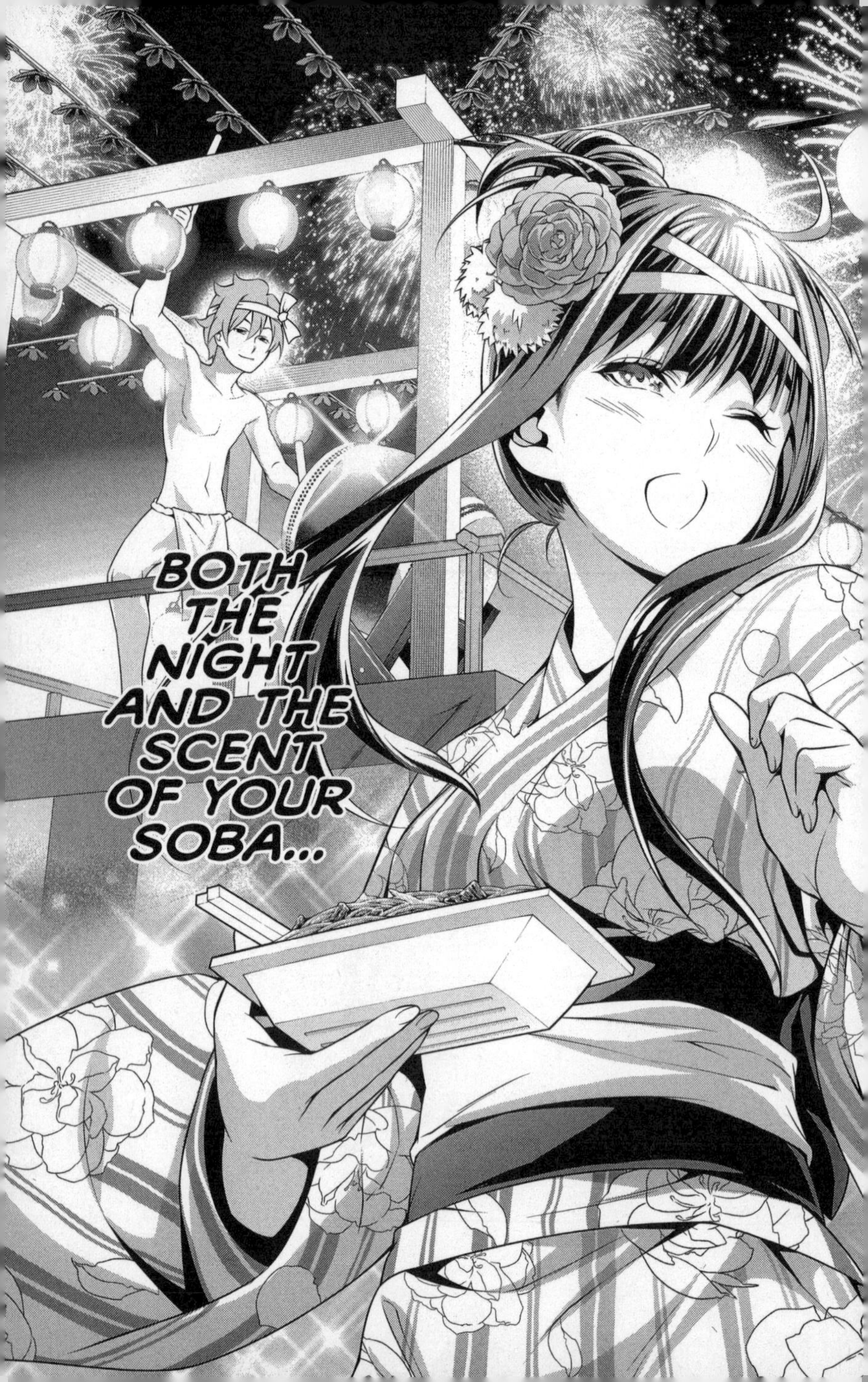
BOTH THE NIGHT AND THE SCENT OF YOUR SOBA...

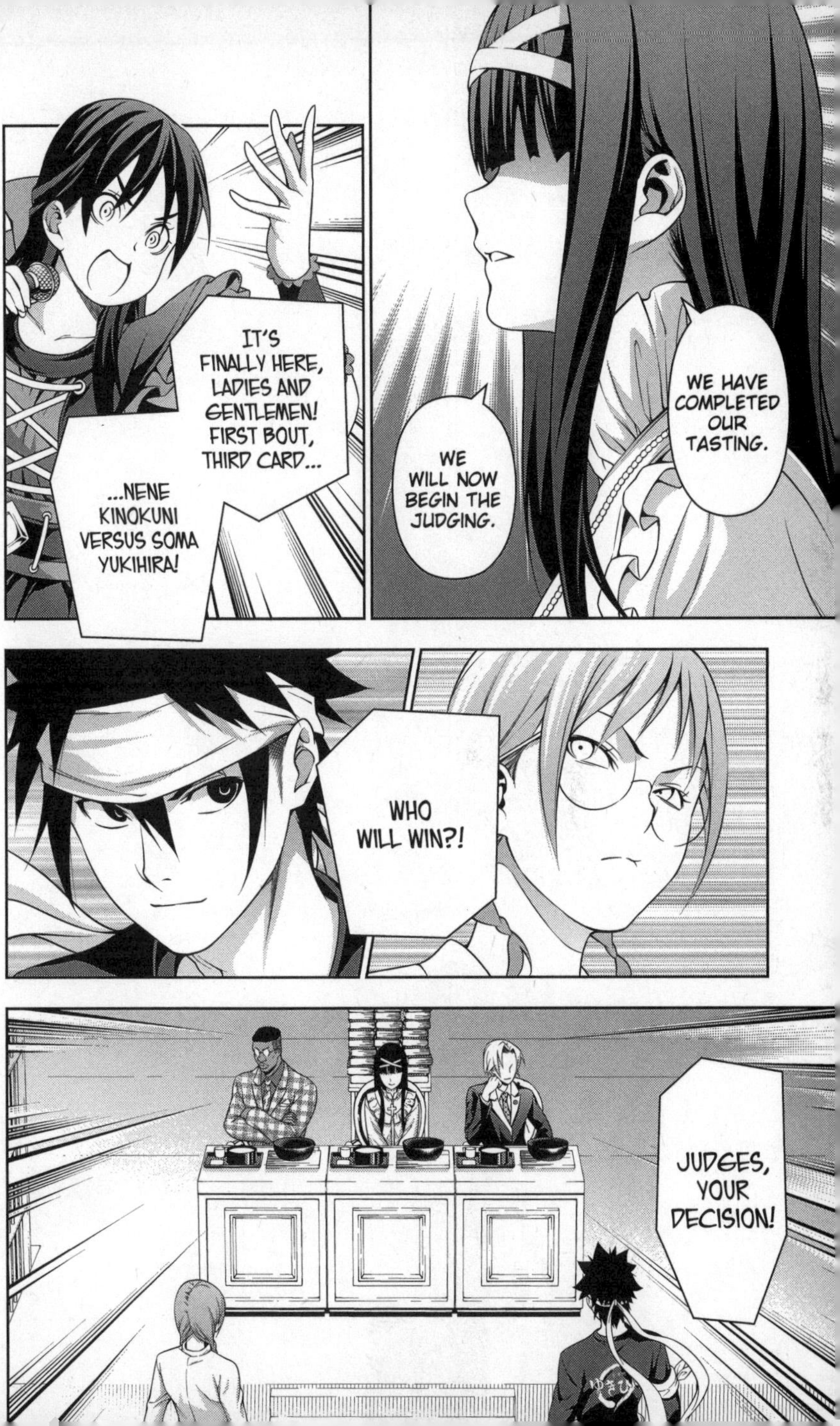
WE HAVE COMPLETED OUR TASTING.
WE WILL NOW BEGIN THE JUDGING.
IT'S FINALLY HERE, LADIES AND GENTLEMEN! FIRST BOUT, THIRD CARD...
...NENE KINOKUNI VERSUS SOMA YUKIHIRA!
WHO WILL WIN?!
JUDGES, YOUR DECISION!

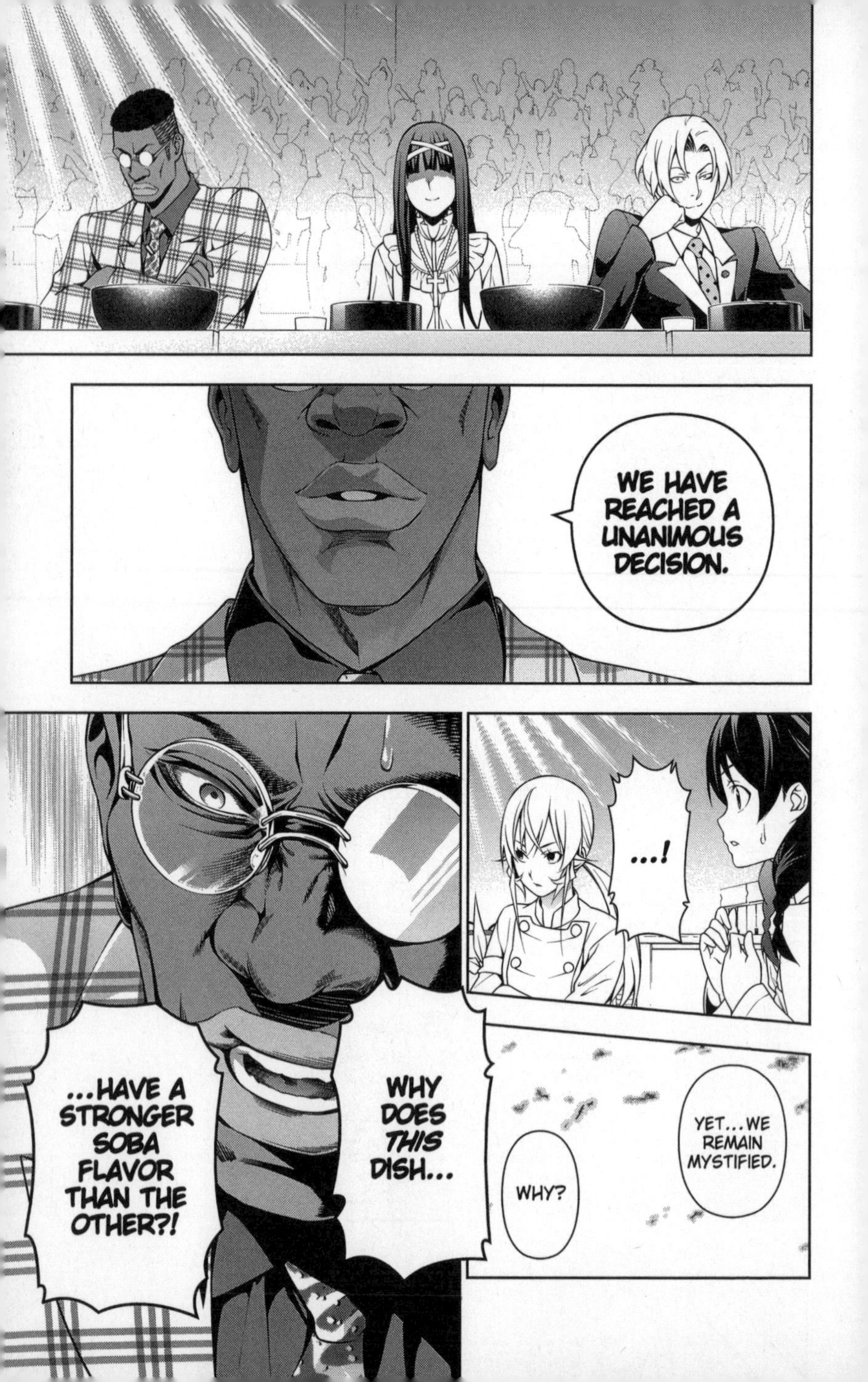
WE HAVE REACHED A UNANIMOUS DECISION.
...!
YET...WE REMAIN MYSTIFIED.
WHY?
WHY DOES *THIS* DISH...
...HAVE A STRONGER SOBA FLAVOR THAN THE OTHER?!

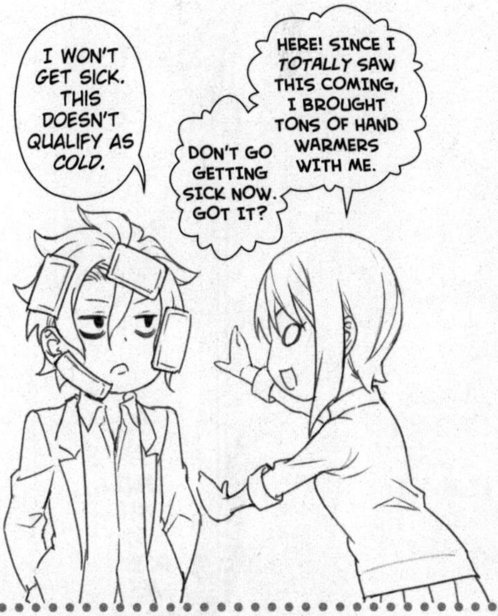
HERE! SINCE I TOTALLY SAW THIS COMING, I BROUGHT TONS OF HAND WARMERS WITH ME.
DON'T GO GETTING SICK NOW. GOT IT?
I WON'T GET SICK. THIS DOESN'T QUALIFY AS COLD.

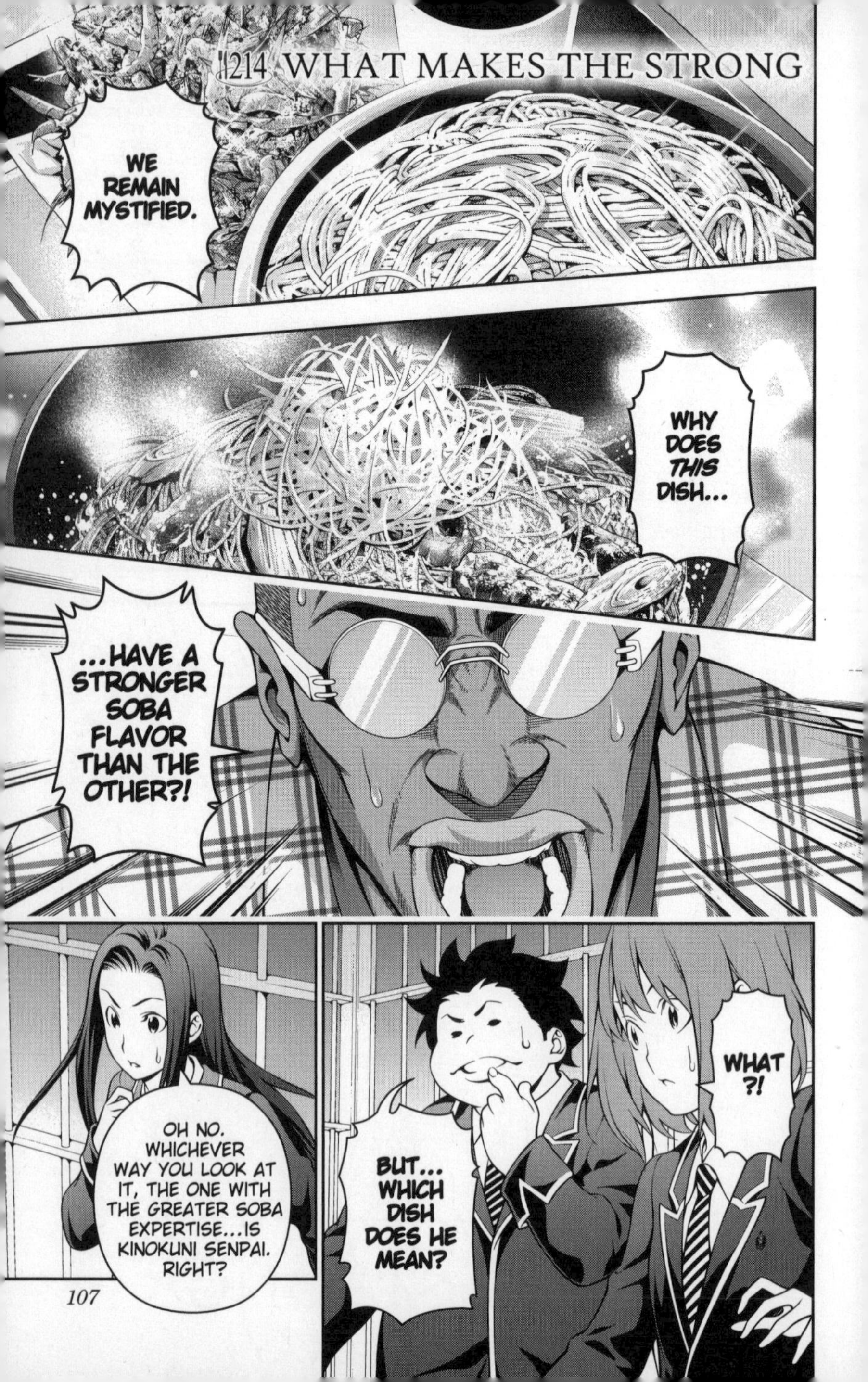
214 WHAT MAKES THE STRONG
WE REMAIN MYSTIFIED.
WHY DOES *THIS* DISH...
...HAVE A STRONGER SOBA FLAVOR THAN THE OTHER?!
WHAT ?!
BUT... WHICH DISH DOES HE MEAN?
OH NO. WHICHEVER WAY YOU LOOK AT IT, THE ONE WITH THE GREATER SOBA EXPERTISE...IS KINOKUNI SENPAI. RIGHT?

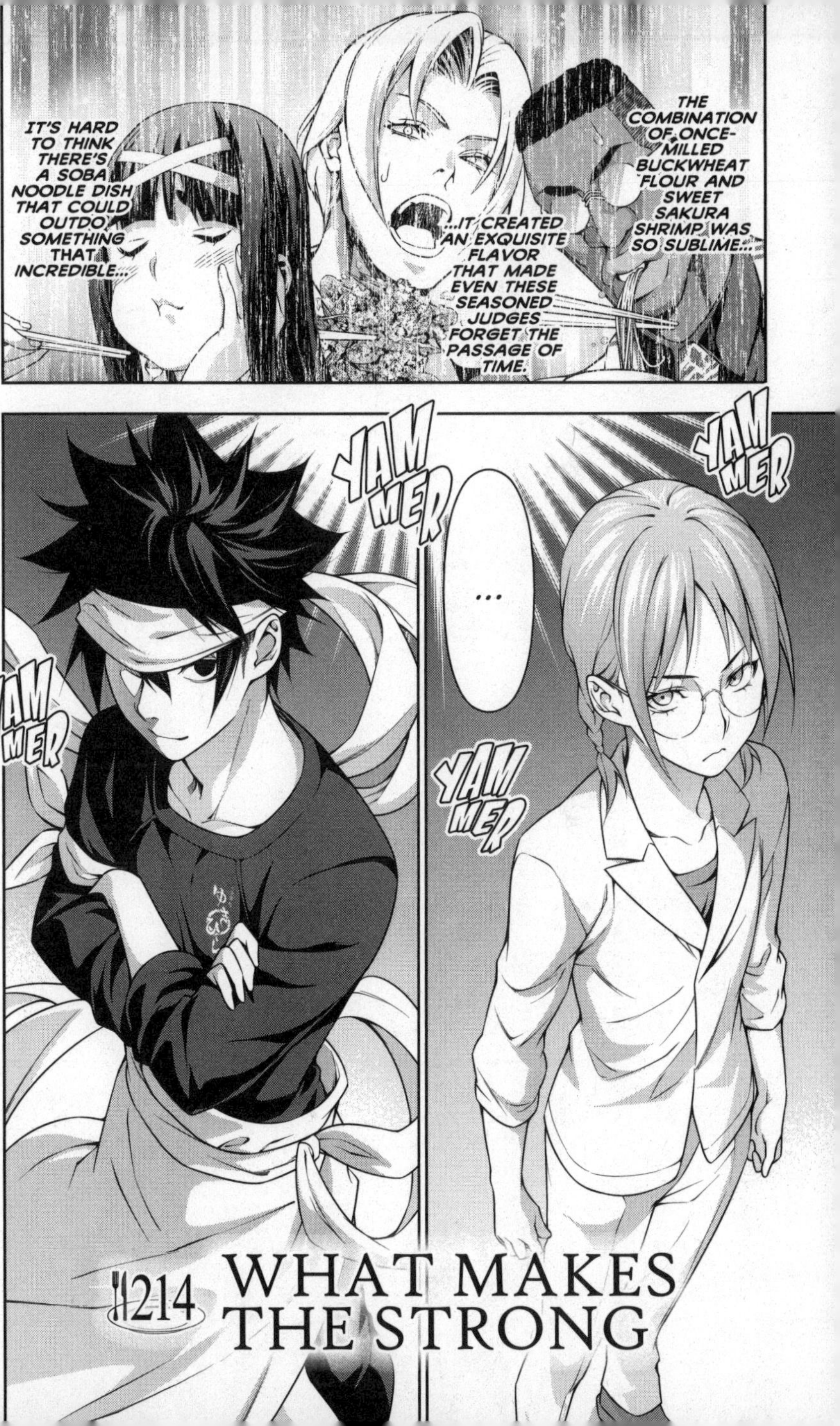
THE COMBINATION OF ONCE-MILLED BUCKWHEAT FLOUR AND SWEET SAKURA SHRIMP WAS SO SUBLIME...
...IT CREATED AN EXQUISITE FLAVOR THAT MADE EVEN THESE SEASONED JUDGES FORGET THE PASSAGE OF TIME.
IT'S HARD TO THINK THERE'S A SOBA NOODLE DISH THAT COULD OUTDO SOMETHING THAT INCREDIBLE...
YAM MER
...
YAM MER
YAM MER
YAM MER
214 WHAT MAKES THE STRONG

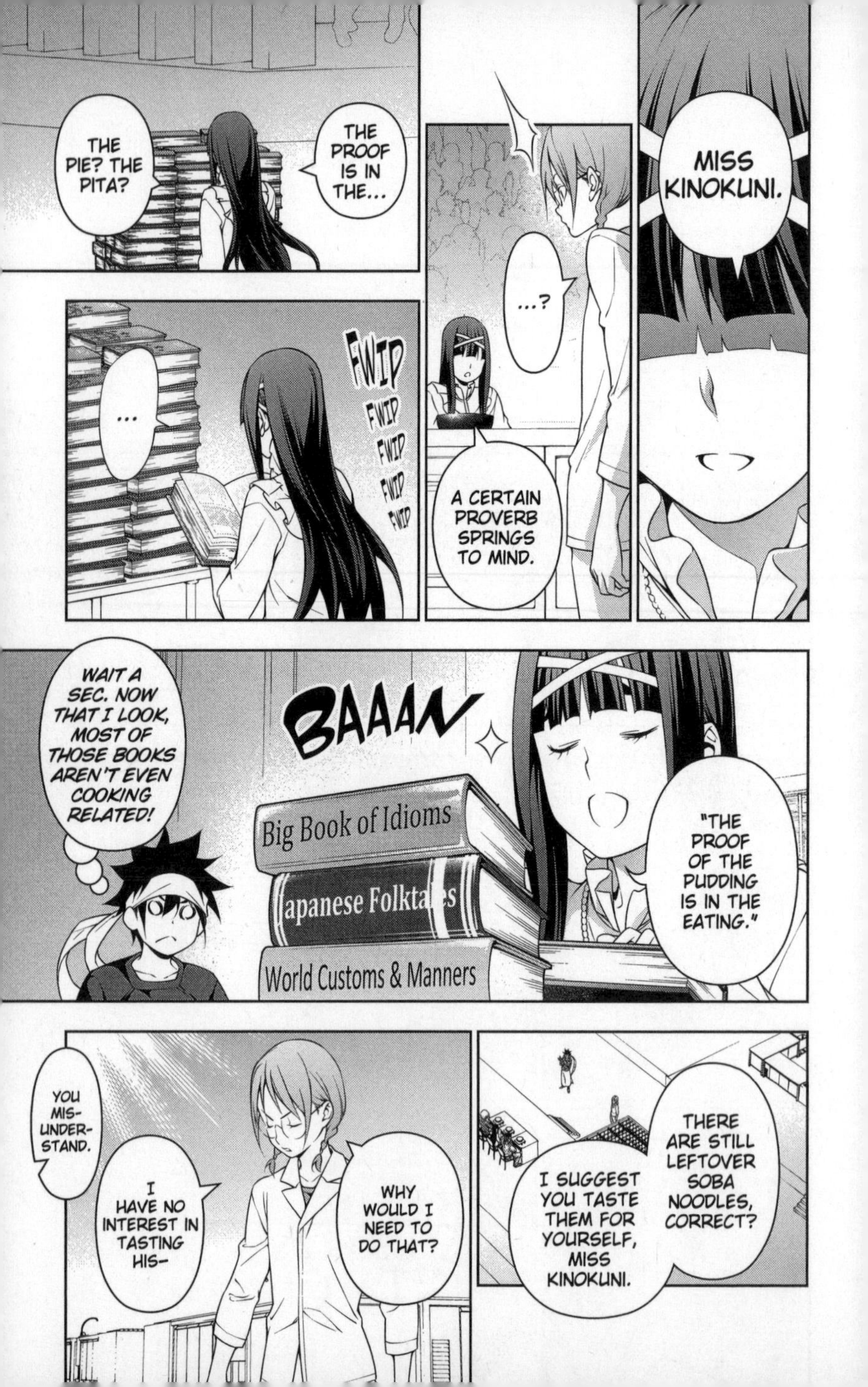
MISS KINOKUNI.
...?
A CERTAIN PROVERB SPRINGS TO MIND.
THE PROOF IS IN THE...
THE PIE? THE PITA?
...
FWIP FWIP FWIP FWIP FWIP
BAAAN
"THE PROOF OF THE PUDDING IS IN THE EATING."
Big Book of Idioms
Japanese Folktales
World Customs & Manners
WAIT A SEC. NOW THAT I LOOK, MOST OF THOSE BOOKS AREN'T EVEN COOKING RELATED!
THERE ARE STILL LEFTOVER SOBA NOODLES, CORRECT?
I SUGGEST YOU TASTE THEM FOR YOURSELF, MISS KINOKUNI.
WHY WOULD I NEED TO DO THAT?
YOU MIS-UNDER-STAND.
I HAVE NO INTEREST IN TASTING HIS-

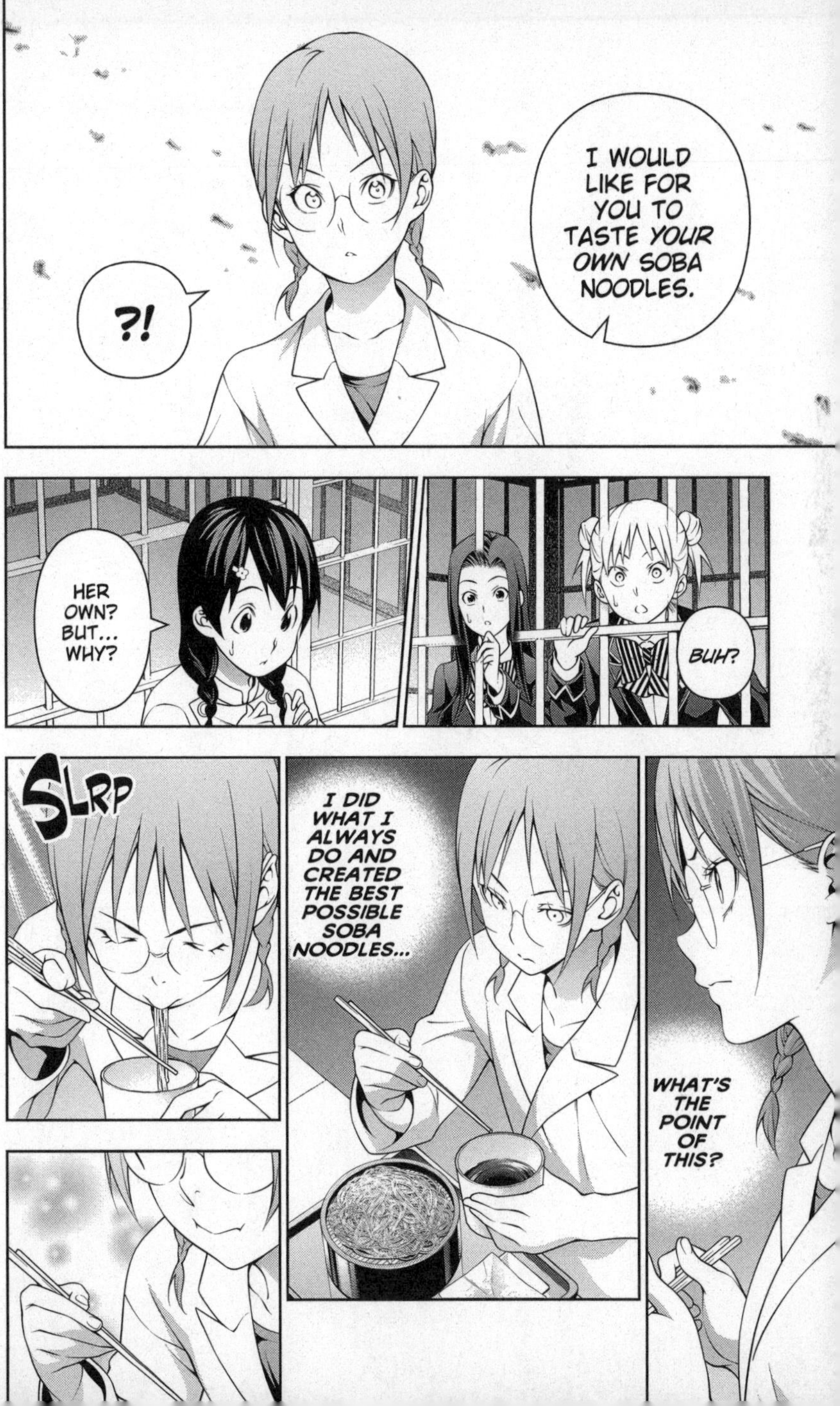
I WOULD LIKE FOR YOU TO TASTE *YOUR* OWN SOBA NOODLES.
?!
BUH?
HER OWN? BUT... WHY?
WHAT'S THE POINT OF THIS?
I DID WHAT I ALWAYS DO AND CREATED THE BEST POSSIBLE SOBA NOODLES...
SLRP

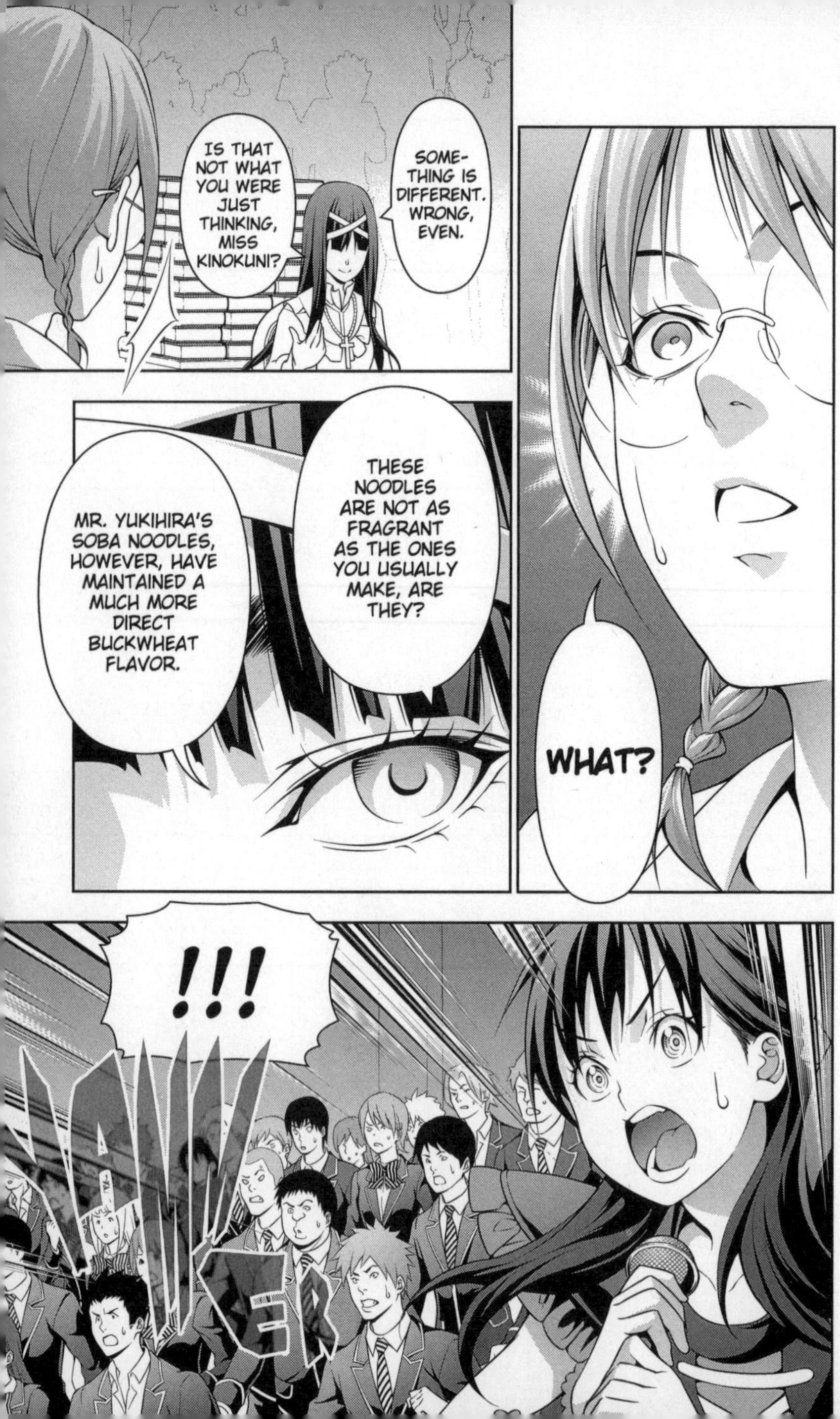
SOME-THING IS DIFFERENT. WRONG, EVEN.
IS THAT NOT WHAT YOU WERE JUST THINKING, MISS KINOKUNI?
WHAT?
THESE NOODLES ARE NOT AS FRAGRANT AS THE ONES YOU USUALLY MAKE, ARE THEY?
MR. YUKIHIRA'S SOBA NOODLES, HOWEVER, HAVE MAINTAINED A MUCH MORE DIRECT BUCKWHEAT FLAVOR.
!!!

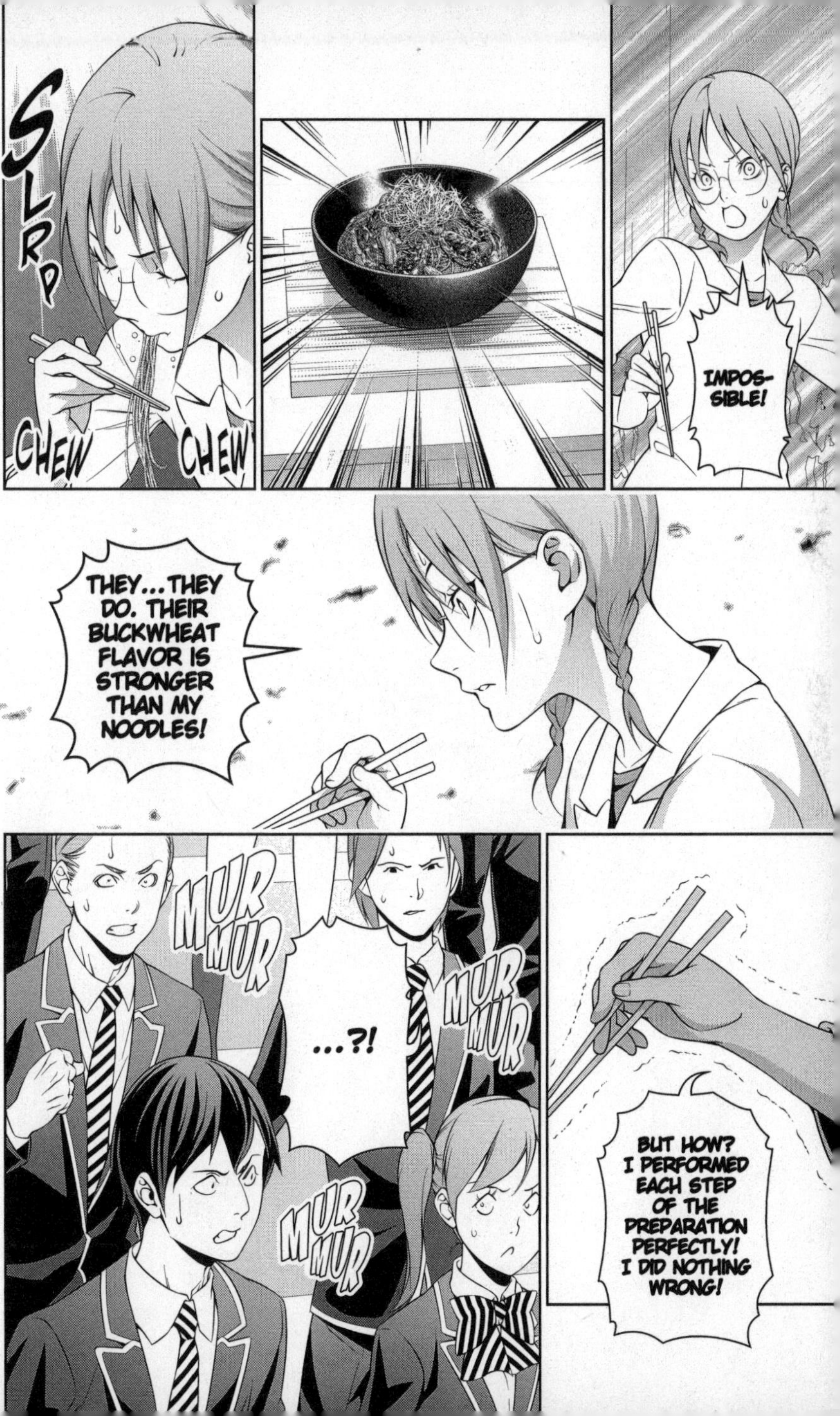
IMPOS-SIBLE!
SLRP
CHEW CHEW
THEY...THEY DO. THEIR BUCKWHEAT FLAVOR IS STRONGER THAN MY NOODLES!
BUT HOW? I PERFORMED EACH STEP OF THE PREPARATION PERFECTLY! I DID NOTHING WRONG!
MUR MUR
MUR MUR
...?!
MUR MUR

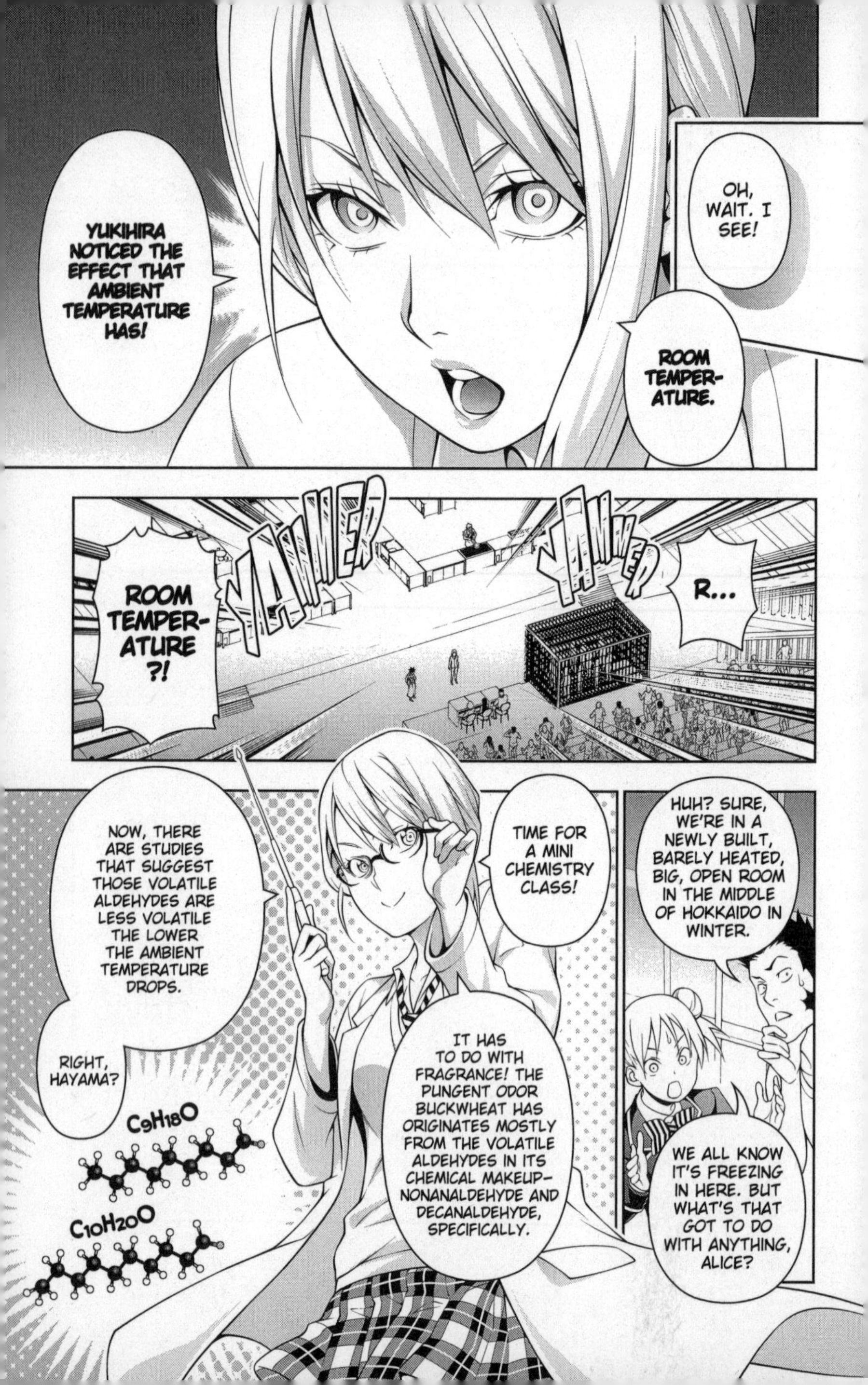

OH, WAIT. I SEE!
ROOM TEMPER-ATURE.
YUKIHIRA NOTICED THE EFFECT THAT AMBIENT TEMPERATURE HAS!
R...
YAMMER
YAMMER
ROOM TEMPER-ATURE ?!
HUH? SURE, WE'RE IN A NEWLY BUILT, BARELY HEATED, BIG, OPEN ROOM IN THE MIDDLE OF HOKKAIDO IN WINTER.
WE ALL KNOW IT'S FREEZING IN HERE. BUT WHAT'S THAT GOT TO DO WITH ANYTHING, ALICE?
TIME FOR A MINI CHEMISTRY CLASS!
IT HAS TO DO WITH FRAGRANCE! THE PUNGENT ODOR BUCKWHEAT HAS ORIGINATES MOSTLY FROM THE VOLATILE ALDEHYDES IN ITS CHEMICAL MAKEUP–NONANALDEHYDE AND DECANALDEHYDE, SPECIFICALLY.
NOW, THERE ARE STUDIES THAT SUGGEST THOSE VOLATILE ALDEHYDES ARE LESS VOLATILE THE LOWER THE AMBIENT TEMPERATURE DROPS.
RIGHT, HAYAMA?
$C_9H_{18}O$
$C_{10}H_{20}O$

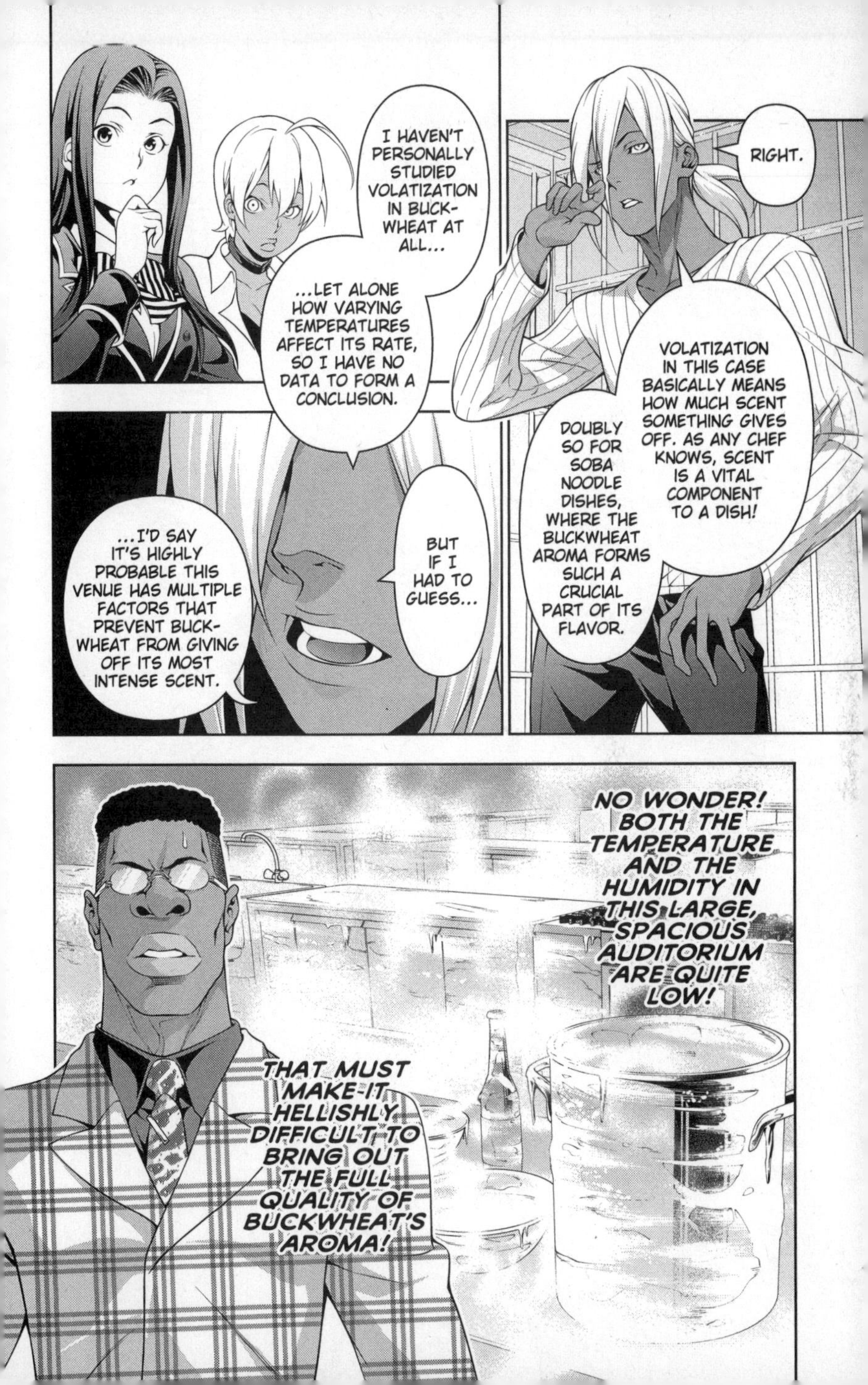
RIGHT.
VOLATIZATION IN THIS CASE BASICALLY MEANS HOW MUCH SCENT SOMETHING GIVES OFF. AS ANY CHEF KNOWS, SCENT IS A VITAL COMPONENT TO A DISH!
DOUBLY SO FOR SOBA NOODLE DISHES, WHERE THE BUCKWHEAT AROMA FORMS SUCH A CRUCIAL PART OF ITS FLAVOR.
I HAVEN'T PERSONALLY STUDIED VOLATIZATION IN BUCK-WHEAT AT ALL...
...LET ALONE HOW VARYING TEMPERATURES AFFECT ITS RATE, SO I HAVE NO DATA TO FORM A CONCLUSION.
BUT IF I HAD TO GUESS...
...I'D SAY IT'S HIGHLY PROBABLE THIS VENUE HAS MULTIPLE FACTORS THAT PREVENT BUCK-WHEAT FROM GIVING OFF ITS MOST INTENSE SCENT.
NO WONDER! BOTH THE TEMPERATURE AND THE HUMIDITY IN THIS LARGE, SPACIOUS AUDITORIUM ARE QUITE LOW!
THAT MUST MAKE IT HELLISHLY DIFFICULT TO BRING OUT THE FULL QUALITY OF BUCKWHEAT'S AROMA!

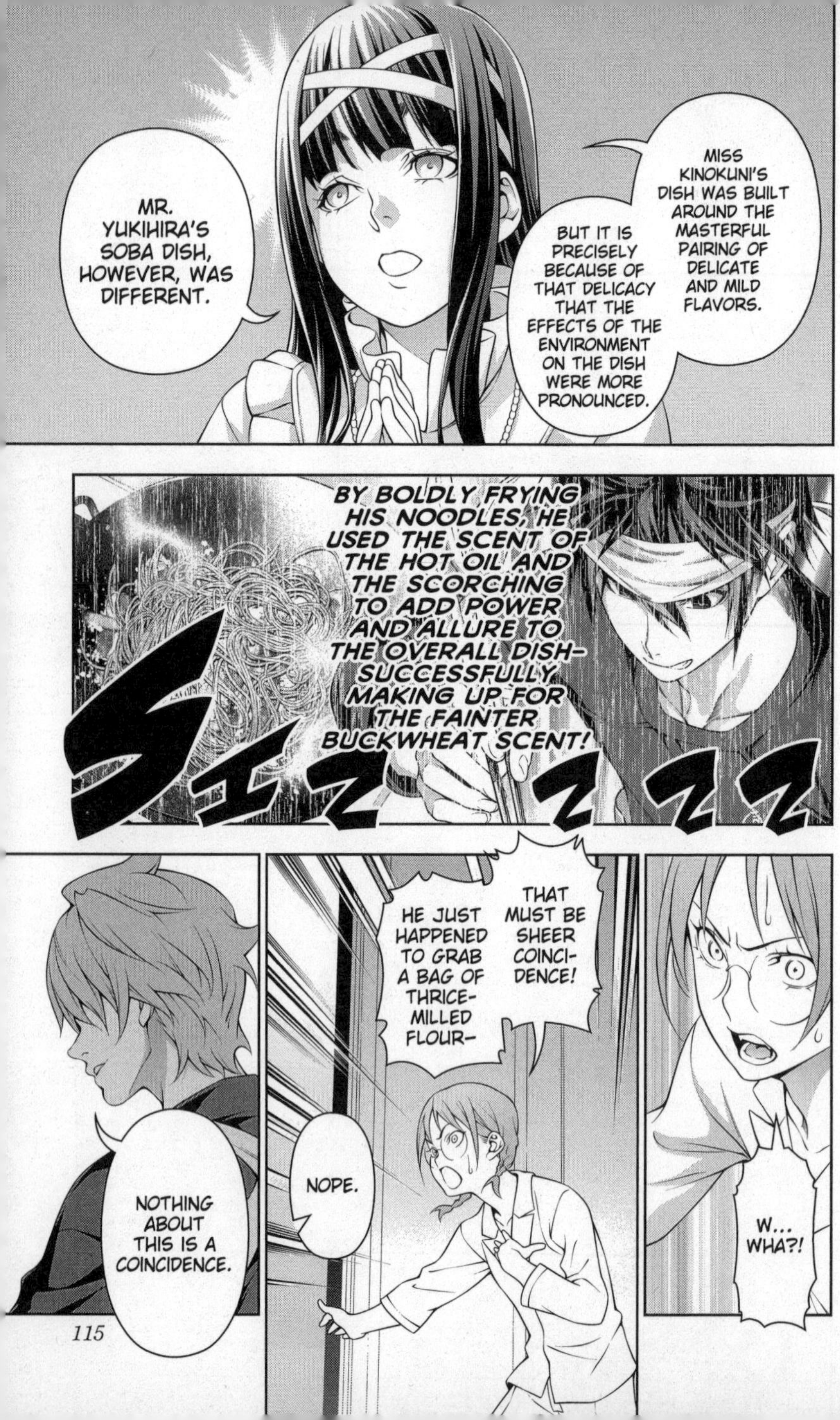
MISS KINOKUNI'S DISH WAS BUILT AROUND THE MASTERFUL PAIRING OF DELICATE AND MILD FLAVORS.
BUT IT IS PRECISELY BECAUSE OF THAT DELICACY THAT THE EFFECTS OF THE ENVIRONMENT ON THE DISH WERE MORE PRONOUNCED.
MR. YUKIHIRA'S SOBA DISH, HOWEVER, WAS DIFFERENT.
BY BOLDLY FRYING HIS NOODLES, HE USED THE SCENT OF THE HOT OIL AND THE SCORCHING TO ADD POWER AND ALLURE TO THE OVERALL DISH–SUCCESSFULLY MAKING UP FOR THE FAINTER BUCKWHEAT SCENT!
W... WHA?!
THAT MUST BE SHEER COINCI-DENCE!
HE JUST HAPPENED TO GRAB A BAG OF THRICE-MILLED FLOUR–
NOPE.
NOTHING ABOUT THIS IS A COINCIDENCE.

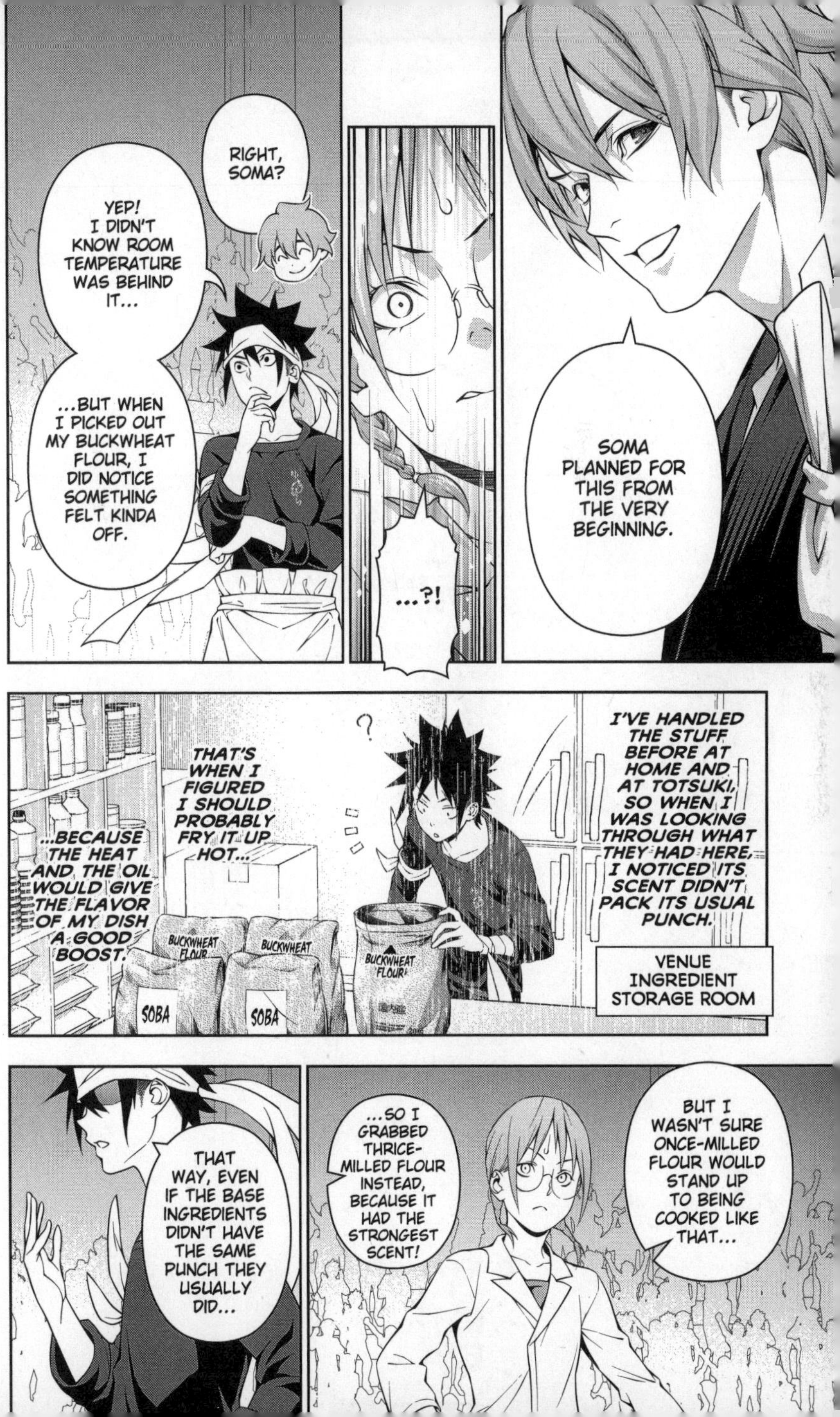
SOMA PLANNED FOR THIS FROM THE VERY BEGINNING.
...?!
RIGHT, SOMA?
YEP! I DIDN'T KNOW ROOM TEMPERATURE WAS BEHIND IT...
...BUT WHEN I PICKED OUT MY BUCKWHEAT FLOUR, I DID NOTICE SOMETHING FELT KINDA OFF.
VENUE INGREDIENT STORAGE ROOM
I'VE HANDLED THE STUFF BEFORE AT HOME AND AT TOTSUKI, SO WHEN I WAS LOOKING THROUGH WHAT THEY HAD HERE, I NOTICED ITS SCENT DIDN'T PACK ITS USUAL PUNCH.
BUCKWHEAT FLOUR
BUCKWHEAT
SOBA
SOBA
THAT'S WHEN I FIGURED I SHOULD PROBABLY FRY IT UP HOT...
...BECAUSE THE HEAT AND THE OIL WOULD GIVE THE FLAVOR OF MY DISH A GOOD BOOST.
BUT I WASN'T SURE ONCE-MILLED FLOUR WOULD STAND UP TO BEING COOKED LIKE THAT...
...SO I GRABBED THRICE-MILLED FLOUR INSTEAD, BECAUSE IT HAD THE STRONGEST SCENT!
THAT WAY, EVEN IF THE BASE INGREDIENTS DIDN'T HAVE THE SAME PUNCH THEY USUALLY DID...

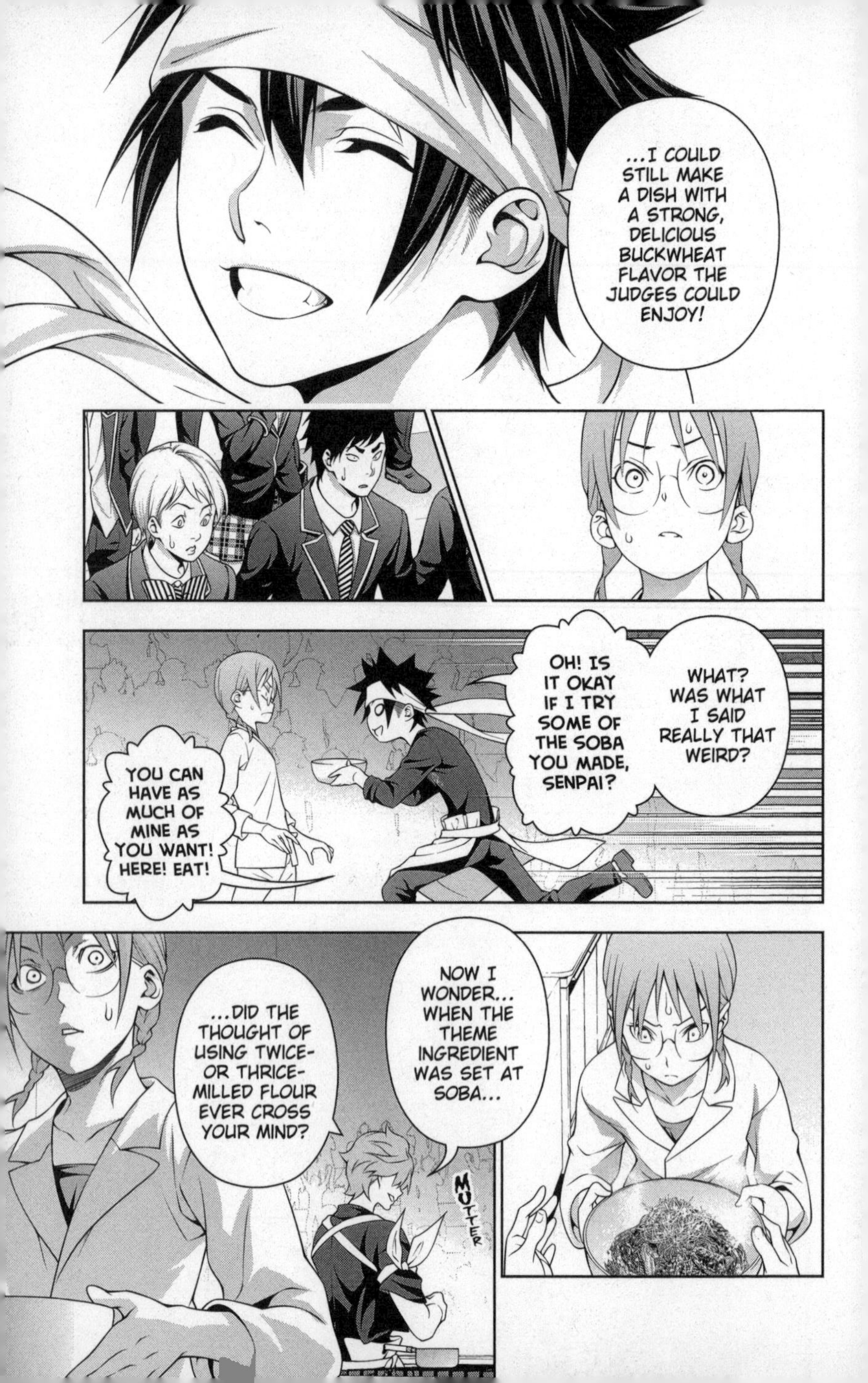
...I COULD STILL MAKE A DISH WITH A STRONG, DELICIOUS BUCKWHEAT FLAVOR THE JUDGES COULD ENJOY!
WHAT? WAS WHAT I SAID REALLY THAT WEIRD?
OH! IS IT OKAY IF I TRY SOME OF THE SOBA YOU MADE, SENPAI?
YOU CAN HAVE AS MUCH OF MINE AS YOU WANT! HERE! EAT!
NOW I WONDER... WHEN THE THEME INGREDIENT WAS SET AT SOBA...
MUTTER
...DID THE THOUGHT OF USING TWICE- OR THRICE-MILLED FLOUR EVER CROSS YOUR MIND?

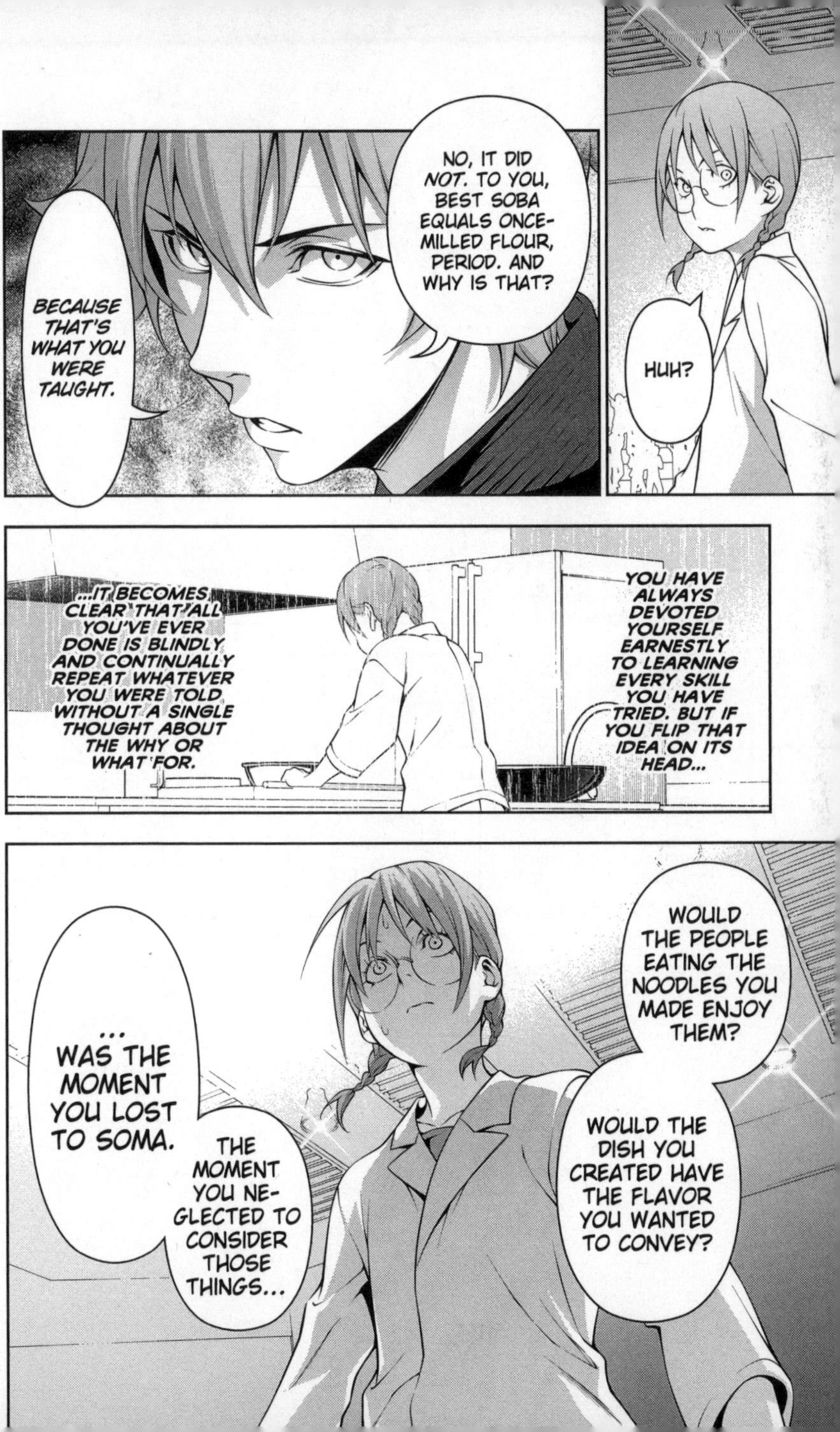
HUH?
NO, IT DID NOT. TO YOU, BEST SOBA EQUALS ONCE-MILLED FLOUR, PERIOD. AND WHY IS THAT?
BECAUSE THAT'S WHAT YOU WERE TAUGHT.
YOU HAVE ALWAYS DEVOTED YOURSELF EARNESTLY TO LEARNING EVERY SKILL YOU HAVE TRIED. BUT IF YOU FLIP THAT IDEA ON ITS HEAD...
...IT BECOMES CLEAR THAT ALL YOU'VE EVER DONE IS BLINDLY AND CONTINUALLY REPEAT WHATEVER YOU WERE TOLD WITHOUT A SINGLE THOUGHT ABOUT THE WHY OR WHAT FOR.
WOULD THE PEOPLE EATING THE NOODLES YOU MADE ENJOY THEM?
WOULD THE DISH YOU CREATED HAVE THE FLAVOR YOU WANTED TO CONVEY?
THE MOMENT YOU NEGLECTED TO CONSIDER THOSE THINGS...
...WAS THE MOMENT YOU LOST TO SOMA.

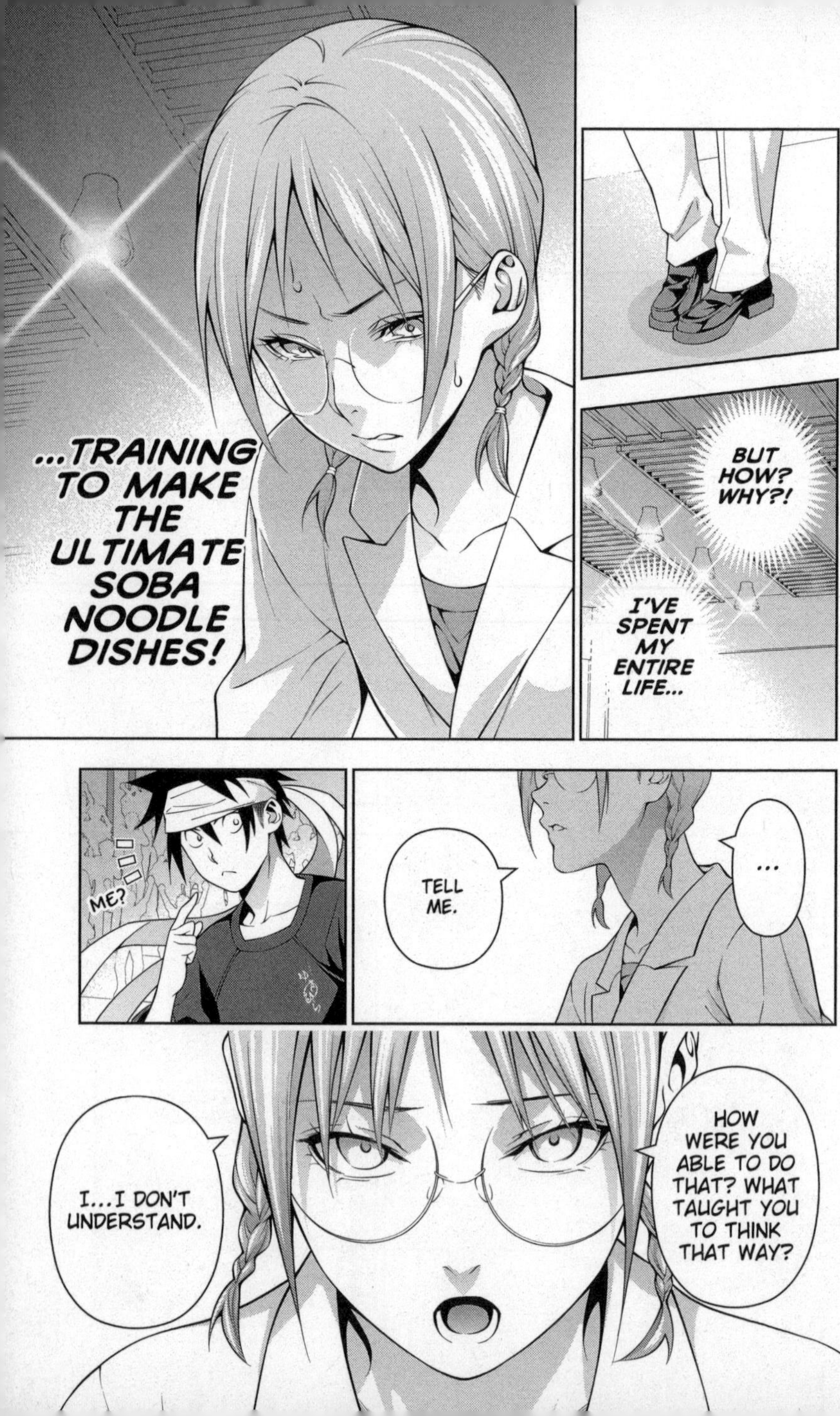
BUT HOW? WHY?!
I'VE SPENT MY ENTIRE LIFE...
...TRAINING TO MAKE THE ULTIMATE SOBA NOODLE DISHES!
...
TELL ME.
ME?
HOW WERE YOU ABLE TO DO THAT? WHAT TAUGHT YOU TO THINK THAT WAY?
I...I DON'T UNDERSTAND.

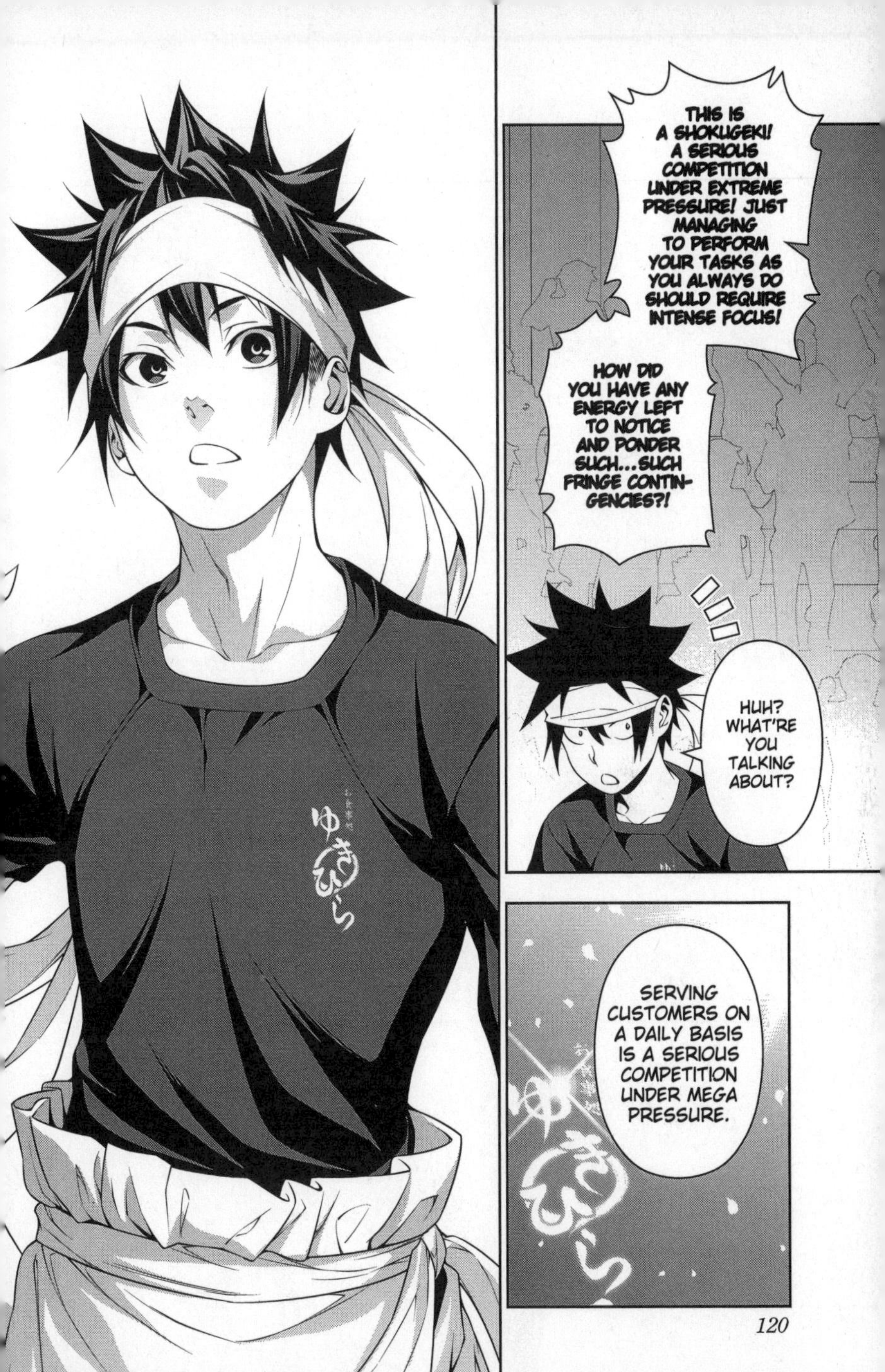
THIS IS A SHOKUGEKI! A SERIOUS COMPETITION UNDER EXTREME PRESSURE! JUST MANAGING TO PERFORM YOUR TASKS AS YOU ALWAYS DO SHOULD REQUIRE INTENSE FOCUS!
HOW DID YOU HAVE ANY ENERGY LEFT TO NOTICE AND PONDER SUCH...SUCH FRINGE CONTIN-GENCIES?!
HUH? WHAT'RE YOU TALKING ABOUT?
SERVING CUSTOMERS ON A DAILY BASIS IS A SERIOUS COMPETITION UNDER MEGA PRESSURE.

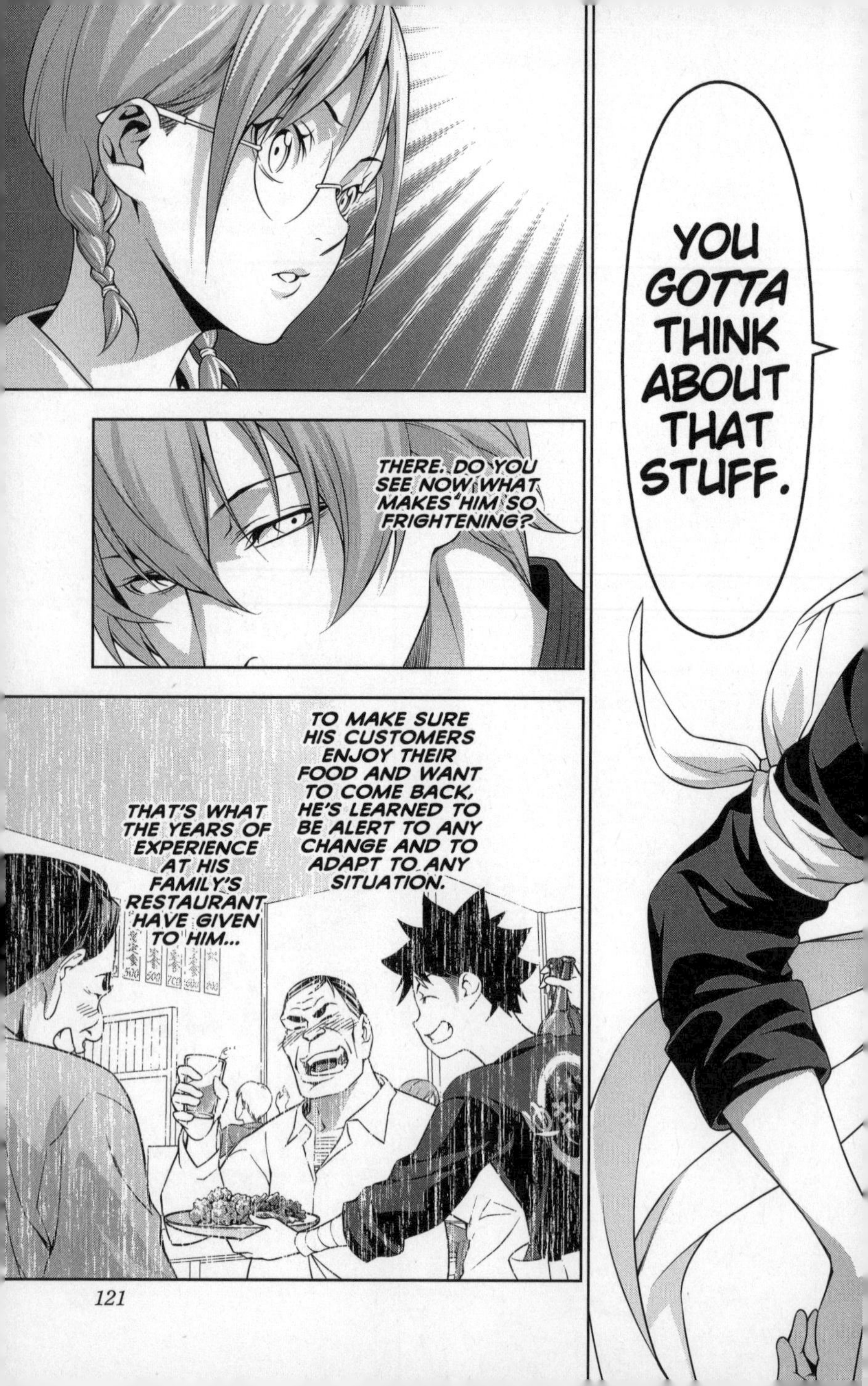
YOU GOTTA THINK ABOUT THAT STUFF.
THERE. DO YOU SEE NOW WHAT MAKES HIM SO FRIGHTENING?
TO MAKE SURE HIS CUSTOMERS ENJOY THEIR FOOD AND WANT TO COME BACK, HE'S LEARNED TO BE ALERT TO ANY CHANGE AND TO ADAPT TO ANY SITUATION.
THAT'S WHAT THE YEARS OF EXPERIENCE AT HIS FAMILY'S RESTAURANT HAVE GIVEN TO HIM...

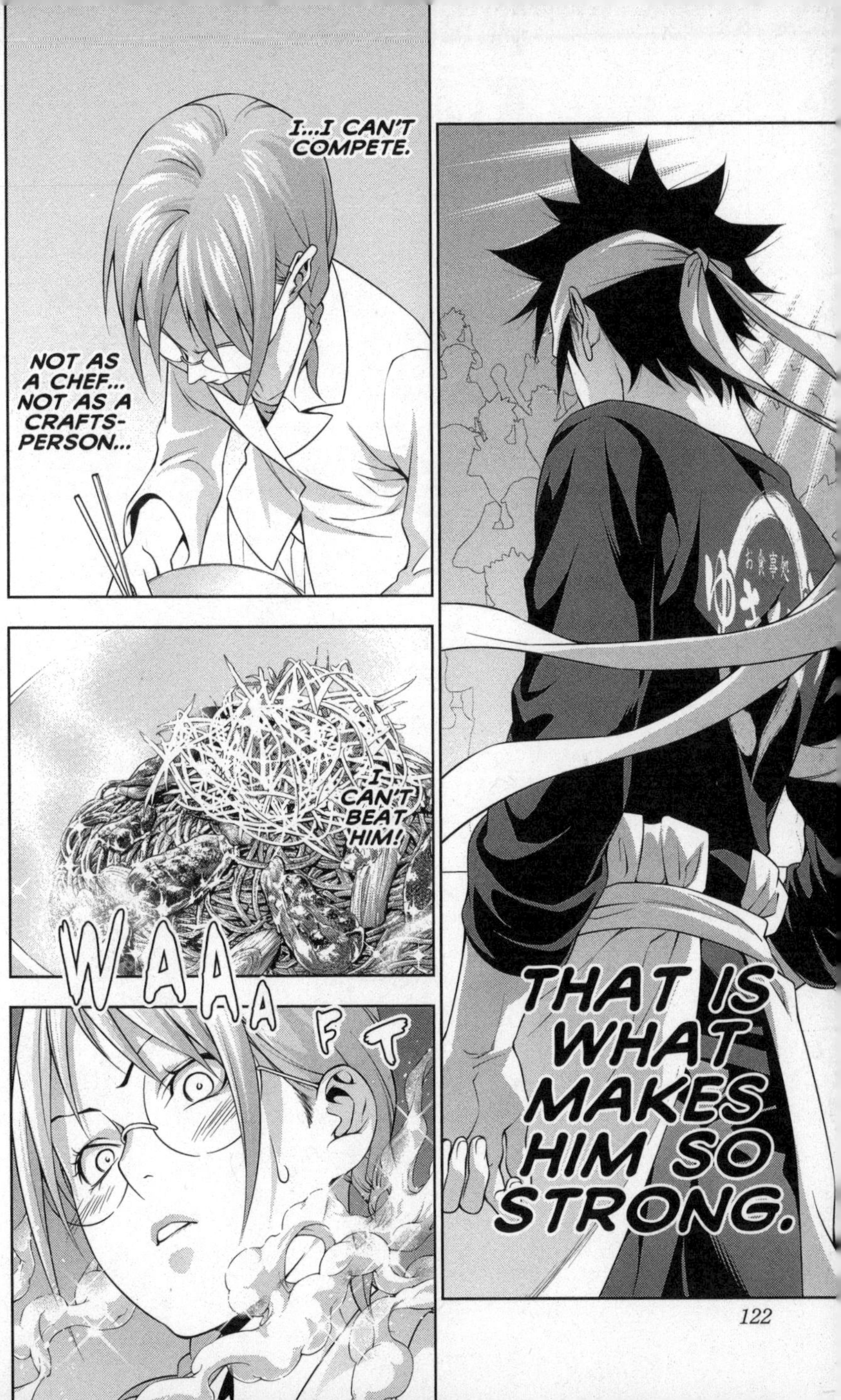
THAT IS WHAT MAKES HIM SO STRONG.
I...I CAN'T COMPETE.
NOT AS A CHEF... NOT AS A CRAFTS-PERSON...
I CAN'T BEAT HIM!
WAAAFT

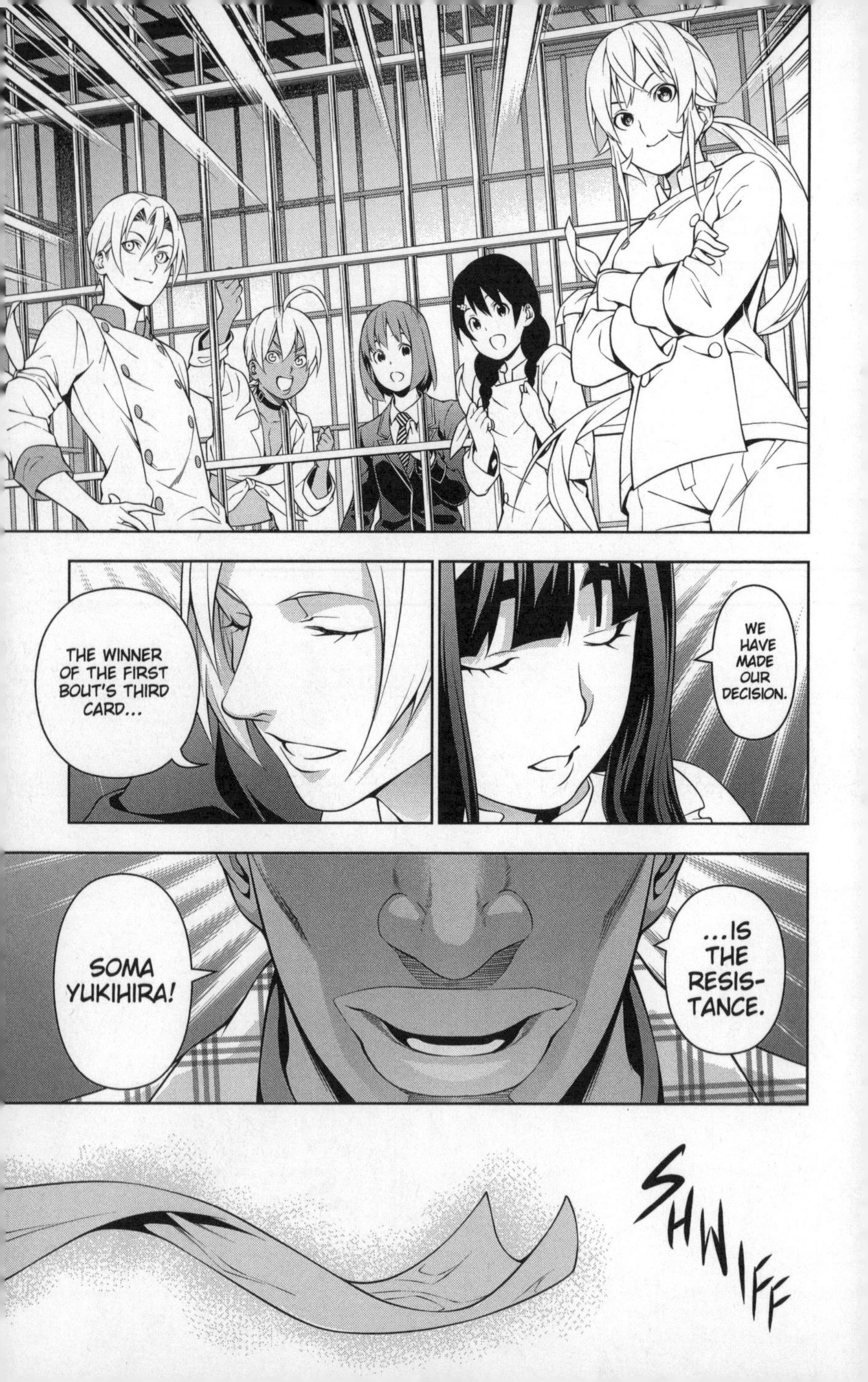
WE HAVE MADE OUR DECISION.
THE WINNER OF THE FIRST BOUT'S THIRD CARD...
...IS THE RESIS-TANCE.
SOMA YUKIHIRA!
SHWIFF

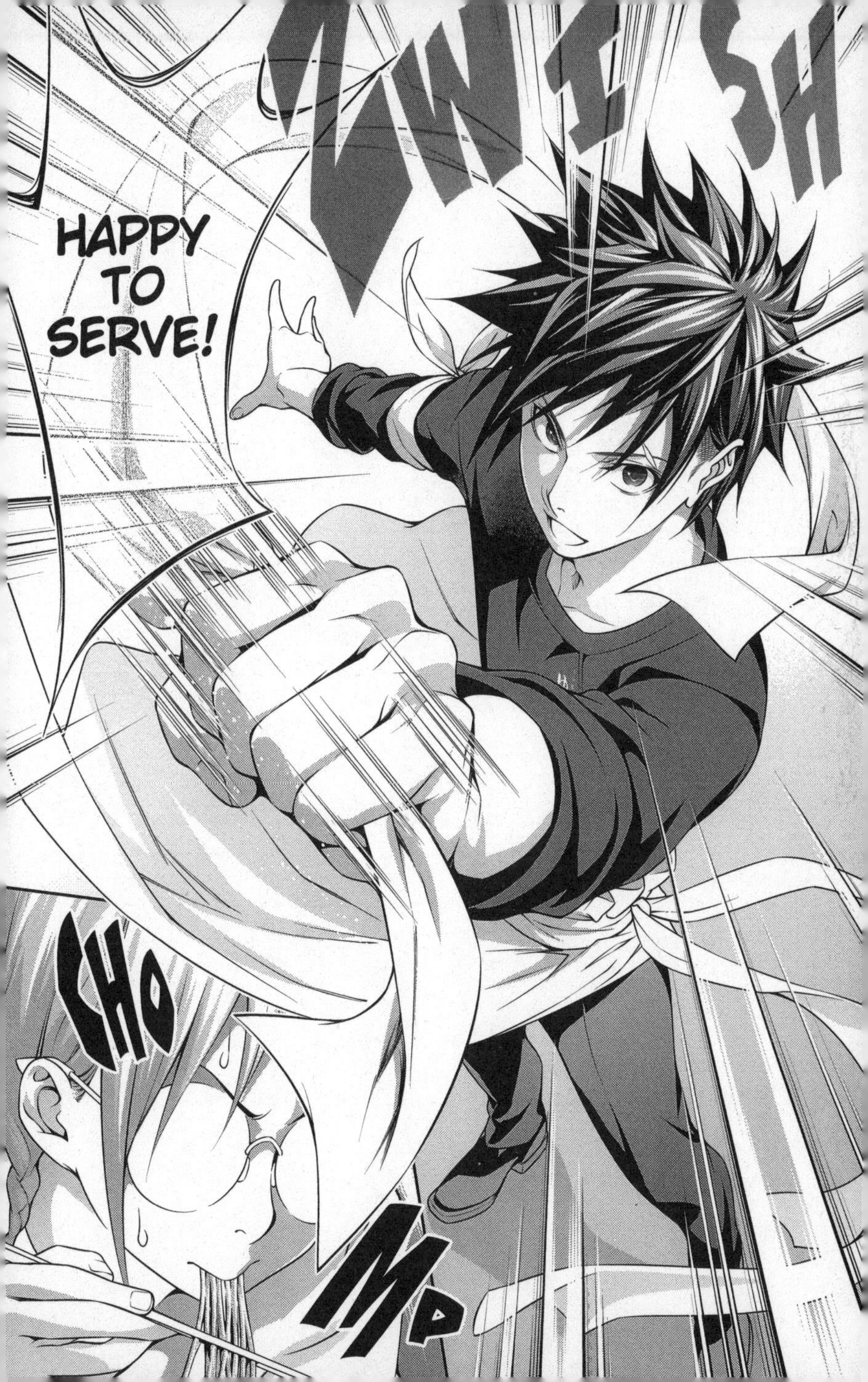
HAPPY TO SERVE!
CHO
MP

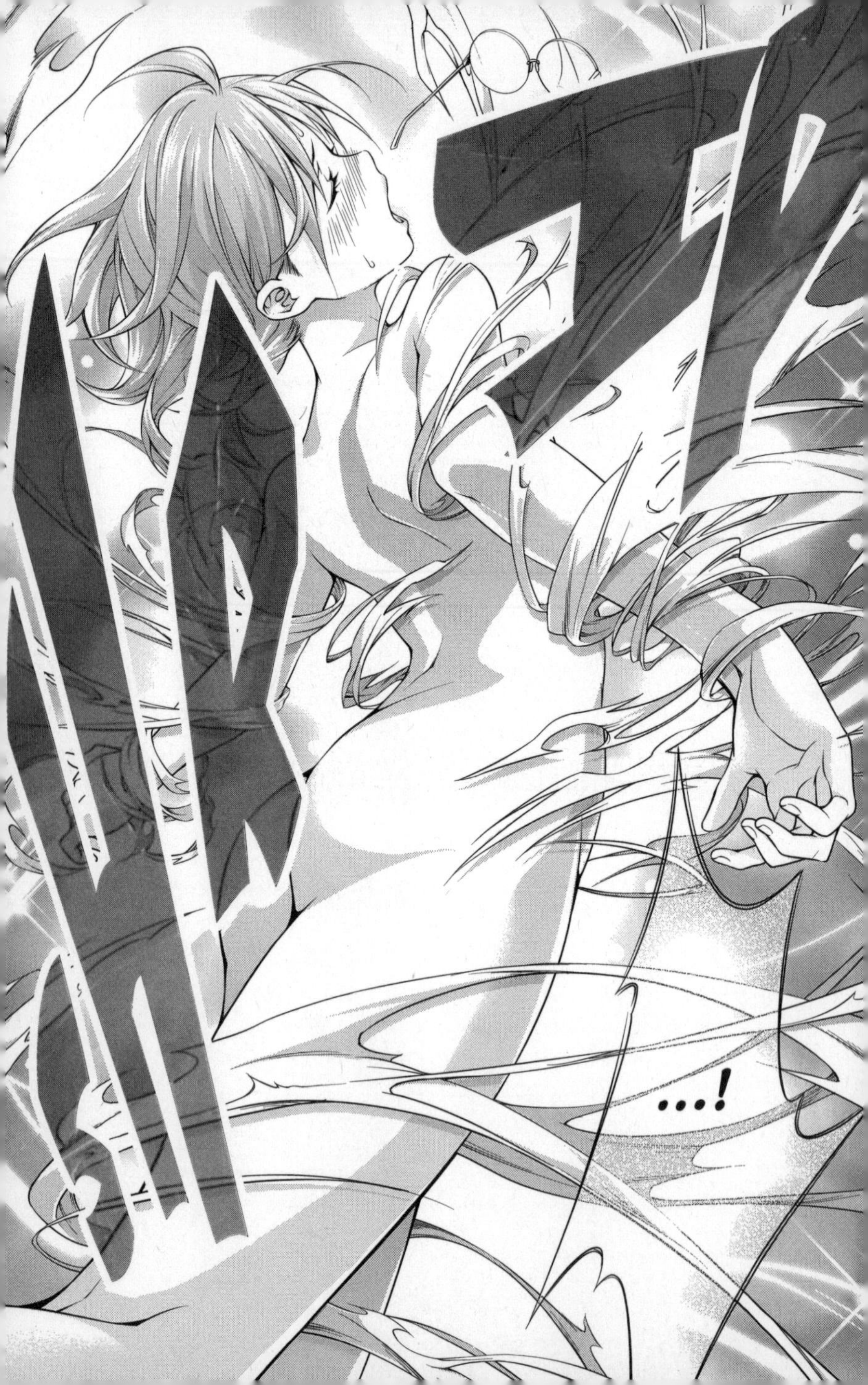
...!

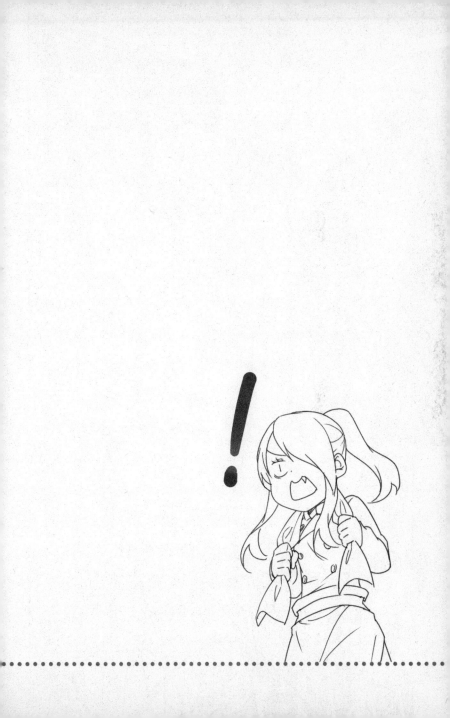

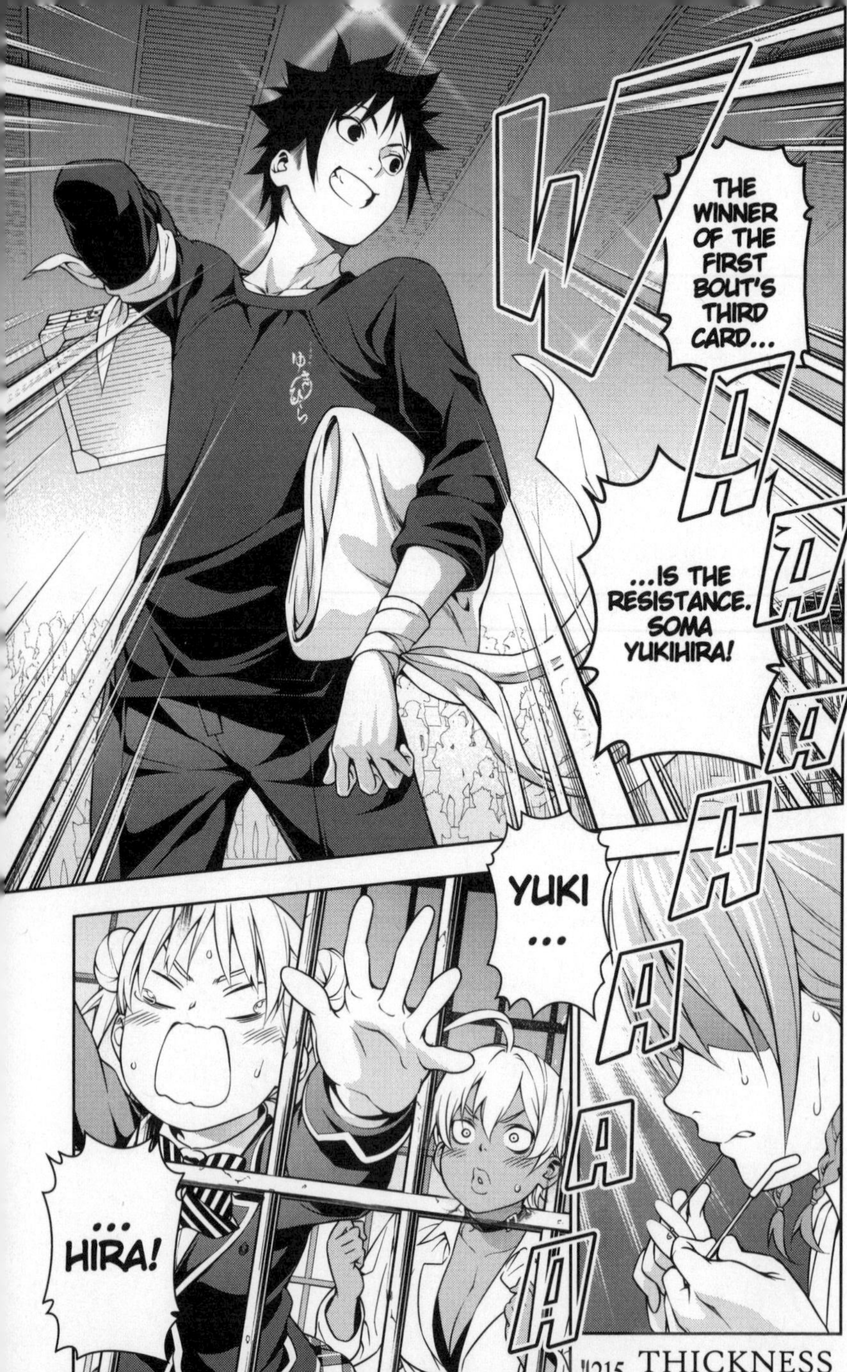
THE WINNER OF THE FIRST BOUT'S THIRD CARD...
...IS THE RESISTANCE. SOMA YUKIHIRA!
WAAAAAAAAA
YUKI...
...HIRA!

215 THICKNESS IS JUSTICE

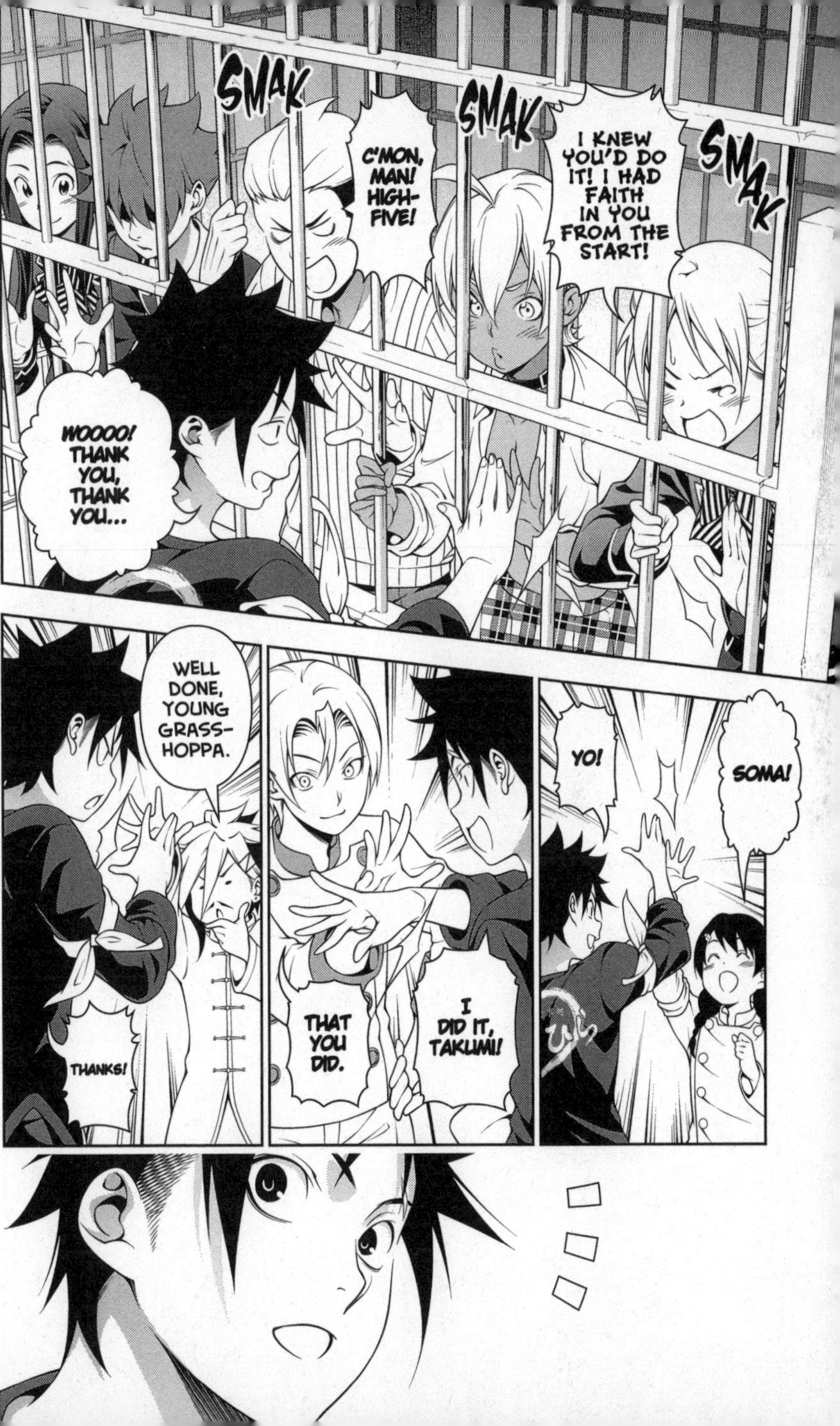
SMAK
I KNEW YOU'D DO IT! I HAD FAITH IN YOU FROM THE START!
SMAK
C'MON, MAN! HIGH-FIVE!
SMAK
WOOOO! THANK YOU, THANK YOU...
SOMA!
YO!
I DID IT, TAKUMI!
THAT YOU DID.
WELL DONE, YOUNG GRASS-HOPPA.
THANKS!

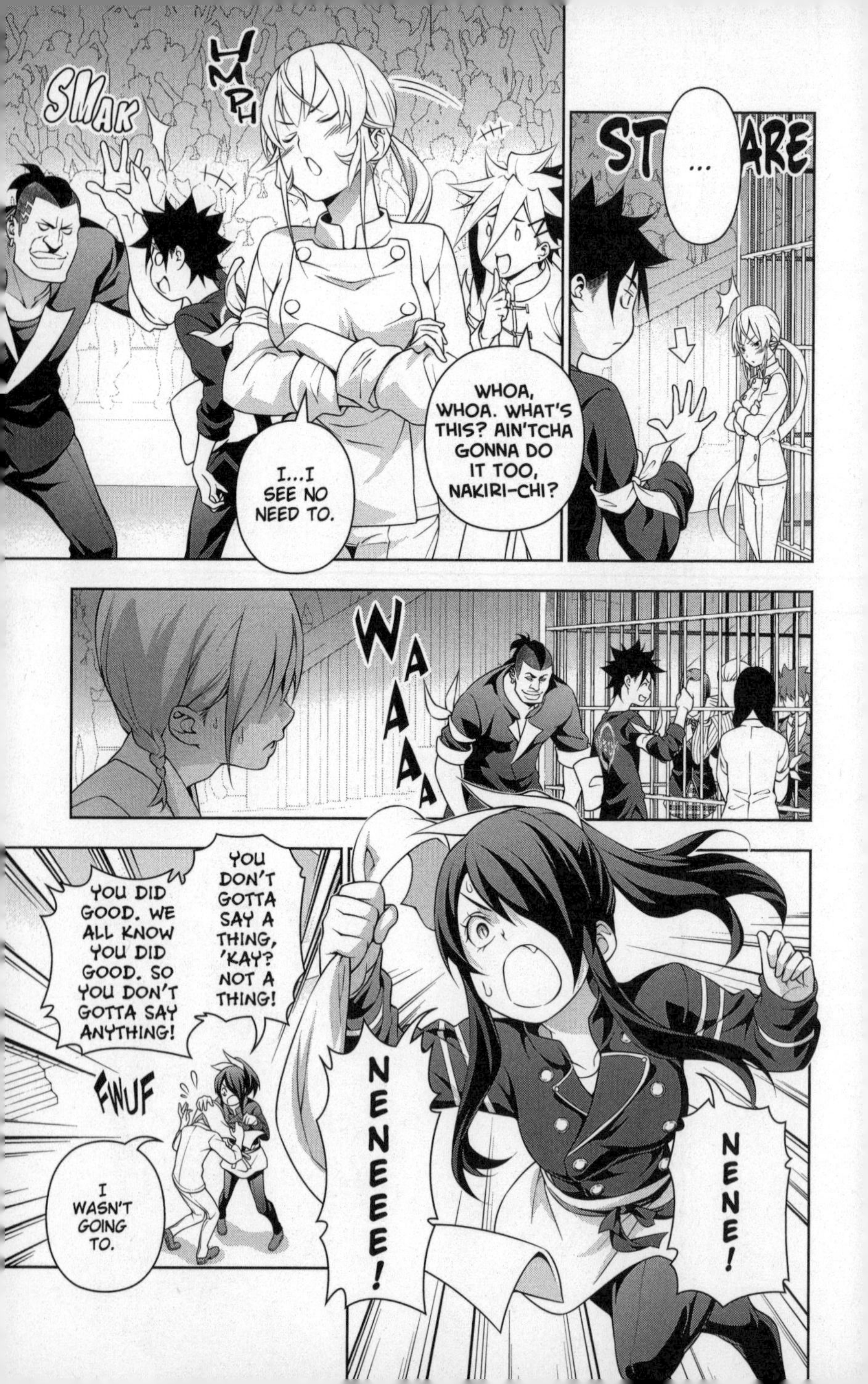
ST ARE
...
HMPH
SMAK
WHOA, WHOA. WHAT'S THIS? AIN'TCHA GONNA DO IT TOO, NAKIRI-CHI?
I...I SEE NO NEED TO.
WAAAA
NENE!
NENEEE!
YOU DON'T GOTTA SAY A THING, 'KAY? NOT A THING!
YOU DID GOOD. WE ALL KNOW YOU DID GOOD. SO YOU DON'T GOTTA SAY ANYTHING!
FWUF
I WASN'T GOING TO.

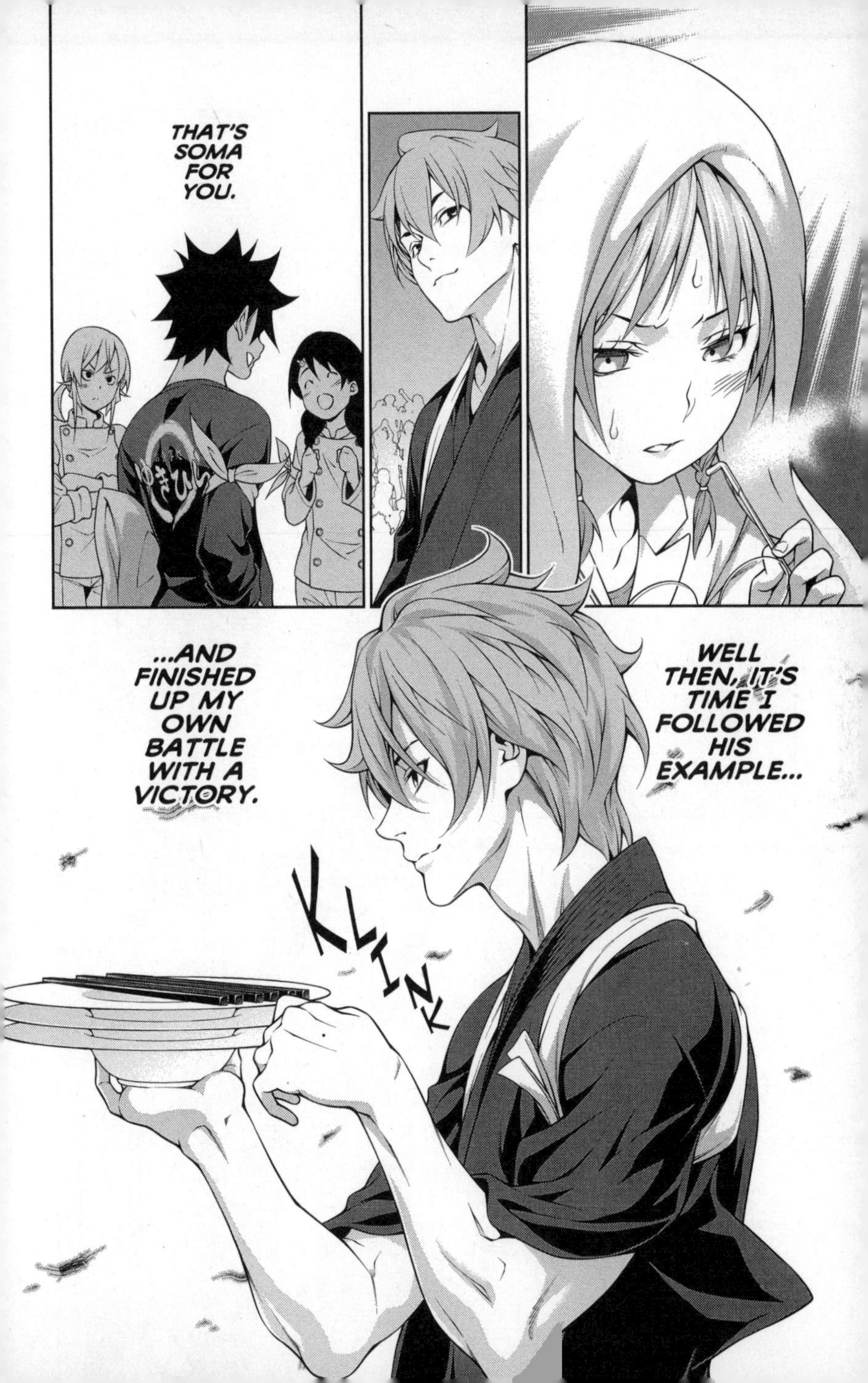
THAT'S SOMA FOR YOU.
WELL THEN, IT'S TIME I FOLLOWED HIS EXAMPLE...
...AND FINISHED UP MY OWN BATTLE WITH A VICTORY.
KLINK

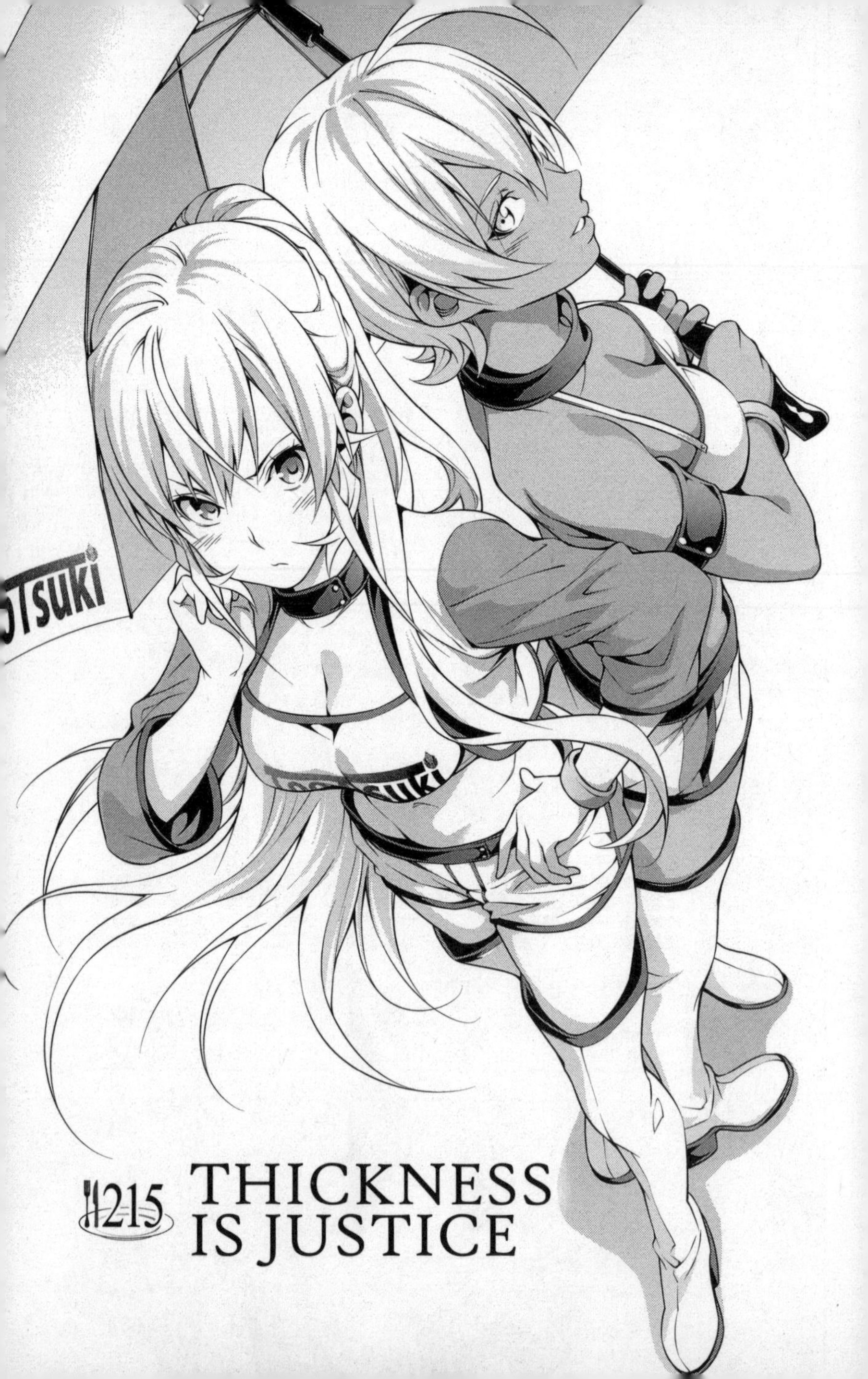
TOTSUKI
TOTSUKI

215 THICKNESS IS JUSTICE

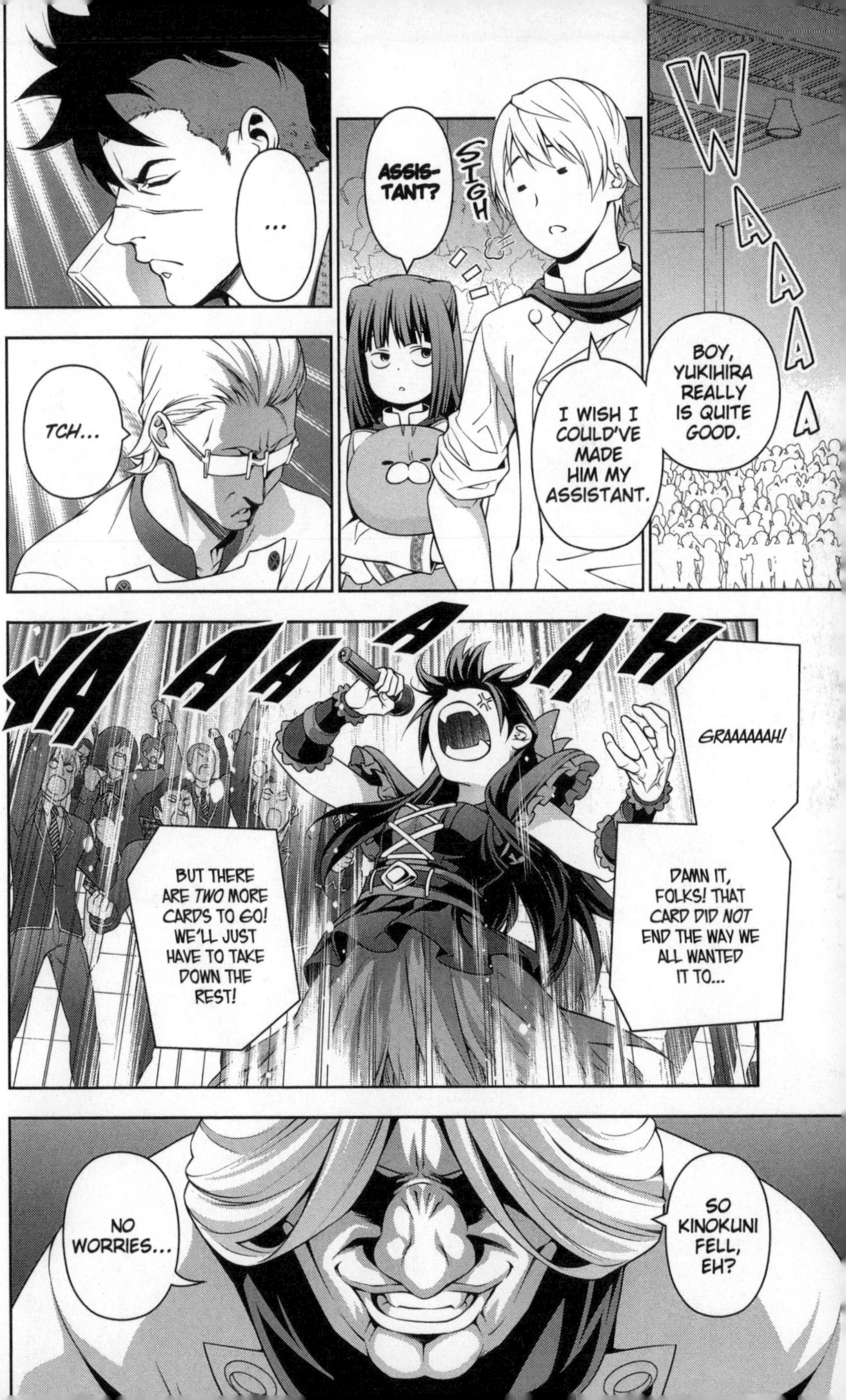
WAAAAAA
BOY, YUKIHIRA REALLY IS QUITE GOOD.
I WISH I COULD'VE MADE HIM MY ASSISTANT.
SIGH
ASSIS-TANT?
...
TCH...
WAAAAAH
GRAAAAAAH!
DAMN IT, FOLKS! THAT CARD DID *NOT* END THE WAY WE ALL WANTED IT TO...
BUT THERE ARE *TWO* MORE CARDS TO GO! WE'LL JUST HAVE TO TAKE DOWN THE REST!
SO KINOKUNI FELL, EH?
NO WORRIES...

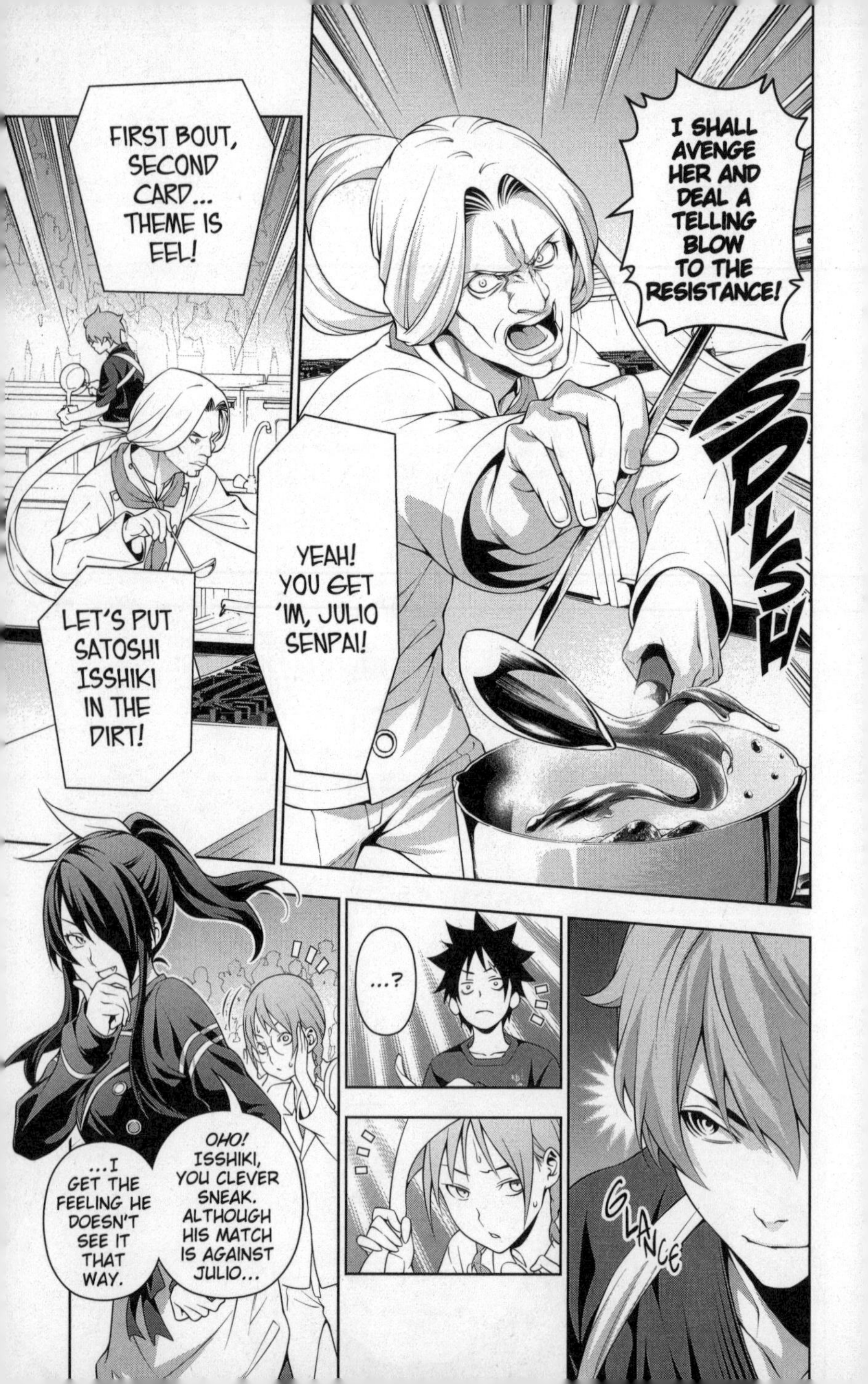
I SHALL AVENGE HER AND DEAL A TELLING BLOW TO THE RESISTANCE!
SPLSH
YEAH! YOU GET 'IM, JULIO SENPAI!
FIRST BOUT, SECOND CARD... THEME IS EEL!
LET'S PUT SATOSHI ISSHIKI IN THE DIRT!
GLANCE
...?
OHO! ISSHIKI, YOU CLEVER SNEAK. ALTHOUGH HIS MATCH IS AGAINST JULIO...
...I GET THE FEELING HE DOESN'T SEE IT THAT WAY.

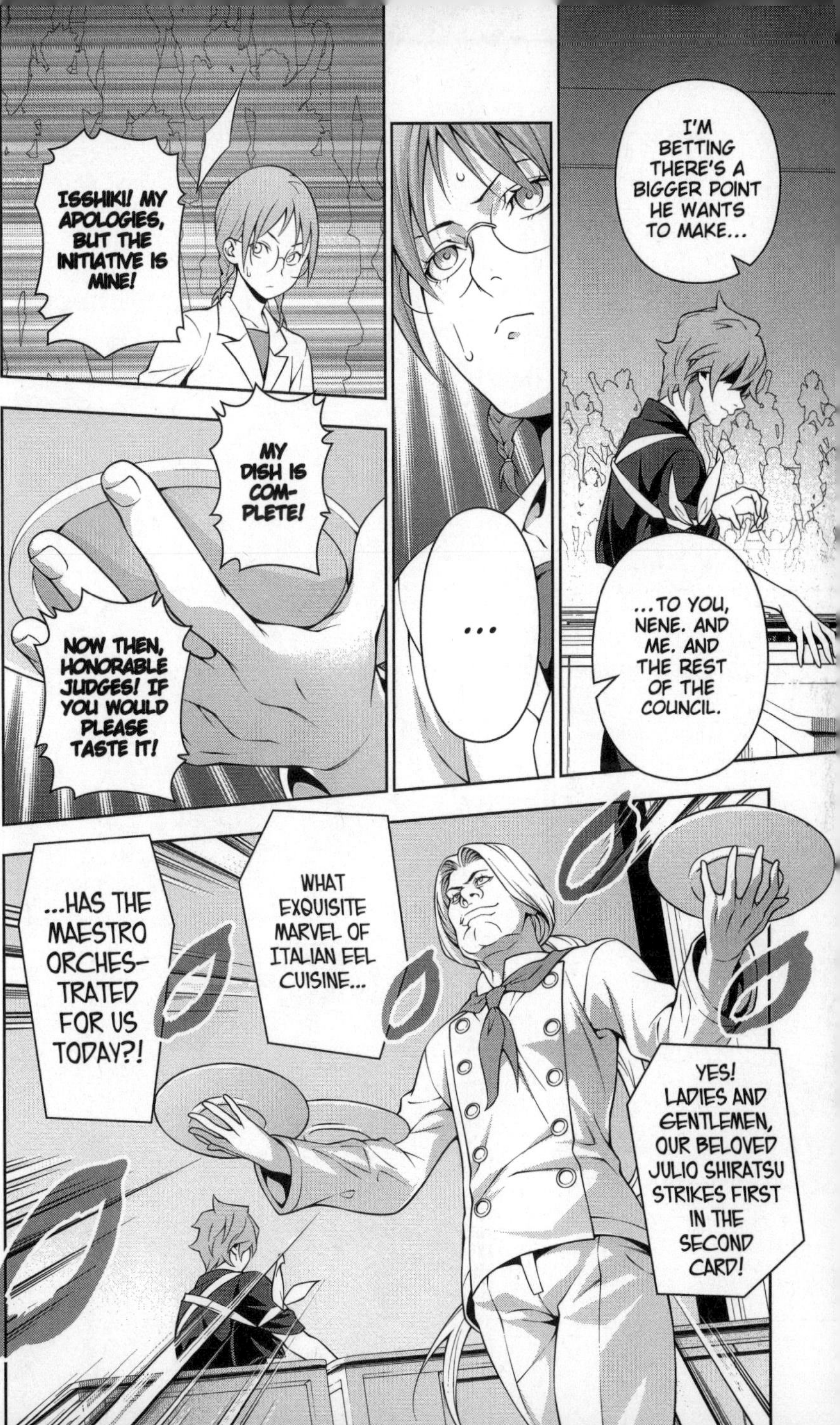
I'M BETTING THERE'S A BIGGER POINT HE WANTS TO MAKE...
...TO YOU, NENE. AND ME. AND THE REST OF THE COUNCIL.
...
ISSHIKI!! MY APOLOGIES, BUT THE INITIATIVE IS MINE!
MY DISH IS COM-PLETE!
NOW THEN, HONORABLE JUDGES! IF YOU WOULD PLEASE TASTE IT!
YES! LADIES AND GENTLEMEN, OUR BELOVED JULIO SHIRATSU STRIKES FIRST IN THE SECOND CARD!
WHAT EXQUISITE MARVEL OF ITALIAN EEL CUISINE...
...HAS THE MAESTRO ORCHES-TRATED FOR US TODAY?!

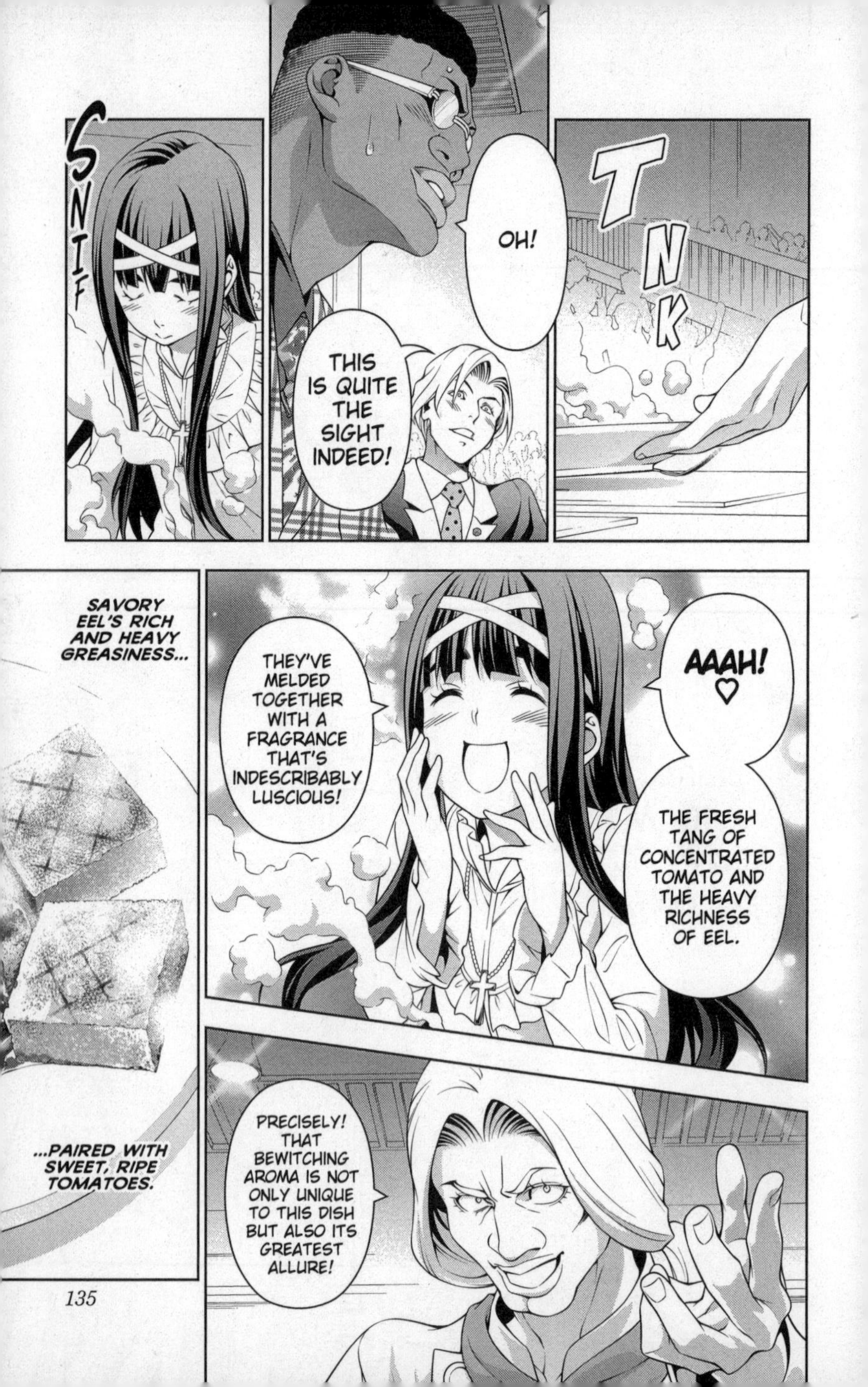
TNK
OH!
THIS IS QUITE THE SIGHT INDEED!
SNIFF
AAAH! ♡
THE FRESH TANG OF CONCENTRATED TOMATO AND THE HEAVY RICHNESS OF EEL.
THEY'VE MELDED TOGETHER WITH A FRAGRANCE THAT'S INDESCRIBABLY LUSCIOUS!
PRECISELY! THAT BEWITCHING AROMA IS NOT ONLY UNIQUE TO THIS DISH BUT ALSO ITS GREATEST ALLURE!
SAVORY EEL'S RICH AND HEAVY GREASINESS...
...PAIRED WITH SWEET, RIPE TOMATOES.

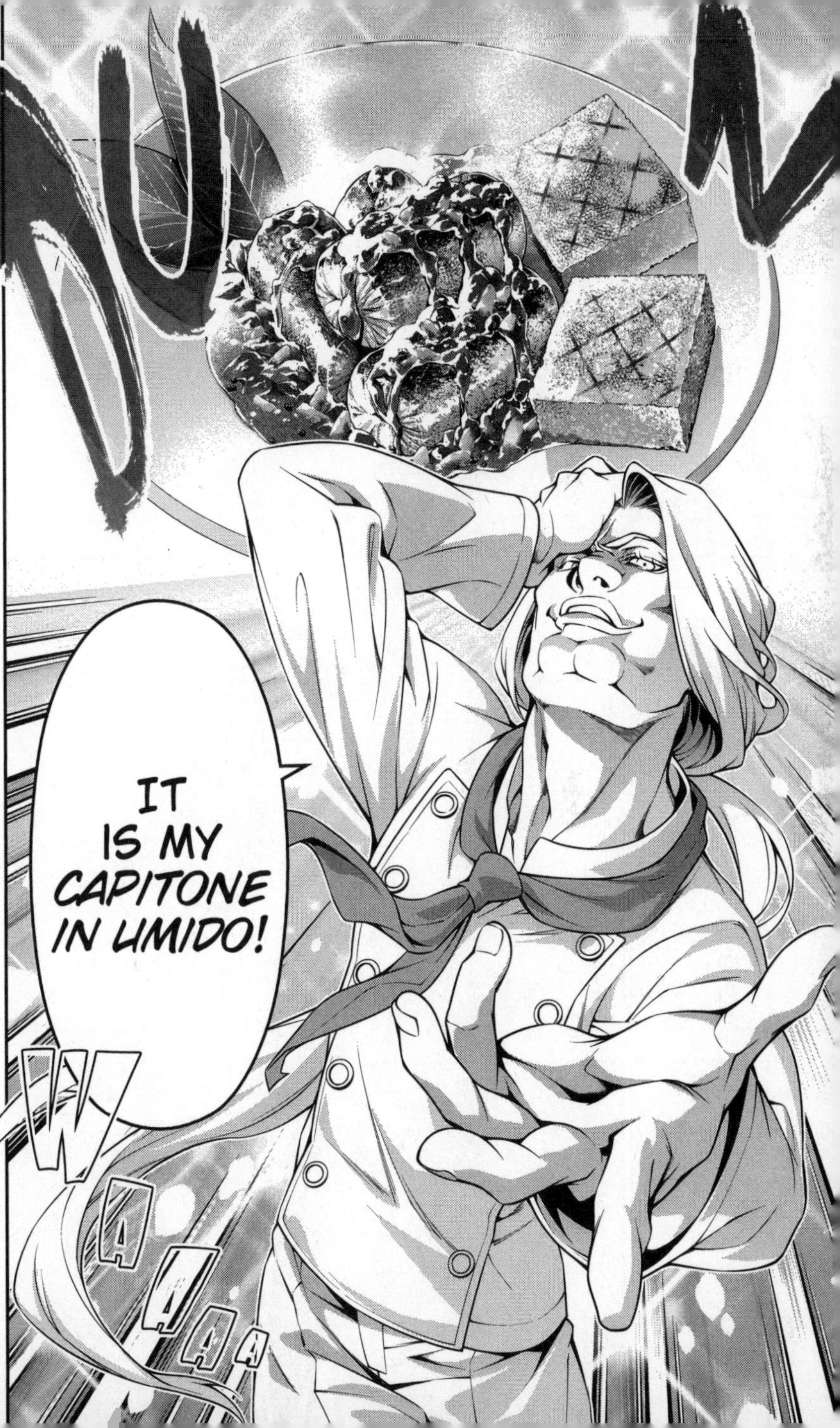
IT IS MY CAPITONE IN UMIDO!
WAAAAA

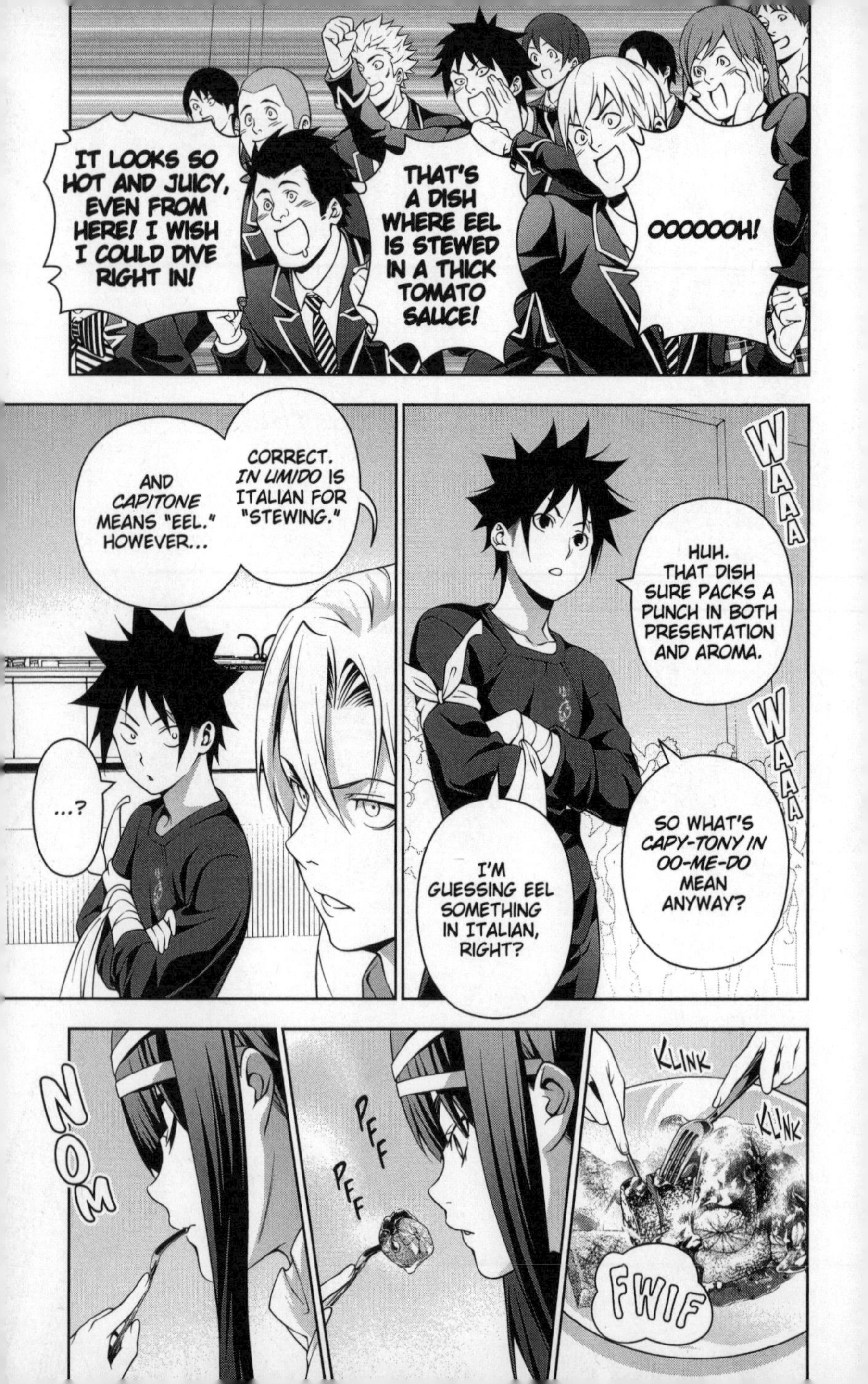
OOOOOOH!
THAT'S A DISH WHERE EEL IS STEWED IN A THICK TOMATO SAUCE!
IT LOOKS SO HOT AND JUICY, EVEN FROM HERE! I WISH I COULD DIVE RIGHT IN!
WAAAA
HUH. THAT DISH SURE PACKS A PUNCH IN BOTH PRESENTATION AND AROMA.
WAAAA
SO WHAT'S *CAPY-TONY IN OO-ME-DO* MEAN ANYWAY?
I'M GUESSING EEL SOMETHING IN ITALIAN, RIGHT?
CORRECT. *IN UMIDO* IS ITALIAN FOR "STEWING."
AND *CAPITONE* MEANS "EEL." HOWEVER...
...?
KLINK
KLINK
FWIF
PFF
PFF
NOM

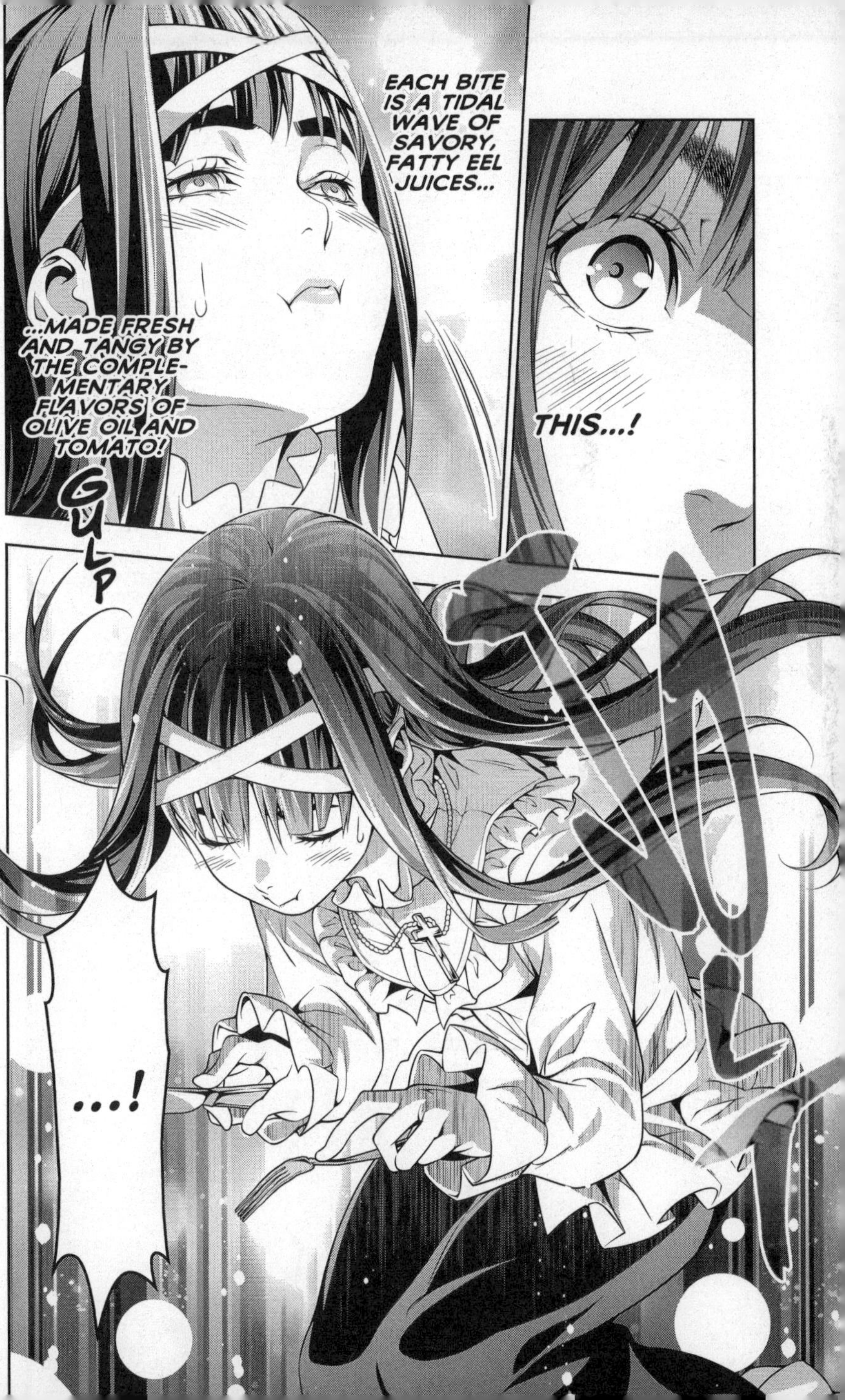
THIS...!
EACH BITE IS A TIDAL WAVE OF SAVORY, FATTY EEL JUICES...
...MADE FRESH AND TANGY BY THE COMPLE-MENTARY FLAVORS OF OLIVE OIL AND TOMATO!
GULP
...!

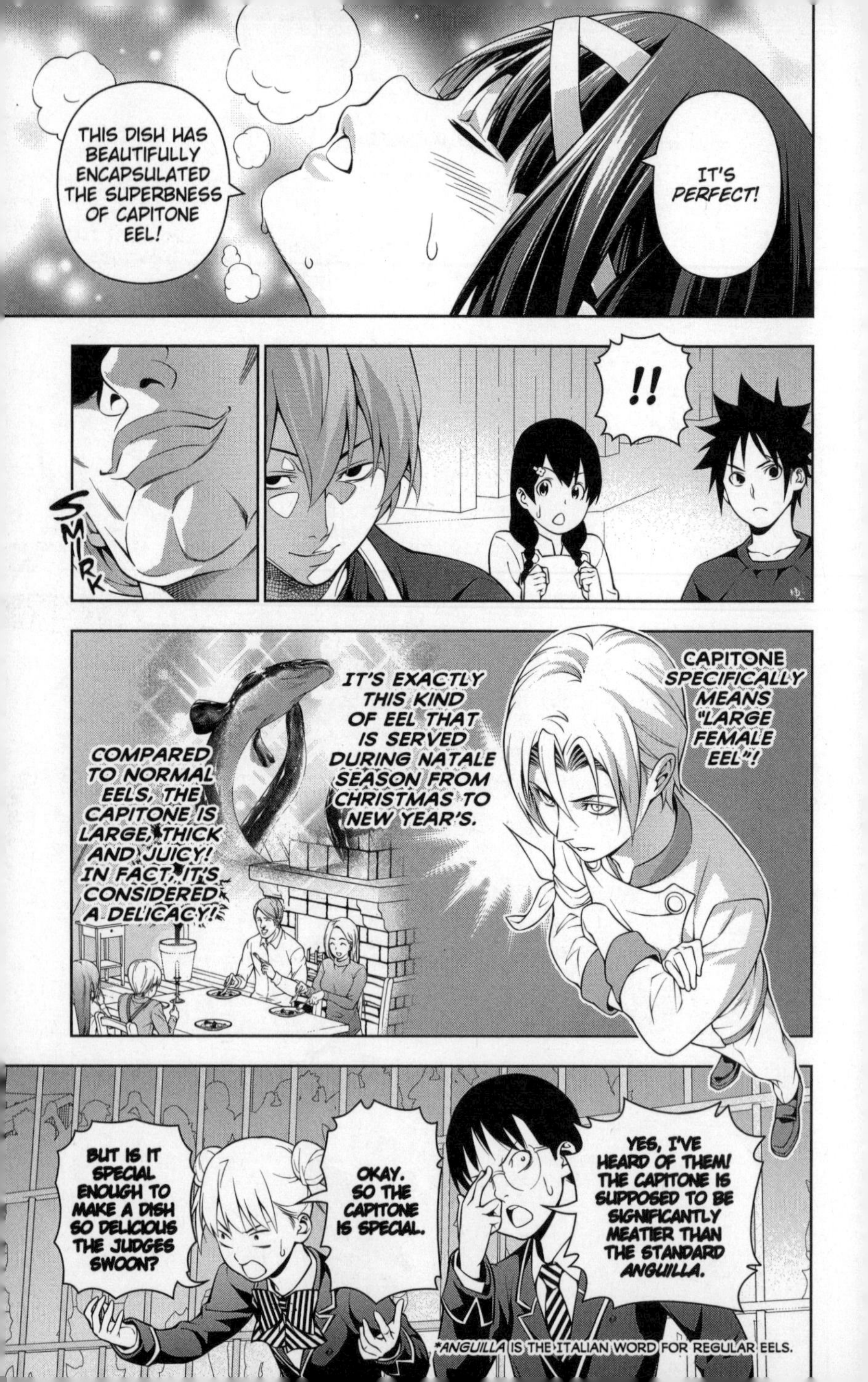
IT'S PERFECT!
THIS DISH HAS BEAUTIFULLY ENCAPSULATED THE SUPERBNESS OF CAPITONE EEL!
!!
SMIRK
CAPITONE SPECIFICALLY MEANS "LARGE FEMALE EEL"!
IT'S EXACTLY THIS KIND OF EEL THAT IS SERVED DURING NATALE SEASON FROM CHRISTMAS TO NEW YEAR'S.
COMPARED TO NORMAL EELS, THE CAPITONE IS LARGE, THICK AND JUICY! IN FACT, IT'S CONSIDERED A DELICACY!
YES, I'VE HEARD OF THEM! THE CAPITONE IS SUPPOSED TO BE SIGNIFICANTLY MEATIER THAN THE STANDARD ANGUILLA.
OKAY. SO THE CAPITONE IS SPECIAL.
BUT IS IT SPECIAL ENOUGH TO MAKE A DISH SO DELICIOUS THE JUDGES SWOON?
*ANGUILLA IS THE ITALIAN WORD FOR REGULAR EELS.

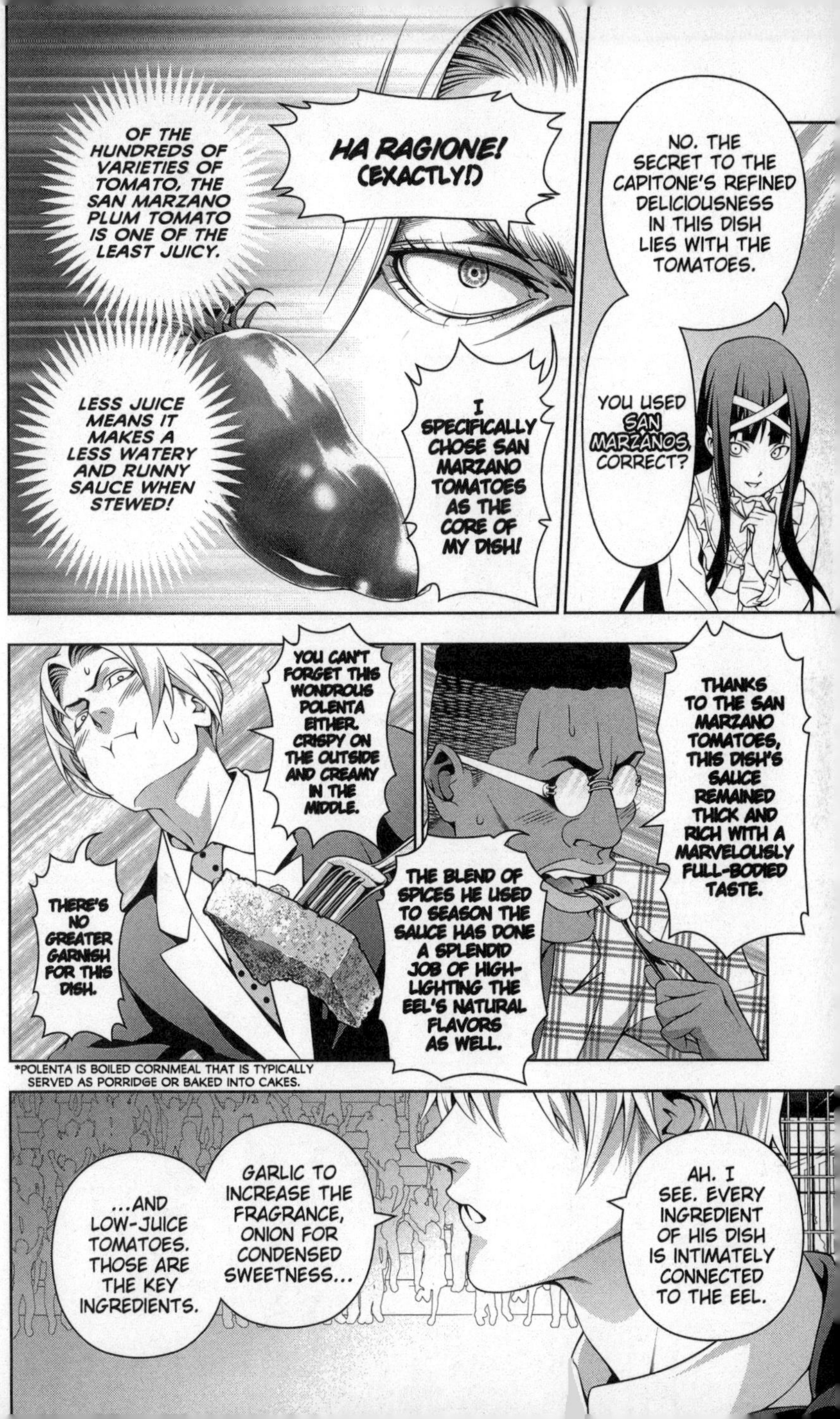
NO. THE SECRET TO THE CAPITONE'S REFINED DELICIOUSNESS IN THIS DISH LIES WITH THE TOMATOES.
YOU USED SAN MARZANOS, CORRECT?
HA RAGIONE! (EXACTLY!)
OF THE HUNDREDS OF VARIETIES OF TOMATO, THE SAN MARZANO PLUM TOMATO IS ONE OF THE LEAST JUICY.
I SPECIFICALLY CHOSE SAN MARZANO TOMATOES AS THE CORE OF MY DISH!
LESS JUICE MEANS IT MAKES A LESS WATERY AND RUNNY SAUCE WHEN STEWED!
THANKS TO THE SAN MARZANO TOMATOES, THIS DISH'S SAUCE REMAINED THICK AND RICH WITH A MARVELOUSLY FULL-BODIED TASTE.
THE BLEND OF SPICES HE USED TO SEASON THE SAUCE HAS DONE A SPLENDID JOB OF HIGH-LIGHTING THE EEL'S NATURAL FLAVORS AS WELL.
YOU CAN'T FORGET THIS WONDROUS POLENTA EITHER. CRISPY ON THE OUTSIDE AND CREAMY IN THE MIDDLE.
THERE'S NO GREATER GARNISH FOR THIS DISH.
AH. I SEE. EVERY INGREDIENT OF HIS DISH IS INTIMATELY CONNECTED TO THE EEL.
GARLIC TO INCREASE THE FRAGRANCE, ONION FOR CONDENSED SWEETNESS...
...AND LOW-JUICE TOMATOES. THOSE ARE THE KEY INGREDIENTS.

*POLENTA IS BOILED CORNMEAL THAT IS TYPICALLY SERVED AS PORRIDGE OR BAKED INTO CAKES.

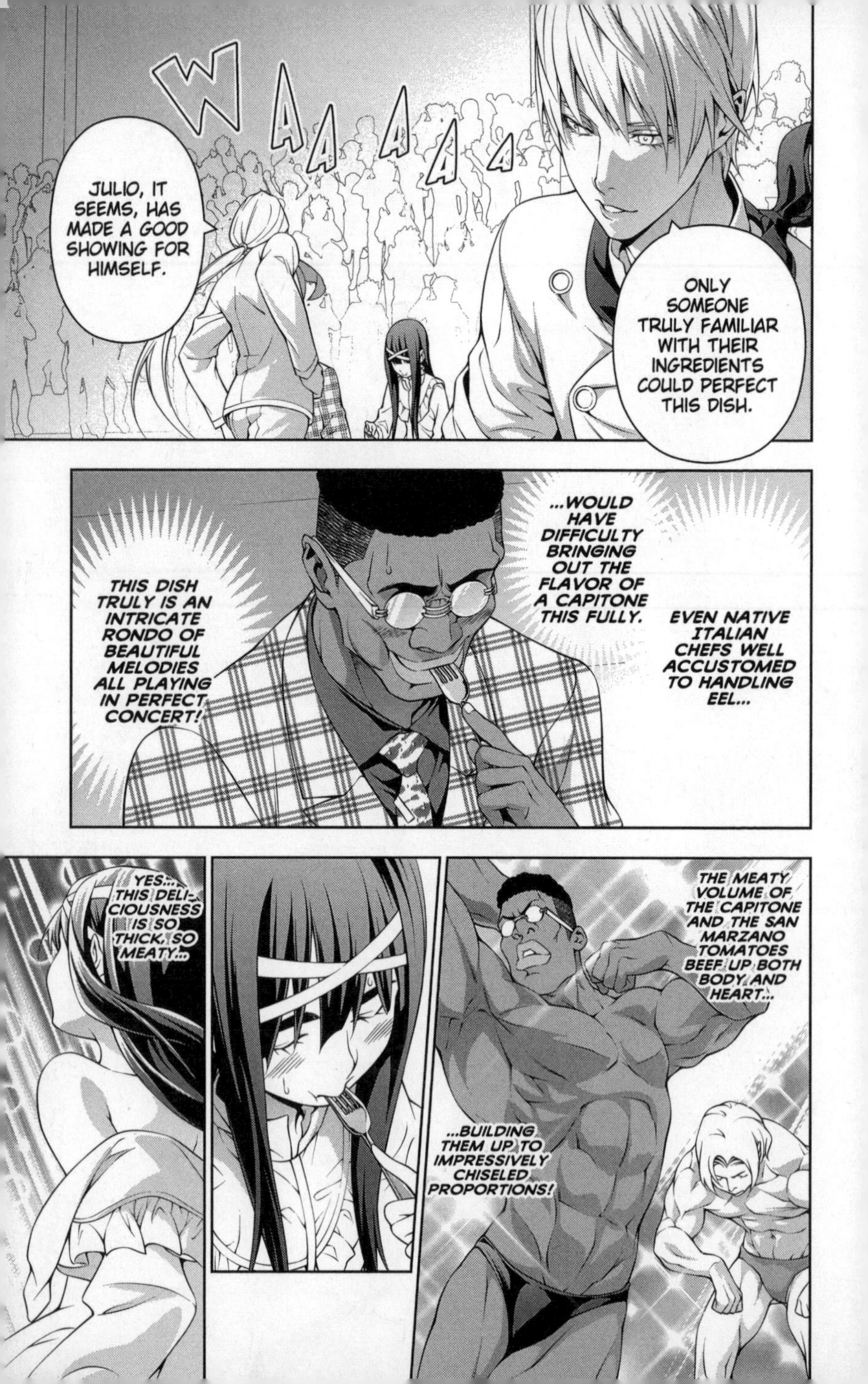
WAAAAAA
JULIO, IT SEEMS, HAS MADE A GOOD SHOWING FOR HIMSELF.
ONLY SOMEONE TRULY FAMILIAR WITH THEIR INGREDIENTS COULD PERFECT THIS DISH.
EVEN NATIVE ITALIAN CHEFS WELL ACCUSTOMED TO HANDLING EEL...
...WOULD HAVE DIFFICULTY BRINGING OUT THE FLAVOR OF A CAPITONE THIS FULLY.
THIS DISH TRULY IS AN INTRICATE RONDO OF BEAUTIFUL MELODIES ALL PLAYING IN PERFECT CONCERT!
THE MEATY VOLUME OF THE CAPITONE AND THE SAN MARZANO TOMATOES BEEF UP BOTH BODY AND HEART...
...BUILDING THEM UP TO IMPRESSIVELY CHISELED PROPORTIONS!
YES... THIS DELI-CIOUSNESS IS SO THICK, SO MEATY...

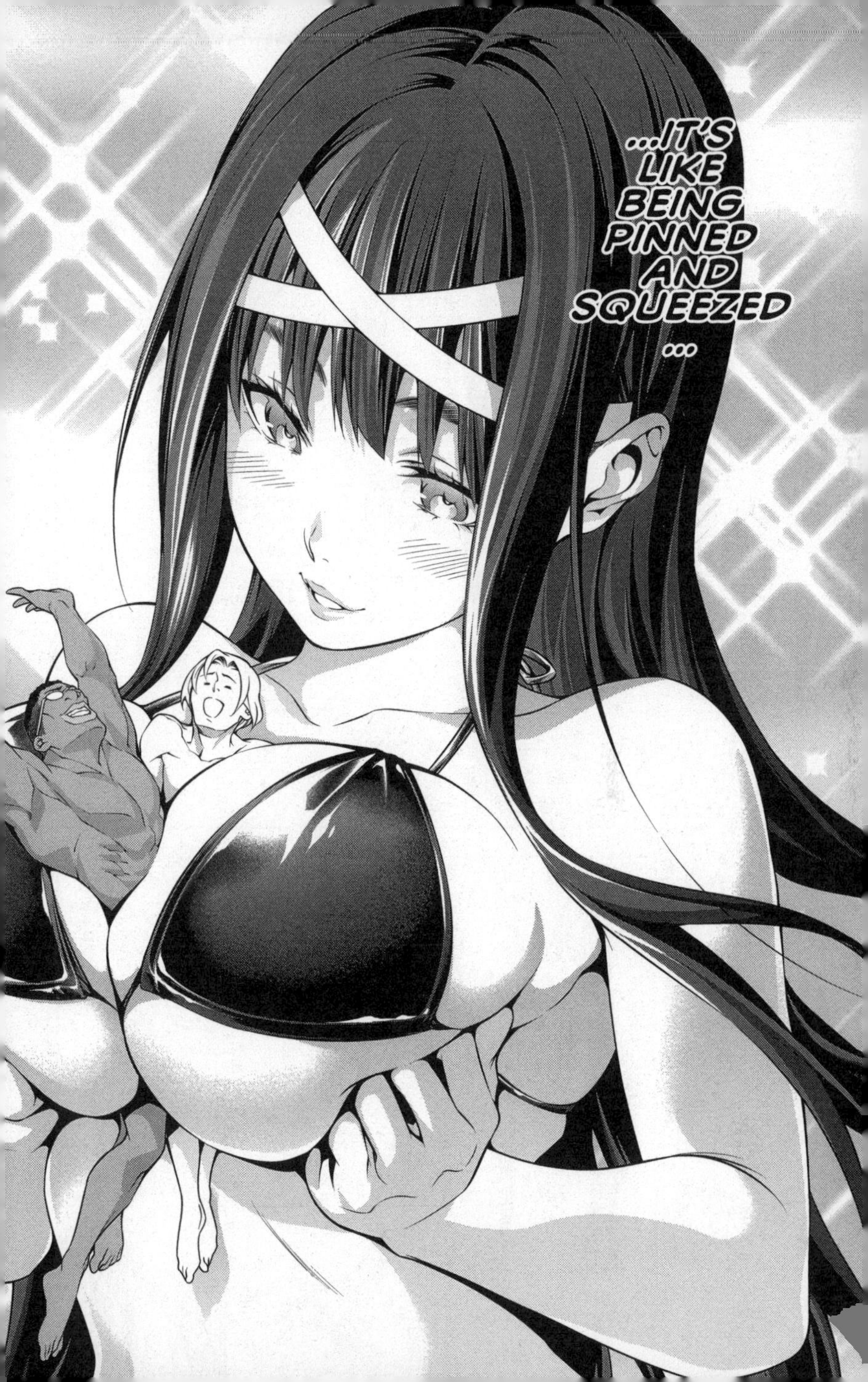
...IT'S LIKE BEING PINNED AND SQUEEZED ...

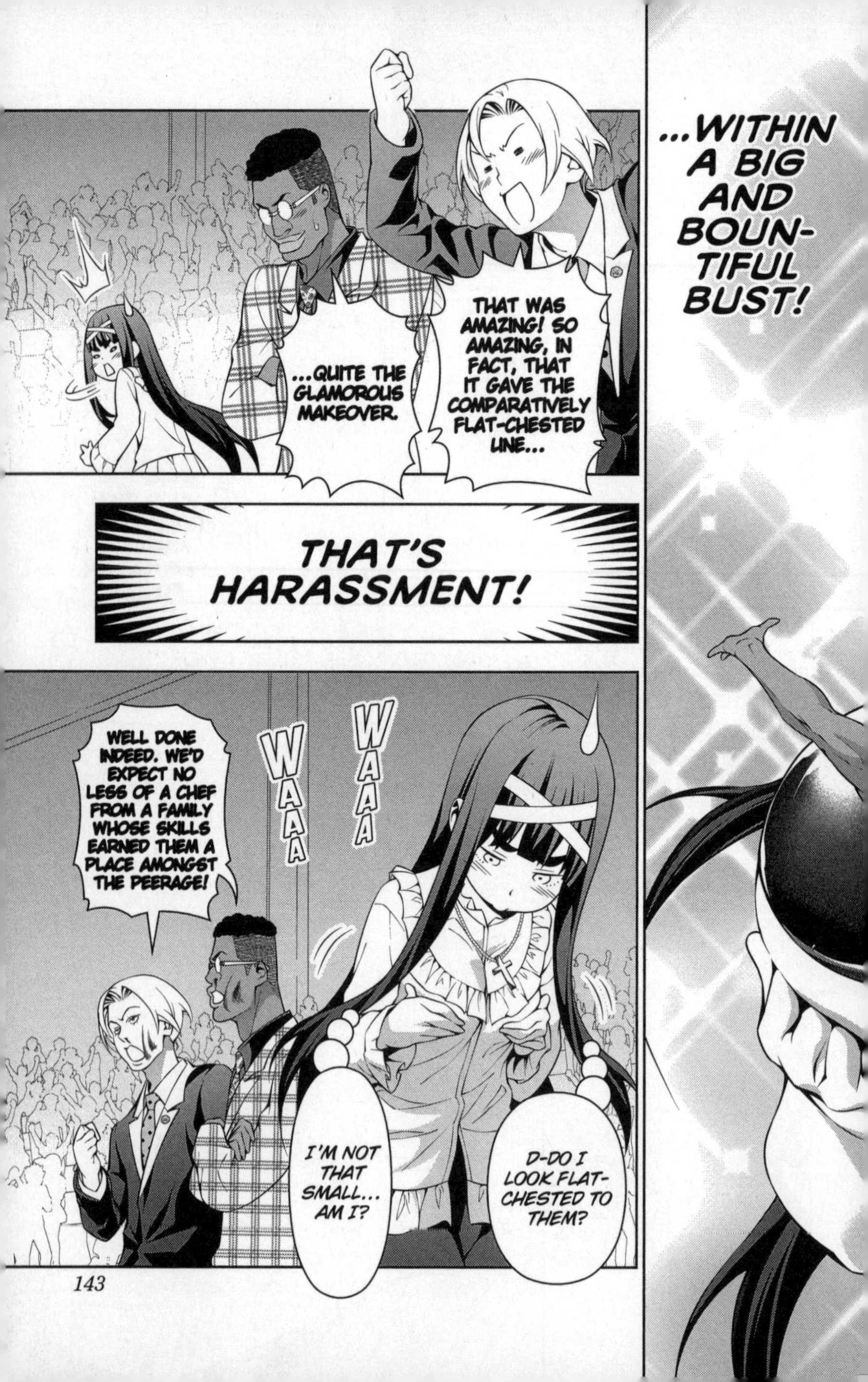
...WITHIN A BIG AND BOUN-TIFUL BUST!
THAT WAS AMAZING! SO AMAZING, IN FACT, THAT IT GAVE THE COMPARATIVELY FLAT-CHESTED LINE...
...QUITE THE GLAMOROUS MAKEOVER.
THAT'S HARASSMENT!
WAAAA
WAAAA
WELL DONE INDEED. WE'D EXPECT NO LESS OF A CHEF FROM A FAMILY WHOSE SKILLS EARNED THEM A PLACE AMONGST THE PEERAGE!
D-DO I LOOK FLAT-CHESTED TO THEM?
I'M NOT THAT SMALL... AM I?

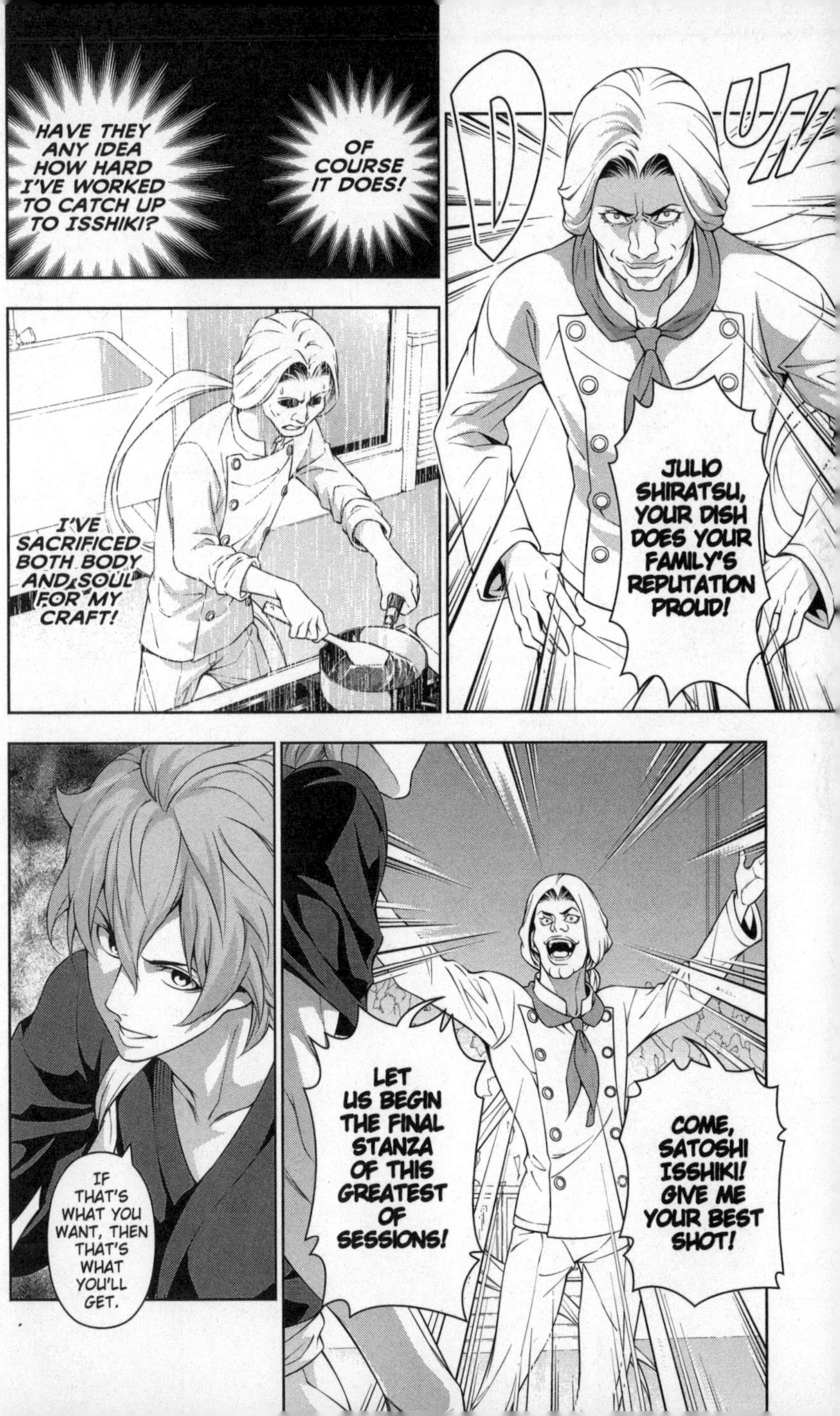
D-UN
JULIO SHIRATSU, YOUR DISH DOES YOUR FAMILY'S REPUTATION PROUD!
OF COURSE IT DOES!
HAVE THEY ANY IDEA HOW HARD I'VE WORKED TO CATCH UP TO ISSHIKI?
I'VE SACRIFICED BOTH BODY AND SOUL FOR MY CRAFT!
COME, SATOSHI ISSHIKI! GIVE ME YOUR BEST SHOT!
LET US BEGIN THE FINAL STANZA OF THIS GREATEST OF SESSIONS!
IF THAT'S WHAT YOU WANT, THEN THAT'S WHAT YOU'LL GET.

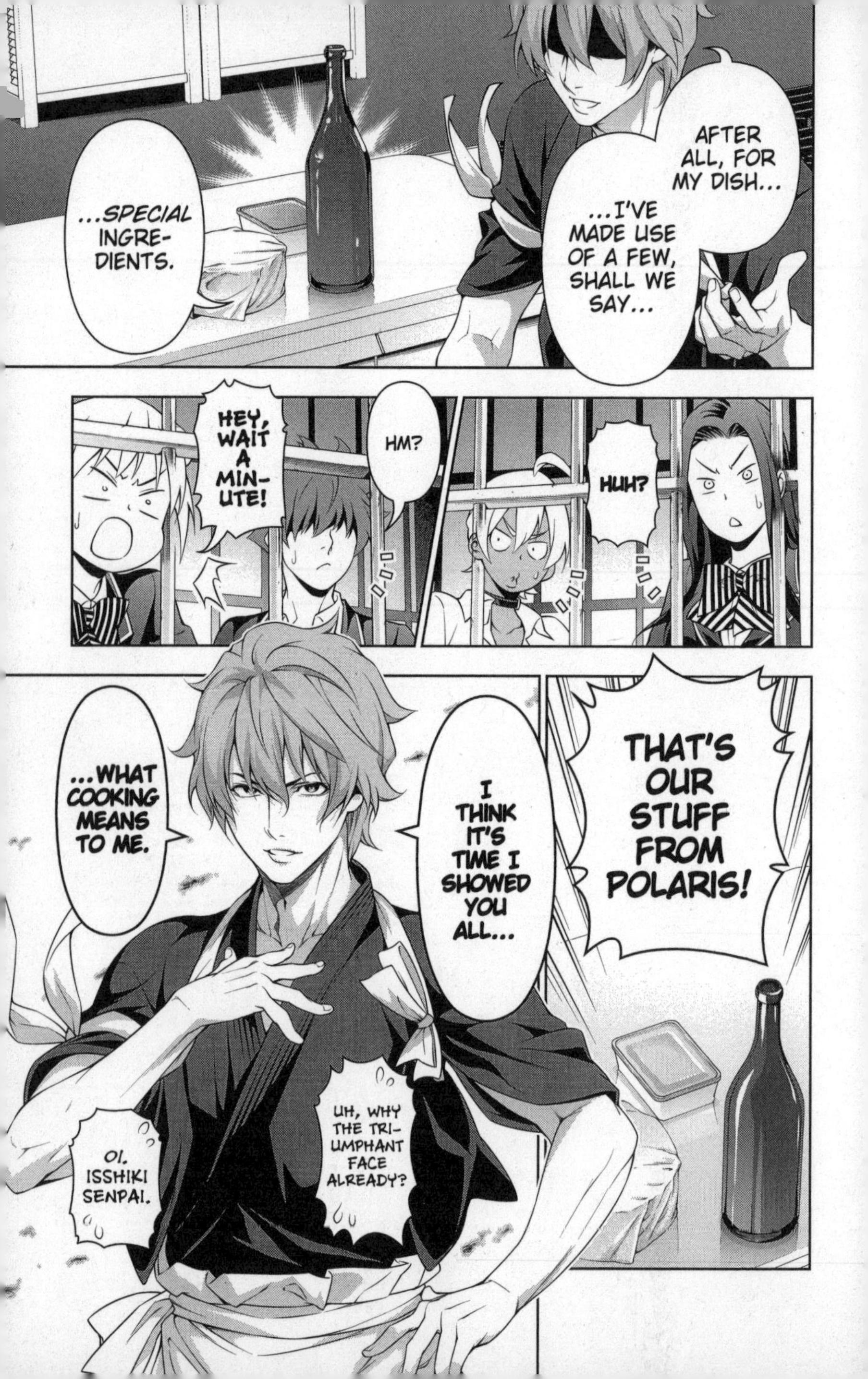
AFTER ALL, FOR MY DISH...
...I'VE MADE USE OF A FEW, SHALL WE SAY...
...SPECIAL INGRE-DIENTS.
HUH?
HM?
HEY, WAIT A MIN-UTE!
THAT'S OUR STUFF FROM POLARIS!
I THINK IT'S TIME I SHOWED YOU ALL...
...WHAT COOKING MEANS TO ME.
UH, WHY THE TRI-UMPHANT FACE ALREADY?
OI. ISSHIKI SENPAI.

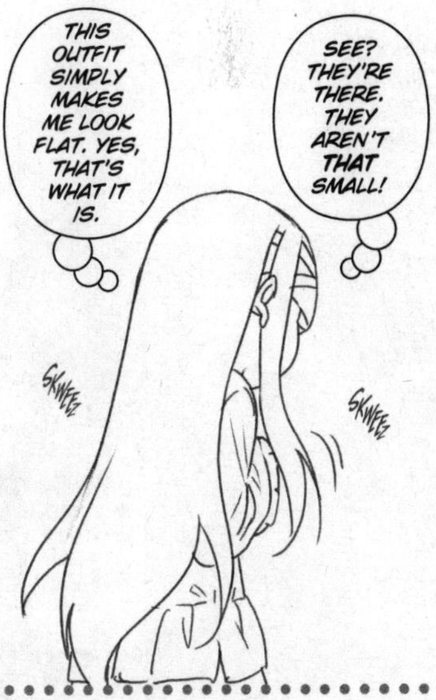
SEE? THEY'RE THERE. THEY AREN'T THAT SMALL!
THIS OUTFIT SIMPLY MAKES ME LOOK FLAT. YES, THAT'S WHAT IT IS.
SKWEEZ
SKWEEZ

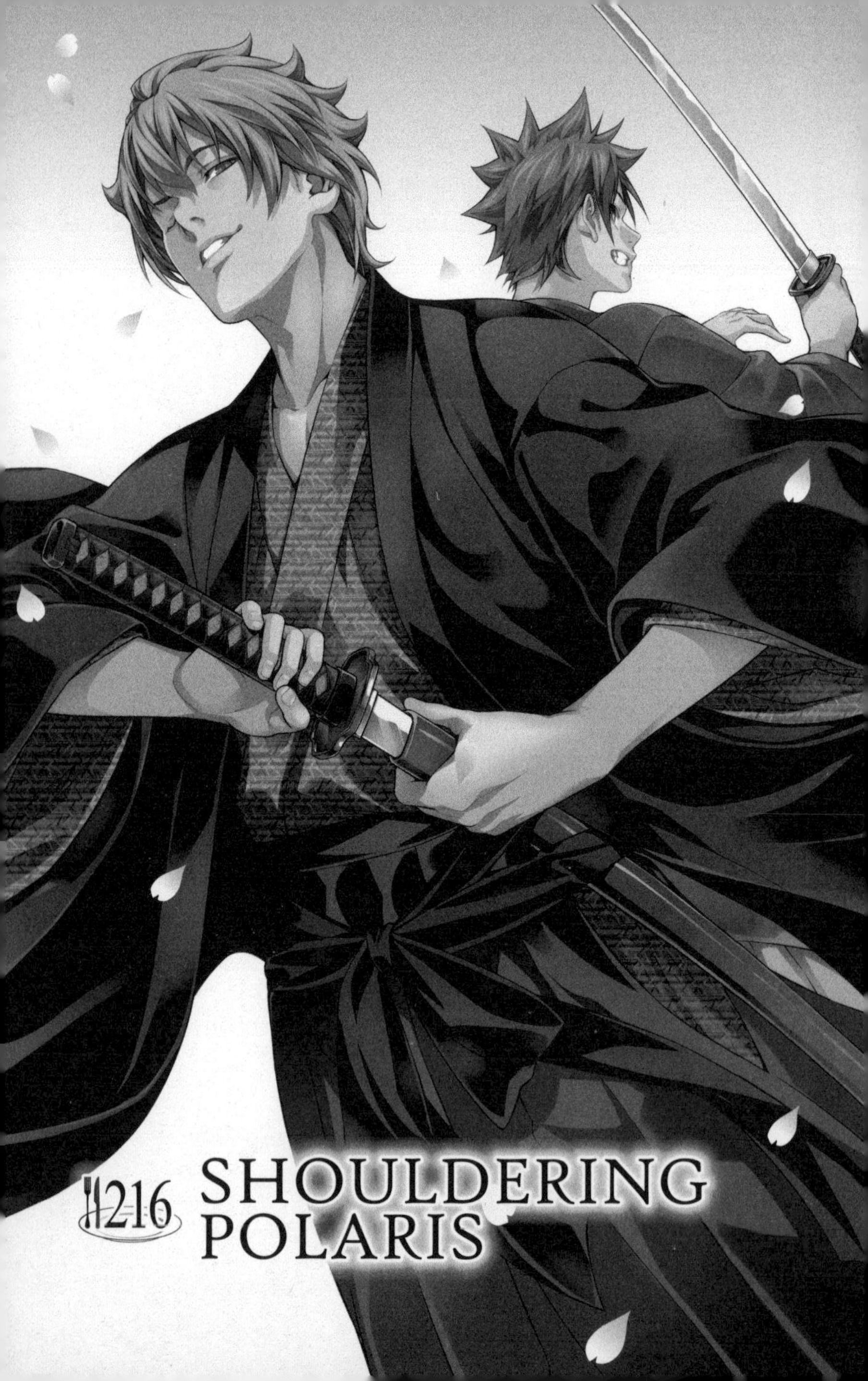
216
SHOULDERING
POLARIS

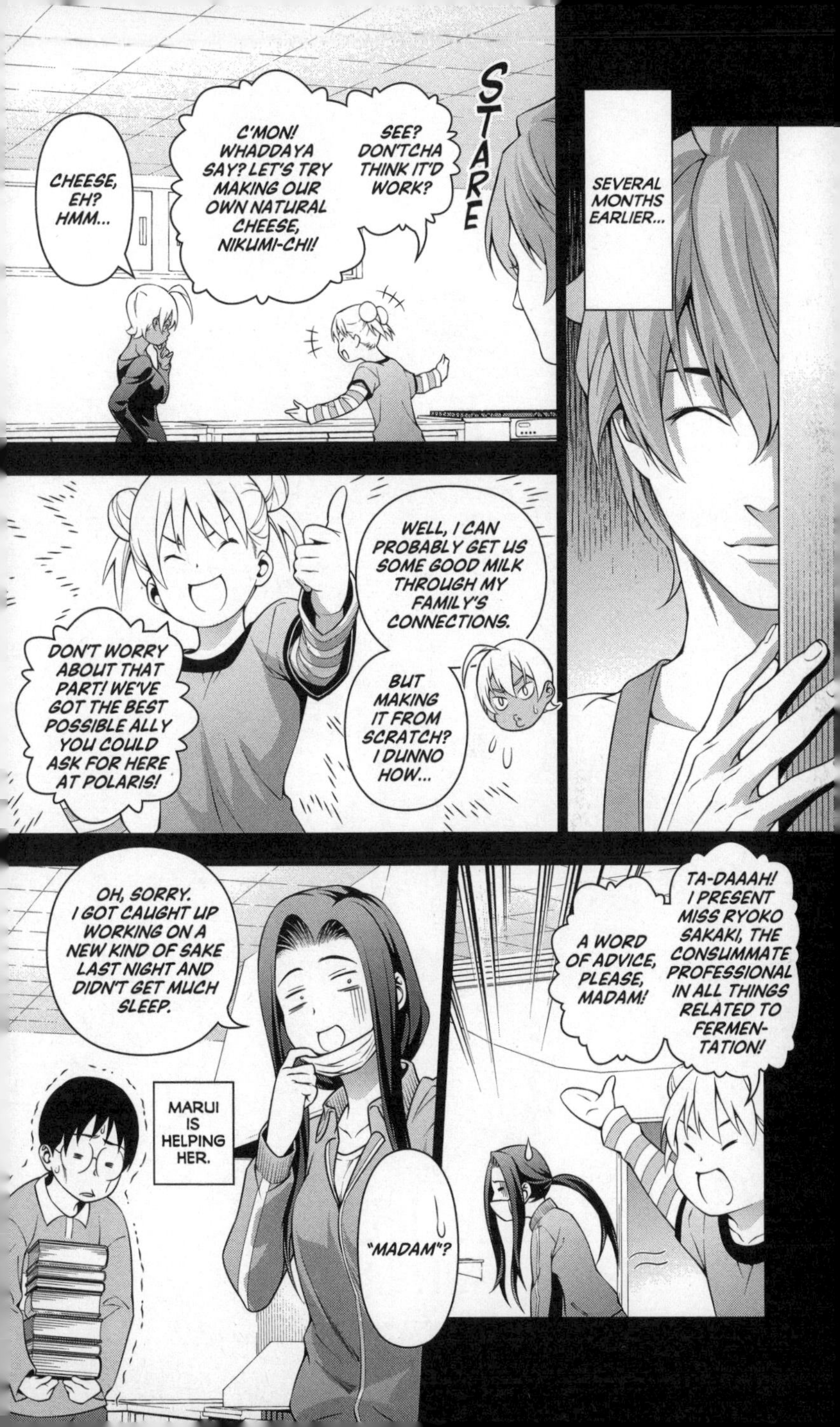
SEVERAL MONTHS EARLIER...
STARE
C'MON! WHADDAYA SAY? LET'S TRY MAKING OUR OWN NATURAL CHEESE, NIKUMI-CHI!
SEE? DON'TCHA THINK IT'D WORK?
CHEESE, EH? HMM...
WELL, I CAN PROBABLY GET US SOME GOOD MILK THROUGH MY FAMILY'S CONNECTIONS.
BUT MAKING IT FROM SCRATCH? I DUNNO HOW...
DON'T WORRY ABOUT THAT PART! WE'VE GOT THE BEST POSSIBLE ALLY YOU COULD ASK FOR HERE AT POLARIS!
TA-DAAAH! I PRESENT MISS RYOKO SAKAKI, THE CONSUMMATE PROFESSIONAL IN ALL THINGS RELATED TO FERMENTATION!
A WORD OF ADVICE, PLEASE, MADAM!
"MADAM"?
OH, SORRY. I GOT CAUGHT UP WORKING ON A NEW KIND OF SAKE LAST NIGHT AND DIDN'T GET MUCH SLEEP.
MARUI IS HELPING HER.

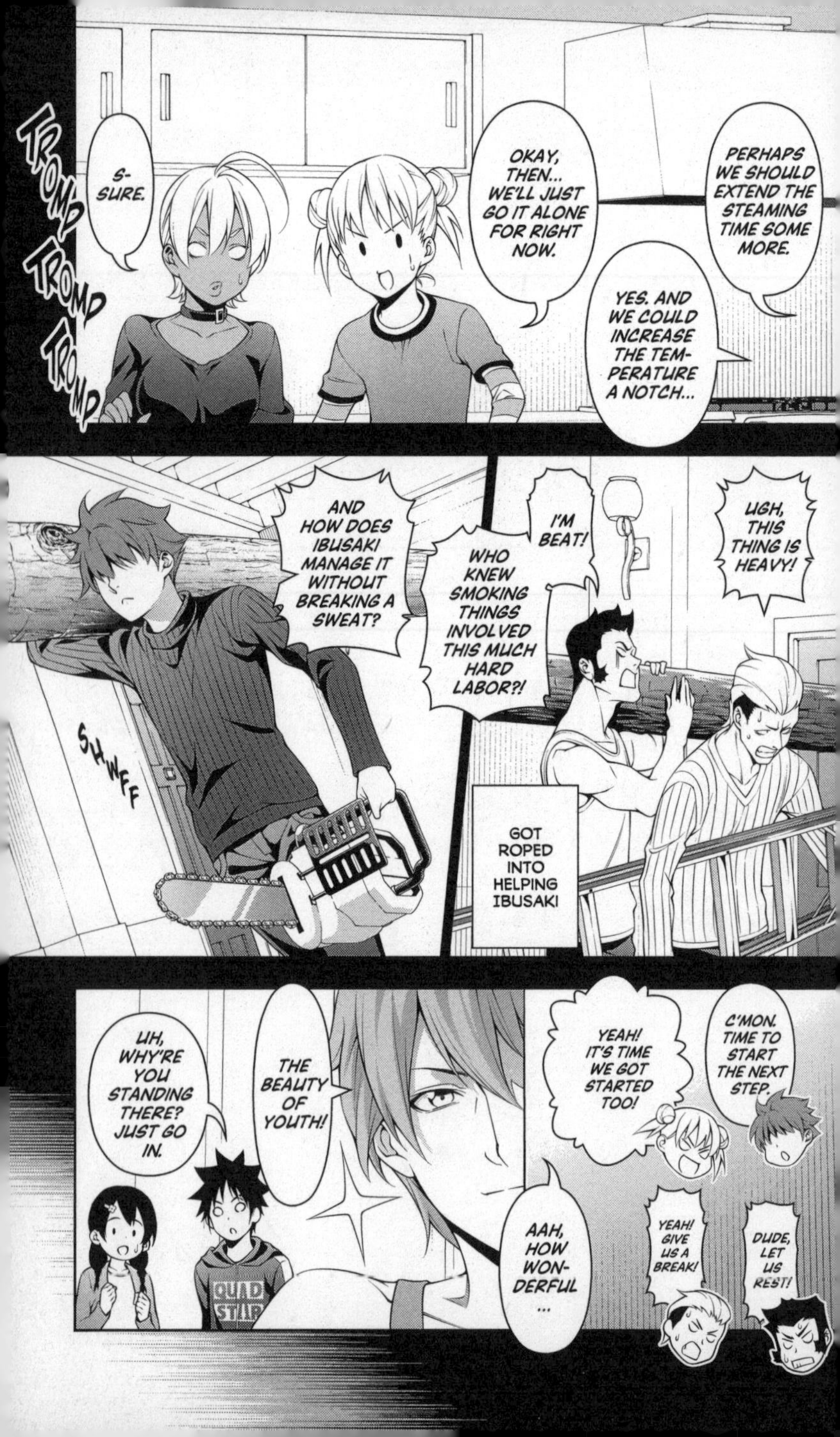
PERHAPS WE SHOULD EXTEND THE STEAMING TIME SOME MORE.
YES. AND WE COULD INCREASE THE TEM-PERATURE A NOTCH...
OKAY, THEN... WE'LL JUST GO IT ALONE FOR RIGHT NOW.
S-SURE.
TROMP TROMP TROMP TROMP
UGH, THIS THING IS HEAVY!
I'M BEAT!
WHO KNEW SMOKING THINGS INVOLVED THIS MUCH HARD LABOR?!
GOT ROPED INTO HELPING IBUSAKI
AND HOW DOES IBUSAKI MANAGE IT WITHOUT BREAKING A SWEAT?
SHWFF
C'MON. TIME TO START THE NEXT STEP.
YEAH! IT'S TIME WE GOT STARTED TOO!
DUDE, LET US REST!
YEAH! GIVE US A BREAK!
AAH, HOW WON-DERFUL ...
THE BEAUTY OF YOUTH!
UH, WHY'RE YOU STANDING THERE? JUST GO IN.

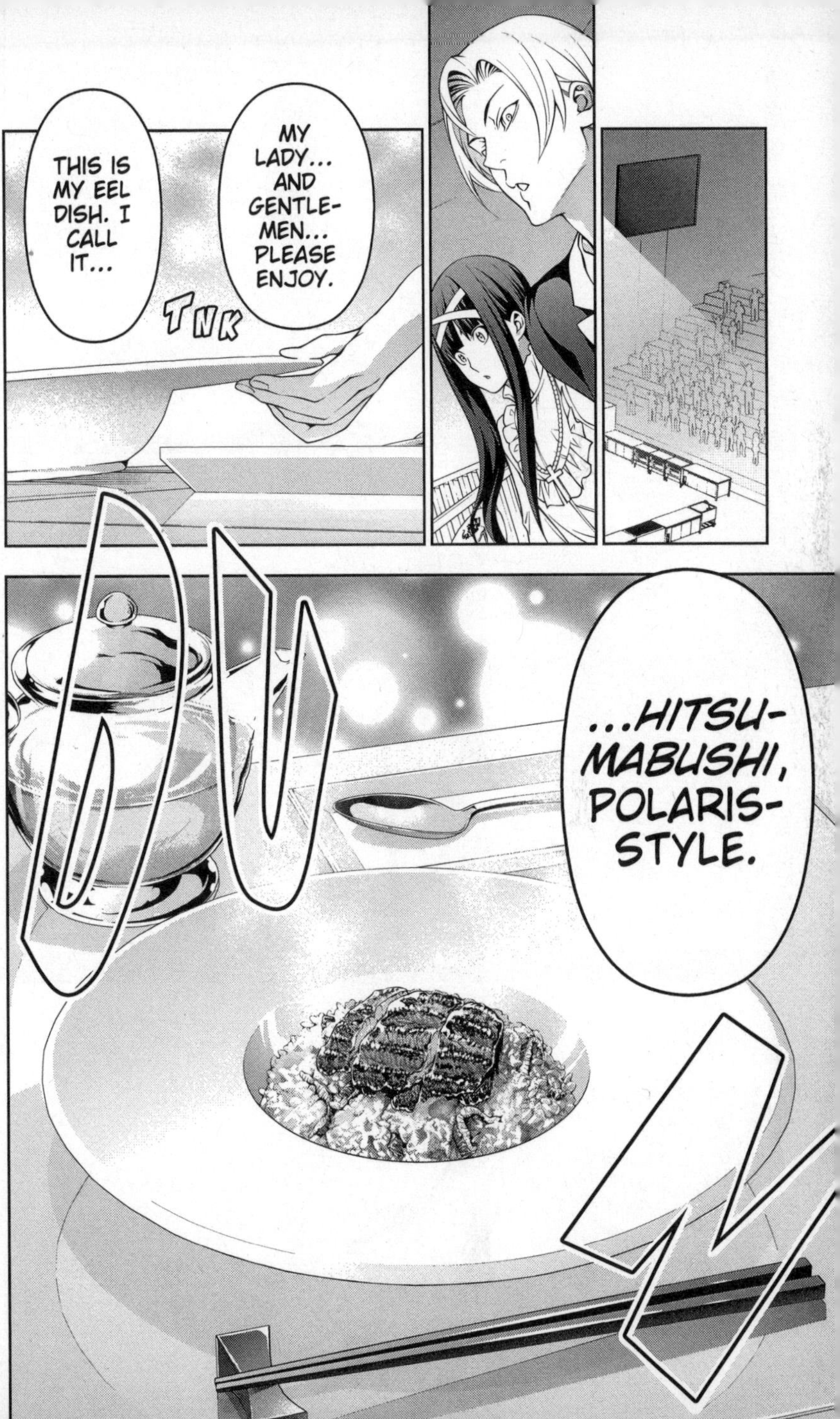
MY LADY... AND GENTLE-MEN... PLEASE ENJOY.
THIS IS MY EEL DISH. I CALL IT...
TNK
...HITSU-MABUSHI, POLARIS-STYLE.

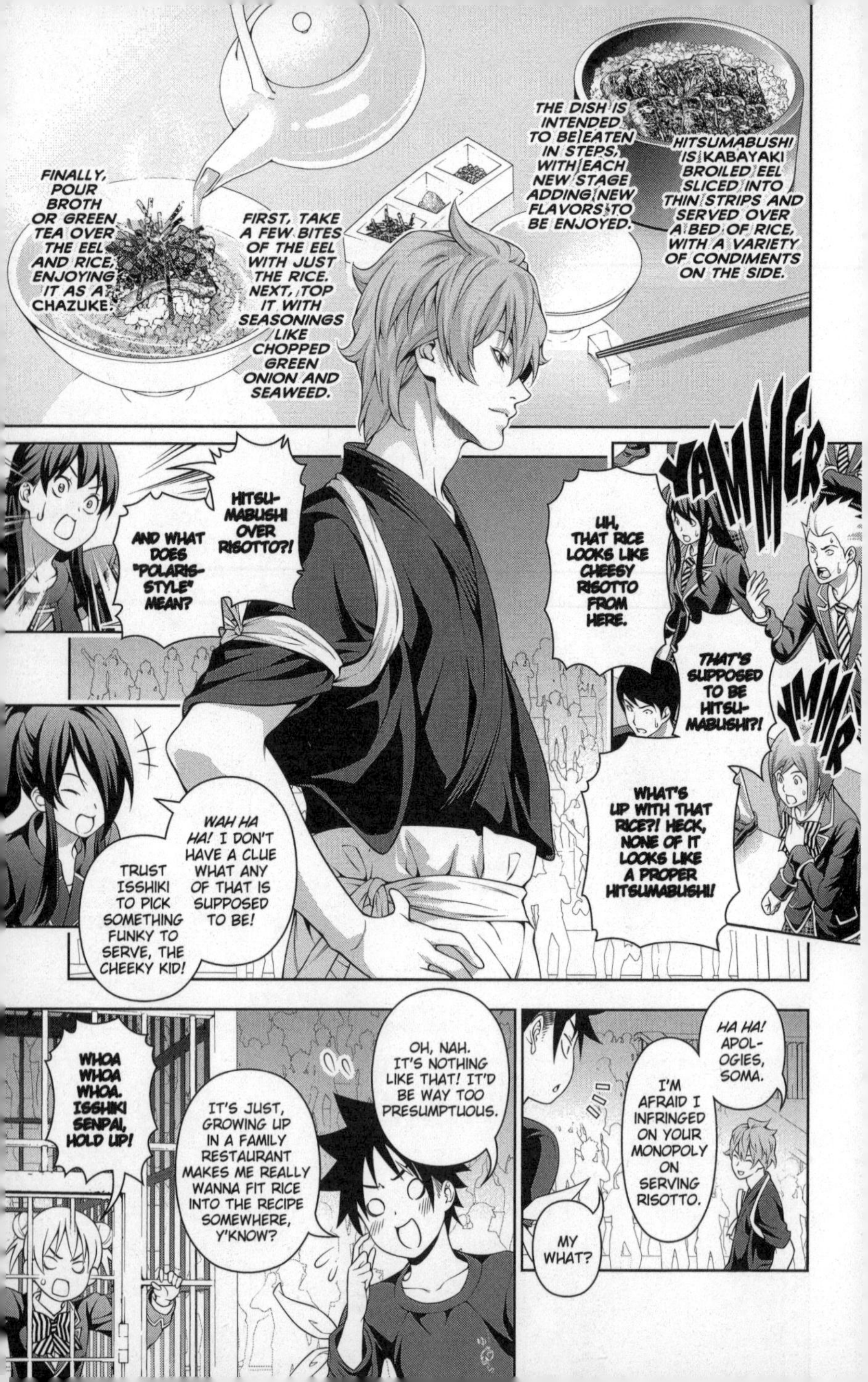
HITSUMABUSHI IS KABAYAKI BROILED EEL SLICED INTO THIN STRIPS AND SERVED OVER A BED OF RICE, WITH A VARIETY OF CONDIMENTS ON THE SIDE.
THE DISH IS INTENDED TO BE EATEN IN STEPS, WITH EACH NEW STAGE ADDING NEW FLAVORS TO BE ENJOYED.
FIRST, TAKE A FEW BITES OF THE EEL WITH JUST THE RICE. NEXT, TOP IT WITH SEASONINGS LIKE CHOPPED GREEN ONION AND SEAWEED.
FINALLY, POUR BROTH OR GREEN TEA OVER THE EEL AND RICE, ENJOYING IT AS A CHAZUKE.
YAMMER
UH, THAT RICE LOOKS LIKE CHEESY RISOTTO FROM HERE.
THAT'S SUPPOSED TO BE HITSU-MABUSHI?!
YMMR
WHAT'S UP WITH THAT RICE?! HECK, NONE OF IT LOOKS LIKE A PROPER HITSUMABUSHI!
HITSU-MABUSHI OVER RISOTTO?!
AND WHAT DOES "POLARIS-STYLE" MEAN?
WAH HA HA! I DON'T HAVE A CLUE WHAT ANY OF THAT IS SUPPOSED TO BE!
TRUST ISSHIKI TO PICK SOMETHING FUNKY TO SERVE, THE CHEEKY KID!
HA HA! APOLOGIES, SOMA.
I'M AFRAID I INFRINGED ON YOUR MONOPOLY ON SERVING RISOTTO.
MY WHAT?
OH, NAH. IT'S NOTHING LIKE THAT! IT'D BE WAY TOO PRESUMPTUOUS.
IT'S JUST, GROWING UP IN A FAMILY RESTAURANT MAKES ME REALLY WANNA FIT RICE INTO THE RECIPE SOMEWHERE, Y'KNOW?
WHOA WHOA WHOA. ISSHIKI SENPAI, HOLD UP!

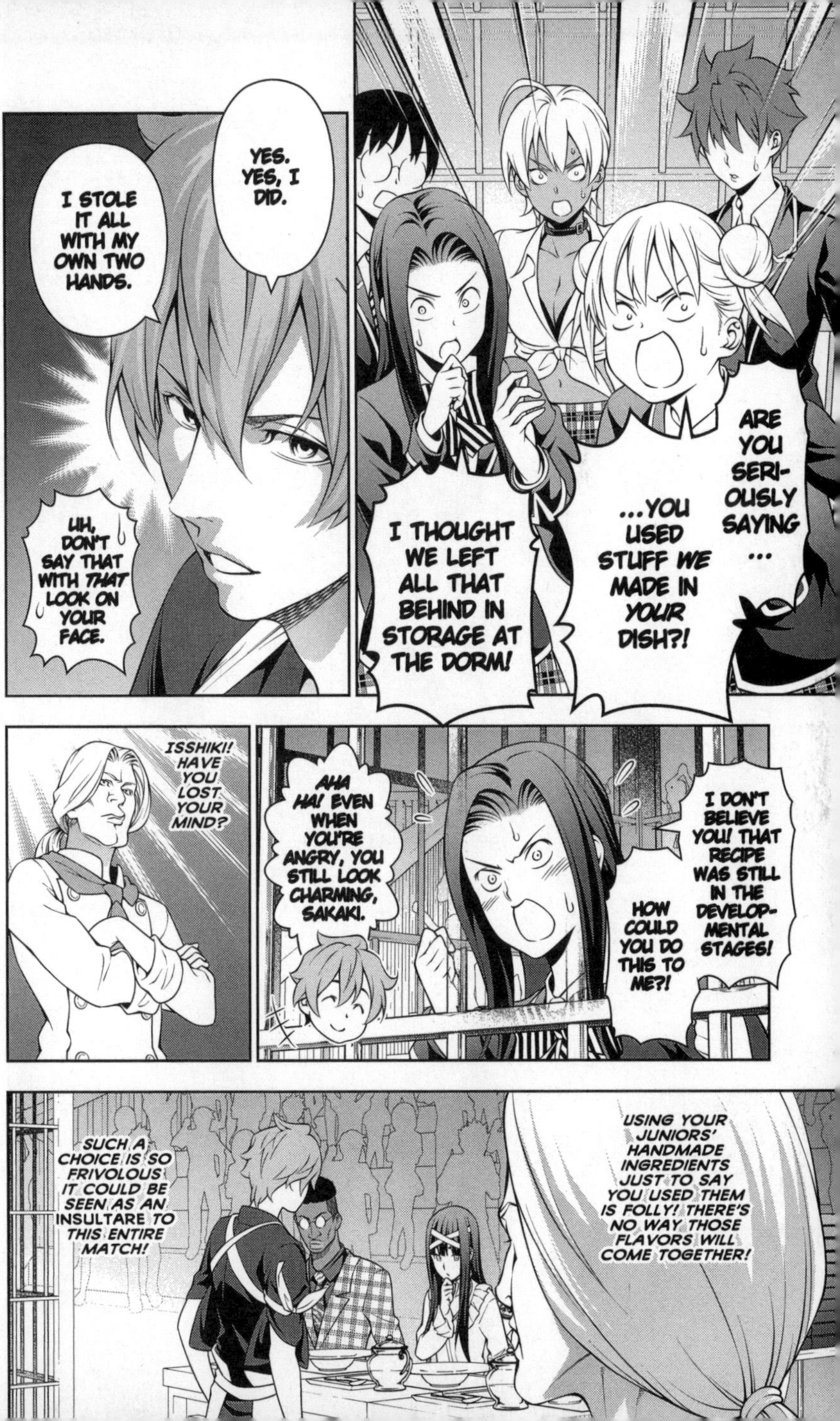
ARE YOU SERI-OUSLY SAYING...
...YOU USED STUFF WE MADE IN YOUR DISH?!
I THOUGHT WE LEFT ALL THAT BEHIND IN STORAGE AT THE DORM!
YES. YES, I DID.
I STOLE IT ALL WITH MY OWN TWO HANDS.
UH, DON'T SAY THAT WITH THAT LOOK ON YOUR FACE.
I DON'T BELIEVE YOU! THAT RECIPE WAS STILL IN THE DEVELOP-MENTAL STAGES!
HOW COULD YOU DO THIS TO ME?!
AHA HA! EVEN WHEN YOU'RE ANGRY, YOU STILL LOOK CHARMING, SAKAKI.
ISSHIKI! HAVE YOU LOST YOUR MIND?
USING YOUR JUNIORS' HANDMADE INGREDIENTS JUST TO SAY YOU USED THEM IS FOLLY! THERE'S NO WAY THOSE FLAVORS WILL COME TOGETHER!
SUCH A CHOICE IS SO FRIVOLOUS IT COULD BE SEEN AS AN INSULTARE TO THIS ENTIRE MATCH!

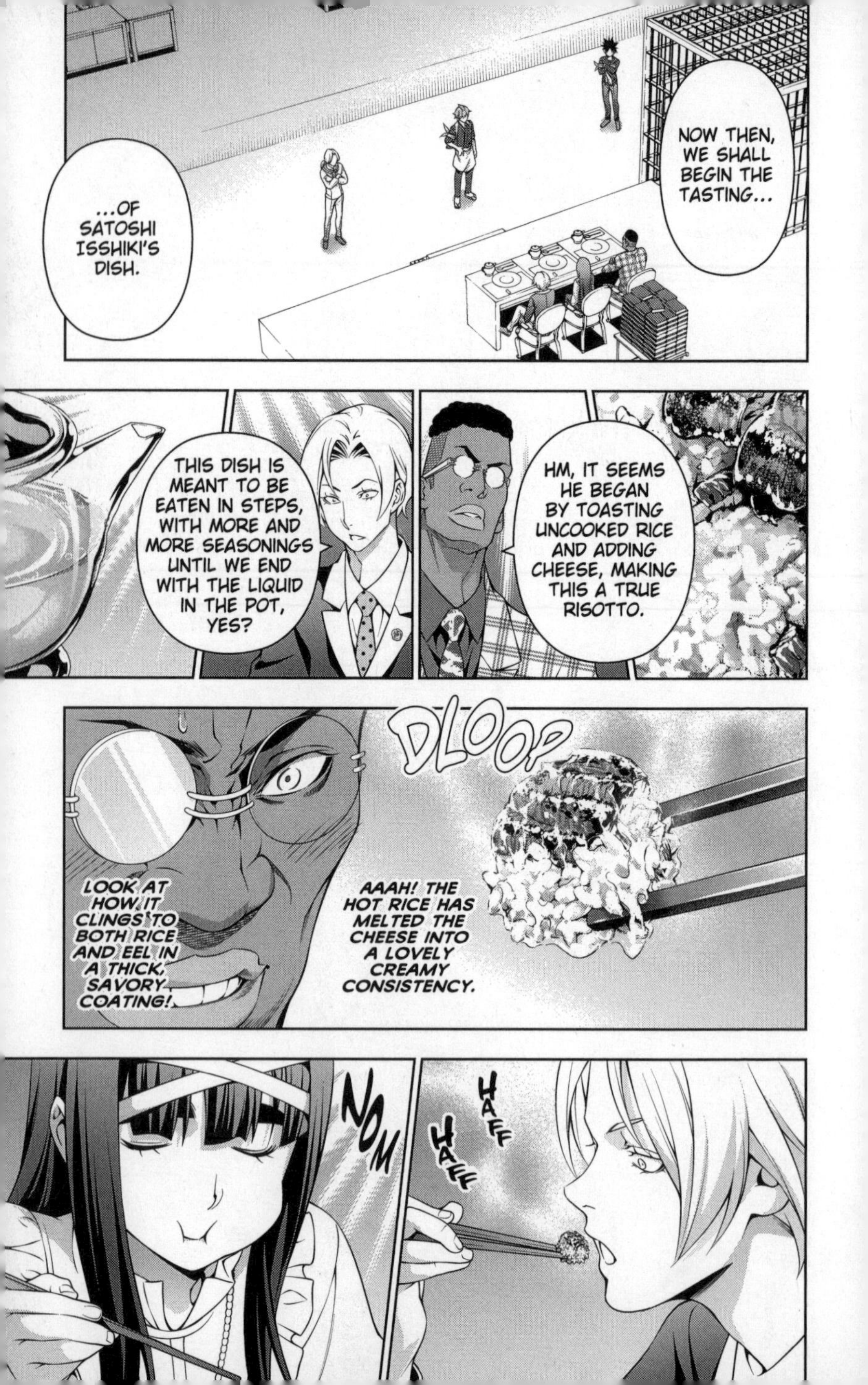
NOW THEN, WE SHALL BEGIN THE TASTING...
...OF SATOSHI ISSHIKI'S DISH.
HM, IT SEEMS HE BEGAN BY TOASTING UNCOOKED RICE AND ADDING CHEESE, MAKING THIS A TRUE RISOTTO.
THIS DISH IS MEANT TO BE EATEN IN STEPS, WITH MORE AND MORE SEASONINGS UNTIL WE END WITH THE LIQUID IN THE POT, YES?
DLOOP
AAAH! THE HOT RICE HAS MELTED THE CHEESE INTO A LOVELY CREAMY CONSISTENCY.
LOOK AT HOW IT CLINGS TO BOTH RICE AND EEL IN A THICK, SAVORY COATING!
HAFF
HAFF
NOM

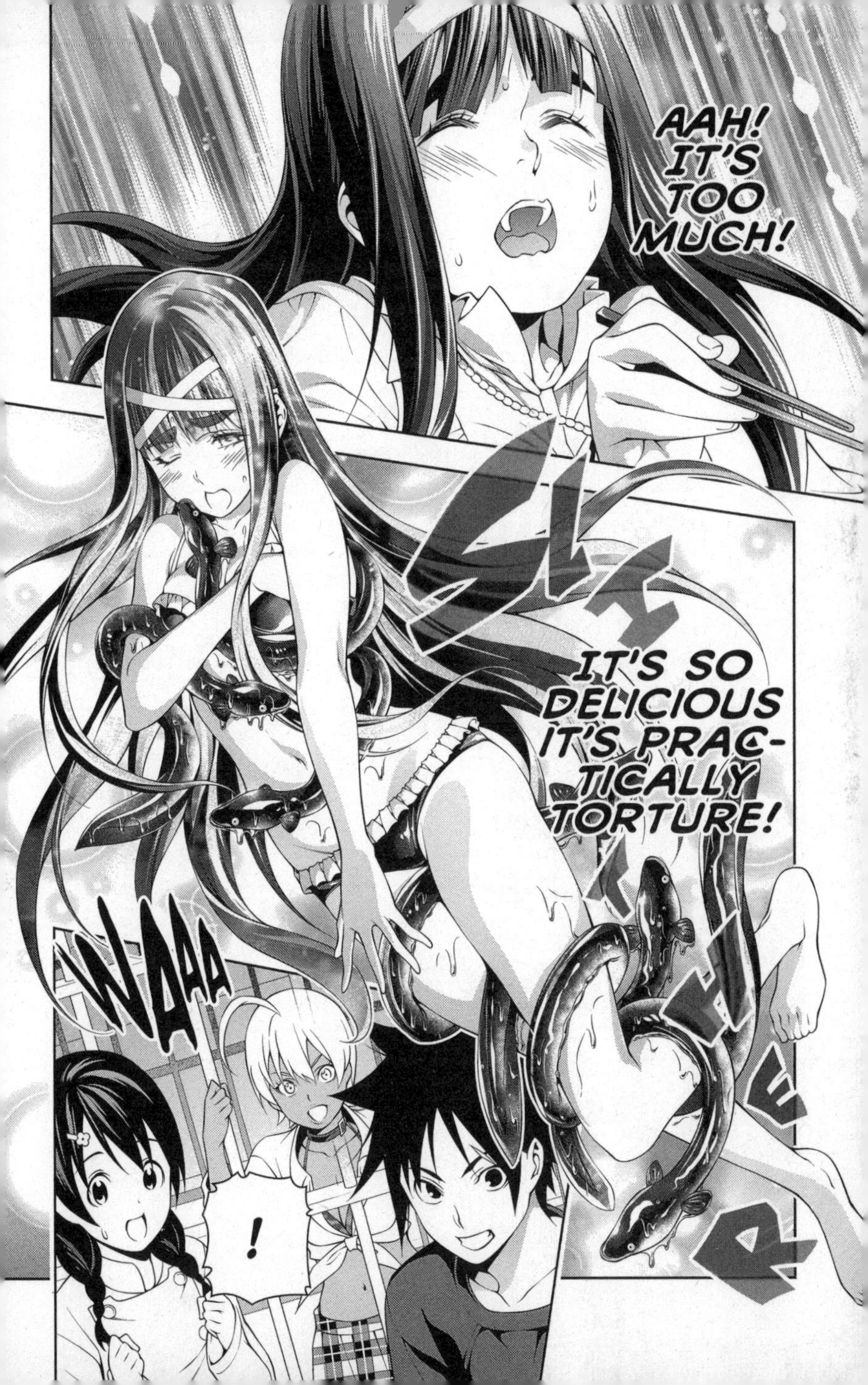
AAH! IT'S TOO MUCH!
IT'S SO DELICIOUS IT'S PRAC-TICALLY TORTURE!
WAAA
!

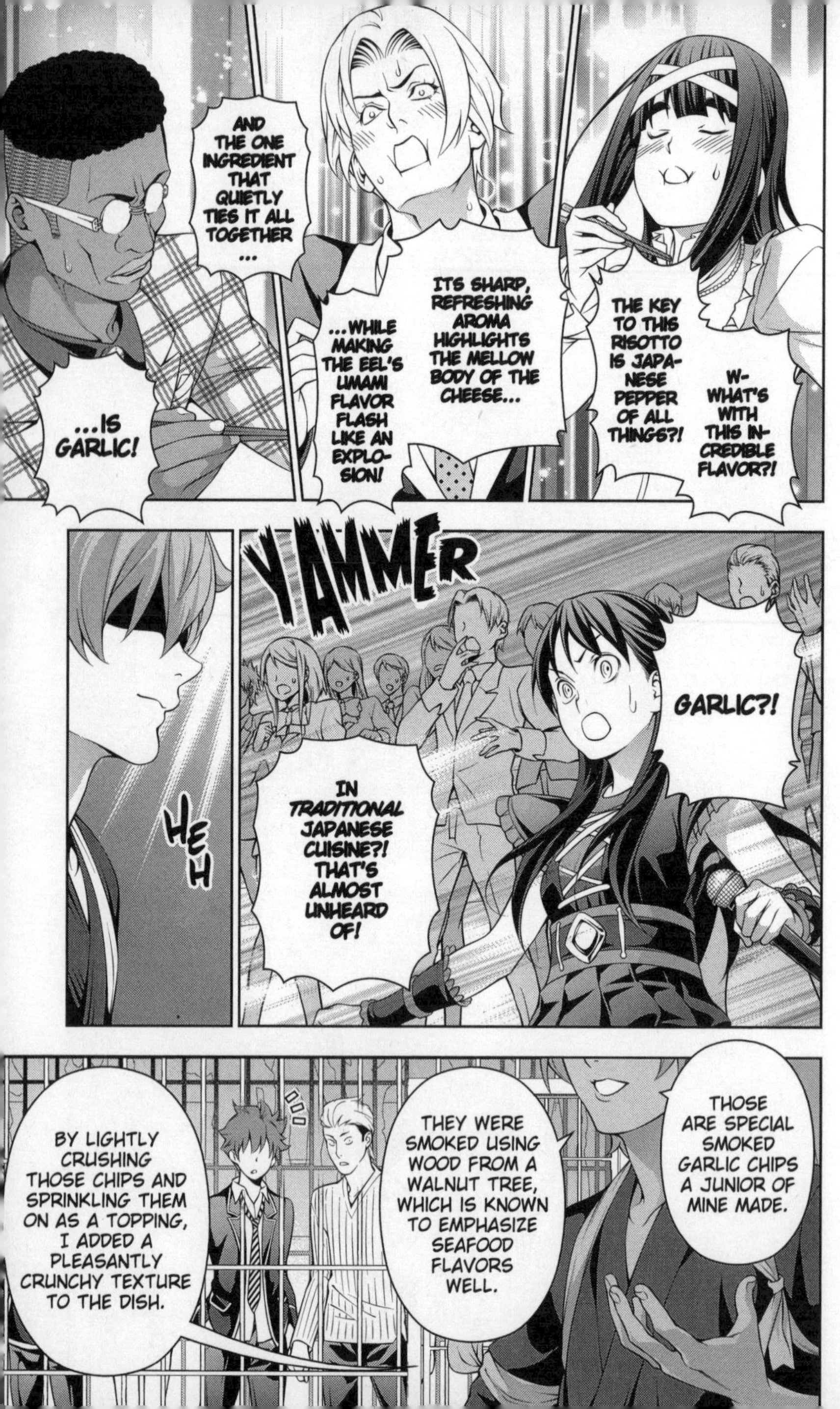
W-WHAT'S WITH THIS INCREDIBLE FLAVOR?!
THE KEY TO THIS RISOTTO IS JAPANESE PEPPER OF ALL THINGS?!
ITS SHARP, REFRESHING AROMA HIGHLIGHTS THE MELLOW BODY OF THE CHEESE...
...WHILE MAKING THE EEL'S UMAMI FLAVOR FLASH LIKE AN EXPLOSION!
AND THE ONE INGREDIENT THAT QUIETLY TIES IT ALL TOGETHER ...
...IS GARLIC!
YAMMER
GARLIC?!
IN *TRADITIONAL* JAPANESE CUISINE?! THAT'S ALMOST UNHEARD OF!
HEH
THOSE ARE SPECIAL SMOKED GARLIC CHIPS A JUNIOR OF MINE MADE.
THEY WERE SMOKED USING WOOD FROM A WALNUT TREE, WHICH IS KNOWN TO EMPHASIZE SEAFOOD FLAVORS WELL.
BY LIGHTLY CRUSHING THOSE CHIPS AND SPRINKLING THEM ON AS A TOPPING, I ADDED A PLEASANTLY CRUNCHY TEXTURE TO THE DISH.

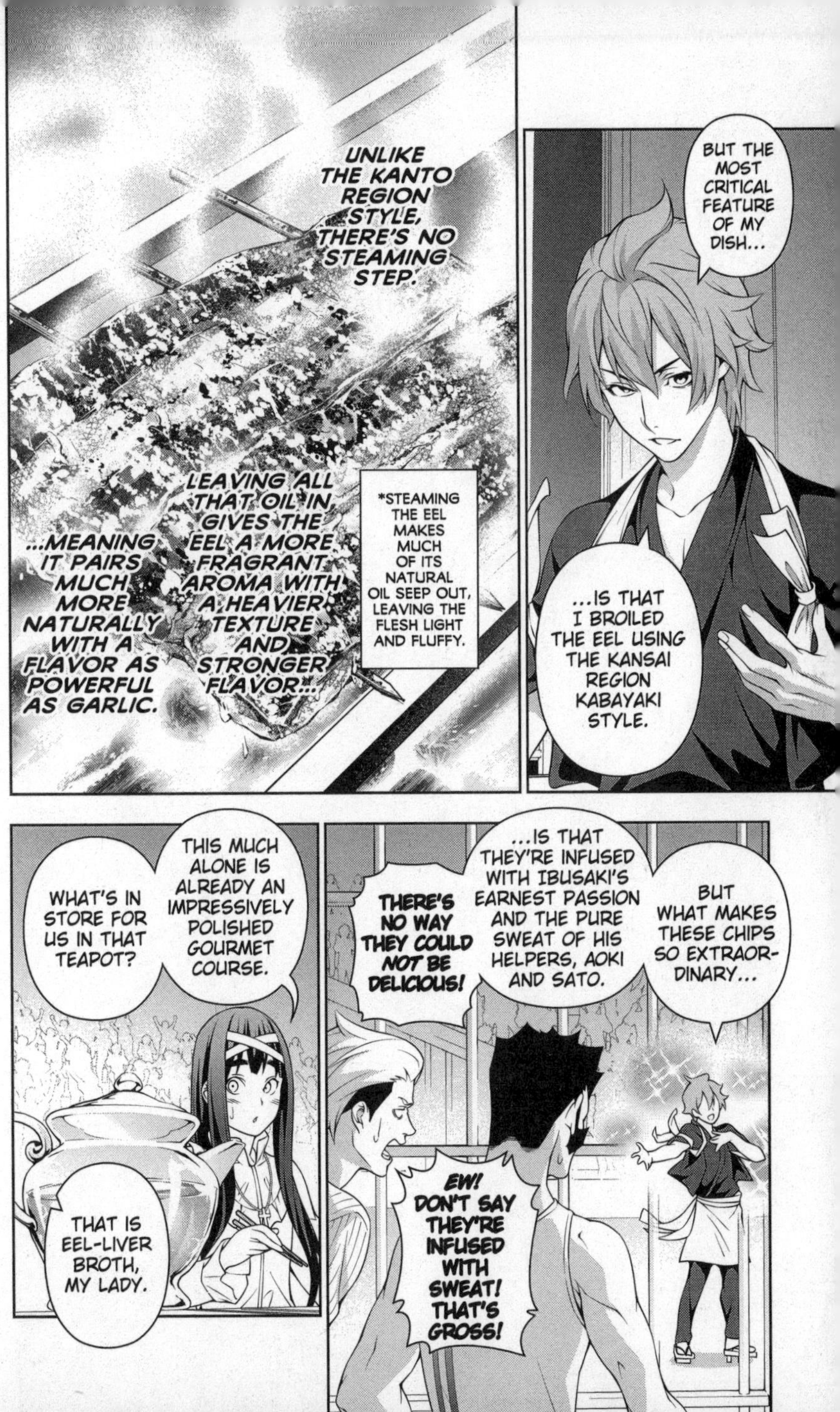
BUT THE MOST CRITICAL FEATURE OF MY DISH...
...IS THAT I BROILED THE EEL USING THE KANSAI REGION KABAYAKI STYLE.
UNLIKE THE KANTO REGION STYLE, THERE'S NO STEAMING STEP.
*STEAMING THE EEL MAKES MUCH OF ITS NATURAL OIL SEEP OUT, LEAVING THE FLESH LIGHT AND FLUFFY.
LEAVING ALL THAT OIL IN, GIVES THE EEL A MORE FRAGRANT AROMA WITH A HEAVIER TEXTURE AND STRONGER FLAVOR...
...MEANING IT PAIRS MUCH MORE NATURALLY WITH A FLAVOR AS POWERFUL AS GARLIC.
BUT WHAT MAKES THESE CHIPS SO EXTRAOR-DINARY...
...IS THAT THEY'RE INFUSED WITH IBUSAKI'S EARNEST PASSION AND THE PURE SWEAT OF HIS HELPERS, AOKI AND SATO.
THERE'S NO WAY THEY COULD NOT BE DELICIOUS!
EW! DON'T SAY THEY'RE INFUSED WITH SWEAT! THAT'S GROSS!
THIS MUCH ALONE IS ALREADY AN IMPRESSIVELY POLISHED GOURMET COURSE.
WHAT'S IN STORE FOR US IN THAT TEAPOT?
THAT IS EEL-LIVER BROTH, MY LADY.

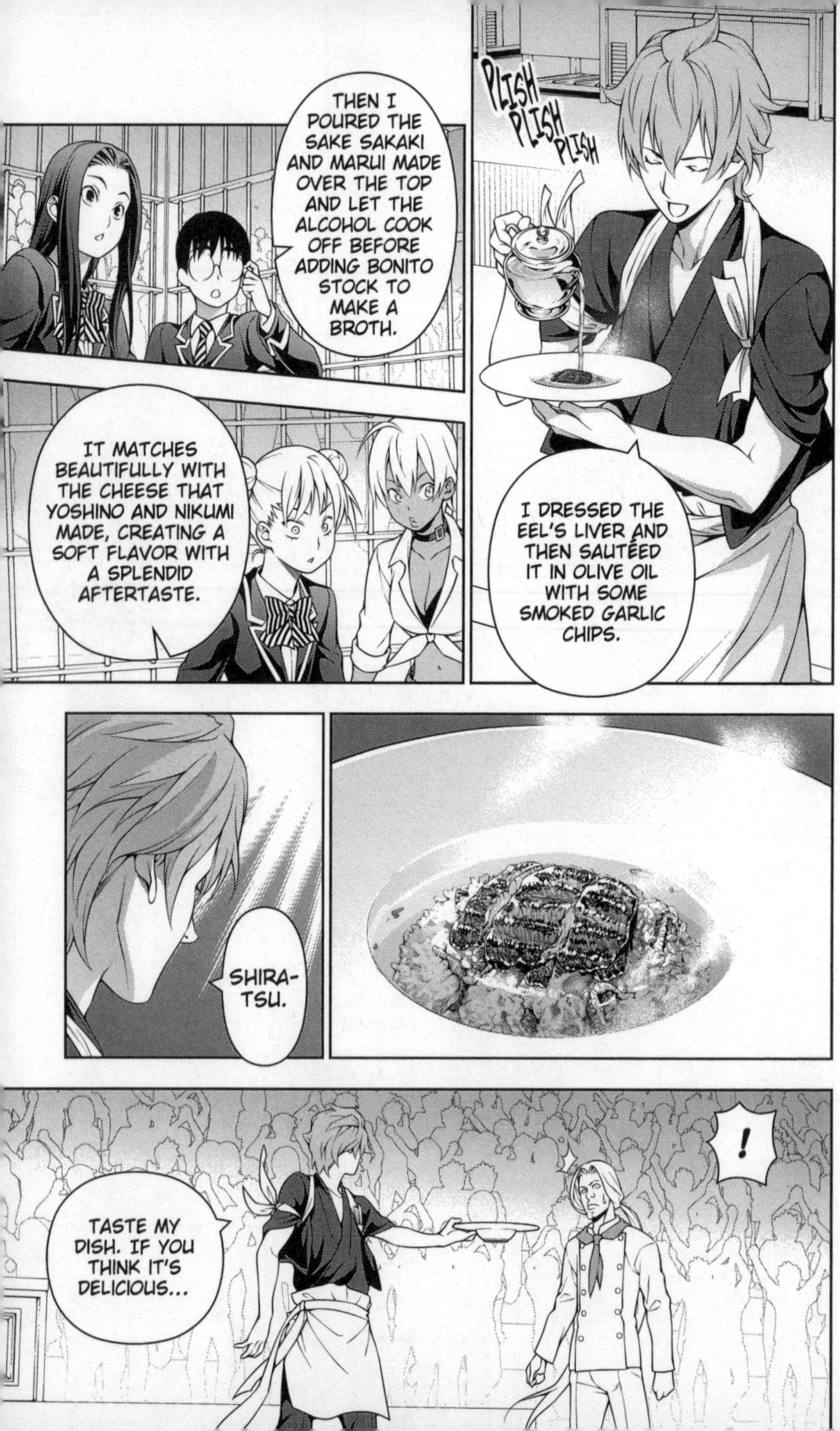
PLISH PLISH PLISH
I DRESSED THE EEL'S LIVER AND THEN SAUTÉED IT IN OLIVE OIL WITH SOME SMOKED GARLIC CHIPS.
THEN I POURED THE SAKE SAKAKI AND MARUI MADE OVER THE TOP AND LET THE ALCOHOL COOK OFF BEFORE ADDING BONITO STOCK TO MAKE A BROTH.
IT MATCHES BEAUTIFULLY WITH THE CHEESE THAT YOSHINO AND NIKUMI MADE, CREATING A SOFT FLAVOR WITH A SPLENDID AFTERTASTE.
SHIRA-TSU.
!
TASTE MY DISH. IF YOU THINK IT'S DELICIOUS...

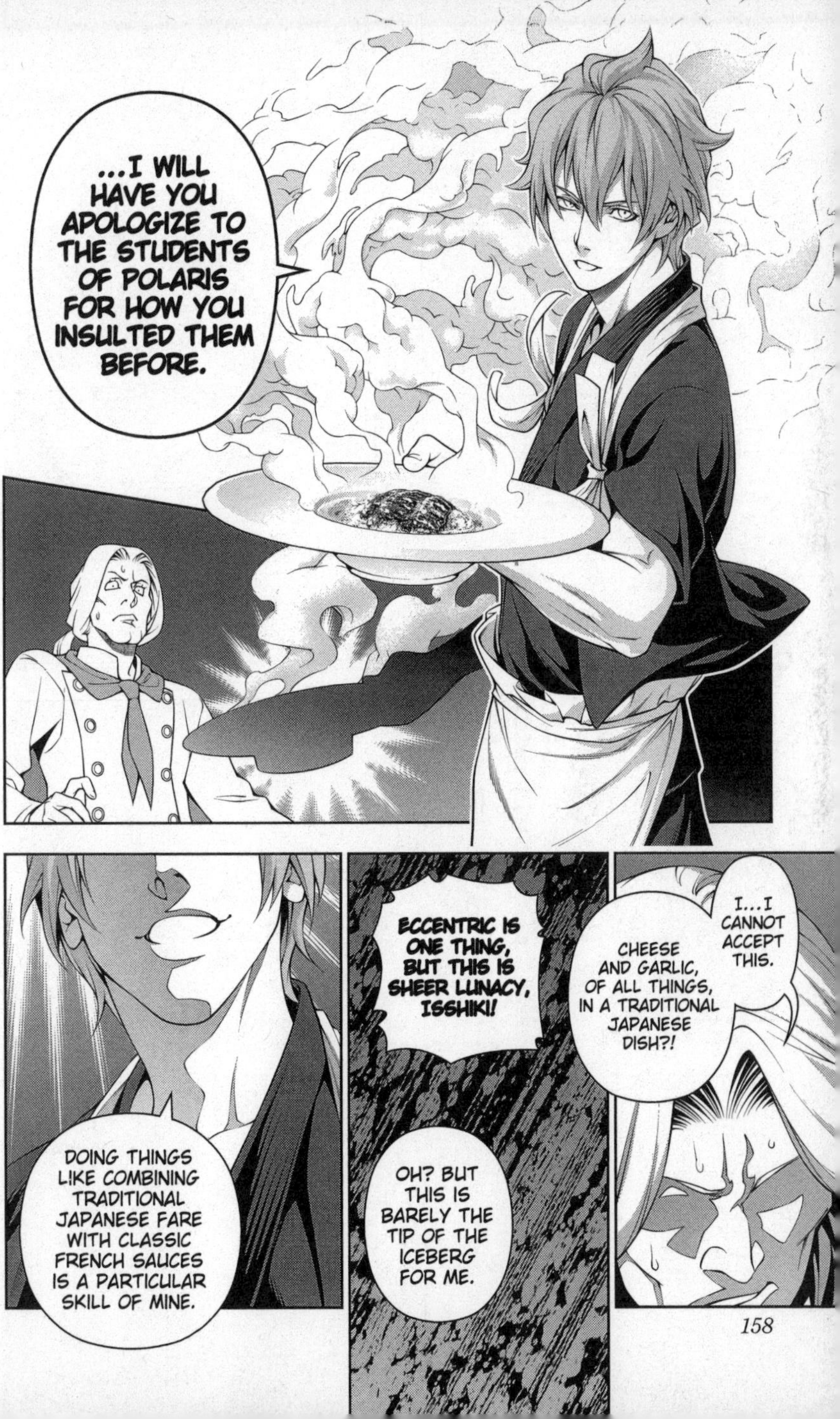
...I WILL HAVE YOU APOLOGIZE TO THE STUDENTS OF POLARIS FOR HOW YOU INSULTED THEM BEFORE.
I...I CANNOT ACCEPT THIS.
CHEESE AND GARLIC, OF ALL THINGS, IN A TRADITIONAL JAPANESE DISH?!
ECCENTRIC IS ONE THING, BUT THIS IS SHEER LUNACY, ISSHIKI!
OH? BUT THIS IS BARELY THE TIP OF THE ICEBERG FOR ME.
DOING THINGS LIKE COMBINING TRADITIONAL JAPANESE FARE WITH CLASSIC FRENCH SAUCES IS A PARTICULAR SKILL OF MINE.

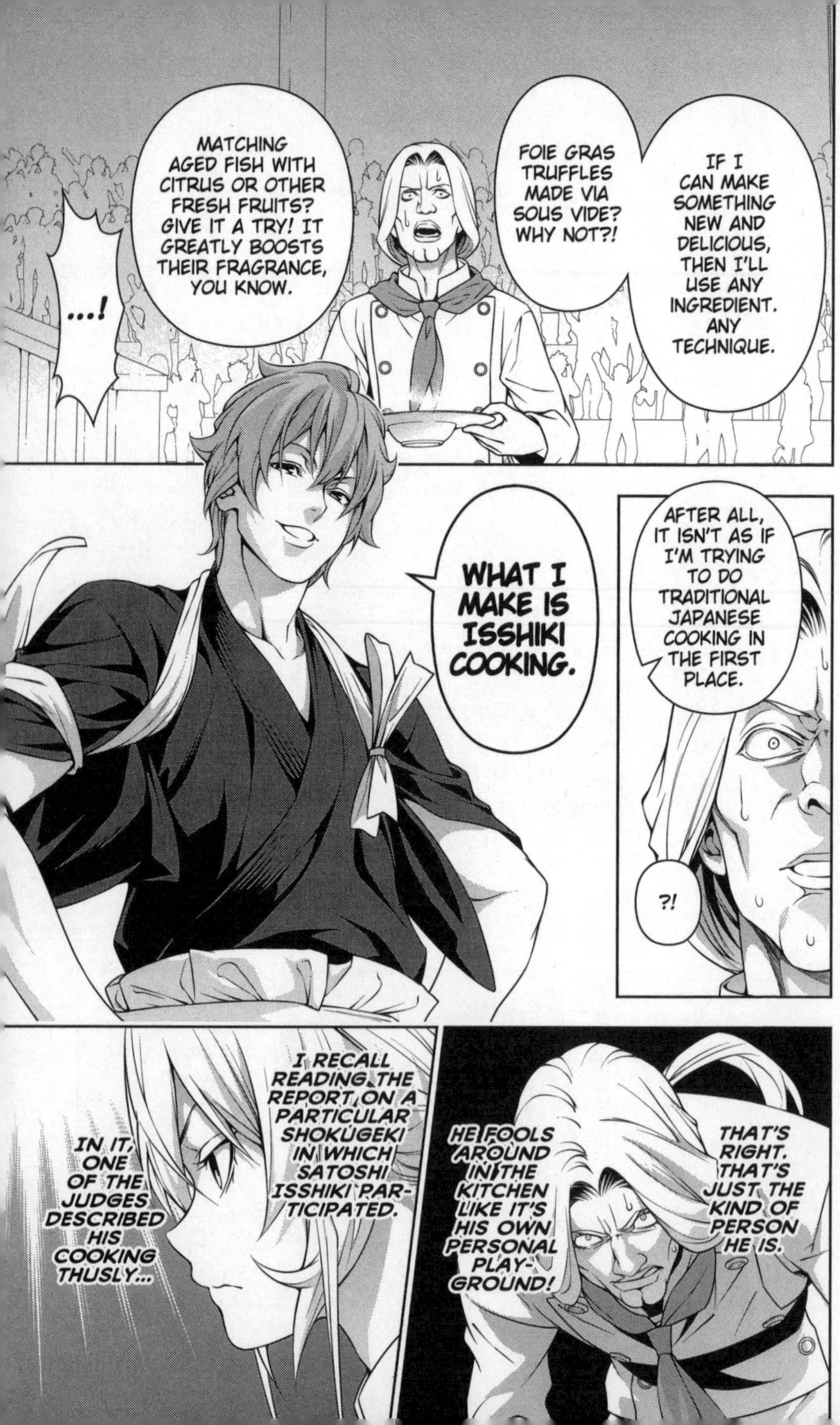
IF I CAN MAKE SOMETHING NEW AND DELICIOUS, THEN I'LL USE ANY INGREDIENT. ANY TECHNIQUE.
FOIE GRAS TRUFFLES MADE VIA SOUS VIDE? WHY NOT?!
MATCHING AGED FISH WITH CITRUS OR OTHER FRESH FRUITS? GIVE IT A TRY! IT GREATLY BOOSTS THEIR FRAGRANCE, YOU KNOW.
...!
AFTER ALL, IT ISN'T AS IF I'M TRYING TO DO TRADITIONAL JAPANESE COOKING IN THE FIRST PLACE.
?!
WHAT I MAKE IS ISSHIKI COOKING.
THAT'S RIGHT. THAT'S JUST THE KIND OF PERSON HE IS.
HE FOOLS AROUND IN THE KITCHEN LIKE IT'S HIS OWN PERSONAL PLAY-GROUND!
I RECALL READING THE REPORT ON A PARTICULAR SHOKUGEKI IN WHICH SATOSHI ISSHIKI PAR-TICIPATED.
IN IT, ONE OF THE JUDGES DESCRIBED HIS COOKING THUSLY...

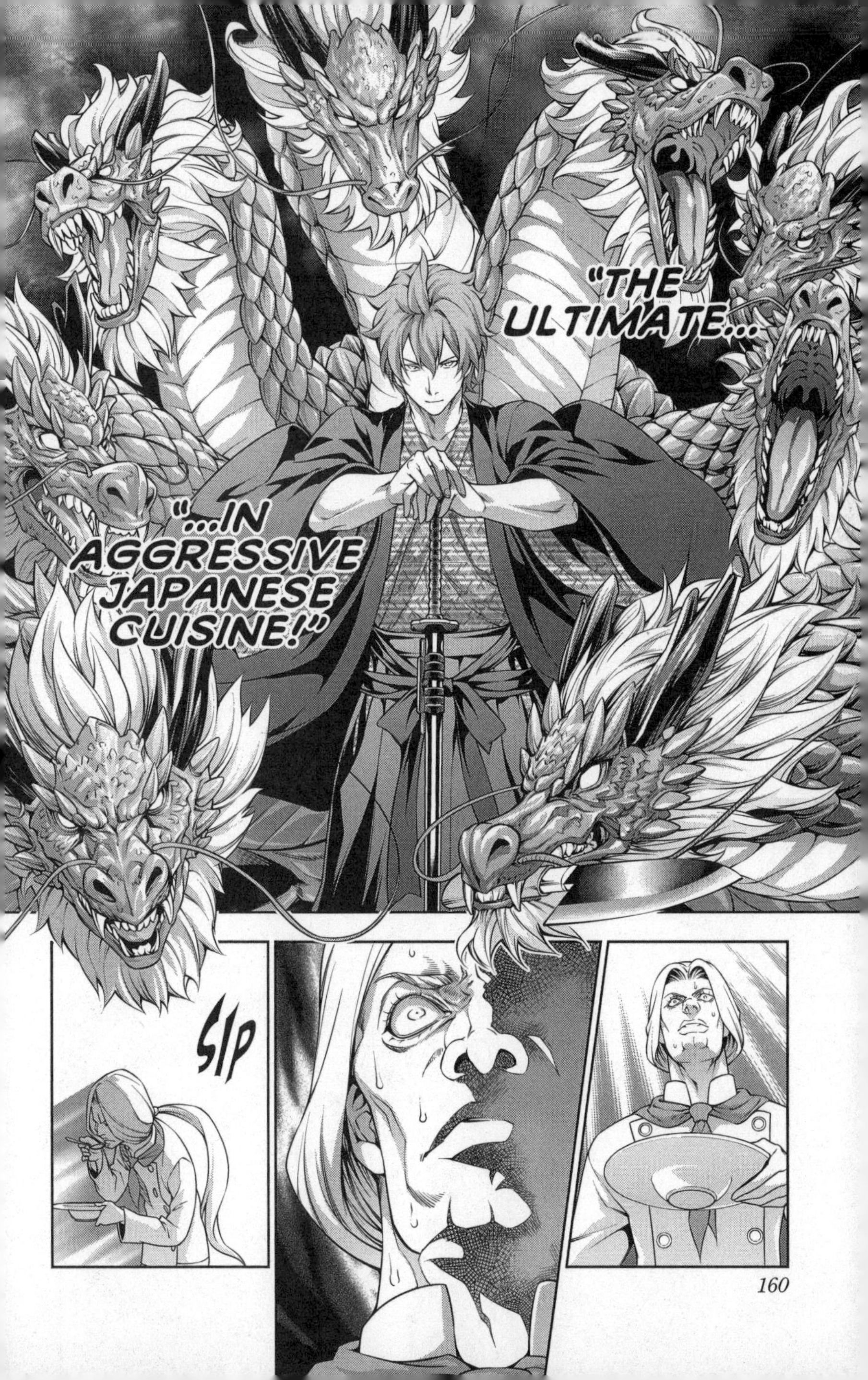
"THE ULTIMATE...
"...IN AGGRESSIVE JAPANESE CUISINE!"
SIP

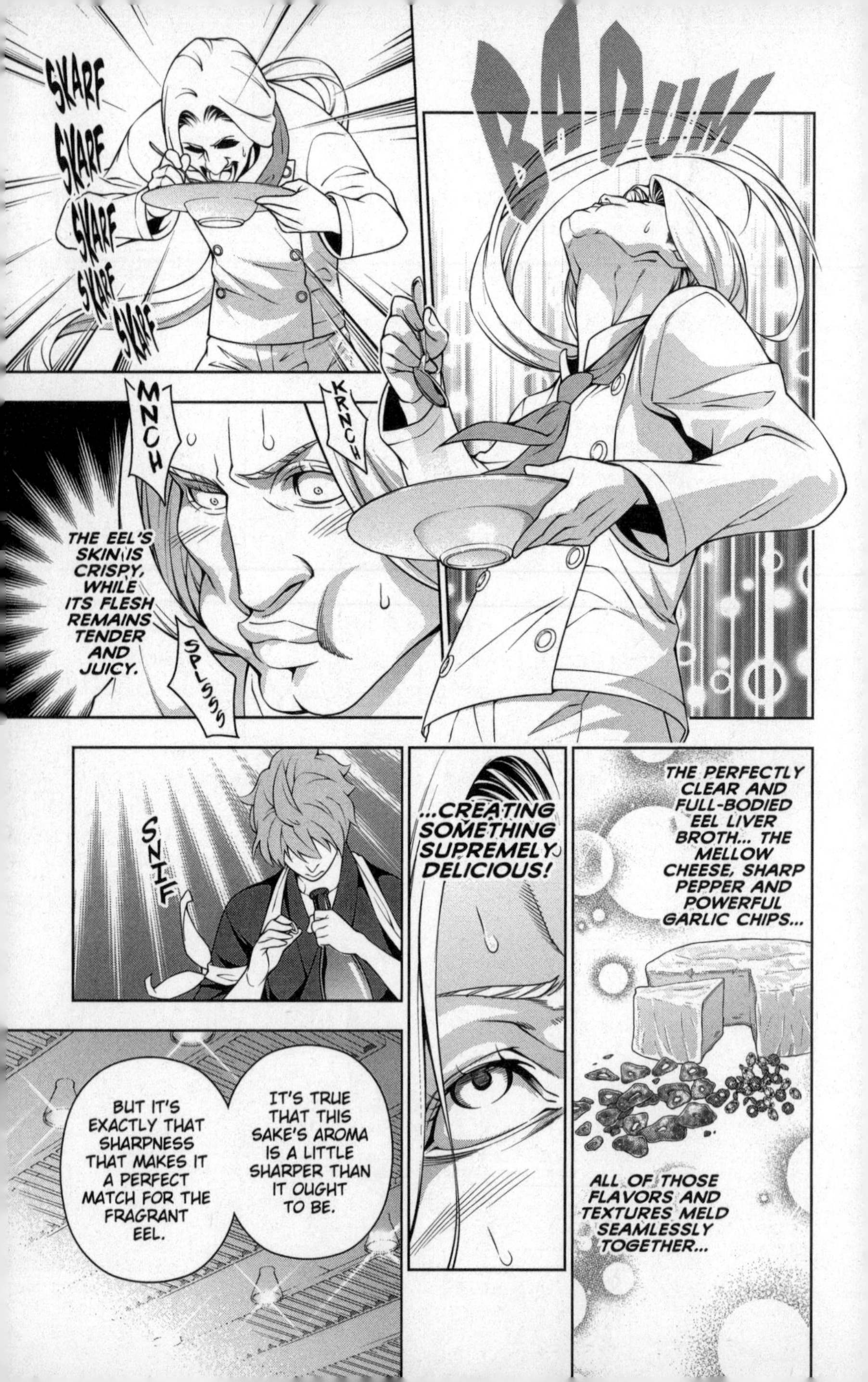
BADUM
SKARF SKARF SKARF SKARF SKARF
KRNCH
MNCH
THE EEL'S SKIN IS CRISPY, WHILE ITS FLESH REMAINS TENDER AND JUICY.
SPLSSS
THE PERFECTLY CLEAR AND FULL-BODIED EEL LIVER BROTH... THE MELLOW CHEESE, SHARP PEPPER AND POWERFUL GARLIC CHIPS...
ALL OF THOSE FLAVORS AND TEXTURES MELD SEAMLESSLY TOGETHER...
...CREATING SOMETHING SUPREMELY DELICIOUS!
SNIF
IT'S TRUE THAT THIS SAKE'S AROMA IS A LITTLE SHARPER THAN IT OUGHT TO BE.
BUT IT'S EXACTLY THAT SHARPNESS THAT MAKES IT A PERFECT MATCH FOR THE FRAGRANT EEL.

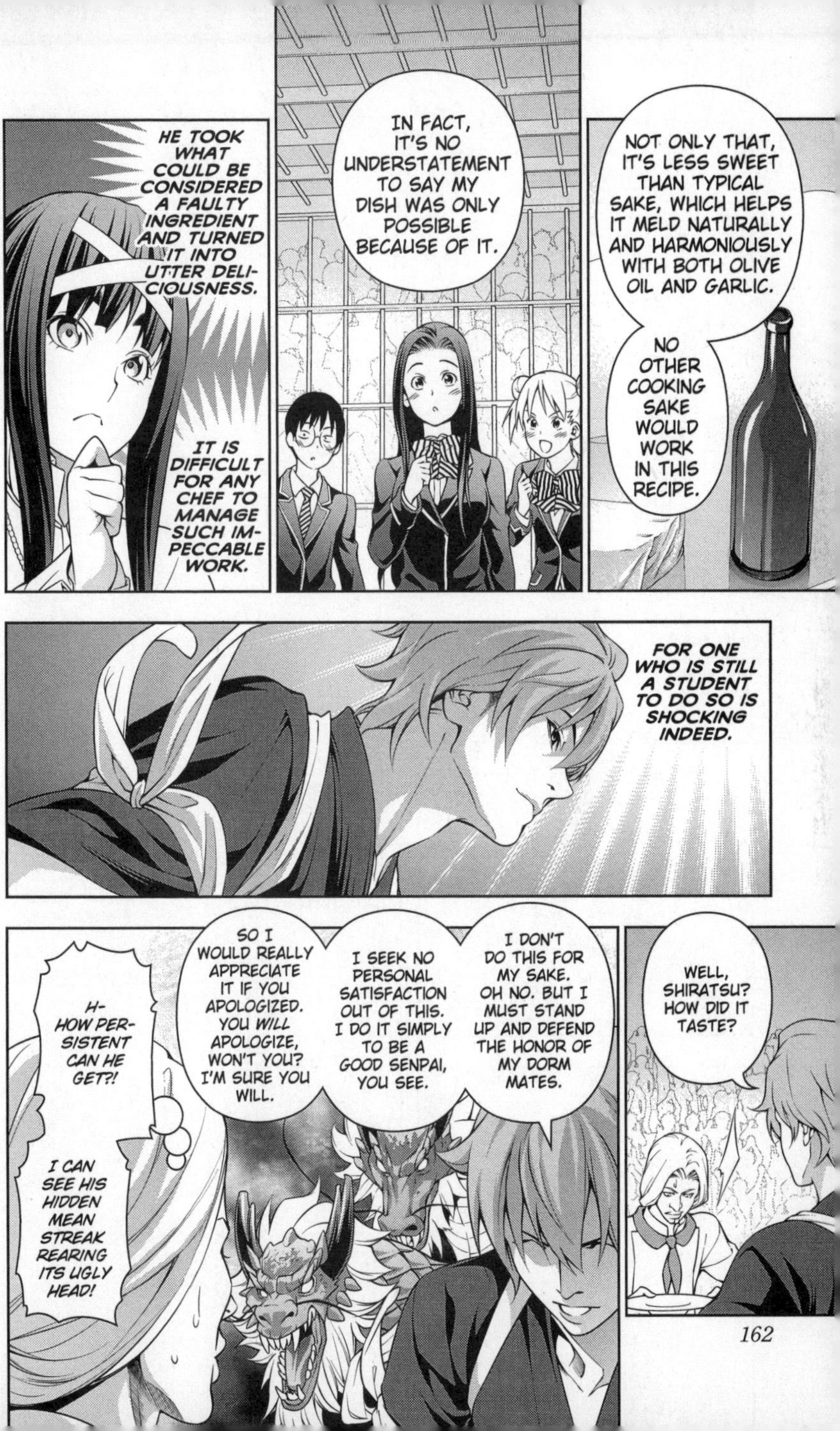
NOT ONLY THAT, IT'S LESS SWEET THAN TYPICAL SAKE, WHICH HELPS IT MELD NATURALLY AND HARMONIOUSLY WITH BOTH OLIVE OIL AND GARLIC.
NO OTHER COOKING SAKE WOULD WORK IN THIS RECIPE.
IN FACT, IT'S NO UNDERSTATEMENT TO SAY MY DISH WAS ONLY POSSIBLE BECAUSE OF IT.
HE TOOK WHAT COULD BE CONSIDERED A FAULTY INGREDIENT AND TURNED IT INTO UTTER DELI-CIOUSNESS.
IT IS DIFFICULT FOR ANY CHEF TO MANAGE SUCH IM-PECCABLE WORK.
FOR ONE WHO IS STILL A STUDENT TO DO SO IS SHOCKING INDEED.
WELL, SHIRATSU? HOW DID IT TASTE?
I DON'T DO THIS FOR MY SAKE. OH NO. BUT I MUST STAND UP AND DEFEND THE HONOR OF MY DORM MATES.
I SEEK NO PERSONAL SATISFACTION OUT OF THIS. I DO IT SIMPLY TO BE A GOOD SENPAI, YOU SEE.
SO I WOULD REALLY APPRECIATE IT IF YOU APOLOGIZED. YOU *WILL* APOLOGIZE, WON'T YOU? I'M SURE YOU WILL.
H-HOW PER-SISTENT CAN HE GET?!
I CAN SEE HIS HIDDEN MEAN STREAK REARING ITS UGLY HEAD!

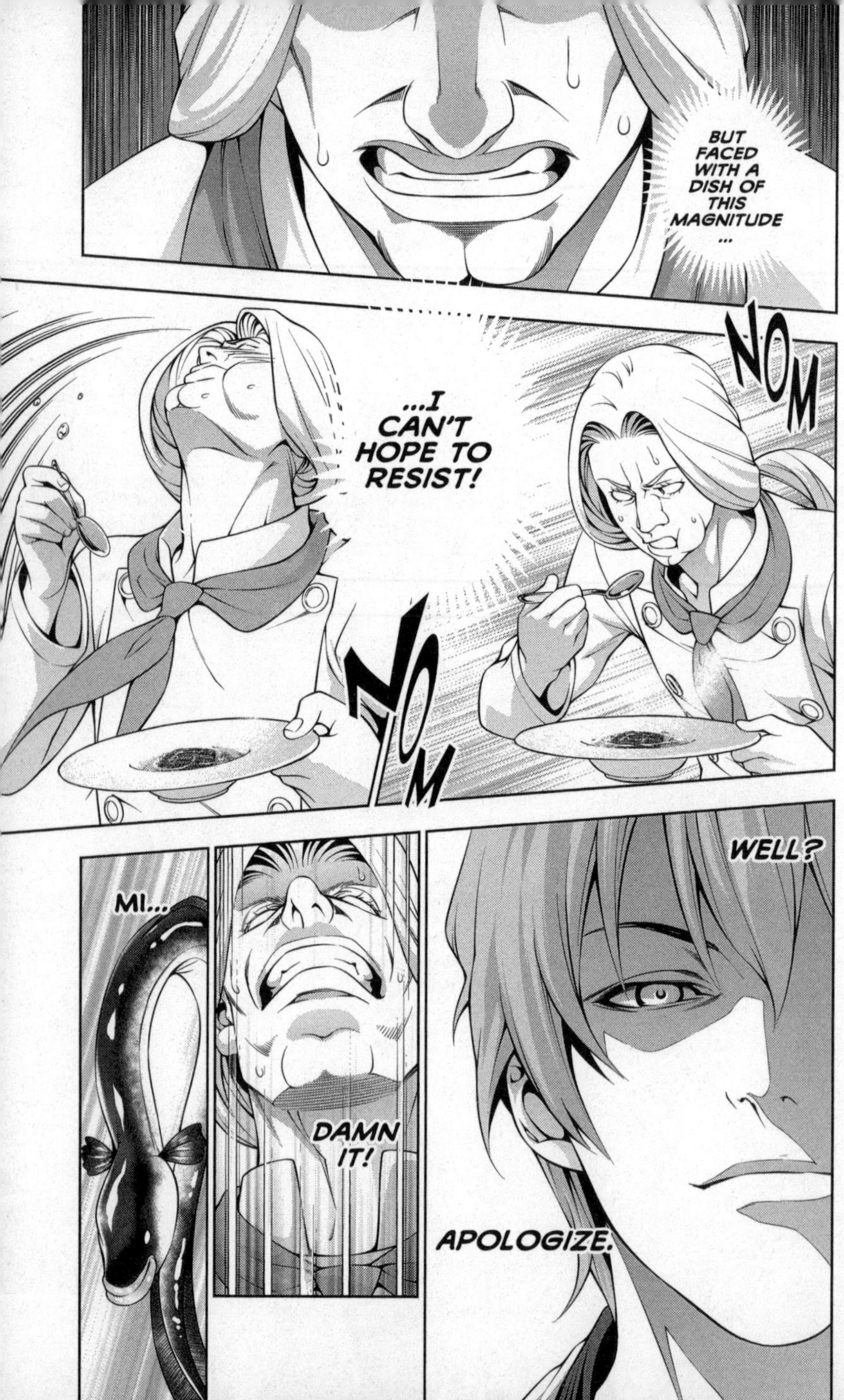
BUT FACED WITH A DISH OF THIS MAGNITUDE ...
NOM
...I CAN'T HOPE TO RESIST!
NOM
WELL?
APOLOGIZE.
DAMN IT!
MI...

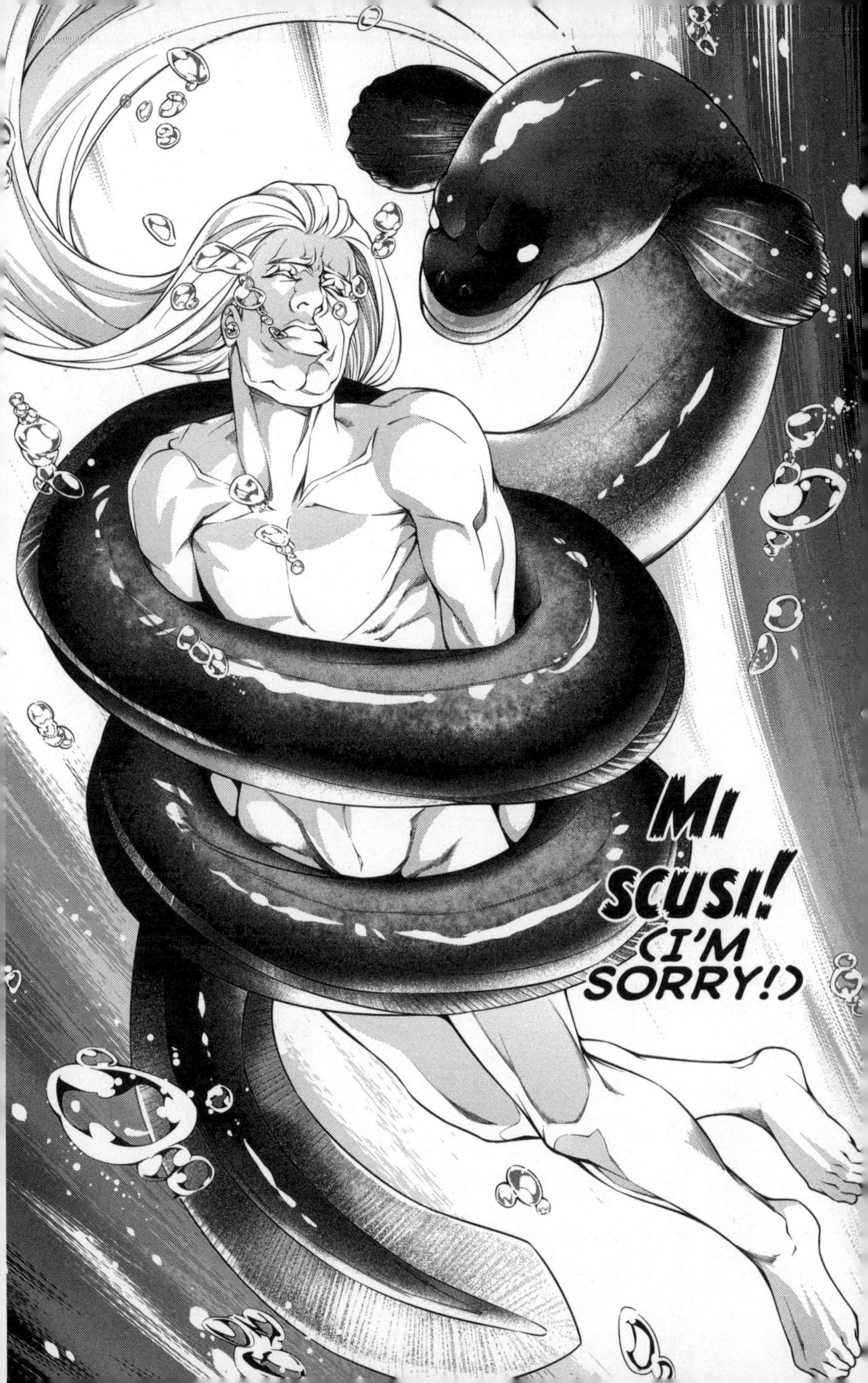
MI SCUSI!
(I'M SORRY!)

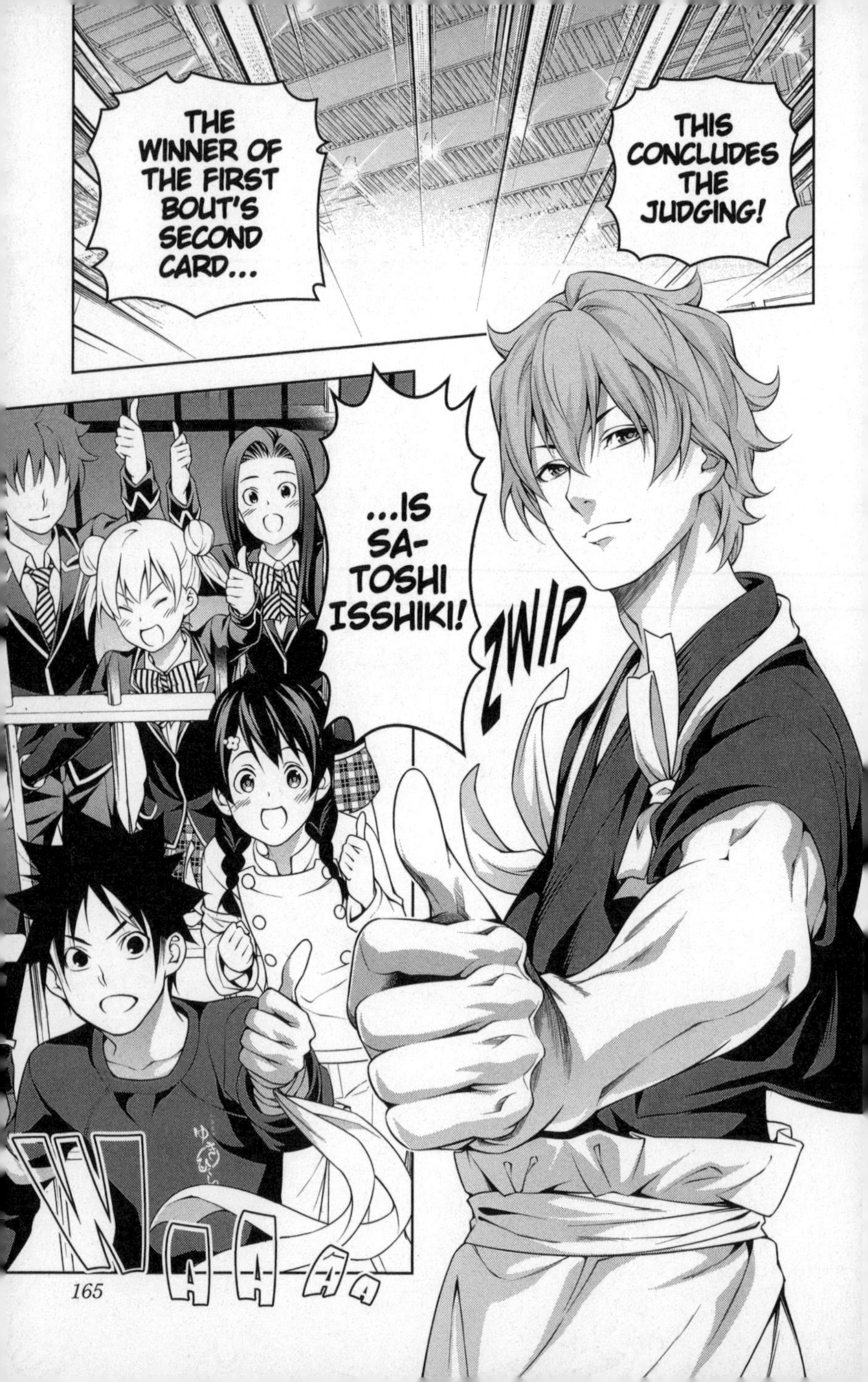
THIS CONCLUDES THE JUDGING!
THE WINNER OF THE FIRST BOUT'S SECOND CARD...
...IS SA-TOSHI ISSHIKI!
ZWIP
WAAAA

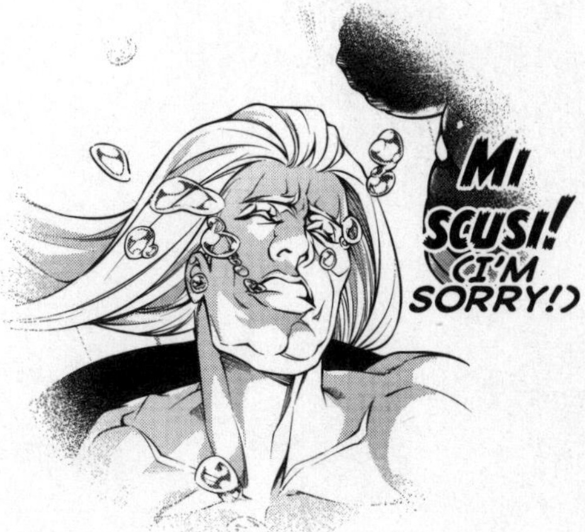
MI SCUSI!
(I'M SORRY!)

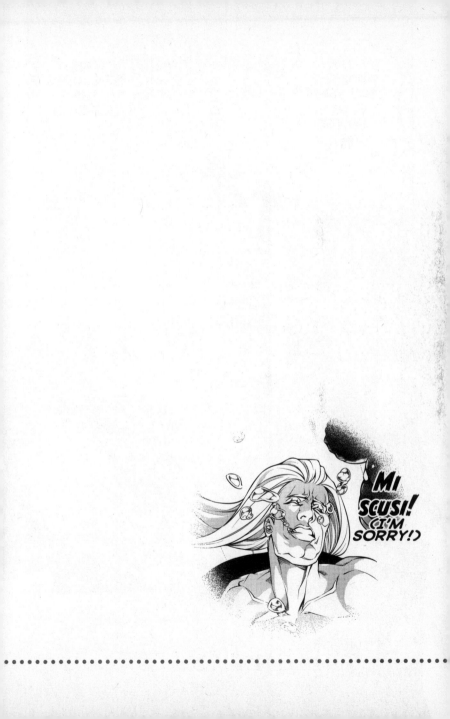

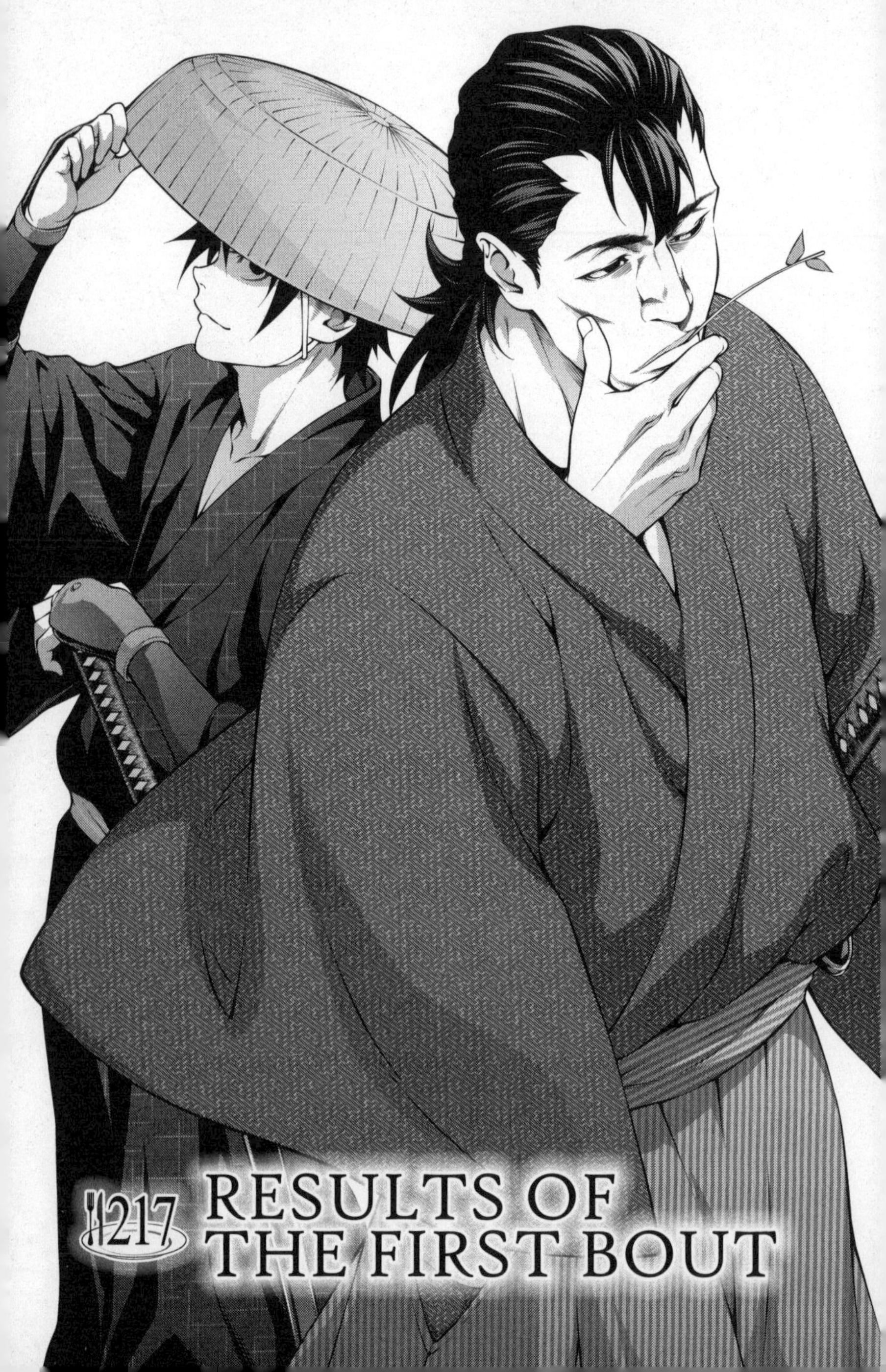
217
RESULTS OF
THE FIRST BOUT

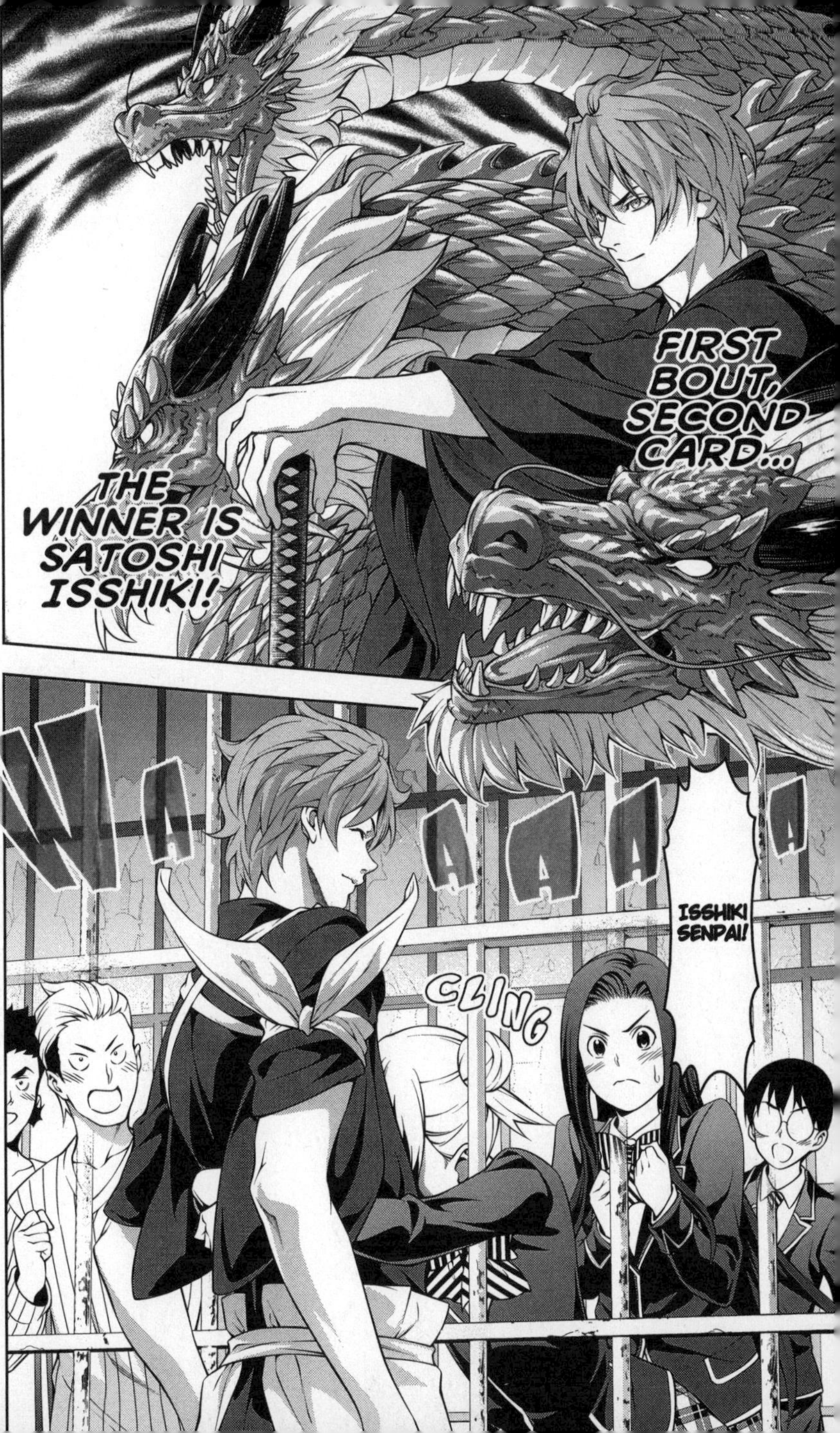
FIRST BOUT, SECOND CARD...
THE WINNER IS SATOSHI ISSHIKI!
WAAAAA
ISSHIKI SENPAI!
CLING

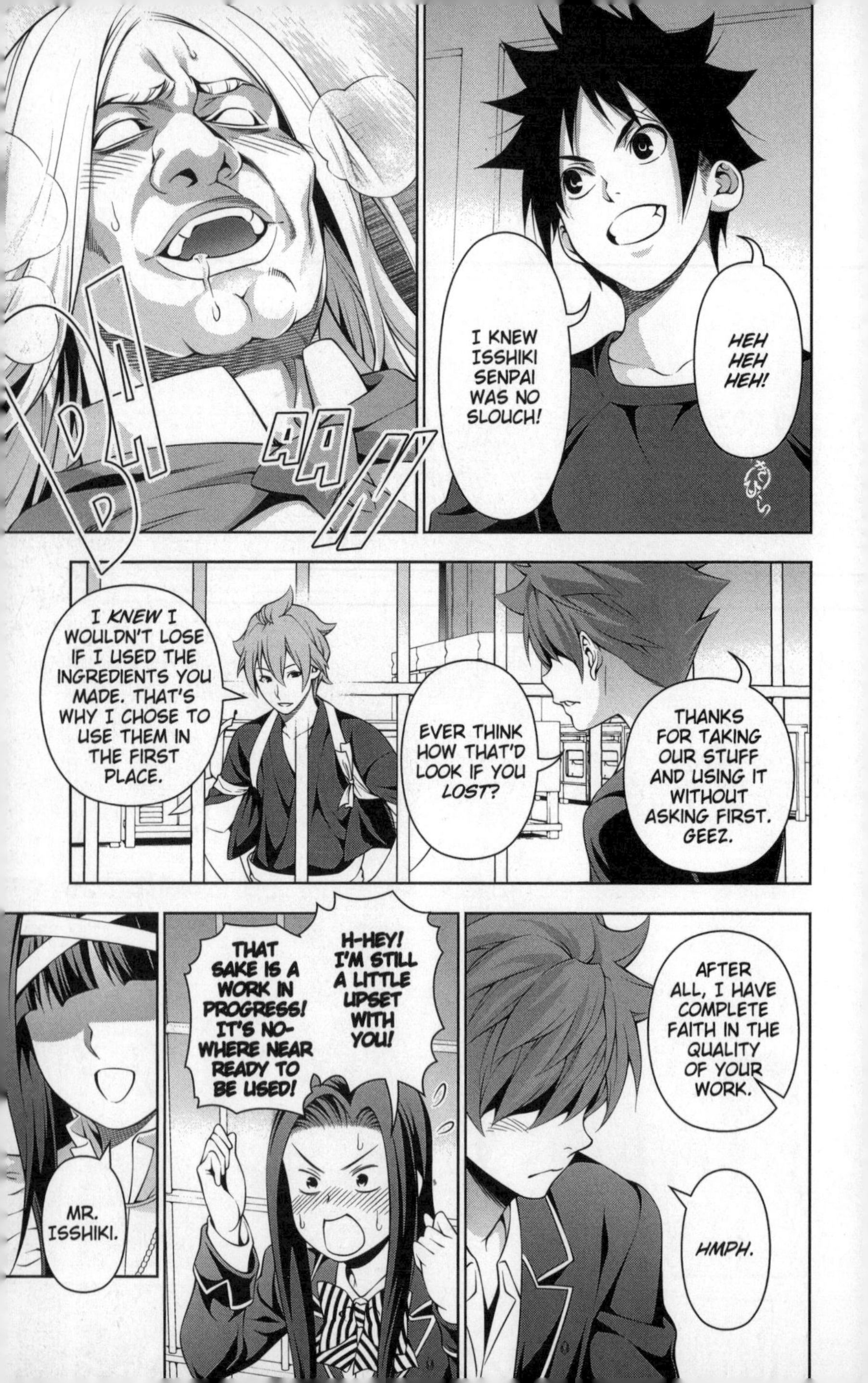
HEH HEH HEH!
I KNEW ISSHIKI SENPAI WAS NO SLOUCH!
THANKS FOR TAKING OUR STUFF AND USING IT WITHOUT ASKING FIRST. GEEZ.
EVER THINK HOW THAT'D LOOK IF YOU *LOST*?
I *KNEW* I WOULDN'T LOSE IF I USED THE INGREDIENTS YOU MADE. THAT'S WHY I CHOSE TO USE THEM IN THE FIRST PLACE.
AFTER ALL, I HAVE COMPLETE FAITH IN THE QUALITY OF YOUR WORK.
HMPH.
H-HEY! I'M STILL A LITTLE UPSET WITH YOU!
THAT SAKE IS A WORK IN PROGRESS! IT'S NOWHERE NEAR READY TO BE USED!
MR. ISSHIKI.

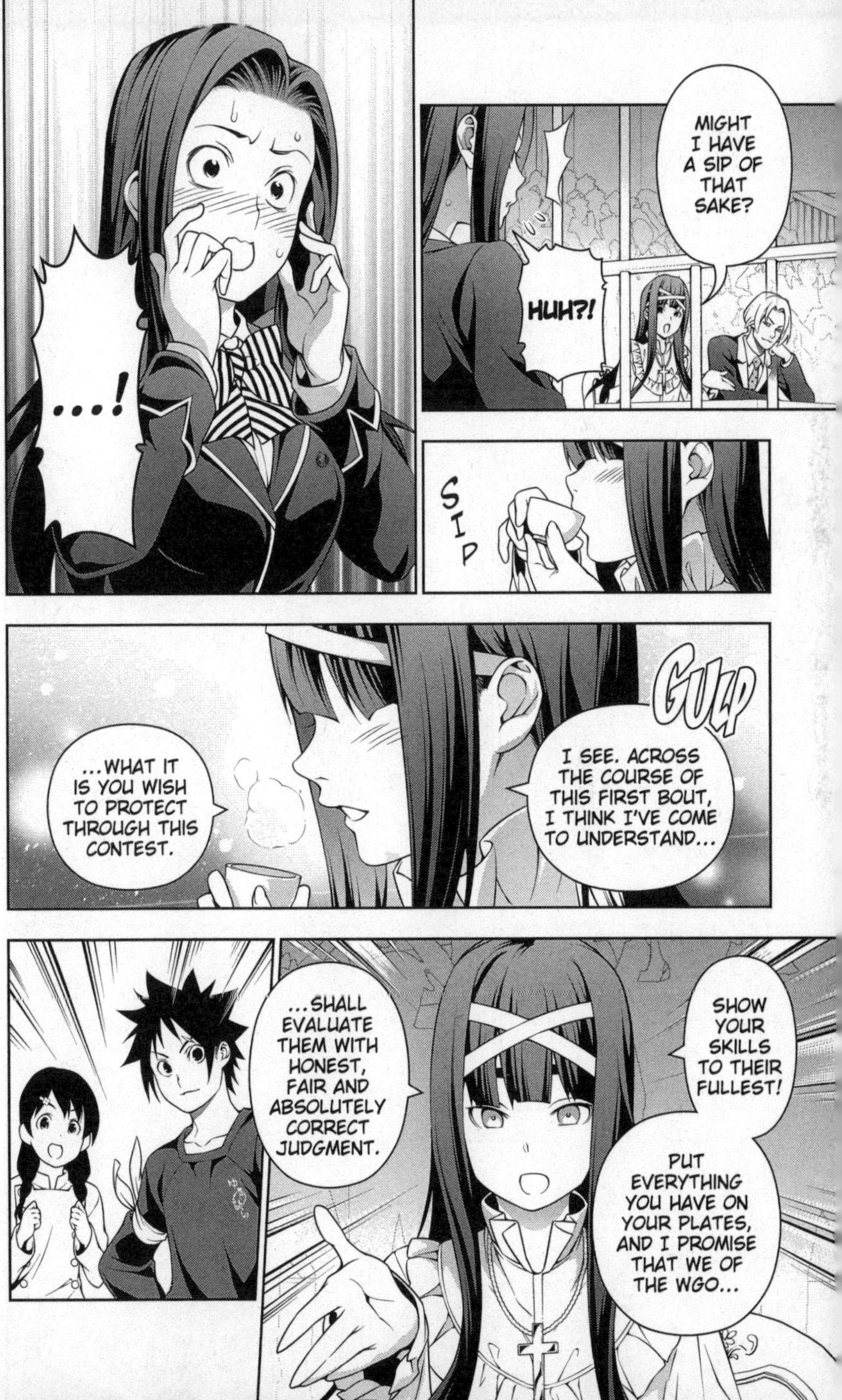
MIGHT I HAVE A SIP OF THAT SAKE?
HUH?!
SIP
...!
GULP
I SEE. ACROSS THE COURSE OF THIS FIRST BOUT, I THINK I'VE COME TO UNDERSTAND...
...WHAT IT IS YOU WISH TO PROTECT THROUGH THIS CONTEST.
SHOW YOUR SKILLS TO THEIR FULLEST!
PUT EVERYTHING YOU HAVE ON YOUR PLATES, AND I PROMISE THAT WE OF THE WGO...
...SHALL EVALUATE THEM WITH HONEST, FAIR AND ABSOLUTELY CORRECT JUDGMENT.

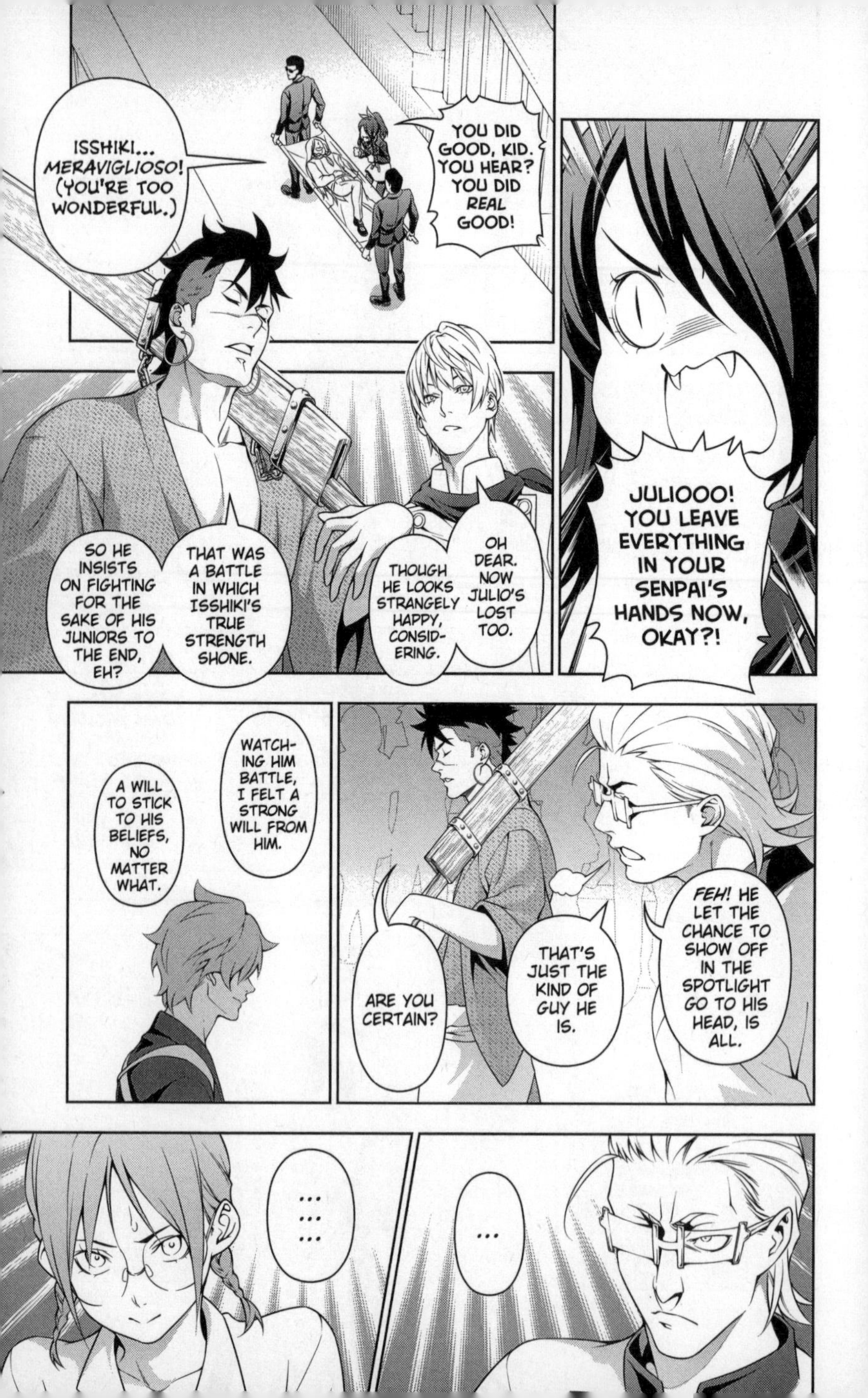
JULIOOO! YOU LEAVE EVERYTHING IN YOUR SENPAI'S HANDS NOW, OKAY?!
YOU DID GOOD, KID. YOU HEAR? YOU DID *REAL* GOOD!
ISSHIKI... *MERAVIGLIOSO!* (YOU'RE TOO WONDERFUL.)
OH DEAR. NOW JULIO'S LOST TOO.
THOUGH HE LOOKS STRANGELY HAPPY, CONSID-ERING.
THAT WAS A BATTLE IN WHICH ISSHIKI'S TRUE STRENGTH SHONE.
SO HE INSISTS ON FIGHTING FOR THE SAKE OF HIS JUNIORS TO THE END, EH?
FEH! HE LET THE CHANCE TO SHOW OFF IN THE SPOTLIGHT GO TO HIS HEAD, IS ALL.
THAT'S JUST THE KIND OF GUY HE IS.
ARE YOU CERTAIN?
WATCH-ING HIM BATTLE, I FELT A STRONG WILL FROM HIM.
A WILL TO STICK TO HIS BELIEFS, NO MATTER WHAT.
...
...
...
...

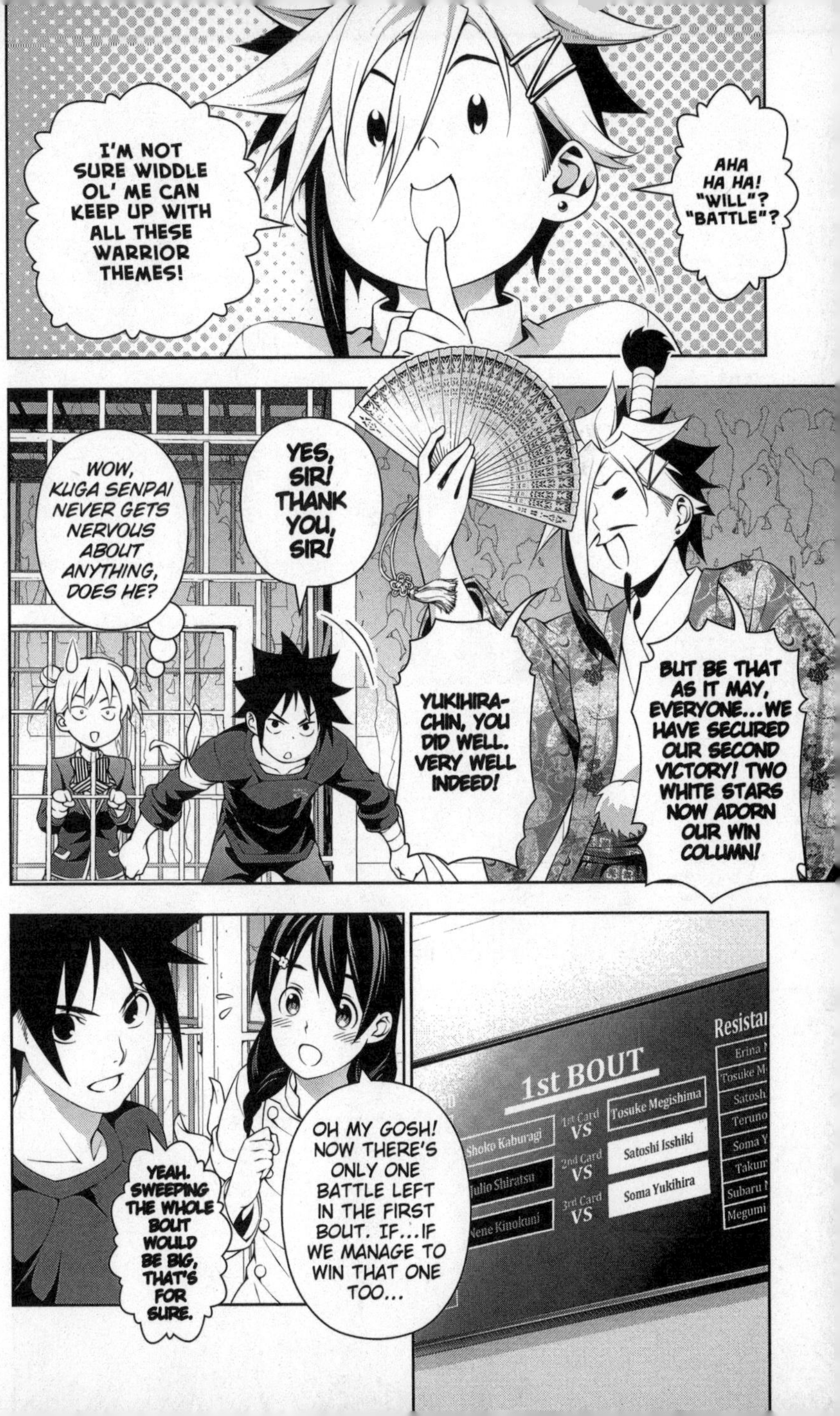
AHA HA HA! "WILL"? "BATTLE"?
I'M NOT SURE WIDDLE OL' ME CAN KEEP UP WITH ALL THESE WARRIOR THEMES!
BUT BE THAT AS IT MAY, EVERYONE...WE HAVE SECURED OUR SECOND VICTORY! TWO WHITE STARS NOW ADORN OUR WIN COLUMN!
YUKIHIRA-CHIN, YOU DID WELL. VERY WELL INDEED!
YES, SIR! THANK YOU, SIR!
WOW, KUGA SENPAI NEVER GETS NERVOUS ABOUT ANYTHING, DOES HE?
1st BOUT
Shoko Kaburagi
1st Card
VS
Tosuke Megishima
Julio Shiratsu
2nd Card
VS
Satoshi Isshiki
Nene Kinokuni
3rd Card
VS
Soma Yukihira
OH MY GOSH! NOW THERE'S ONLY ONE BATTLE LEFT IN THE FIRST BOUT. IF...IF WE MANAGE TO WIN THAT ONE TOO...
YEAH. SWEEPING THE WHOLE BOUT WOULD BE BIG, THAT'S FOR SURE.

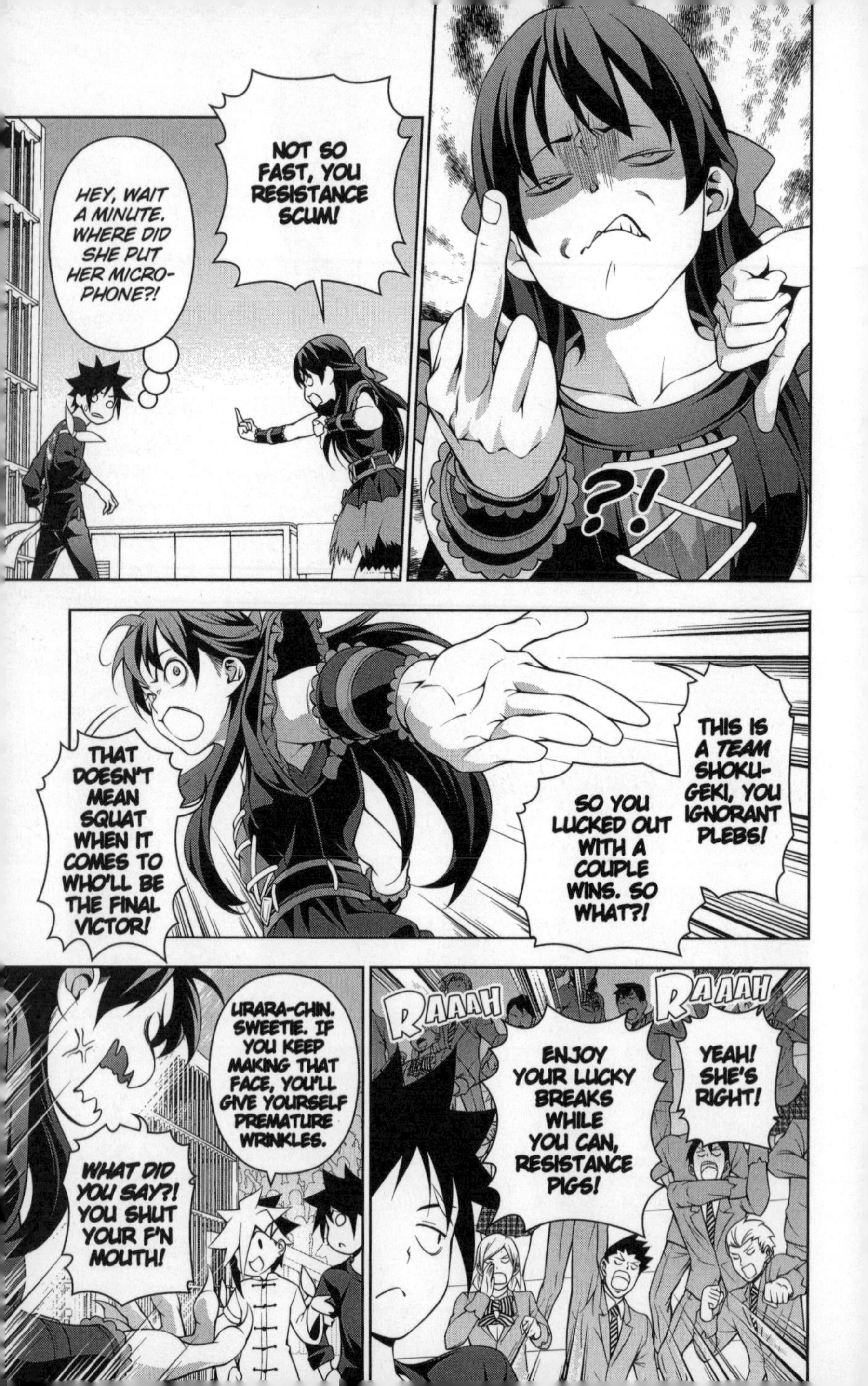
?!
NOT SO FAST, YOU RESISTANCE SCUM!
HEY, WAIT A MINUTE. WHERE DID SHE PUT HER MICRO-PHONE?!
THIS IS A *TEAM* SHOKU-GEKI, YOU IGNORANT PLEBS!
SO YOU LUCKED OUT WITH A COUPLE WINS. SO WHAT?!
THAT DOESN'T MEAN SQUAT WHEN IT COMES TO WHO'LL BE THE FINAL VICTOR!
RAAAH
YEAH! SHE'S RIGHT!
RAAAH
ENJOY YOUR LUCKY BREAKS WHILE YOU CAN, RESISTANCE PIGS!
URARA-CHIN. SWEETIE. IF YOU KEEP MAKING THAT FACE, YOU'LL GIVE YOURSELF PREMATURE WRINKLES.
WHAT DID YOU SAY?! YOU SHUT YOUR F'N MOUTH!

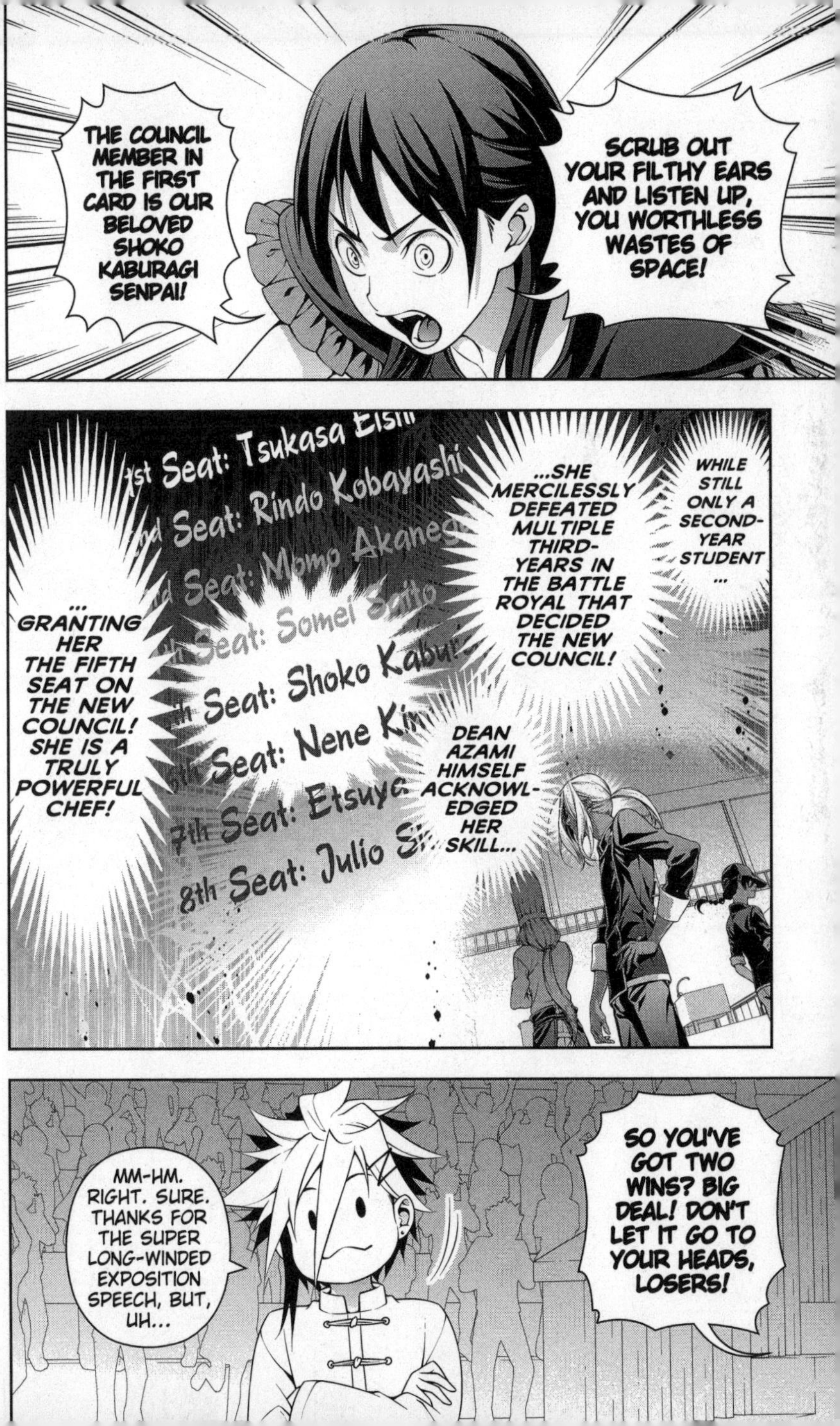
SCRUB OUT YOUR FILTHY EARS AND LISTEN UP, YOU WORTHLESS WASTES OF SPACE!
THE COUNCIL MEMBER IN THE FIRST CARD IS OUR BELOVED SHOKO KABURAGI SENPAI!
WHILE STILL ONLY A SECOND-YEAR STUDENT...
...SHE MERCILESSLY DEFEATED MULTIPLE THIRD-YEARS IN THE BATTLE ROYAL THAT DECIDED THE NEW COUNCIL!
DEAN AZAMI HIMSELF ACKNOWLEDGED HER SKILL...
1st Seat: Tsukasa Eishi
Seat: Rindo Kobayashi
Seat: Momo Akane
Seat: Somei Saito
Seat: Shoko Kabur
Seat: Nene Ki
7th Seat: Etsuya
8th Seat: Julio S
...GRANTING HER THE FIFTH SEAT ON THE NEW COUNCIL! SHE IS A TRULY POWERFUL CHEF!
SO YOU'VE GOT TWO WINS? BIG DEAL! DON'T LET IT GO TO YOUR HEADS, LOSERS!
MM-HM. RIGHT. SURE. THANKS FOR THE SUPER LONG-WINDED EXPOSITION SPEECH, BUT, UH...

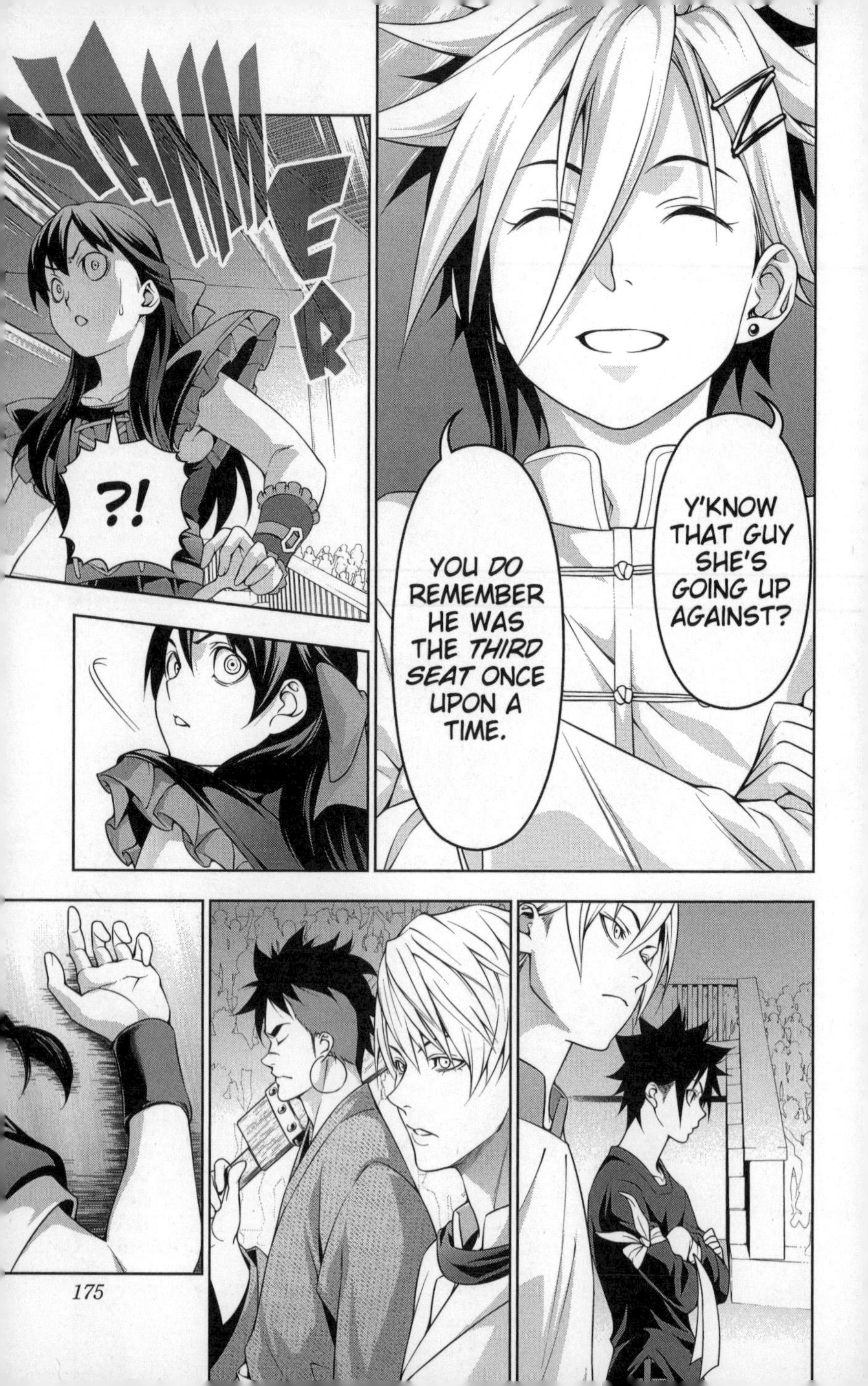
Y'KNOW THAT GUY SHE'S GOING UP AGAINST?
YOU DO REMEMBER HE WAS THE *THIRD SEAT* ONCE UPON A TIME.
?!

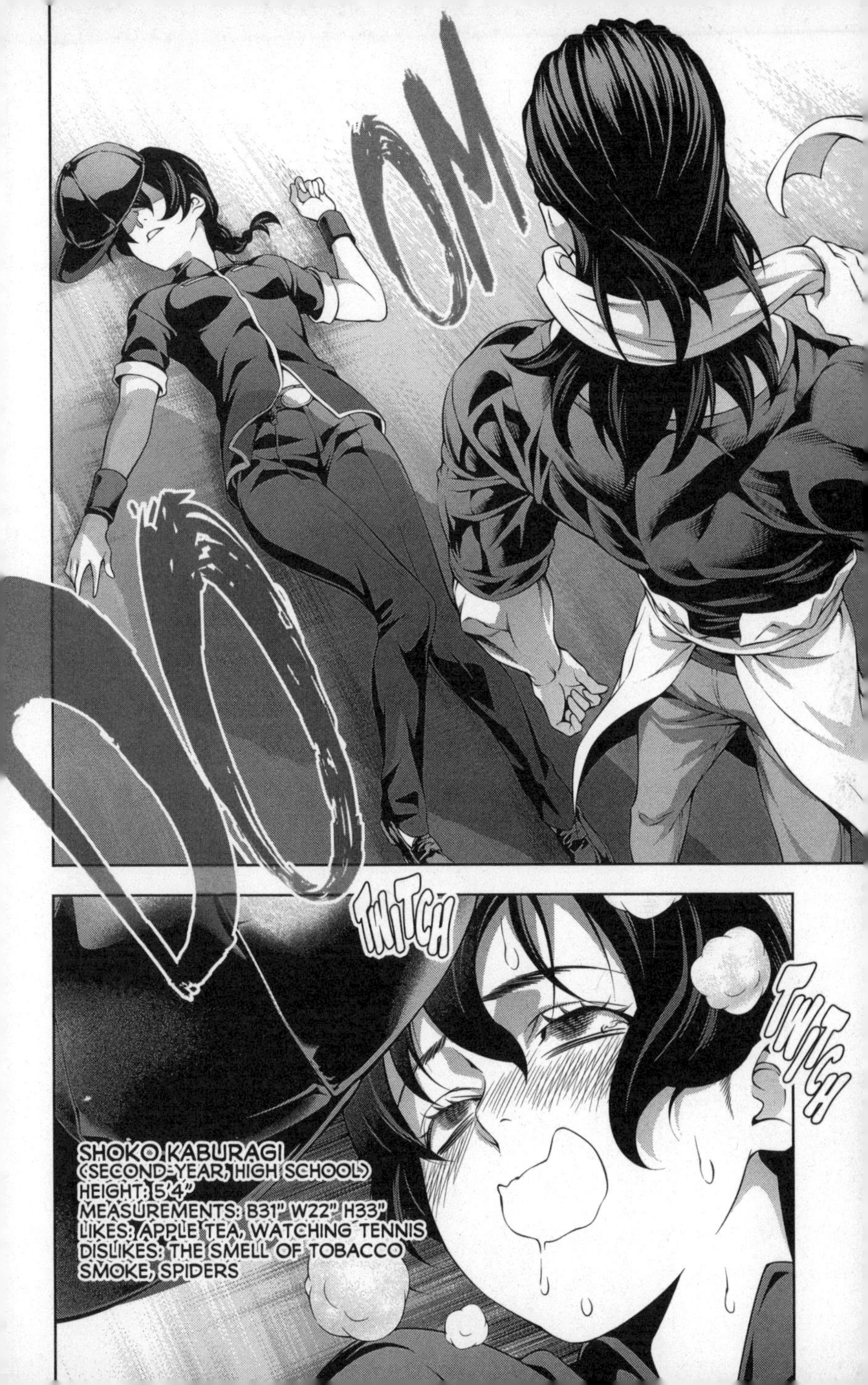
DOOOM
TWITCH
TWITCH
SHOKO KABURAGI
(SECOND-YEAR, HIGH SCHOOL)
HEIGHT: 5'4"
MEASUREMENTS: B31" W22" H33"
LIKES: APPLE TEA, WATCHING TENNIS
DISLIKES: THE SMELL OF TOBACCO SMOKE, SPIDERS

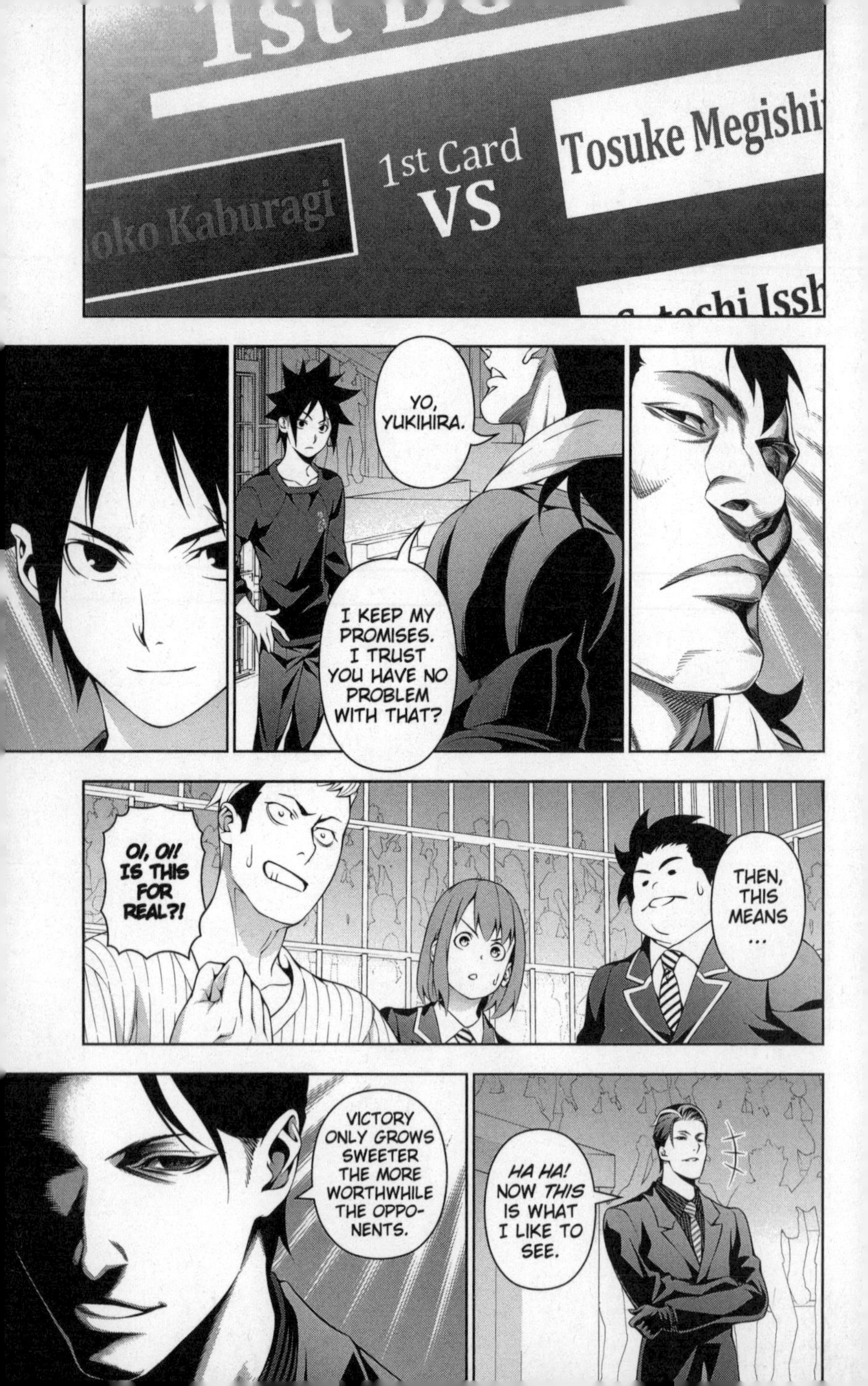
Tosuke Megishi
1st Card
VS
oko Kaburagi
YO, YUKIHIRA.
I KEEP MY PROMISES. I TRUST YOU HAVE NO PROBLEM WITH THAT?
THEN, THIS MEANS ...
OI, OI! IS THIS FOR REAL?!
HA HA! NOW *THIS* IS WHAT I LIKE TO SEE.
VICTORY ONLY GROWS SWEETER THE MORE WORTHWHILE THE OPPO-NENTS.

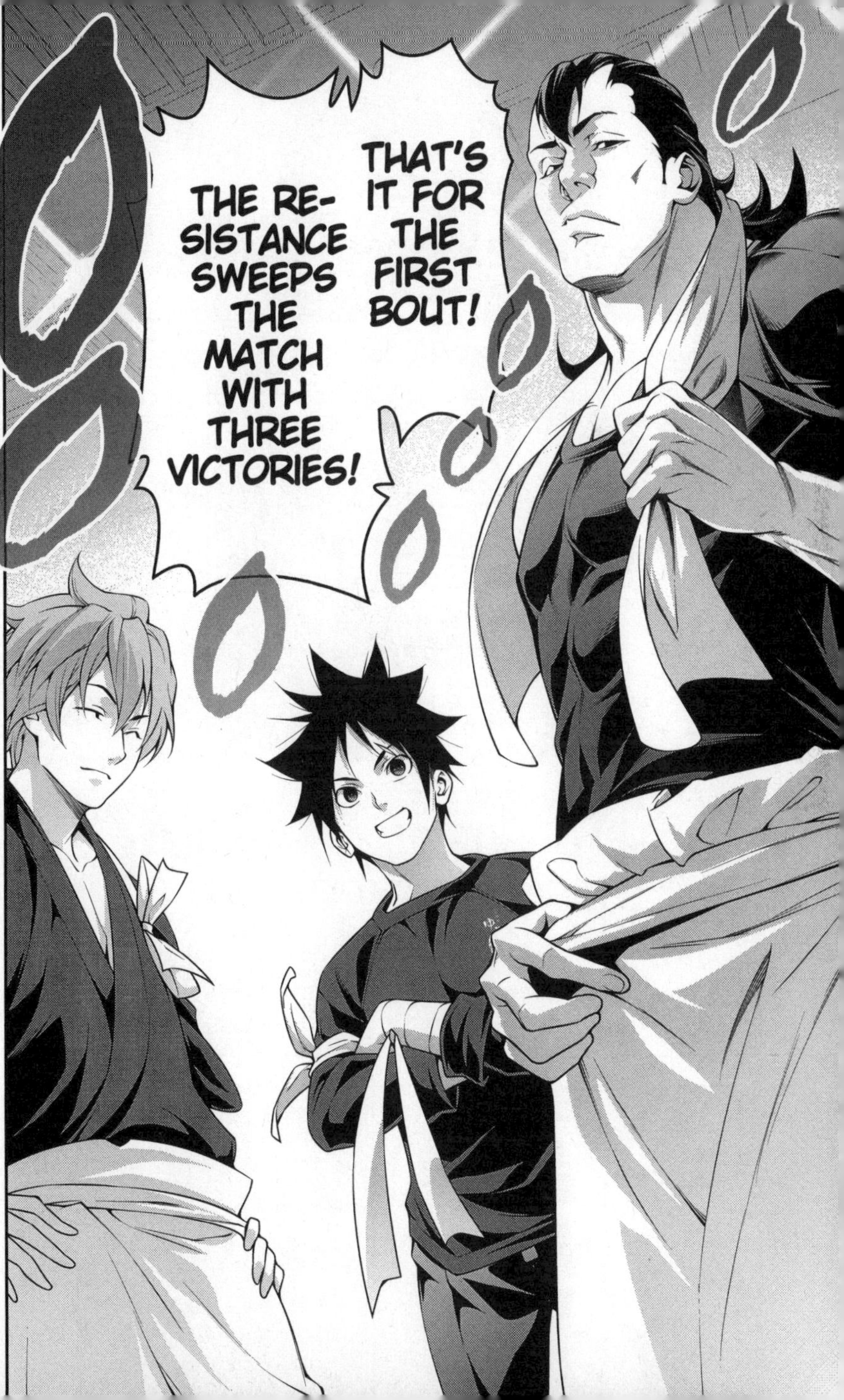
THAT'S IT FOR THE FIRST BOUT!
THE RE-SISTANCE SWEEPS THE MATCH WITH THREE VICTORIES!

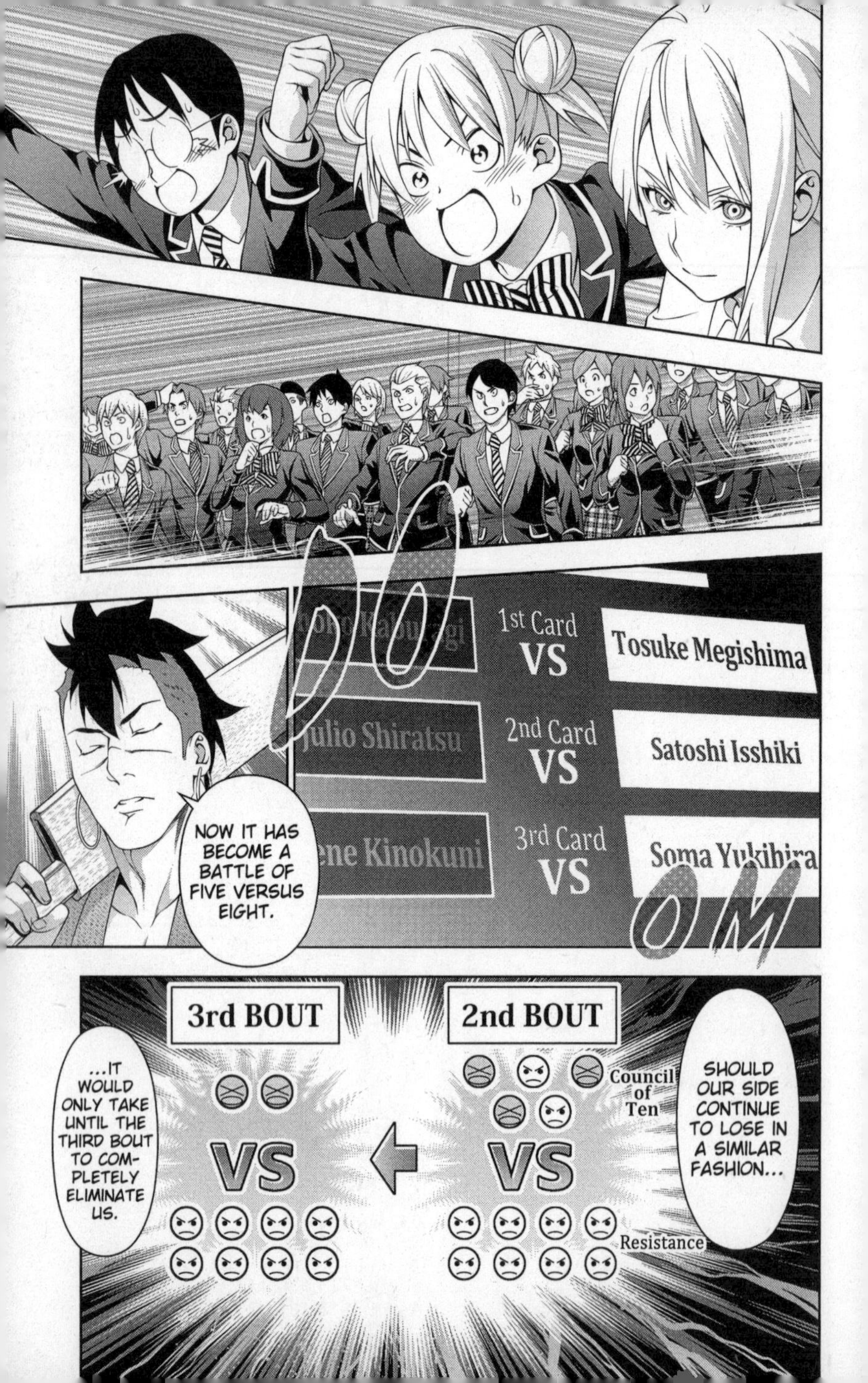
1st Card VS Tosuke Megishima
ulio Shiratsu 2nd Card VS Satoshi Isshiki
3rd Card VS Soma Yukihira
DOOM
NOW IT HAS BECOME A BATTLE OF FIVE VERSUS EIGHT.
SHOULD OUR SIDE CONTINUE TO LOSE IN A SIMILAR FASHION...
2nd BOUT
Council of Ten
VS
Resistance
3rd BOUT
VS
...IT WOULD ONLY TAKE UNTIL THE THIRD BOUT TO COMPLETELY ELIMINATE US.

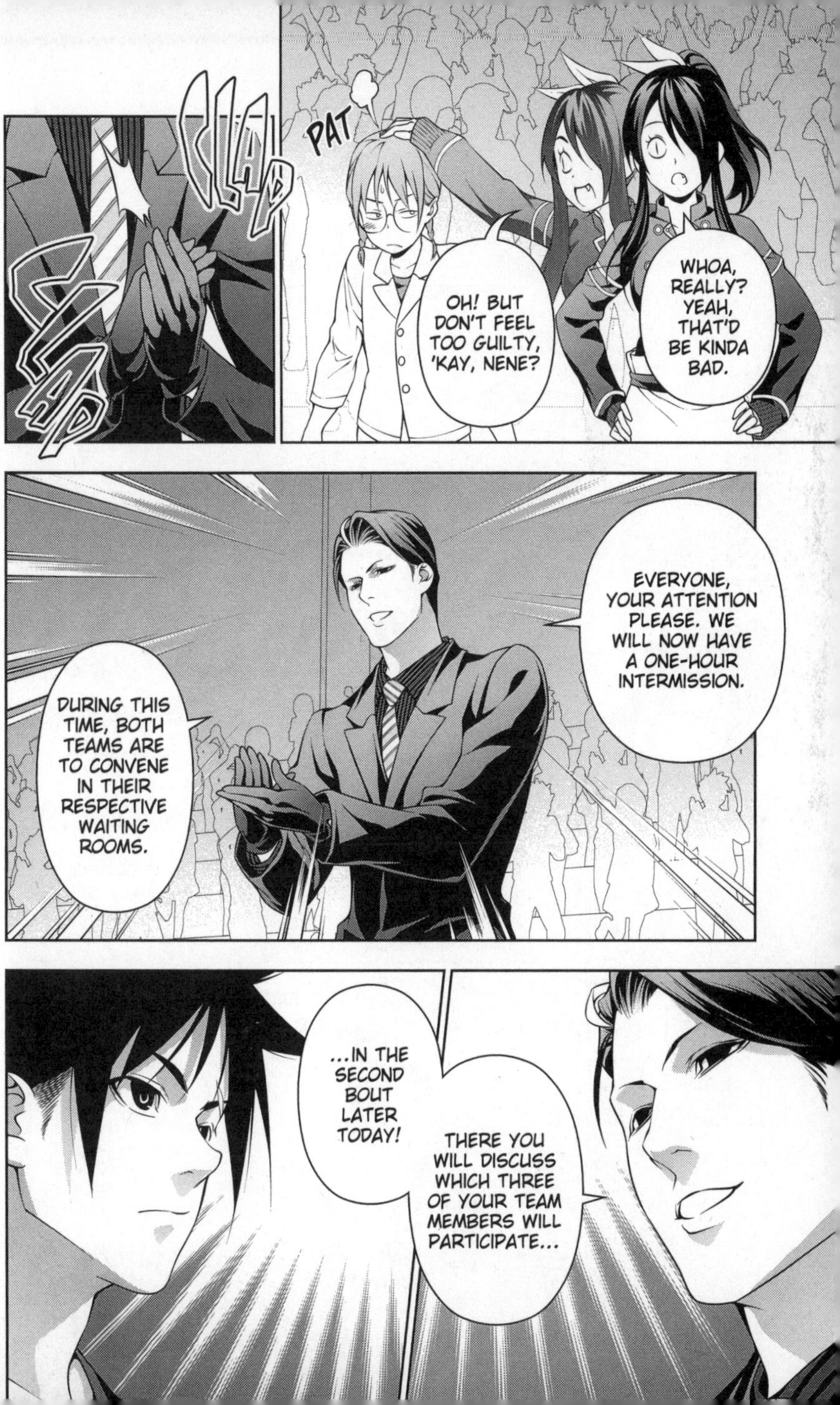
WHOA, REALLY? YEAH, THAT'D BE KINDA BAD.
PAT
OH! BUT DON'T FEEL TOO GUILTY, 'KAY, NENE?
CLAP
CLAP
EVERYONE, YOUR ATTENTION PLEASE. WE WILL NOW HAVE A ONE-HOUR INTERMISSION.
DURING THIS TIME, BOTH TEAMS ARE TO CONVENE IN THEIR RESPECTIVE WAITING ROOMS.
THERE YOU WILL DISCUSS WHICH THREE OF YOUR TEAM MEMBERS WILL PARTICIPATE...
...IN THE SECOND BOUT LATER TODAY!

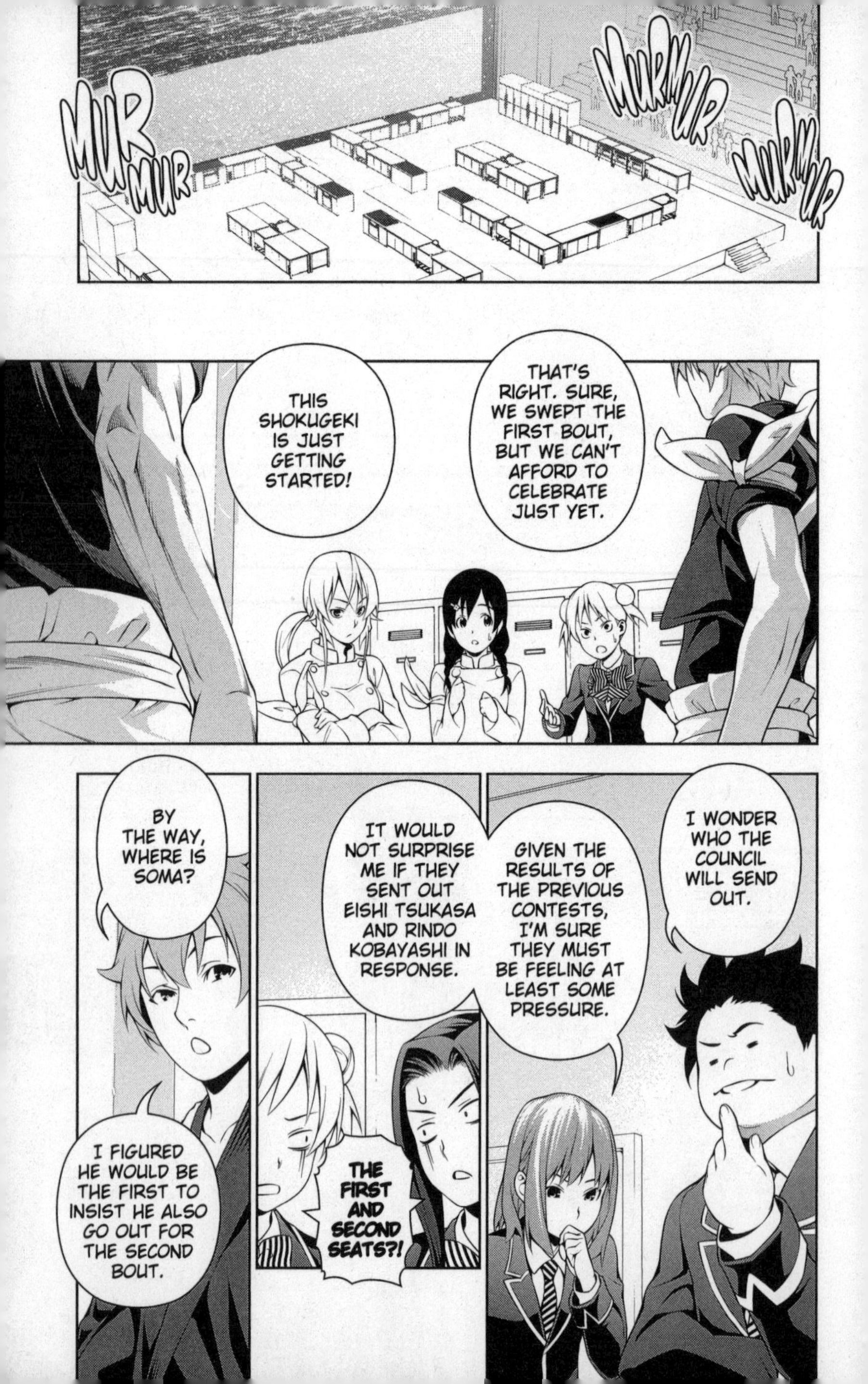
MURMUR
MURMUR
MUR MUR MUR
THAT'S RIGHT. SURE, WE SWEPT THE FIRST BOUT, BUT WE CAN'T AFFORD TO CELEBRATE JUST YET.
THIS SHOKUGEKI IS JUST GETTING STARTED!
I WONDER WHO THE COUNCIL WILL SEND OUT.
GIVEN THE RESULTS OF THE PREVIOUS CONTESTS, I'M SURE THEY MUST BE FEELING AT LEAST SOME PRESSURE.
IT WOULD NOT SURPRISE ME IF THEY SENT OUT EISHI TSUKASA AND RINDO KOBAYASHI IN RESPONSE.
THE FIRST AND SECOND SEATS?!
BY THE WAY, WHERE IS SOMA?
I FIGURED HE WOULD BE THE FIRST TO INSIST HE ALSO GO OUT FOR THE SECOND BOUT.

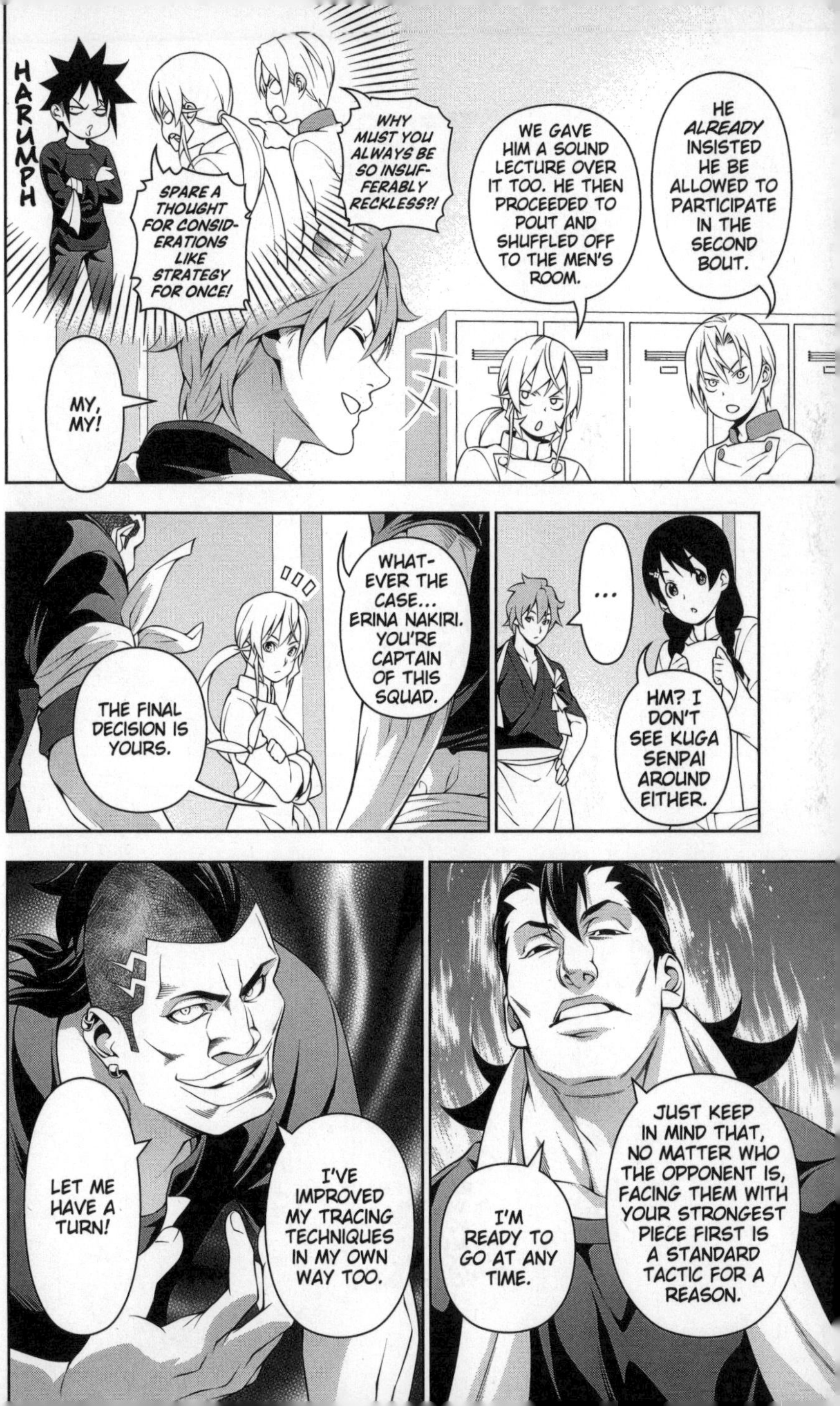
HE ALREADY INSISTED HE BE ALLOWED TO PARTICIPATE IN THE SECOND BOUT.
WE GAVE HIM A SOUND LECTURE OVER IT TOO. HE THEN PROCEEDED TO POUT AND SHUFFLED OFF TO THE MEN'S ROOM.
WHY MUST YOU ALWAYS BE SO INSUFFERABLY RECKLESS?!
SPARE A THOUGHT FOR CONSIDERATIONS LIKE STRATEGY FOR ONCE!
HARUMPH
MY, MY!
...
HM? I DON'T SEE KUGA SENPAI AROUND EITHER.
WHATEVER THE CASE... ERINA NAKIRI. YOU'RE CAPTAIN OF THIS SQUAD.
THE FINAL DECISION IS YOURS.
JUST KEEP IN MIND THAT, NO MATTER WHO THE OPPONENT IS, FACING THEM WITH YOUR STRONGEST PIECE FIRST IS A STANDARD TACTIC FOR A REASON.
I'M READY TO GO AT ANY TIME.
I'VE IMPROVED MY TRACING TECHNIQUES IN MY OWN WAY TOO.
LET ME HAVE A TURN!

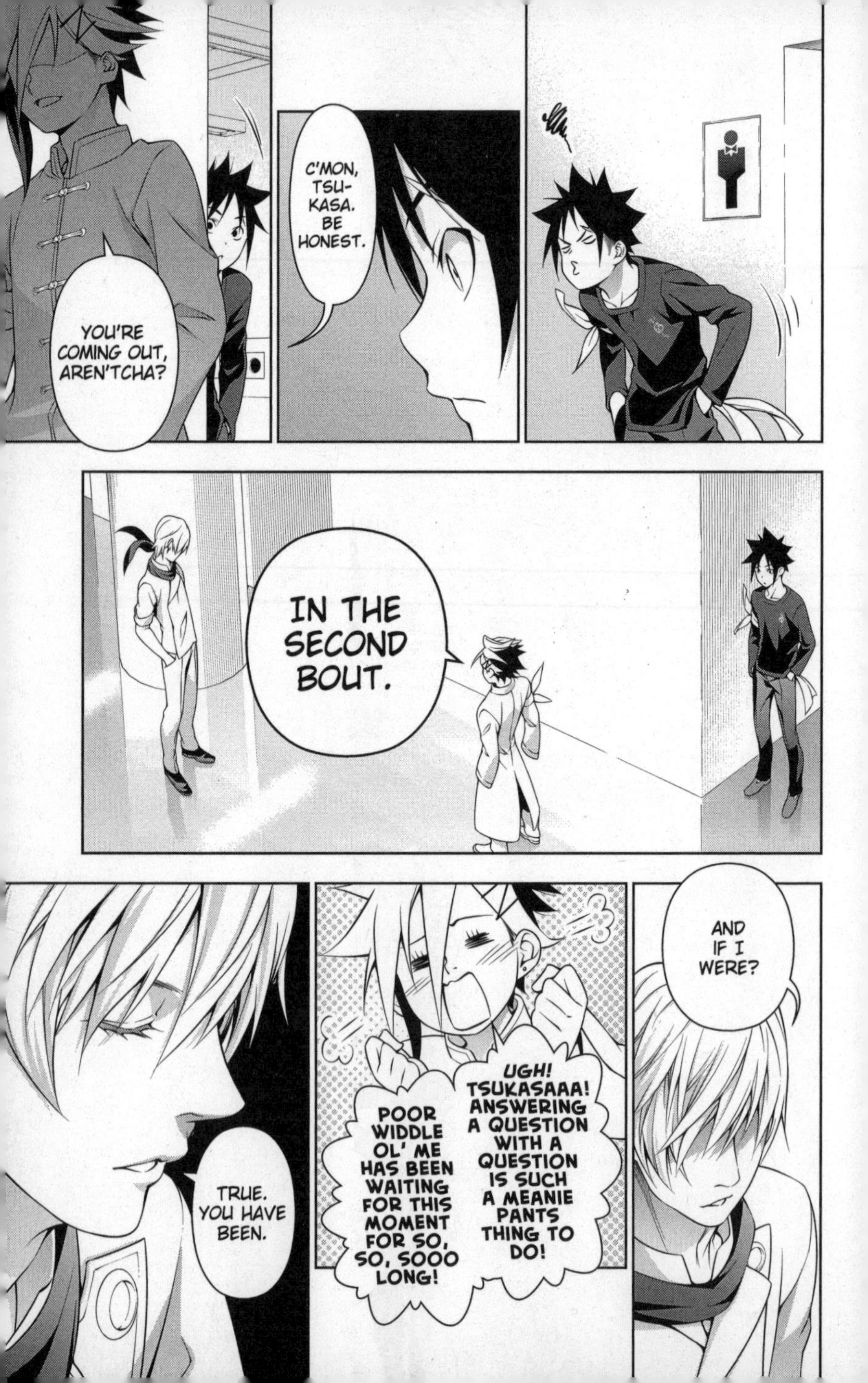
C'MON, TSU-KASA. BE HONEST.
YOU'RE COMING OUT, AREN'TCHA?
IN THE SECOND BOUT.
AND IF I WERE?
UGH! TSUKASAAA! ANSWERING A QUESTION WITH A QUESTION IS SUCH A MEANIE PANTS THING TO DO!
POOR WIDDLE OL' ME HAS BEEN WAITING FOR THIS MOMENT FOR SO, SO, SOOO LONG!
TRUE. YOU HAVE BEEN.

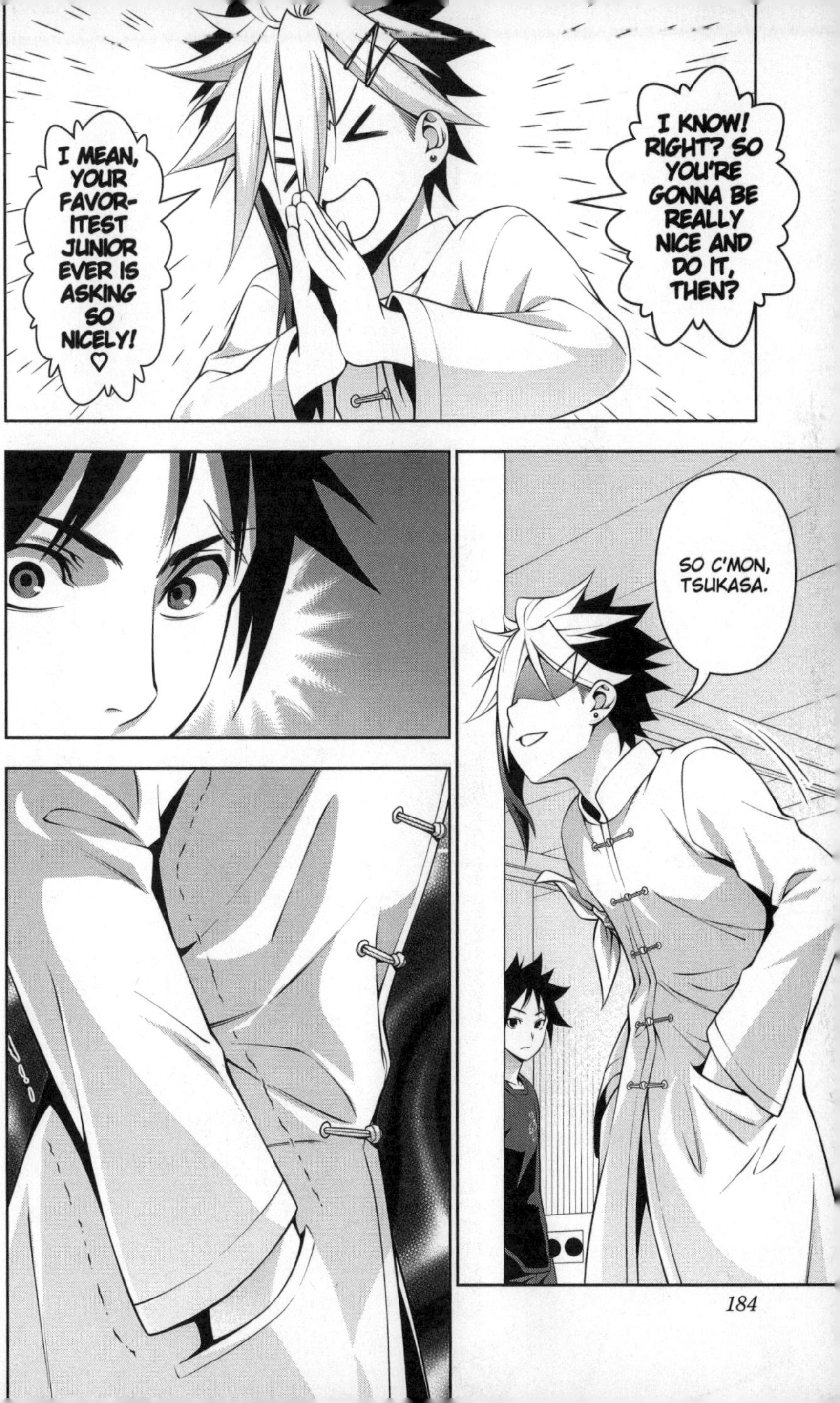
I KNOW! RIGHT? SO YOU'RE GONNA BE REALLY NICE AND DO IT, THEN?
I MEAN, YOUR FAVOR-ITEST JUNIOR EVER IS ASKING SO NICELY! ♡
SO C'MON, TSUKASA.

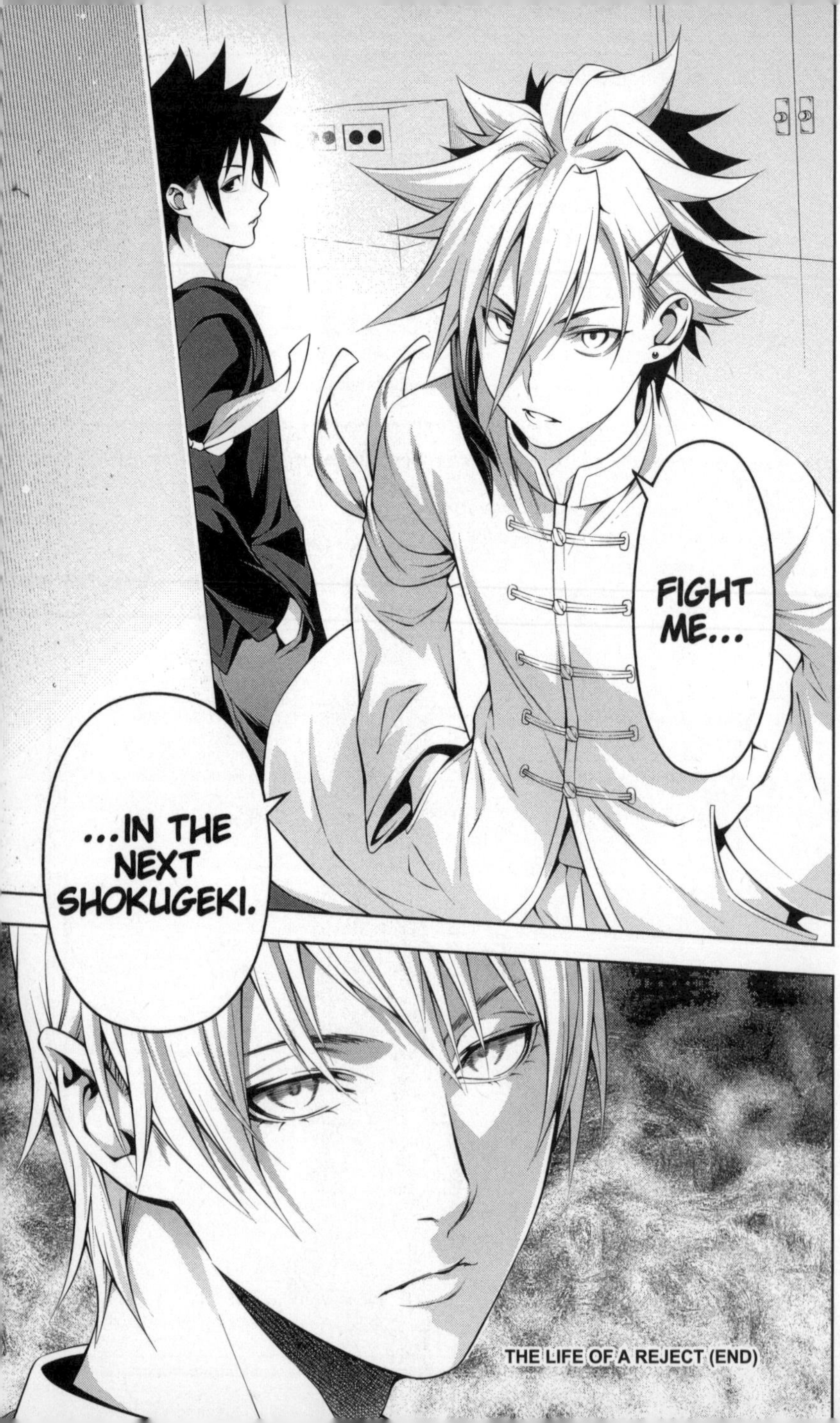
FIGHT ME...
...IN THE NEXT SHOKUGEKI.
THE LIFE OF A REJECT (END)

ARTIST: YUTO TSUKUDA RECIPE BY: YUKI MORISAKI

OOH! OW!
FWOOOO
OUCH! HOT!
SIZZZZZ

VOLUME 25 SPECIAL SUPPLEMENT!

PRACTICAL RECIPE #1

YUKIHIRA-STYLE RICE BOWL FRIED SOBA

‹MAKE AT HOME IN A FRYING PAN!›

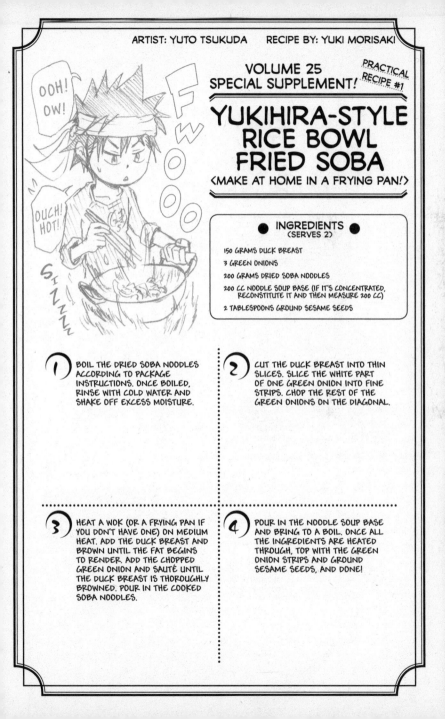

● INGREDIENTS ●
(SERVES 2)

150 GRAMS DUCK BREAST

3 GREEN ONIONS

200 GRAMS DRIED SOBA NOODLES

200 CC NOODLE SOUP BASE (IF IT'S CONCENTRATED, RECONSTITUTE IT AND THEN MEASURE 200 CC)

2 TABLESPOONS GROUND SESAME SEEDS

1. BOIL THE DRIED SOBA NOODLES ACCORDING TO PACKAGE INSTRUCTIONS. ONCE BOILED, RINSE WITH COLD WATER AND SHAKE OFF EXCESS MOISTURE.

2. CUT THE DUCK BREAST INTO THIN SLICES. SLICE THE WHITE PART OF ONE GREEN ONION INTO FINE STRIPS. CHOP THE REST OF THE GREEN ONIONS ON THE DIAGONAL.

3. HEAT A WOK (OR A FRYING PAN IF YOU DON'T HAVE ONE) ON MEDIUM HEAT. ADD THE DUCK BREAST AND BROWN UNTIL THE FAT BEGINS TO RENDER. ADD THE CHOPPED GREEN ONION AND SAUTÉ UNTIL THE DUCK BREAST IS THOROUGHLY BROWNED. POUR IN THE COOKED SOBA NOODLES.

4. POUR IN THE NOODLE SOUP BASE AND BRING TO A BOIL. ONCE ALL THE INGREDIENTS ARE HEATED THROUGH, TOP WITH THE GREEN ONION STRIPS AND GROUND SESAME SEEDS, AND DONE!

THE PROMISED NEVERLAND

STORY BY KAIU SHIRAI
ART BY POSUKA DEMIZU

Emma, Norman and Ray are the brightest kids at the Grace Field House orphanage. And under the care of the woman they refer to as "Mom," all the kids have enjoyed a comfortable life. Good food, clean clothes and the perfect environment to learn—what more could an orphan ask for? One day, though, Emma and Norman uncover the dark truth of the outside world they are forbidden from seeing.

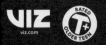

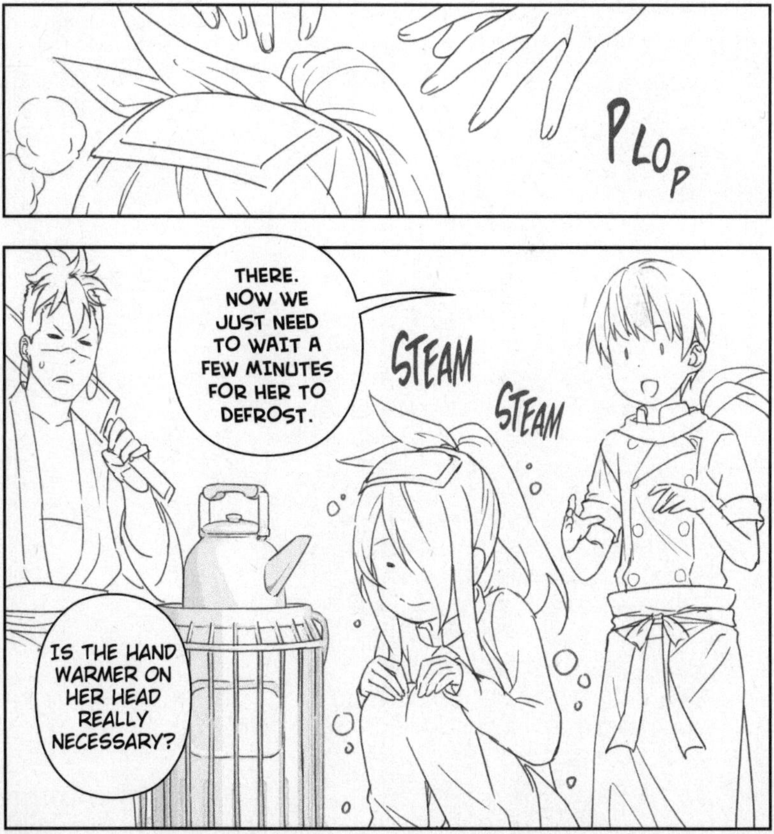
PLOP
THERE. NOW WE JUST NEED TO WAIT A FEW MINUTES FOR HER TO DEFROST.
STEAM
STEAM
IS THE HAND WARMER ON HER HEAD REALLY NECESSARY?

(END)

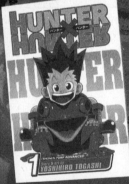
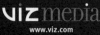
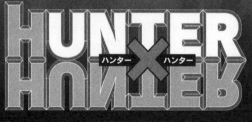

You're Reading in the Wrong Direction!!

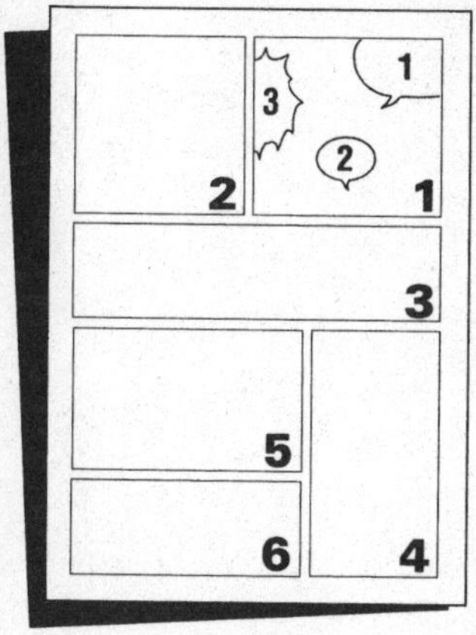
1
2
3
1
2
3
4
5
6

Whoops! Guess what? You're starting at the wrong end of the comic!

...It's true! In keeping with the original Japanese format, **Food Wars!** is meant to be read from right to left, starting in the upper-right corner.

Unlike English, which is read from left to right, Japanese is read from right to left, meaning that action, sound effects and word-balloon order are completely reversed... something which can make readers unfamiliar with Japanese feel pretty backwards themselves. For this reason, manga or Japanese comics published in the U.S. in English have sometimes been published "flopped"—that is, printed in exact reverse order, as though seen from the other side of a mirror.

By flopping pages, U.S. publishers can avoid confusing readers, but the compromise is not without its downside. For one thing, a character in a flopped manga series who once wore in the original Japanese version a T-shirt emblazoned with "M A Y" (as in "the merry month of") now wears one which reads "Y A M"! Additionally, many manga creators in Japan are themselves unhappy with the process, as some feel the mirror-imaging of their art skews their original intentions.

We are proud to bring you Yuto Tsukuda and Shun Saeki's **Food Wars!** in the original unflopped format.

For now, though, turn to the other side of the book and let the adventure begin...!

—Editor

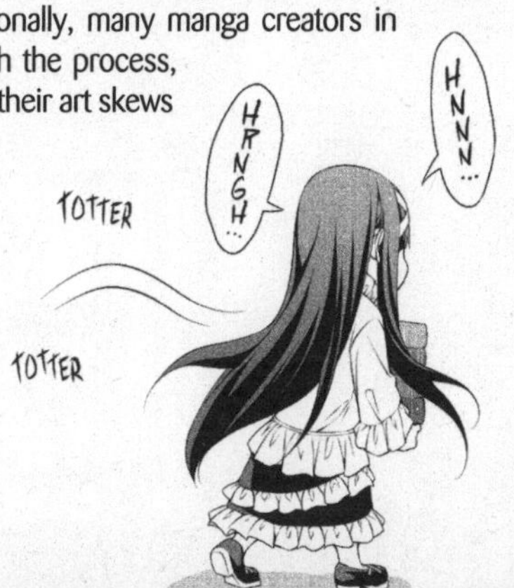
HNNN...
HRNGH...
TOTTER
TOTTER